KU-044-779

YANA ROWLAND

THE TREATMENT OF THE THEMES OF MORTALITY IN THE POETRY OF THE BRONTË SISTERS

2006

For my parents,
Maya and Atanas

To Julian Wolfreys,

With gratitude for the
support and the
warm welcome!

Yana Rowland,

February
2008

© Yana Rowland, author, 2006
© Plovdiv University Press, 2006

ISBN-10: 954-423-362-8
ISBN-13: 978-954-423-362-4

ACKNOWLEDGEMENTS

My sincere gratitude goes to, firstly, **MY PARENTS**, who have given me all the support – spiritual, professional and physical – which I needed in order to complete this PhD project and thus quench my critical thirst.

I am also greatly indebted to **Professor Leonée Ormond** (*King's College, London*), who has generously supported my work ever since it emerged as just an idea-in-project and until it materialized into a literary product.

I have found particularly valuable the support I have received from my official supervisor, Professor Julia Stefanova (*The St. Kliment Ohridski University of Sofia*), whose criticism of my work has proved extremely productive to its overall structure and presentation. I should also like to thank Professor Stefana Rusenova (*University of Sofia*), for suggesting important ideas, from which the book, I hope, has benefited.

I also have to thank all my *colleagues and friends from The Paisij Hilendarski University of Plovdiv*, who have answered and clarified a wide range of questions I have had to face in the process of investigating the theme of this research, and have given me the best of their support in preparing my PhD thesis for publication. These are: Professor Kleo Protohristova, Professor Albena Hranova, Professor Ivan Tchobanov, Professor Zaprian Kozludzov, Professor Zivko Ivanov. Also, my colleagues from the English Department: Professor Hristo Grancharov, Yordan Kosturkov, Atanas Manchorov. I should like to thank my colleague from the Russian Department Dr Mayya Kuzova. My words of gratitude also go to: Gergina Krasteva, Professor Krassimira Tchakarova, Tzveta Temelkova.

I am particularly grateful to my colleague, Dr Dimitar Krastev, for his generous technical assistance in the preparation of the publication of this book.

I should like to express my gratitude to Dr Radoslava Ilcheva (*The Institute of Literary Studies at The Bulgarian Academy of Arts, Sofia*), whose help in the final stages of my PhD project proved invaluable. I thank my colleague Professor Roussi Nikolov (Department of French at the University of Plovdiv), who aided me in deciphering crucial French criticism by Paul Ricoeur and who also stimulated my confidence in using literary criticism in French.

I am also very grateful to my high-school teachers, Georgi Georgiev, Dr Rachel Behar, Liubov Nizamova, Evgeniya Il'initchna Ivanova, who lavishly encouraged and maintained in me zest for languages and literature.

I also have to thank one person, without whose unselfish and prompt medical assistance I may not have been able to enjoy the blessing of motherhood and thus perceive the *Other*, the humane, the more important side of the term 'professional development' – Dr Svetlozar Stratev MD (*St. Mina Maternity Home, Plovdiv*).

My words of thanks also go to my grandparents, who have supported me in every possible way and always.

And I have to thank **Ani**, my daughter, for being there, for being *my* daughter, and for helping me harness the temptation to feel self-satisfied and self-important…

Yana Atanasova Rowland
Plovdiv, June 2006

CONTENTS

3.

LIST OF ABBREVIATIONS

Theoretical Works

AIG   *Avtor I Geroi v estetitcheskoi deiatel'nosti*:
Bakhtin, M. M., in: Sobraniye sotchinenij, t. 1,
Filosofskaya estetika 1920h godov (Moskva:
Russkie Slovari, RAN, 2003).

KFP   *K filosofii postoupka* (same edition as above)

SUZ   *Sein Und Zeit*: Heidegger, Martin, *Sein und Zeit*
[in Russian: *Bityie I Vremia*], Moskva:
Ad Marginem 1997

Note on the text editions
Unless otherwise indicated, all quotations from, and references to,
the Brontë sisters' (and to Branwell Brontë's) poetic works come from:

- **Chitham, Edward, (ed.) *The Poems of Anne Brontë*
(Macmillan, 1979).**

- **Hatfield, C.W., (ed.) *The Complete Poems of Emily Jane
Brontë* (New York: Columbia University Press, 1941).**

- **Winnifrith, Tom, (ed.) *The Poems of Charlotte Brontë* (Basil
Blackwell for the Shakespeare Head Brontë, 1984).**

- **Winnifrith, Tom, (ed.) *The Poems of Patrick Branwell Brontë*
(Basil Blackwell for the Shakespeare Head Brontë, 1983).**

Unless otherwise indicated, all quotations from, and references to, the <u>Brontë sisters' major prose fiction works</u> come from:

AG	*Agnes Grey*: Brontë, Anne, in: *Four Novels of the Brontë Sisters* (Spring Books, Butler & Tanner Ltd, 1976).
JE	*Jane Eyre*: Mason, Michael (ed.) *Jane Eyre*, by Charlotte Brontë (Penguin Books, 1996).
P	*The Professor*: Glen, Heather (ed.), *The Professor*, by Charlotte Brontë (Penguin Boks, 1989).
Sh	*Shirley:* Brontë, Charlotte, *Shirley* (Wordsworth Classics, 1995).
TWH	*The Tenant of Wildfell Hall*: White, Kathryn (ed.), *The Tenant of Wildfell Hall*, by Anne Brontë, (Wordsworth Classics, 1996).
V	*Villette*: Minogue, Sally (ed.), *Villette*, by Charlotte Brontë (Wordsworth Classics, 1999).
WH	*Wuthering Heights*: Brontë, Emily, *Wutheri Heights* (Hertfordshire: Wordsworth Classics 1992).

FOREWORD

The present study, entitled ***The Treatment of the Themes of Mortality in the Poetry of the Brontë Sisters***, hopes to be a purposeful and thorough investigation of <u>the problem of Death</u> in the poetic heritage of the three sisters, conducted in a comparative fashion. Whilst critically emphasizing in a new manner the originality, authenticity and autonomy of each sister's poetic merits, it argues Anne's, Charlotte's and Emily's membership in one common literary venture that resulted in a unique literary product. This literary product could be perceived to have legitimized itself through the three sisters' faith in the verity of *Being as Co-Being*, embraced by the three sisters as a philosophy of Life. In accordance with the latter, Being is only and always validated as Being in the context of the search for one *dialogic whole*: between the *living/Survivor/Mourner* and the *dead/the missing person*, between *child* and *mother*, between *the sinner* and *the dead beloved*, between *Man* and God, between *Man* and *Nature*, between *two friends* etc.

I hereby hope to be able to offer a new paradigm of reading English poetry in a given literary period. What is defended in the present study is the value of <u>the problem of Death as a gradually emerging chief philosophic discourse in English poetry of the late 18th–19th centuries</u> – on the basis of a comparative examination of certain major representatives alongside the Brontë sisters' poetic achievements. In this sense, the book also contains the idea-in-project of a kind of a new anthologization, new selection and restructuring of major poetic works of the period in hand with the purpose of a more extensive and larger-scale presentation of this concrete theme of research.

One task of the present study is to defend the originality of the somewhat underrated literary merits of *all* the three sisters' poetry (and not just of Emily's, which is traditionally recognized, or of their prose fiction heritage solely) with the conviction, that a prerequisite for the Brontës' legitimate presence in the literary world is the depth and the scale of their developing themes of *Mortality*. This thematic area, which I believe, is central to the works of all the three sisters, contains a surprisingly rich spectrum of motifs, symbols and images, which additionally suggests that Anne, Charlotte and Emily possessed ample philosophical awareness. This thematic focus discovers that the Brontë sisters' works harmonize with such characteristic topics and motifs of 19th-century Western European literature as, for instance: *solitude and alienation; orphanhood and the problem of the missing parent; the impossibility of maintaining dialogue/communication; the chronotopal value of the grave; the metamorphic essence of the traditionally topologically defined concepts of Heaven and Hell* (which were beginning to get „interiorized", i.e. they were beginning to be perceived as variable states of the human mind).

One contribution I hope to be able to make with the present book is to offer a new approach in treating the poetry of the Brontë sisters, and in this link, a new approach in treating English poetry of the late 18th–19th centuries (The Romantics and the Victorians). The innovativeness could be seen in the application of the ideology (themes, ideas, concepts, terms) of modern European ontophilosophy and existential ethics (represented here by Martin Heidegger, Emmanuel Levinas, Jacques Derrida and, mostly, Mikhail Bakhtin) on a specific literary material. This is a way to prove both the significance of the chosen theme of research, as well as the uniqueness of the Brontë sisters themselves, as interpreted in the logic of the symptomatic for the contemporary era integrative mode of thinking, evident in interdisciplinary studies. The borderline position, which the problem of *Mortality,* of *Death,* occupies (it is as relevant in philosophy as it is in literature), proves extremely fruitful, it is hemmed with a wide range of sub-motifs and thematic variations, the most crucial of which I hope to have critically covered in this book.

I trust that the book would be useful guide to all scholars (students and professionals alike), who take deeper interest in the Brontës and in English literature of the 19th century. I strongly hope that it would be beneficial to all those who, at one point or another in their lives, have pondered, nay... hesitated over the validity and the purpose of one's existence in the absence of *an Other...* Whilst being exclusive in the way it wields specific literary and philosophical terminology, the book is all-inclusive in that it addresses a common existential problem. The commonest of all, in fact...

Introduction

„The realization of one's own mortality
is an indicator of man's authenticity.
The understanding and the experience of the event of Death,
the „insertion" and appropriation of Death
within culture is a process which not only runs parallel
to the pace of man's Life,
but in fact humanizes Life[1]."

The present research is a critical investigation of the poetry of Emily, Charlotte and Anne Brontë. The topic to be researched is **the treatment of themes of Mortality in the poetic works of the Brontë sisters**, as those are to be found in the traditionally acknowledged 1941, 1979, 1983 and 1984 editions of their poetic works (as already specified in the list of abbreviations that precedes the introduction). The choice of the theme of research is motivated by my desire to present the poetry of Emily, Charlotte and Anne Brontë in a specific manner. The empirical basis for such research is the Bronte children's dramatic worlds of Angria and Gondal. A literary product of their juvenile plays, **Angria** and **Gondal**[2] evolved further into poetic phenomena of a high calibre, which

---

[1] Demichev, A. *(in Russian) Diskoursij smerti. Vvedenie v filosofskuiu tanatologiu, Sankt-Peterburg:* Inopress 1997, p. 5 (my translation of the selected piece) . **Here and henceforth, the quotations of critical sources will appear as follows: name of author, followed by the year of publication, followed by the relevant page(s): e.g. <u>Plasa, C., 2004. p. 15</u>. When first mention is made of a work, a full bibliographical reference will be given. After that – as explained above. All the critical sources quoted/ referred to in this manner are included in the bibliography at the end of the present research in a due manner. For reasons of clarity, the Latin alphabet is also used to transliterate titles of Bulgarian/ Russian critical sources referred to. On the other hand, in the bibliography a clear division is made between English critical sources v/s Bulgarian/ Russian sources. In the bibliography, therefore, the specific titles will be written in the appropriate language. Ostensibly a complication, the latter technique in fact aims at broadening the target readership of this critical investigation of the poetic works of the Brontë sisters, which, I hope, would become available and intriguing to a Bulgarian and a non-Bulgarian-speaking critical audience alike. The latter is also the reason for this critical work to appear in English, rather than in Bulgarian, with the hope that the range of critics likely to approach it would thus become wider. As a non-native speaker of English, I am aware of the perils which lurk beneath any such undertaking, yet I am convinced that that is the most adequate manner to present the theme of the present research.**
[2] A fuller and more detailed explanation of the choice of the contexts of *Angria* and *Gondal* as the main canvas for researching the themes of mortality in the Brontë sisters' poetry follows in, respectively, the introduction to the chapters about Charlotte Brontë and then about Emily Brontë.

consequently encouraged Charlotte Brontë to publish select poetic pieces by herself and her sisters in the first combined edition of the Brontë sisters' poetry of 1846[3]. The fact that Angria and Gondal resulted from the Brontë children's <u>collaboration in their playtime</u> has been reflected in the various editions ever since. One proof of the latter is the fact that the editions of their poetry vary in the editor's opinion on the authorship and on the authenticity of a number of poems (a fact which is discussed separately where necessary further on). Independent of the latter, all the editions are unanimous in admitting that Emily, Charlotte, Anne and Patrick Branwell (their notorious artist brother) intended to create a literary world of their own. The way Gondal and Angria exist nowadays – mainly in a compilation of poetic fragments and verse narratives – could be described as a „purified" version of the four Brontës early literary collaboration in drama. The established fact of Branwell Brontë's contribution to the latter (most vivid in his literary partnership with his sister Charlotte) will be given due consideration if/where appropriate. It would serve to support my insistence on the depth of <u>the Brontës' literary infatuation with Mortality and with Death – the philosophic discourse which best discloses their ontological growth.</u>

The thematic specificities of Angria and Gondal are subjected to a more thorough discussion in the appropriate chapters. That is, **Angria** forms the introductory part of the chapter about Charlotte Brontë. **Gondal** is the introduction to Part III of the present research (the part dedicated to Emily Brontë) – a major critical undertaking which endeavours to present Emily Brontë as the one of the family with the subtlest and most unique feel for, and awareness of, *Mortality* <u>– the theme that became, in effect, the Brontës' hermeneutical „tool" for interpreting existence.</u>

<u>The general choice of the theme of research is motivated by a desire to present</u> **the poetry of the Brontë sisters as one common literary phenomenon** – <u>something that has not yet been attempted.</u> The comparative analysis of the theme of research is to emphasize my belief that *Mortality* <u>**has a categorical significance in the Brontë sisters' philosophy of Being perceived as Co-Being**. It is that theme which penetrates through, and unites, their novels</u> (including most of Charlotte

---

[3] A contemporary reprint of the latter, which I quote, is: *The Works of the Brontë Sisters*, introduction by Kathryn White (Wordsworth Poetry Library, 1995).

Brontë's unfinished novels and Emily and Charlotte Brontë's *Belgian essays*[4]). In this sense, <u>Emily's, Charlotte's and Anne's poetry can be treated as a preamble to their novels[5] which reveal each writer's purposeful and persistent study of death as symptomatic of man's maturation and existential awareness.</u> I therefore claim that each sister's poetic input (which reads as a distinct literary unit) was followed by a prose fiction unit (rather voluminous in Charlotte Brontë's case), so that the two would form a common entity. Therefore, where necessary, references and comparisons are to be made to the Brontë sisters' prose fiction works relevant. The latter, however, is but a marginal aim of the present investigation, which is by no means to eclipse the numerous and already critically acclaimed studies of the Brontë sisters' prose fiction heritage, which have, in one way or another, endeavoured to throw some light on the relevance of the knotty issue of *DEATH* as the Brontë sisters' haunt and obsession. Yet my faith in the heuristic element in researching the themes of *Mortality* in the Brontë sisters' poetic works stretches as far as to see that subject area as the core of their prose fiction heritage too. In the <u>context of Brontë studies such perception is, I trust, innovative.</u> *Mortality/Death* is the most obvious contextual field which reveals the Brontë sisters' ethical and aesthetic development. The latter has certainly remained until present a hidden territory of research of the Brontës – certainly the case in respect of a comparative study of the Brontë sisters' poetry, which is what the present thesis strives to be.

<u>There will be an emphasis on presenting the development of the themes of *Mortality* within the context of Angria and Gondal which could thus offer a diachronic perspective on the overall creative and moral development of Emily, Charlotte and Anne Brontë.</u> As much as the present

---

[4] As far as Charlotte Brontë's unfinished novels are concerned, the present research has found of some interest the following: *The Story of Willie Ellin* (1853) and *Emma* (published 1860). *The Belgian Essays (The Belgian Devoirs)* were written as homework by Charlotte and Emily during their stay at Pensionnat Heger in Brussels during 1842. Although not intended for publication, their profundity and philosophic strain have given the critic enough reasons to categorise them as literary works with rights of their own. The edition of *the Belgian Devoirs* (Essays) followed throughout is: <u>Lonoff, Sue (ed.) *The Belgian Essays. Charlotte and Emily Brontë. A Critical Edition* (Yale University Press, 1996).</u>

[5] Namely: Charlotte Brontë's *Jane Eyre (1847), Shirley (1849), Villette (1853), The Professor (1857)*; Emily Brontë's *Wuthering Heights (1847)* and Anne Brontë's *Agnes Grey (1847) and The Tenant of Wildfell Hall (1849).*

study of the Brontë sisters' poetry is away from the methodological framework of psychoanalysis, yet I feel that at this point it would be valuable to reiterate Professor Isaak Passi's study on Freud. Professor Passi argues that, according to Freud, an act of creativity, or the literary act, (whose core is fancy) is a kind of surrogate for an artist's erstwhile games during his/her playtime as a child. In the case of the Brontë children, to regurgitate an already established fact, Angria and Gondal sprung up as their bedtime plays evolved. Those plays were initiated in 1826, after their father, the Rev. Patrick Branwell Brontë, brought to Haworth a set of 12 wooden soldiers, whom the children named after famous historical persona and made haste to mould as literary characters of their own *Young Men's Plays* (now preserved in fragments). Needless to say, *Gondal* and *Angria* far exceed what Freud might have termed „the escapist-adaptive" purpose for the Brontës' overall artistic development. In the contemporary critical world they are treated as acclaimed literary autonomies, whose philosophic complexity could be observed in their devotedness to the problem of *the Other's Death* – the basis for *the Survivor's* ontological maturation.

A crucial point argued throughout the present study is that **the poetic heritage of each of the Brontë sisters is definitely dominated by a particular lyrical persona.** I believe that a closer analysis of the emergence and of the development of Gondal and Angria provides the scholar with the appropriate contextual background for the investigation of the evolution of *THE MOURNER/THE SURVIVOR* – the principal lyrical persona in the Brontë sisters' poetry (perceived as one common thematic whole, but also as one unit consisting of three unique literary entities). For this main lyrical persona the main hermeneutical „tool" for interpreting existence is DEATH – *the Other's Death*, which he/she is given to cherish and to read over and over again – a lifetime Duty not only in respect of the memory of that *Dead Other*, but also with regard to *the Survivor's* possible successors. Naturally, each of the three Brontë sisters' main lyrical persona bears specific features of character, yet the three sisters share a common belief in the ethic and aesthetic significance of the *MOURNER*. At this point, a terminological clarification needs to be made. The term *„lyrical persona"* applies to the whole of the Brontë sisters' poetic heritage, which chronologically exceeds the contextual limits of Gondal/Angria. This chief lyrical persona, already defined as „*THE MOURNER/THE SURVIVOR*", is philosophically ampler and belongs to a higher order in comparison to concrete main lyrical personae of either Gondal or Angria. In this sense, **Augusta Geraldine Alme[i]da (Gondal's Queen)** is only one variation of the MOURNER/SURVIVOR. Gondal and Angria are, nonetheless, so deeply and irrevocably interwoven into the texture of the Brontë sisters' poetry as a whole (this is least evident in Anne Brontë's case) that the nature of the main lyrical persona inevitably relies on the specificities of the main lyrical personae of Angria and particularly of Gondal, whose fate, indeed, is to OUTLIVE *the OTHER*. Another term applicable is „*lyrical speaker*" (introduced in Bulgarian literary criticism by professor Nicola Georgiev in his critical study *Analysis of the Lyrical Work*[ii]). The lyrical speaker may be observed to lurk as a third party between the author (the poet) and the specific lyrical personae (Angrian and Gondalian): describing their emotions, feelings and reflections, but at times dropping an odd confession about his/her own self (one example is the commentator who appears towards the end of Emily Brontë's poem *The Death of A.G.A.*, 1841–1844). Emotionally, this lyrical speaker rather resembles *THE MOURNER*, so that although he/she may be structurally higher than each single persona, yet he/she often merges with the voice of a lyrical persona (for instance, in Emily Brontë's poetry Augusta herself might well be a commentator of Life, as though she is perched on a high position and watches everything from a bird's eye view). Last, but not least, it should be mentioned that in that confessional portion of each sister's poetic heritage which is independent of the context of either Gondal or Angria, the confessions and lyrical digressions belong to what may be termed a „*Lyrical Self*", who talks about himself/herself through his/her reflections on the theme of DEATH, and on *the Other's Death* in particular. This Lyrical Self's search for a moral authority, for an external referee, brings him/her close to some of Gondal's and of Angria's main lyrical personae (as well as to the Lyrical Speaker) – they all feel the need to share, to confess, to make penitence, to tell their stories – before the END seizes that invaluuable opportunity from them.

It is beyond doubt that the theme of the present research is relevant on a larger scale – it offers a view on the development of **English literary history of mid-18th–19th centuries:** a period in which the thematic focus on Death and Mortality is rather obvious. One secondary task of my research is to substantiate my belief that Mortality/Death is the most adequate thematic link between the Brontë sisters' poetry and the literary context, in which the genius of each one of them rises. A particular favourite of the Romantic poets' (and in the broader 19th-century European context), the themes of *Mortality/Death* are contained in a philosophic duality which marries, and makes exist simultaneously, CHANGE and PERMANENCE. On the one hand, the tripartite formula „*dying–deathbed–grave"* is charged with the idea of transition, of resurrection, of prolongation of earthly existence (through merging with Nature's Pan), but on the other – with the notion of permanent decay, of irreversible dissolution (i.e. the body's irrevocable physical corruption[6]). In this respect, the merit of the Brontë sisters' poetry lies in their conscientious recognition of the importance of the notion of Death as inescapable in the formation of the individual's strife for *Being* amongst, and thanks to, *Other* individuals who define the limits and limitations (both physical and philosophic) of one man's life. Logically, one more statement to defend would be that the themes of *Mortality* not only underpin a „diachronic cut" of the development of the Brontë sisters' literary genius, but also of the development of English literature of the mid 18th–late 19th-centuries. At that, the Brontë sisters' attitude towards Death far exceeds a simplistic argument which might read their poetry as merely a desire to surmount man's imperfection and transience, or else to gain immortality through a spontaneous dissolution in Nature's ever active void of mutability. I would argue that, to the Brontës, the awareness of Death is that thematic component of man's consciousness which transforms *Life* from being an Option into being a *Duty*. The Duty to accomplish a wholesome harmonious selfhood through an active and responsible relation to *someone Other than You*, who is at all times both an antecedent and a

---

[6] Cf Wheeler, Michael, *Heaven, Hell and the Victorians* (CUP, 1994), p. 183. Michael Wheeler also offers an excerpt from William Wordsworth's *Excursion*:

Death and its two-fold aspect! wintry-one,
Cold, sullen, blank, from hope and joy shut out;
The other, which the ray divine hath touched,
Replete with vivid promise, bright as spring.
(ibid. p. 28)

successor to *Your Being*, which is thus only qualified as *Co-Being*. That *OTHER* individual – the „mirror" of the Self and an objectifier of reality – verifies Being as such. Without him/her living equals Non-Being, as it is deprived of *a Redeemer* at *the furthermost line of existence called Death*. One of the tasks of this thesis is to prove that Emily's, Charlotte's and Anne's poetry shows that each sister followed a different route, yet all the three eventually reached the above conclusions.

I see the crucial experimental element of the present research in my attempt to closely examine and emphasize the relevance of the themes of *Mortality* in an interdisciplinary manner – within a certain period of English literary history (and with a particular interest in the Brontë sisters' poetic input) alongside the investigation of certain major concepts of **modern ontophilosophy and existential ethics**. Such methodology of research which employs immediately the merits and theoretical achievements on the given topic of **Martin Heidegger, Emmanuel Levinas, Jacques Derrida and Mikhail Bakhtin**[7] and accommodates those within the field of studying English Romantic and Early Victorian Poetry[8] appears innovative. I have embraced this methodology of research with the conviction that it is the most adequate one to reveal the Brontë sisters' ontological search and growth. Additionally, the theme of the

---

[7] Whilst I have familiarized myself with the appropriate translations of Bakhtin's works in the English language, I mostly make references – often almost too literal – to his works, relying, however, on my personal and professional/academic knowledge of Russian, in which I have read his major essays. I consider that a fair and exact explanation of Bakhtin's views with their original in Russian in mind should pose as no shortcoming to a critical work which is written in English by a non-native speaker of English. All the main terms of Bakhtin's theory I use in my research I have verified through a diligent comparison to their equivalents in English. And I consider direct quotations from the official translations of his works in English to be too far-fetched a tool for presenting his theory, which, it ought to be clarified, is only used as a theoretical skeleton to a critical investigation which is focused specifically on three English female poets of the 19th century. Heidegger's *Sein Und Zeit*, it must also be pointed out, is referred to in accordance with its Russian translation /the 1997 edition/: this one is the most comprehensive translation of Heidegger's monograph extant. Neither the English, nor the Bulgarian versions are as well equipped with explanatory notes and critical specifications as this one is. Again, as a non-native speaker of English, German, or Russian, my interest in Heidegger was from the angle of theory, rather than from a practical angle, which is why the references are made in good earnest to the Russian edition of *Sein Und Zeit*. The same logic applies to Levinas' works, which I greatly know by their translations in the Russian language.

[8] The literary period in hand has been approached in depth by almost all contemporary literary schools. This fact will be paid due respect in the survey of the criticism available on the Brontës in the thematic area of Mortality/Death, which follows the introduction.

present thesis is a good opportunity to examine the validity of one certain aspect of modern philosophy and ethics – *ontology* – on the level of an analysis of English poetry of the mid 18th–19th centuries. There is a contemporary rise of interest towards the themes of Death/Mortality, and I hereby join one apparent academic and artistic reaction against one tendency of the modern world to alienate this theme from matters of everyday concern with the naïve hope that one could postpone Death as such. The other tendency of the modern world, which I fervently adhere to, is to discuss the theme of Death/Mortality in order to make it more familiar and to incorporate it in an attempt to unite man's efforts to achieve a more harmonious, considerate and altruistic lifestyle[iii].

An additional factor in support of the argument of <u>the significance of the theme of research is its practical validity</u>. To paraphrase Hans-Georg Gadamer (*Wahrheit Und Methode*), Death is a classical theme, because it signifies itself and treats itself through its own happening, through its own realization. Death befalls each individual not as an uttering about something long lost, not as an evidence of something which once was: it addresses Modernity as though it was coined especially to objectify this very moment. Death, as a discourse, is classical because, sadly, it requires no efforts to overcome some historical distance. Death is itself the mediator between the Past/History and Modernity[iv] and yet it is never confirmed as such by the direct bearer of its effects but always by a Survivor, who could never confirm for a fact his/her own contact with Death either. <u>From an ethical point of view</u>, then, an occasion of Death summons man to demonstrate empathy towards a phenomenon of which no one has a direct experience whilst being alive. This is a paradox which did not remain unnoticed by the Brontë sisters, as the structure of both Gondal and Angria would demonstrate. In both Angria and Gondal the alternating elimination and resuscitation of certain lyrical personae demonstrate their creators' struggle to find one firm and unequivocal route which would lead the individual towards ontological perfection – in art, but in reality too (it would suffice to recall the numerous names under which A.G.A. appears in Gondal – Sidonia's deity, Rosina of Alcona, Geraldine, Rochelle etc. – a confirmation of Emily Brontë's hesitation over her authorial right to punish/abolish this sinisterly charismatic lyrical persona who thematically functions as Gondal's axis). The overall weight and value of the theme of research find support in the fact that DEATH proves to have been an issue of intense debate and disagreement between some major religious denominations and philosophic movements of 18th–19th-century England[9] (more details are to be provided in relevant chapters further on). The present research, therefore, endeavours to highlight certain aspects of the Brontë sisters' religious input in the development of *the philosophic discourse of Mortality/Death*.

*   *   *

The critical approach in a certain work of research is generally considered to be a matter of free choice. In this case I choose ***ontophilosophy* and *existential ethics* (represented by Martin Heidegger, Emmanuel Levinas, Jacques Derrida and Mikhail Bakhtin), which could alternatively be termed *Dialogism*.** Yet on the matter of freedom of choice in Life, I should like to adhere to Hans-Georg Gadamer's *hermeneutics*, according to which an individual's appearance is more or less a matter of accident – the horizon which is allotted to one is an open entity which haunts one so long as one is alive – it sustains itself, but it also mutates, it evolves. One immediate consequence of the latter is that the meaning of a text is always „higher" (i.e. broader, ampler) that its author's treatment of it: the act of interpreting a text is always also a productive attitude towards it (an not just a reproductive one). Exactly because of this it should be a responsible attitude. The critic chooses to depict an image in a certain manner which then becomes a part of that image itself – so representation is an act of participation in Being, it is, as Gadamer calls it „*Dabeisein"*. Participation means partiality towards a given viewpoint about life – such that it would bring about Being's growth, evolution, abundance and wholesomeness. The employment of ontophilosophy in the case of analyzing *Mortality/ Death* in the Brontë sisters' poetry is, to my deep belief, what the essence of *Being*, which is what the three sisters broadly deal with in their poetic heritage (as understood by the Brontës in the relation „*Mourner – Dead Other")* would really profit from. Such an approach, whose focus is on the contents, and

---

[9] Those would include: Calvinism, Methodism, Evangelicalism, the Oxford movement; Pantheism and Deism etc.

not on the form, contains a minimal dose of an imposition on the literary empirical material available itself, which, without losing its authenticity, would unfold so as to show the three sisters' unique treatment of Death. The Brontë sisters' perseverance in exploring Death and Mortality seems logical in view of their historical, social, philosophic and literary environment, whose orientation was towards matters existential, rather than purely aesthetic (like the purpose of art, for example – a question that certainly gathered head towards the turn of the 19th century). It therefore makes sense to take into deep consideration the overall literary and biographical contexts of the poetry of the Brontë sisters, as well as the specificities of the personalities of Emily, Charlotte and Anne Brontë – insofar as those are accessible to the critic from their works extant, from the biographical data about these three poets, as well as from relevant criticism which has accumulated until present. In other words, the critical approach in the present study detaches itself from any attempt to artificially manipulate the text with the sole purpose of being original in saying something which has never been said before, or in saying something which appears quite groundless yet intriguing because it contradicts all critical viewpoints already expressed. The choice of the methodology of research is made with the belief that one could never really have the last word about a literary work. In this sense, the contemporary taste for deconstructing the text would appear rather amateurish, being a good linguistic exercise, but missing out on in depth philosophic analysis, missing out on an adequate hermeneutical treatment of the literary, philosophic and historical background against which the Brontë sisters really stand out. A critic's desire to merely deconstruct this poetic heritage is, to my mind, egotistical and prejudiced. A technique which always offers categorically new ideas, but does so at the expense of neglecting the covert but ever present *Other* participant (the reader, the interlocutor, the author, the other critic etc.) is a weakness of nature. And *Otherness* is, as was mentioned earlier, to dominate in *a dialogic attitude* to Art, as well as to Life. <u>The method of research could therefore be defined as focused on the **contents** of the works</u> (both the contents of their creation and the contents of their expression), <u>rather than on their formal characteristics</u>. Analysis of the formal characteristics of a given poem is more sporadic in this research than may be expected, and is undertaken only whenever the form is obviously and indivisibly interwoven into the contents and the kernel meaning of a given idea/concept[vi]. As stated earlier, there is a conscientious striving to trace down the development of one major lyrical persona, of one man's life, in each of those poetic worlds – with the purpose of elucidating the ontological value of the theme of *Mortality* in man's Being. A theme which speaks of the phenomenon with the uttermost capacity to finalize, summarize and condense a lifetime experience and turn it into one (non-) accomplished fate. Indeed, *Death* – as the flawless „tool" which moulds Life into a lifetime, into a biography[vii].

I believe I have reached the point where it would be necessary and useful to highlight some of the main ideas and concepts relevant to the theme of *Mortality,* as developed by the four philosophers mentioned above. Embarking on such rather lengthy introductory part, I anticipate certain criticism. Superficially, every such more or less detailed theoretical „digression" at this initial stage of the research hides the risk of „dissolving" the real focus of the introduction. Whilst I abide by the perception that the introduction to a major research must clearly declare the theme, the tasks of research and the motivation for the choice of the theme of research, I would like, additionally, to pay special attention to the methodology of research. I believe that because the theoretical basis of the research (namely, modern ontophilosophy) is innovative to Brontë studies, and because it utilizes simultaneously extensive monographic studies of four different major 20th-century philosophers, it is worth dedicating the next three quarters of the introduction to an overview of how those might be summarized with regard to the present theme of research, i.e. see how they may relate to the Brontë sisters' poetry. I trust that the research itself, as well its possible target readership, would benefit from a summary of my main theoretical points, which should, indeed, be placed initially, rather than anywhere else.

* * *

First published in **1927**, **Martin Heidegger's** *Sein und Zeit* (*Being and Time*, abbreviated throughout this thesis as *„SUZ"*, the 1997 edition) reads as his thorough and in depth presentation of his **phenomenology**, which unfolds as **ontology**[viii]. Heidegger starts his discussion of the phenomenon of Mortality through an analysis of the concept of ***care***[10]. **Care** *unlocks* man's existence in that it confirms life's relativism. Heidegger proposes *care* as one exemplification/ phenomenon of objective reality, yet it is also highlighted through his fascination with the original meaning of the present participle *phenomenon,* which in Greek means „looking as though/ appearing like." Verbally uttered, or executed in truth, it is subject to degeneration (Cf Heidegger *Sein und Zeit,* [in Russian] *Bityie I Vremya,* Moskva: AD MARGINEM 1997, pp. 27–29), as it could never be exemplified in two fully identical ways. This ambiguity, Heidegger continues, is best demonstrated in the phenomenon of Death because it is the one that most obviously and undeniably depends on two individuals whose task is to confirm it. However, **Death,** like everything else, is not substance. For, if Death were substance, it would not require another substance to confirm it. In this sense, Death's counterpoint would be God – a being who is unconditional because it is prior to any hermeneutical urge, to any urge to interpret (*SUZ,* p. 92). In Cartesian terms, Death lies in both *res cogitans* (the *I* item, the individual's consciousness), and in *res extensa* (the existent external world – ibid. p. 98). Death can only be declared for a fact in view of someone else's presence, which reveals that Death's nature is one of an event (or, what Bakhtin would term „*so-bytiye", i.e. „co-existence", „co-being"*). The above reflections could throw some light onto Emily Brontë's interpretation of the phenomenon of *mutability,* as the latter emerges as an issue in her earliest poetic period of 1837–1839. *Mutability* is doubly relevant and invokes melancholy in a human being's mind, because, first of all, as a natural phenomenon, it is ingrained in Life's evolution, but also because man realises the latter predominantly in his/her mind (i.e. mutability becomes relevant in a unique verbal manner for each individual: this diversity makes it unstable a phenomenon in itself; compare especially poems H2, H3, H4, H54, H147 and H31 in Hatfield's 1941 edition of Emily Brontë's verse).

The analytics of ***Being*** is closely interrelated with that of ***presence,*** which implies living amongst *Others* whilst recognizing the need for a

---

[10] It is only within a caring circle of *other* individuals that man could at all dare interpret **the meaning of Being,** which is what *ontology* deals with. „The phenomenology of presence is indeed *hermeneutics* in the original meaning of this word (…)" The phenomenon of presence bears an ontological advantage to all other phenomena (Cf Heidegger, M., SUZ, 1997, pp. 36–37).

positive appropriation of the Past, which is what would enhance the factual verifiability of each one presence. Heidegger's perception of *presence* is that presence is an *'event'*, or an act of *'co-being'*[11] (SUZ, pp. 21, 38). As such, it is subject to temporal limits, but then <u>temporality is a transcendent truth too</u>. Time is directly linked to Space because the spatial boundaries of an event/ an object depend on the temporal and temporary status of the observer/ the participant. In this case, the World reveals itself as an entity continuously undergoing various shifts and alterations, so that Space alone could not be a good marker of one man's consciousness and inner world, of one man's identity. <u>Space only co-constitutes the World, but does not create or define it – man' *Presence* does (SUZ, pp. 109–113). Physical matter is thus trapped, or rather, positioned, within an „ontological vice".</u> Consequently, *Presence* is never merely physical presence, but is *co-presence, co-being, co-existence. Other individuals* constitute a whole to which one is given access so that one might achieve Co-Being. Therefore the lack of *an Other* (caused by that Other's death, or when one is trapped in a state of solitude) is an event too. Since that Other's lack could only really and definitely be experienced by a human being for whom that Other would have been the „other" constitutive element in the act of Co-Being. Thus <u>Death</u> (as the Other's Death, which causes solitude) causes a <u>defective model of Co-Being</u> to emerge for the Survivor (SUZ, pp. 118–120).

Whilst trying to naturally escape Death, <u>every presence contains the *idea* of Death</u>. In its existence, **Dasein** (i.e. every *Being as Presence*) Heidegger argues, represents a constant process of dying (SUZ, pp. 251–252). ***Being towards Death*** <u>is in effect Being towards a possibility which makes every Presence unique in its own way</u>. It would appear that the notion of Death has an alienating effect on one's mind, whilst in this conscientiously achieved state of solitude one manages to escape from the anonymity of Co-Being (i.e. of Being with, and for the sake of, Others). The Russian literary critic Tatiana Shtitsova observes also that Heidegger's *Mit-*

---

[11] Indeed, in English both the word *'event'* and the word *'co-being/co-existence'* are possible translations of the Russian word *'sobytije'* (which is how Heidegger's ideas on the matter in German have been treated in Russian). 'Event' would emphasise temporality and verifiability, whereas 'co-being' would stress the notion of the importance of the existence of a second being/ second observer/ second participant.

Sein is in obvious conflict with the ideal which defines the ontological interpretation of existence, but in the long run, this conflict is productive, because it leads (for Bakhtin and his followers) towards recognizing the need of the Other in the impasse of insurmountable solitude (Cf Shitsova, Tatiana. /in Russian/ *Sobytije v filosofii Bakhtina*. Minsk. I. I. Logvinov. 2002, pp. 207–208). The strife towards accomplishing Death as a possibility implies suicide, and suicide would deprive the individual of his/her chance to realize his/her Presence in a wholesome manner. Death should therefore remain at all times *a possibility only,* so that Presence should mean anticipation, rather than fulfilment (SUZ, p. 261). Whilst still alive, an individual's Presence happens constantly and is never Past, as such. Presence becomes Past only when it is no more available, is no more ready at hand, which is why the still existent presence could never establish itself in an empirically verifiable manner (SUZ, p. 328). Our world, which is Time's subject, is a „multiple" of the phenomenon of presence (SUZ, p. 365).

The world, the rest of people – the Self's true external component – has the privilege of owning the knowledge of finality, i.e. of Death (SUZ, p. 62). Since Presence could never be accomplished its end is always imminent, is always forthcoming. Heidegger believes that Death is best described as *that which is forthcoming.* And, as presence is in effect anticipation of the future, then ultimately, presence is the unavoidable anticipation of death – the unconditional possibility of both Being and reaching the limit of Being (SUZ, p. 250). If one were to paraphrase Hans-Georg Gadamer, Death is a perfect example of an *experience*: its validity is confirmed each time it happens, yet each time it happens in a different, in another manner. Death is that which could be defined as *the other experience,* or as *The Experience Itself.* Typically, each one experience of Death contains negativity, because it both verifies and refutes its previous appearances, yet this very negativity proves productive (Gadamer, 1988, pp. 414, 416, 419). Until we experience Death we are dogmatic, but when we do, we are no more... to relate this Experience, this Event, in a non-dogmatic manner[12]. Ironically, as a possibility, Death cannot give presence

---

[12] Influenced by Kant's *Critique of Pure Judgement*, Heidegger believes that truths are confirmed for a fact not by objects contemplated, but by the thought about those. That is, consciousness is prior to physics. In this sense, truth is „available" so long as presence is. Therefore man's personality is

anything to accomplish: _Death is the possibility of the impossibility_ (SUZ, p. 262) – the innermost place of Bakhtin's polemic with Heidegger, as would be revealed later.

To use the notion of Death in order to live _for the sake of the Other_, rather than _after/without the Other_[ix] is what Bakhtin would argue in his aesthetics. Heidegger also meets the opposition of **Paul Ricoeur**, who questions the efficiency of such a deep focus on the idea of the End as leading man's evolution. To Ricoeur, the idea of the imminent End feels a constraint, rather than a stimulus for Being. His argument is that in _Sein und Zeit_ Heidegger appears to be oblivious of the phenomenon of _birth_, the knowledge of which is much greater an impetus for man to enjoy a lifetime of mutuality than Death can ever be. In addition, Ricoeur sees that such insistence on the dominance of the knowledge of Death is not far from creating an idea about a Future as containing the undeniable possibility for Death _imposed_ on man, i.e. for murder – the ultimate threat, unpredictable and detrimental. In other words, the Future also contains the possibility of Death as a non-option, but as something which could be externally executed on one – by another individual (Cf Ricoeur, Paul, _La mémoire, l'histoire, l'oubli_, Editions du Seuil, 2000, /in Russian/ _Pamiat', istoria, zabvenie_. Moskva. Izdatel'stvo gumanitarnoi literaturij. 2004, pp. 498–499, p. 503).

To return to the argument which I used to introduce Heidegger's theory, _Being-in-the-world_ means _Care_. So, Presence is underpinned with the idea of Care (SUZ, pp. 195–196). That is why Being is always Co-Being. The ontological significance of Care, Heidegger affirms, is seen in the phenomenon of _Temporality_ (SUZ, p. 364). Death is that ingredient of Temporality that should intensify man's Being understood as Care – within a certain period of time, after a certain/certain individuals who would be categorized in relation to him/her as Other(s). One crucial ingredient of the phenomenon of Care is _Forgiveness_ – extensively explored by all the Brontë sisters in their mature works (e.g. Anne Brontë's _The Power of Love_ 1846, „_Believe not those who say_" – 1848 and „_A dreadful darkness closes in_" 1849, or Emily Brontë's „_Why ask to know the date –_

---

open to _the Other_ insofar as man's presence is detectable. Truth, Heidegger argues, dies with the expiration of every presence (SUZ, pp. 203, 213, 226).

the clime" 1846). It is paradoxical that the practice of forgiving *the Other* shortens the forgiver's own lifetime. That is, the recognition of the uniqueness of *that Other* is executed with the notion of the possible/feasible lack/Death/ of this Other in the forgiver's mind. That introduces the concept of Non-Being as inevitable to the still living man too. A *dialogic understanding of Death* implies knowledge and remembrance of the phenomenon of Death, but not the voluntarily executed Death (which the Brontë sisters' early works naïvely worship as a sure route to avoid desecration by one reaching old age[13]).

In practice, the only guarantee that *Death* could be had in an ontologically comprehensible manner is by virtue of becoming the Survivor after, or the witness of, another individual's Death – in order to confirm that Death for a fact. For Heidegger, *Non-Being-in-the-World* still implies Being, but Being-as-an-item (SUZ, p. 237–238). Such possible itemization of an individual does not, nonetheless, take away from his/ her relevance to the people who are still alive[14]. *The Art of Death* is not the Art of Dying, but the art of remembering that „you, too, will die". This unique fruit of knowledge[x] summons man to contemplate Death as inevitability, but an inevitability which should urge one to live more bravely: to make oneself more readily useful to the Other – the true way to liberate oneself from Death's actual grip.

One particular point of the analysis of Death which Heidegger

---

[13] The hermeneutics of Death in the Contemporary Age has completely drifted away from the treatment which Death received in the tradition of the Old Greek epic. According to the latter, the status of a hero was granted to one who succeeded in avoiding dying old, but who embraced Death earlier. Not to come to terms with Death as a natural conclusion of man's life, but to voluntarily accept to bear its effects whilst being young is what the Greeks considered a heroic encounter with Death (the essence of the voluntarily chosen death in the fate of a number of major personae in Homer's epic *The Iliad*). The truly negative element of dying was hidden in the fact that the living might become oblivious of a deceased individual – when his/her name would be remembered by the living no more and thus the departed person's reputation would be ruined. The sincerely devoted *Survivor* in Ancient Greece was therefore required to act as a receptacle of the memory of the dead hero – he would remind the World about *the dead one* and thus guard his memory which would thus defeat *Mortality* (Cf Vernant, Jean-Pierre *L'Individu, La Mort, L'Amour*, [in Bulgarian] Individat, Smartta, Liubovta. Sofia. Nov Balgarski Universitet. 2004, pp. 62–65).

[14] This argument feels even more solid in view of the realisation that with Death, a certain individual's presence may not have finished, may not have utilised the whole of his/her potential. For, after all, one's Presence, Heidegger argues, may have been violated, and may have been denied an opportunity to unfold. On the other hand, just because someone has died does not automatically mean that that person has reached spiritual maturity (SUZ, p. 244).

reaches appears particularly relevant to the Brontë sisters' philosophy. Namely, that *Co-Being* contains the notion that <u>one Presence is interchangeable with another within the same dichotomy</u>. Presence could never really be complete because Co-Being is possible only when the two individuals are on the same side of Existence (SUZ, pp. 239, 242). Death leaves the Survivor with a feeling of loss, but never the loss of one's own existence: as soon as a dichotomy of Co-Being is being destroyed, there immediately emerges an opportunity for another such dichotomy to form through a new acquisition in it (SUZ, pp. 238–239). In their poetry, Emily, Charlotte and Anne Brontë endeavour to fill up this free ontological position left after the Other's Death. However, fill it in not by another individual (which is where they could be seen to disagree with Heidegger). They do that through the introduction of the so-called *missing lyrical persona*. Oftentimes that is the Ghost of the dead parent/beloved, which steps over the boundary between the dead and the living in order to satiate the Mourner's sense of incompleteness. Interestingly enough, Emily Brontë's Nature contains that ingredient of *Otherness* which is always primary and authorially protective over man (e.g. *the Wind* plays such role in many of her poems[15]). Charlotte Brontë sees the missing Other as *the ghost/ the female visitant/ the silent Nun* – the dead woman who finalizes the *Survivor's* existence (often a man) whilst charging it with the knowledge of the unique phenomenon of Co-Being which now appears broken and irreparable (see especially the poems: *Gilbert* – around 1843, and *Well, the day's toils are over, with success* – 1837). For Anne Brontë *the Survivor's* tragedy is in that she outlives the better one, the nobler one. The missing lyrical persona for her is *the dead mother, the husband*, but particularly prominent is Anne's choice of *Christ* as capable of bestowing universal pardon to man. The Brontë sisters overcome what would normally be seen as the paralyzing fear of Death through their insistence on the active and feasible role the *Dead Other* plays in the Survivors' dutiful ontological growth.

For Heidegger, *Death* is the ultimate ontological regulator of *Time*. It is an availability which makes one's time on earth worth its while: as the

---

[15] See the poems: Alone I sat, the summer day 1837; O evening, why is thy light so sad; Shall Earth no more inspire thee 1841; Lines 1837.

utmost boundary of existence, Death is man's chance to complete the Option of Being as Co-Being[16] (SUZ, p. 435). Heidegger's *Dasein* faces Death but does not cross the boundary of Death: it is, after all, Being that happens during Life. Death means completion, but within the semiotics of real life and for Survivors[xi]. The awareness of Death draws contours around Life: the awareness of Death has the storage capacity to transform Life into fate, into a meaningful span of Time on Earth[xii].

Again, it would appear logical to start the presentation of **Emmanuel Levinas'** vision of Death with an emphasis on the phenomenon of *Care* (one of Heidegger's concepts). There are a number of Levinas' works I have used in this research: those were mainly written in the period late 1940s – early 1970s and they all seem to revolve around issues like: Time, Otherness, Transcendence. One way to start the discussion of Levinas' perception of Death would be to clarify his belief that the individual's quality of being responsible to, and for the sake of, another human being should always dominate and act prior to one's urge to merely be intentional as a subject (Cf Levinas, E. [in Bulgarian] *Houmanizam kam drougia tchovek.* Izdatelstvo SONM. 1997, p. 79). As Paul Ricoeur argues, one's identity, albeit being grammatically definable through the personal pronoun „I", or through the reflexive pronoun „Self/Oneself", contains No indication as to some permanent and immutable core of one's personality (Cf Ricoeur, Paul, *Soi-même come un autre*, Editions du Seuil, 1990, [in Bulgarian] *Samiat sebe si kato niakoi Drug.* Pleven. „EA" AD. 2004, p. 11). Paying close attention on Levinas' theory of Otherness, Ricoeur continues: the attestation that one is oneself should, on all levels, be verified through the awareness that one is active, that one „*suffers*" *reality* for the sake of another. The question „*Who*" should at all times be subordinate to the questions „*What*" and „*Why*" (Cf Ricoeur, ibid., p. 42). *Self-awareness* remains an option unfulfilled, is only an act of thinking, until the moment when it is objectified through the dialogic structure which the reference to *the Other* introduces (Cf Ricoeur, ibid., p. 272). There is no Self without an Other who summons man to be responsible (Cf Ricoeur, ibid., p. 295). The feeling of *duty* towards *the Other*, Levinas argues,

---

[16] In the context of the Brontë sisters' poetry, a confirmation of the latter idea is found, for example, in Anne Brontë's mature poem *A Word to the Calvinists* (1843).

instills such power in one's lifetime (always a limited span of time) as is capable of incapacitating Death in the face of man's endless Care and love for the Other person[17] (Cf Levinas, Emmanuel. [in Bulgarian] *Sobstveni imena*. SONM. 1997, p. 91).

Unlike Heidegger, Levinas believes that living should be *Being-in spite of-Death*, rather than *Being-towards-Death*. Thus Being becomes intentional through the strife to disseminate Good – the only element of Life which the knowledge of Death is powerless to destroy (Cf Ricoeur, *La mémoire...*, 2004, p. 503). The uttermost expression of man's potential to be good is to demonstrate sensitivity and sensibility towards another person's Death (Levinas, E. [in Bulgarian] *Drougost I transtsendentnost*. SONM 1999, p. 165). The experience of outliving another person is a sure reminder of one's own finality, an in effect, an evidence of one's own Self (as still alive). The ontological superiority of *the Other* person over „Me" becomes most obvious at the moment of Death which is the moment of liminal doubt: doubt in the adequacy of reality without the Other[18]. Does one actually possess the right to exist solely for himself/ herself? Levinas' answer is negative (Cf Levinas, E. *De l'existence à l'existant. Totalité et Infini*. P. Fontaine, 1947; [in Russian] *Total'nost' I beskonetchnost'*. Moskva – Sankt-Peterburg. 2000, p. 359). *The Other* is the kernel ingredient in morality. The Other's Being and well-being precedes any debate about the independence of man's mind. With no Otherness available, man's individuality is shattered (ibid. p. 362; see also Levinas, E. [in Russian] *Vremia I drougoi*. Visshaya Religiozno-Filosofskaya Shkola. Sankt-Peterburg 1998, p. 69). In a group of early poems of Charlotte Brontë's which deal with the theme of the lost home the lyrical Self is trying find rescue under the spiritually enlightening and protective influence of The Other which elevates his spirit above its carnal case (see especially the

---

[17] Again, Paul Ricoeur maintains that *Care* is not an element attached externally to one's *self-awareness*, to one's identity, to one's self-respect, but that it makes possible for the dialogic dimension of self-awareness to unfold so that Care and self-awareness ought never to be considered as separate items but only within the logic of one common whole (Cf Ricoeur, *Samiat Sebe si...*2004, pp. 284–285).

[18] We tend to transfer the knowledge of the Other on ourselves which helps us realise the uniqueness of our own lives: „*I am, first of all and above all, indispensable to the Other*" (Cf Ricoeur, *Samiat Sebe si...*, 2004, pp. 305–305). In the irreparable experience of the loss of *the Other* we get to know the essence of our own Being.

16.

poems *But once again, but once again,* 1836 and *Richard's Song,* 1833).
Further on, a more mature variation of the sought for Other in Charlotte
Brontë's poetry appears to be *the female ghost,* which embodies the poet's
ideas about purity and moral perfection. The female ghost is the one
mourned, irrevocably lost and unapproachable because belonging to a
higher order of existence (see, for instance, the poem *Matin* 1830).

Another aspect of Death Levinas emphasizes is that <u>Death is „*the
naught of knowledge.* (…) it does not enter the human mind (…) it is
an event without a project"</u> (Cf Levinas, Emmanuel. *Drougost i
transtsendentnost.* 1999, p. 161). In practice, Death contains no
possibility whatsoever. He thus apostrophizes and corrects Heidegger:
Death is not *the total possibility of impossibility,* but the „*utter
impossibility of possibility"* (ibid. p. 163). Clearly enough, the matter is
not merely limited within some kind of linguistic equilibrium – possibility,
impossibility etc. Death always contains, potentially, the promise of the
impossibility of the existence of any one person who may have previously
survived/outlived someone Other. <u>Yet, so long as a survivor is alive, Death
matters only through *the Other individual's death*</u> (i.e. the death of the
parent, the relative, the friend, the wife/ husband, at last – the death of any
one stranger whom each one man meets so as to, at least once, relate
himself/herself to it). Logically, one *can only be perceived as a survivor
with regard to some other individual's Death.* **To remember that
„you, too, will die, and die after someone Other than You –
that is an ethical attitude to life"** (ibid. p. 173). It is in view of the
certainty of Death that *the Other* (and his/ her actual/ possible death)
„challenges the egotistical spontaneity of the self-contained mind"[xiii].
Ostensibly, the phenomenon of Death presents an insoluble paradox to the
artist's imagination, because how could one find the creative power to give
substance to something one could never have a direct personal experience
of during one's own lifetime?! It seems that an empathetic attitude to an
event of Death is not enough to ignite the artistic impulse to describe
something to which any Survivor has no access anyway. Yet Levinas' answer
to that is that *the Other* and the responsibility towards that Other during a
Lifetime itself is each author's/poet's/creator's/man's chance to gain access
to the utterly impossible. It is *the Other* that gives one the chance to own
Time whilst also outlining and indeed limiting it. In the Bulgarian context of

literary criticism, Professor Atanas Buchkov re-iterates Levinas: „I am responsible for *the Other's Death* in as much as I include myself in that Death" (Cf Buchkov, Atanas. *Aporiite v „Smartta na edna ptitza"*. Plovdivski Universitet „P. Hilendarski". Naoutchni trudove. Tom 41. kniga 1. 2003). In fact *the Other's Death* is the only Death ever feasible and meaningful for man – „*the Other's Death inside Me – My Death*" (ibid). In this context, the Survivor's despair born out of the absence of the Other is the organizing centre of the literary act as such[19].

The artist always struggles to itemize Death, to make it qualify as an object[xiv]. That is also evident in Emily Brontë's alternating elimination and resuscitation of Gondal's main lyrical persona, A.G.A. There is the poet's attempt to examine the phenomenon of Death as both observer and bearer of its effects. The poet now merges with A.G.A. (in many personal lyrics and confessional poems), now stands apart from her, recounting versions of her Death. The merging of *author – hero*, or in lyrics – of *poet – lyrical persona*, speaks of the poet's toils over defining the boundaries and value of Life as it happens.

Further on, the structured image of Time, as Levinas believes, is defined by the place of Death in man's life. The division of Time into Present v/s Non-Present is not merely a physical concept. The fact that Death is never Present Time for the dead individual is true not because of the physical gap left after each person's death, or because of a body representing nothing after expiration. Rather, Death is never the Present because the dead individual is incapable of grasping the reality of Death in a conscious way so as to respond to it, to answer it. Being dead is therefore equal to being irresponsive (Cf Levinas, Emmanuel. *Vremia I Drougoi.* 1998, pp. 71–72). That is why the Future always befalls us and never comes gradually. The Future is something Other – Other than what we are (ibid. pp. 76, 81). Where Levinas deviates from Heidegger is in that he stresses upon the unexpectedness of Death, which is always overwhelming to man and could not be the aim of man's Being. The contemporary

---

[19] It would be interesting to note that, in an article on Arthur Schopenhauer (which pays special tribute to his essay *On Death and Its Relation to the Indestructibility of Our True Nature*) Richard Taylor summarizes that representations of pain and suffering (and not of happiness) prove rather more beneficial for the overall impact and strength of a literary work than do representations of happiness and of luck (Cf Richard Taylor in: Smart, N., /ed./ Nineteenth-Century Religious Thought in the West /CUP, 1985/).

Russian philosopher Andrey Demichev observes that, unlike Heidegger, Levinas' perception of Death is characterized by a strong feeling of uneasiness about it, of fear which tightens the horizon of choice for man because man feels vulnerable like a child deprived of maternal care. Death cannot be therefore captured fully even in our imagination: it always befalls us as something totally different, totally other than what we are used to (Cf Demichev, 1997, pp. 59–60). In young Anne Brontë's poetry one could detect a fear of the Present, which results from the painful realisation that a Present divested of the Presence of one's dearest people is a gap, is Noneity. The departure of the Mother, in particular, leaves the Survivor apprehensive about the unfamiliar Future – would Mourner and Mourned succeed in reuniting[20].

The Present, according to Levinas, should demonstrate remembrance and forgiveness towards the Past[xv]: it ought to forgive anything that would have been qualified as wrong whilst *the Other* was still alive. Forgiveness – a moral category central to the Brontë sisters' philosophy – is seen as a tool capable of reversing Time, so that the Past at all times would justify the Survivor's Present. Thus, **_Eternity is the eternal experience with „someone other than you."_** That is why the idea of Eternity is above all a social link, rather than a mathematical division of Time (Cf Levinas, *Totalité…* 2000, p. 298). In practice, Eternity happens through *eternal Otherness*. In effect, Eternity is a concept built upon the faith in some higher, supreme subjectivity which once – in an act of unlimited generosity and altruism – gave birth to the subject we now know as „*Man"* (Ibid., p. 268). Man should like to hope that this *Primary Subjectivity,* which may indeed adequately be referred to as *God,* is the source of humanity. To it Levinas juxtaposes *the Noneity of the night*: the impersonality of the time of darkness which deprives the subject of its physical outlines, of its shape and so reminds one very strongly of the physical effects Death has on a body after a while. The impersonality of this time of darkness Levinas calls *the Il y a* (in English „there is") *of the night* (from a grammatical point of view this structure is impersonal). The

---

[20] Anne Brontë demonstrates rather obviously her Evangelical belief in treating present life as a pilgrimage towards Death as towards the moment of achieving spiritual completion (Cf W. G. G. James in: /ed./ Gregor, I. *Gossip and Subversion in Nineteenth-Century British Fiction* /New York: St. Martin's Press 1980/, pp. 229–230).

Night is frightening to man because it denies one any opportunity whatsoever in differentiating subject and object. It is the time when nothing can be declared for sure to be in motion and therefore nothing can be seen as capable of declaring even the physicality, the silhouette of a subject, of a human being. The subject is exposed to his/her own Self, to his/her own Being, at last – to the overwhelming void of the Universe's mighty Being (Ibid. pp. 34–35, p. 37). Such impersonality invokes not fear of Death, but fear of being denied the right to be a subject (because in the dark one could not differentiate between other subjects and objects that would normally constitute a Subject's daytime life). In the Brontë sisters' poetry this seemingly impersonal nighttime accommodates *the ghost persona* – the mediator between Being and non-Being. Even though a creature „half-existent", it again emphasizes Levinas' formula that „***Being does not have a gate through which one could step out of it once and for all.***" „*To realize the thought of non-Being would mean not to see non-Being, but in fact to die*" (Levinas, ibid. pp. 39, 68). The Ghost – the epitome of the eschatological concept of *Being beyond the Present*, is a direct translator of the existential formula of *Care and Responsibility*. It comes back to check up on the Survivor, but also to remind him/her that *being alive* implies undeniable and unconditional care for *someone Other than You*. The Brontë sisters' interpretation of what Levinas refers to as *ultima latex* ("last moment" – Lat.) is not the moment of collision between the Subject and the Subject's complete *otherness* which might be thought of as entirely unfamiliar or alien (Cf Ricoeur, *La mémoire...*, 2004, p. 503). The Ghost's presence in the Brontë sisters' poetry could be categorized as didactic and protective. It brings revelation to the Survivor: it discloses the meaning of Life. There are specificities in Emily's *Ghost* compared to Charlotte's *Ghost* which will be looked into in due course. Whilst Emily's Ghost acts in the ambience of deeper introspection, Charlotte's yields revelations to Life which have more rigorous social dimensions (e.g. it invokes thoughts about the detrimental influence of placidity and indifference in Life, as for instance in the poems: *Stanzas on the Fate of Henry Percy*, 1834, and „*Lady-Bird! Lady-bird! Fly away home*", 1837). Emily's ghost is more of a replica of the Mourner's self who would be quite happy with a controversially constructed Earth, which, however, is true bliss. Emily's Ghost is also

18.

juxtaposed to a judgemental God who is traditionally believed to dictate man's future. Most importantly, however, the Ghost indicates the three sisters' awareness of the chronotopal value of the grave/the tomb/the deathbed in their poetry. The *grave* is the receptacle of the missing Other – at once the Redeemer and the judge of the worthiness of the Survivor's existence.

For **Jacques Derrida,** Death is unavoidable at any point in one's life, is always imminent, which is why the process of maturation and of getting ontological awareness is in the individual's conscious acceptance of his/her fate as a mortal (Derrida, Jacques, *Apories* /Èditions Galilee, 1996/; [translated in Bulgarian] Aporii. *Umirane – Otchakvane predelite na istinata.* Sofia. IK „Kritika i humanizam". 1998, p. 19). In his last interview[21] Derrida in fact admits to have failed his own project to learn to live – because to master the skill to live would mean to master dying, to come to terms with the idea of one's own absolute finality – with no hope for resurrection or redemption – neither regarding oneself, nor in fact any other person. Or, as Hans-Georg Gadamer emphasizes, „*experience*" means in the long run *the experience of man's finality.* He is „*experienced*" who remembers he is final and has no power over Time and the Future. The experienced person knows that all plans man builds during a lifetime are unreliable and fragile, are limited – this knowledge and experience form for one the experience of one's own historicity (Cf Gadamer, *Wahrheit Und Methode,* 1988, pp. 420–421).

First, in his *Apories* (1996, translated in Bulgarian as: Aporii. *Umirane – otchakvane predelite na istinata. IK „Kritika I humanizam".* **1998**) Derrida argues that as a mortal, every man can be taken to represent a context of *Being* which is not definitive and limitative as to the purpose of existence in general. Death, therefore, contains an element not only of unpredictability and uncertainty, but also of *option, of choice*[22] as

---

[21] This was published in *Lu Monde,* on 19th August 2004 and then translated in Bulgarian and published in: the *Kultura* newspaper (# 35, 24th September 2004, pp. 10–11).

[22] It would be interesting to mention that J.P. Vernant observes that in the epic tradition of Ancient Greece the element of *choice of Death* was motivated by the insurmountable desire to avoid dying old. Because, dying old, or staying alive for as long as one could until old age, hid for the Greeks no tempting opportunities for individuation. Quite the opposite, to be someone would mean to become a hero, and the hero would at all costs avoid staying alive for too long. What mattered was to die beautifully. In this sense, the greatest disaster would be not to deprive the enemy of his/her life, but

to its verifiability (Cf Derrida, *Apories*, 1998, p. 24). That is true because in its essence Death is both pre-scripted (it befalls everyone) and contingent (no one could know for sure the moment of one's own death – Cf Eagleton, T. *Sweet Violence. The Idea of the Tragic* /Blackwell Publishing, 2003/, pp. 115–116, 121). Death implies openness, unfinishedness/incompleteness (quite similar to Heidegger's *Dasein* concept). Man's desire to see his own Death recognized is implausible, for to recognize Death there should be a recipient, a viewer. And the dead man cannot be a recipient of his/her own death. That is why Death never belongs to the life span of the dead man (Cf Derrida, *Apories*, 1998, pp. 69, 73). *Time*, as an item of personal belonging, as something that can be observed and therefore had, cannot include the instant of personal Death. In her study on Derrida Yelena Gurko underlines that not even the subtlest phenomenological study is capable of crossing over, and exploring, the boundary of Death. Death is something that cannot be conceptualized in the illusory world of différance – language is incapable of giving a truthful presentation of man's Death (Cf Gurko, 2001, p. 170). The secret of Death has always watched over man – even before man has learned to keep the secret of that secret – through history, culture, through language (ibid. p. 168).

When Derrida concludes that man's inquisitive and questioning attitude to Death is what makes him „open towards the meaning of Being" (Cf *Apories* 1998, pp. 88–89, 103), he invokes comparison to Heidegger's notion of Life as *Being-towards-Death*. Yet more specifically, he argues that, as there could be no two people (i.e. Survivor and Dead man) to witness one and the same Death at the same time, no claim could be made as to Death's topography, or as to man overstepping a certain borderline in the process of dying. Maurice Blanchot would have said (in his observations over the German poet Reiner Maria Rilke): „*Death never happens to me (…) Death is something I could never truly relate to (…) because Death is its own fragmentation, its own deceit (…)*"[cxvi]. This elusiveness, ingrained in the nature of every occasion of Death, is what potentially makes every man's life irreplaceable and „*Other*"[cxvii] in respect of the individuals who are entitled to outlive him/her. In his last interview

---

to deprive him/her of the opportunity to die beautifully – young, as a hero (Cf Vernant, 2004, pp. 66, 80).

Derrida summarizes that each man is "sentenced to outlive an Other": living means outliving, or living after the Other's Death. Whilst we outlive we carry the trait, the legacy and the last will of the dead man, which should make us ultra-responsible to *the Other*. Yet ourselves, whilst still alive, we never know who will come into our own trait, into the legacy of what we have believed – or whether at all there would be inheritors, followers of our own *Being*... (Cf Derrida, in: *Kultura*, 2004, pp. 10–11). In the logic of these reflections, the act of recognizing and thus of sharing (with another person) the awareness of one's own temporality, of one's own finality is what equalizes the fate of each two people: of the Survivor and the Dead Man, or of the Survivor and the Sufferer/the Victim (Cf Ricoeur, *Samiat sebe si...*, 2004, p. 303).

This is how some of the above reflections may relate to the Brontë sisters' poetry. In Anne Brontë's early poetic search (around 1838) there lurks the Lyrical Self's desire to appropriate and authenticate Death in a particular feasible instance: to counteract the biological order of events. Ominously enough, in the poem *Lady of Alzerno's Hall* (1838) the woman could be perceived to almost will her own husband's death: she prefers the certainty of the knowledge about his Death to the aggravating hopes and conjectures about his whereabouts and well-being. To Emily Brontë Death is obviously even less insurmountable: Death's recurrence is only a confirmation of the mechanism of living, but that does not in itself preclude the element of option as to when a Death should happen. Emily Brontë's poetry is so densely packed with descriptions of Death (of dying and of burial practices) as in fact the onlooker is almost invited to merge with the dead person and to visit the world beyond (see the poem *Start not! Upon the minster wall*, and in particular the poems: *R. Alcona to J. Brenzaida* – 1845, and *Death, that struck when I was most confiding* – 1845). Emily is more than tempted to consider factual probability and verifiability of Death to be non-essential characteristics. She gradually does away with the then popular Evangelical perception of Death as the threshold to either Heaven or Hell with her own paradigm of the world beyond. Namely, that there exists a private dreamt-for realm where the only thing that counts is an individual's reunion with his/her own soul which has been long lost. This is more of a Paradise on Earth: a realm which copies man's happiest time on Earth, for which the traditionally all-praised Christian Heaven is a poor substitute (see especially the poems: *I'm happiest when most away* and *To Imagination* – 1844). Yet Emily Brontë's mature poetry (of 1844 and afterwards) illustrates how, abandoned and left on its own, the soul would fail to be both penitent and confessor: a schizophrenic division of the Self which guarantees not its recuperation, not its wholeness but its degeneration, its end, so that Death would come non-requested – it would be inevitable (see her poem *O thy bright eyes must answer now* 1844). *Otherness* is what, eventually, turns out to be the sought-for source of regeneration.

To recap, as survivor and dead man are always juxtaposed to each other, it is impossible to state for sure that there is a borderline to cross at the moment of the actual happening of Death. The only certainty Death contains, Derrida concludes, is that it is a life-curtailing truth (Cf Derrida, *Apories* 1998, pp. 18, 22). In this logic, Derrida perceives the search for meaning after Death as aimless: there can be no methodology for such search. Death is a riddle which is to remain insoluble however much one theorizes over it[xviii]. For, My own Death may be imminent but what is truly mine is My Responsibility over, and so participation in, another man's life – this is the true task which embosses the existential contours of My own Being. One point on which Derrida and Heidegger could be seen to agree is that **Death juxtaposes *Self* and *Other* in an ontologically fruitful manner**. And that Death encourages ultimate expectation: that, at last, the union between the two might be accomplished (something which the physical expression of temporality denies). Sadly, the One always awaits *the Other*, since the two never arrive *at That place* at the same time. „*In fact Death is the other name for the unachievable simultaneity (…) At that, the One expecting the Other at this borderline is not the one who arrives there first (…)*" (Derrida, *Apories*, 1998, pp. 93–94). This is the point where Derrida's vision about Death is well applicable within the Romantic poets' painful perception of the fragmentariness of Being and of meaning. For both Death is the ultimate metaphor for incompletion which subjugates any other experience of unfinishedness/incompleteness.

Here, it would be interesting to mention, that in Mikhail Bakhtin's understanding, it is typical for the fate of the Romantic lyrical persona to be presented in fragments, in a glimpse, which speaks of incompletion as ingrained in Life (Cf Bakhtin, M. M. [in Russian] *Sobranie sotchinenii.*

Tom 1. Filosofskaya Estetika 1920h godov. Moskva. Izdatel'stvo „Russkie slovari, Yaziki slavianskoi kul'turi". RAN. 2003, *AIG*, p. 230). Emily Brontë's Augusta (in Gondal) reflects the poet's effort to present the phenomenon of *Death* in such a way as to demonstrate how *It* subverts all the solid knowledge one thinks one could gain in a lifetime. Death may be a borderline, which, however, this preternatural lyric persona, Augusta, crosses forth and back easily, as the poet would wish to emphasize the doldrums and alienation which befall one after the expiration of the *Other* who is covertly suggested in all the personifications and names Augusta appears under. Augusta's own life could be described as a sequence of occurrences of Death – her own recurrent Death, as well as instances of the Death of those related to her and mostly caused by her. All the same, in Emily Brontë's thinking, if Death were to confirm finality, then what is, supposedly, beyond Death should be a reiteration, rather than a reversal of present Life. For, however negative and malign, the way a lifetime has developed ought never to be a reason for the existence of the traditional purgatory texture of the Heavenly judgement. One is certain: Death cuts up the Self's opportunities in a way which negates a Self's chances for fuller and humane Being (which could happen in the appropriate circumstances; see especially the poems: *Riches I hold in light esteem* – 1841; *At such a time, in such a spot* – 1843, *How clear she shines...* – 1843, *The Death of A.G.A.* – 1841–1844 and in particular *Julian M. and A.G. Rochelle* – 1845). A.G.A. suffers the effects and consequences of her own corrupt and evil lifetime, yet she is that kind of sufferer who, whilst being observed, must wake up one something more than sympathy. To sympathize with the villain whilst rejoicing over the fact that one's fate is different to the villain's, to sigh with relief over the fact that one has been spared Death, is no real empathy (Cf Ricoeur, *Samiat Sebe si...*, 2004, pp. 301–302). To know that one will, sooner or later, follow in *the steps of that evil Other* when the End comes, to thus feel equal to the dead man (and so even more responsible for the living people than one may have done previously) – here is the ethics which Death teaches man.

A crucial point of Derrida's analysis of the phenomenon of Death is the statement that the Culture of the World and of humankind is a culture of the Past with a cult towards Death seen as entity of irrevocably finalized representations of consciousness. All ritualized and institutionalized places of worship are always built with the sole purpose of revering what is gone, which acknowledges Death. *„Bio-ethics, then, is Thanato-ethics, which is, „inevitably, euthanato-ethics"* (Cf Derrida, *Apories* 1998, pp. 67, 87). And although, in practice, one could gain nothing for one's well-being from Death, yet *„only a kind of Being-towards-Death could think, desire, project, i.e. experience Immortality as such"* (ibid. pp. 82, 100). The idea of Mortality/Immortality is the ultimate abode of human thought, the outermost reach of verbal awareness[23] (ibid. pp. 50, 55). Derrida supposes that access to dying could be gained through language – „speak out the fact of Death and you have achieved it" (ibid. pp. 56–57). The latter is impossible in the animal world, because, animals have no verbal way of considering and therefore of reaching Death. To quote the feminist and psychoanalyst Elisabeth Bronfen, „Death (…) is always culturally constructed, always metaphorical". It is a sort of „detextualization": preservation of authority despite „a plurality of interpretations called forth by the fundamental semantic instability of verbal and visual signs" (Cf Bronfen, Elisabeth, *Over Her Dead Body: Death, Femininity and the Aesthetic* /Manchester University Press, 1992/, p. 72, 151). In other words, living requires man at all times to be hermeneutically vigilant (Cf Eagleton, 2003, pp. 260–263).

A note of Charlotte Brontë's from 1850 discloses subtly her reflections about the issue of the feasibility of Death through language, or through Art. Having just read Alfred Tennyson's *In Memoriam*, she votes against any laboratorial literary expression of mourning. She praises this example of fine poetry, yet *„if Arthur Hallam had been somewhat nearer Alfred Tennyson, – his brother instead of his friend, – I should have distrusted this rhymed, and measured, and printed monument of grief. What change the lapse of years may work I do not know; but **it seems to me that bitter sorrow, while recent, does not flow out in***

---

[23] At this point, it feels useful to mention the opinion of the world-known psychoanalyst and literary critic, Julia Kristeva. In her book *Black Sun – Depression and Melancholy* (1987) Kristeva maintains that the practice of mourning and grief over the loss of a dear person acts as a stimulant for one's imagination and creativity. Sinking in grief hides the risk of depressive psychical instability, but it also encourages the process of bearing and forming ideas. The militantly restless spirit of the artist is anxious to depict the World in a new, symbolic manner, and so to master Death through Art (Cf Kristeva, Julia, /translation in Bulgarian from French/ *Tcherno slantze. Depresia i melancholia.* Sofia. GAL-IKO. **1999**, pp. 16, 31, 213, 219).

verse" (as quoted in: Gaskell, Elizabeth, *The Life of Charlotte Brontë* /New York: J. M. Dent & Sons LTD, 1928/, pp. 313–314, my bold type). What Charlotte Brontë's own poetry of 1835–1839 argues is her conviction that, whilst alive, one knows Death only as something imparted to one through the fact of another man's Death. That must whet man's existential awareness – to the point where the only adequate attitude to Life becomes *empathy* and *openness*. *The Other's* presence is sensed more acutely after his/ her death: in what is left after the deceased. It is impossible to foresee what a Self would be in the Future within the limits of the *„dark (...) narrow cell (...)"* of one's own mind (Charlotte Brontë). One could only sense the limits and dimensions of one's own Being through positioning oneself as *„the One who would outlive Me and for whom, and only for whom, My Death could become an event"* (Cf Bakhtin, M. 2003, p. 179). Similarly, Anne Brontë's desire to see whether Death shortens or prolongs a lifetime[24] dissolves and is being ousted by her growing awareness that the only aspect of Being which Death is powerless to destroy is the *Otherness* every man receives as a gift from an Other during one's own lifetime. To remember Levinas once more, what Death cannot do away with is the effect of one man's benevolent attitude towards another person (see Anne's poems: *Vanitas Vanitatis* – 1845, and especially *Self-Communion* – 1847).

In Emily Brontë's case, the euthanatic urge is gradually ousted by the poet's realization that <u>Death, even when freely chosen, proves irreversible</u>. For, Death, like any other event in life, needs an external/outside referee to confirm it. Even the most grievous instance of the Death of the parent/ the child should not act as an urge to project and cause Death everywhere – for that destroys the individual, as well as the world around the individual (see especially poems *I am the only being whose doom* – 1837, *O mother, I am not regretting* – 1837, *From our evening fireside now* – 1839, *Lines by Claudia* – 1839, *A Farewell to Alexandria* – 1839, *The wind, I hear it sighing* – 1839, *On the Fall of Zalona* – 1843, *Come, walk with me*).

Finally, I would also like to draw the reader's attention to one more

---

[24] See especially Anne's poems of 1836–1838 (e.g. *Verses by Lady Geralda* – 1836, *A Voice From the Dungeon* – 1837).

element of Derrida's vision of Mortality, and that is his concern with the dichotomy *„guilt–forgiveness“*. In this regard, Paul Ricoeur's reflections on the latter are quoted (in his monograph over the interrelation between memory and history – already quoted here from the Russian edition of 2004*)*. When considering *ultimate forgiveness,* ultimate pardon, Derrida means something which religion would, strictly speaking, consider a breach of the moral code of justice – forgiveness towards the unforgivable, forgiveness towards an act of the violation of an individual's right to exist, i.e. forgiveness towards an act of murder (Cf Derrida, J. [in Bulgarian] *Viara I Znanie.* Sofia. LIK. **2001**, p. 108). Derrida is convinced that, if pardon were given upon the condition that the sinner would redeem, or after the sinner has begged for this pardon, then pardon is not real pardon. Pardon towards the unforgivable should come spontaneously, being unsought for. If it is real, the responsibility towards *the Other* should have the capacity to testify against and eventually to defeat Death, it should express itself through Love which admits to, yet forgives, the possibility of a repetition of evil, of the greatest evil – even though the sinner may lack self-reproach. Derrida concludes that real pardon, real forgiveness is madness, is *„the madness of the impossible“* (Cf Derrida, *Viara I Znanie,* 2001, pp. 112–113): it simultaneously foresees and forgives evil. Only such unconditional, most spontaneous gesture of forgiveness is capable of preserving Life – through a trust in the grain of Good in a murderer's mind (albeit dormant and inactive – ibid. p. 119). Pardon is as an act of „preserving meaning“, it urges one towards action, it is non-historical because it „interrupts the continuum of cause and effect“[25]: pardon is an act of overcoming the wild and the unconscious (Cf

---

[25] In his lecture formulated as: *Pein de mort et souveraineté. Une déconstruction de l'ontologie* (delivered during an international conference dedicated to Jacques Derrida in Sofia, Bulgaria, in 2001) Derrida lays out his views **in categorical opposition of *the capital punishment*.** Most importantly, he emphasizes *tat the death sentence* speaks of the End, but as determined by a judical decision – this is the End determined by an Other individual, which in itself cannot be the archetype of an act of decision (Cf Derrida in: Znepolski, Ivailo /red./, /in Bulgarian/ Okolo Jacques Derrida. *Tchudovistniat diskurs.* Sofia. „Dom na naukite za tchoveka I obstestvoto“. 2002, pp. 23–24). To quote the Bulgarian philosopher Boyan Manchev, the death sentence invokes in one terror because it imposes on one the necessity of constructing what cannot be constructed, what cannot be imagined. The death sentence asks one to construct that which presents itself as destruction, as absence, as the unfathomable – Death (Cf Manchev, Boyan, *Donner corps à la mort,* ibid., pp. 168–169).

Kristeva, *Tcherno slantze...*, 1999, pp. 213, 218, 219). Further on, the analysis of Emily Brontë's poem *The Death of A.G.A.* (1841–1844) unfolds so as to supports the above ideas.

Some of **Mikhail Bakhtin's** ideas would have been suggested by now in the presentation of Heidegger, Levinas and Derrida. In my research I draw emphatically on Bakhtin's concept of **Otherness**[26] as the core of *the Dialogic principle of Being*. Bakhtin builds up his phenomenology under one growing and common for the development of the European 19th- and 20th-century thought awareness of the importance of *the Other individual* as an actively dialogising philosophic discourse (Cf Mahlin, V. L., in: [in Russian] Tamartchenko et al, *Bakhtinskiy Tesaurus*. Materialij i issledovania. Moskva. Rossiiskij gosudarstvenniy gumanitarniy institut, 1997, pp. 146–147). *The Other* works as a compound category of the existence of Nature, Culture and History, which are simultaneously „*productively limiting*" in respect of „*My inevitable givenness /dannost'* – in Russian/" in Life. *The Other* is what is always available in the world, is what always comes prior to *Me* (ibid. pp. 142–143). *The Other* is the ultimate condition for the existence of the Self on all levels – cultural, historical, legal, aesthetic etc. (ibid. p. 141). *The Other* objectifies reality and is the kernel component in the process of each individual's gaining self-awareness[27]. The existence of *the Other* both engenders the Self and stimulates **empathy** as the only right attitude towards Life which presents itself as Co-Being. In Bakhtin's understanding empathy springs up and develops as an expression of man's conscientious strife to always do one's best in the name of *Someone Other than Myself*: to donate the best of one's potential to that *Other*. Such philosophy votes against self-sustenance and against self-content altogether.

In my research I have employed some of Bakhtin's major ethico-anthropological points, which he mainly formulates in his essay „*Avtor I Geroi v estetitcheskoi deiatel'nosti*" („*Author and hero in*

---

[26] See also Holquist, 1991, p. 18.

[27] Or, to use Ricoeur's formula, „my" ownership over „my" experiences is always distributed over and across the whole paradigm of the grammatical category of Person, i.e. it implies *an Other* who is *not „me"* (Cf Ricoeur, *Samiat Sebe si...*, 2004, p. 285).

Aesthetic Activity[28], abbreviated throughout this research as „*AIG*"*)*, as well as in his unfinished treatise *K filosofii postupka* (*Toward a Philosophy of the Act*, abbreviated throughout this research as „*KFP*"). Naturally, there will be a special emphasis on Bakhtin's formula of „*Being as Co-Being*", on his vision of the ontogenetic authority of the phenomenon of *Otherness*, on the intrinsic sociability of the Self, and certainly on his perception of Death as „*Death for the Other/ The Other's Death*". In this regard, invaluable, indeed, is the contribution Bakhtin made through his unfinished study named „*Toward a Philosophy of the Act*"[29], which has rightly been defined as his „moral philosophy", as his project to present the argumentation for the idea that Being as always „Being among". The dialogic understanding of Being as Co-Being in the context of the dialogic entity „Self-Other" was first developed in this unfinished work of Bakhtin's, which he wrote prior to „*Author and hero...*" and which is clearly of a higher rank. The aim of this philosophic treatise was to investigate the meaning of Being in the broadest sense of the word, and so it is not at all limited in its quality as a work of literary criticism. Here I should also like to emphasize Bakhtin's view that Life precedes Art, so that Art, albeit ontologically responsible, is secondary in comparison to Being. In *Toward a Philosophy of the Act* Bakhtin maintains that *man, as a common mortal, possesses **no alibi in just Being** for the sake of Being, or just Being merely because one was conceived.* Michael Holquist, one of today's best-known Bakhtin's scholars across the Atlantic, summarizes: „Life will not let me be inactive, no matter how dormant I appear (…) in the eyes of others. I cannot be passive even

---

[28] „*Author and hero in aesthetic activity*", in: *Art and Answerability: Early Philosophical Works by M. M. Bakhtin*, /ed./ Holquist, Michael & Liapunov, Vadim (translator), Austin, TX: University of Texas Press, 1990.

[29] Both „*K filosofii postoupka*" and „*Avtor I Geroi v estetitcheskoi deiatel'nosti*" are undated. Critics and literary scholars believe that those two major studies of Mikhail Bakhtin's were most probably written in the period 1919–1924. „*K filosofii postupka*" was translated in English first in 1993 by V. Liapunov, and edited by M. Holquist (Cf *Toward a Philosophy of the Act*, /ed./ Liapunov, V. & Holquist, M. /Austin: University of Texas Press, 1993/). The final version in English uses the word „act", whilst in earlier references made to that work of Bakhtin's (i.e. Gary Saul Morson's & Caryl Emerson's studies of 1989 and 1990) it appears as „deed". Indeed, both „act" and „deed" in English reflect the Russian meaning of „postupok", yet „act" is more general and somewhat neutral, whilst „deed" is more emphatic and implies notions such as: heroism, deliberateness and epic zeal, it seems to me.

when I choose to be passive (...) I have a stake in everything that comes my way". *Being* is at all times an *event* (*„sobytie bytija"*) (Cf Holquist, Michael, *Dialogism – Bakhtin and His World* /New York & London: Routledge, 1991/; see also the term „co-being of being", in: Morson & Emerson, 1989, p. 179). One exists in the true sense of this word only when one realises and justifies one's Life through one's *Duty* towards another human being (to live for the sake of *the Other*, and not in spite of *the Other*). This should be also valid for the „aesthetic mind – as a variation of the practical mind" and is the kernel component of the literary act (Cf Bakhtin, 2003, AIG, p. 120). The „empathetic" understanding of *the Other* is a prerequisite for the emergence of the Hero and for the aesthetic completion of the Hero (the Author must occupy a „meaningful, and not an incidental position" in relation to the World which should be incarnated in the Hero). Every Act of Serving *the Other* is temporally limited. Yet Bakhtin sees Death as a non-optionally available advantage of Living: the advantage of owning someone's life, of possessing the „aesthetic key" for completing another man's image, the grievous privilege-duty of outliving an other human being (or, as Derrida would say, the sentence, the burden of outliving).

According to Bakhtin's aesthetics, the principle of **Einfühlung**[30] is the only right route to perceiving the essence of *the Other*, but without yielding in full to the Other's pain. In order to soothe *that Other*, one must at all times keep at a distance – for fear of losing one's *„surplus of vision"*, also known in English as *„extra vision"*[xix], which is exactly what should always be the technique available to rescue the *Other* (Bakhtin, 2003, AIG, p. 107). This phenomenon Bakhtin calls *„vnenahodimost'"* – /*вненаходимость*/, or *„outsideness"*[31], which every man possesses

---

[30] This term, borrowed from German, could be translated as *„intra-sensing"*, or *„empathy"*, or *„feeling alongside and into someone else's experience"*. It reflects Bakhtin's desire to find a word denoting man's ability, and in fact obligation, to co-experience everything – ill and good – with, and for the sake of, the *Other*.

[31] Alternatively, „vnenahodimost" has been translated in English as: „exotopy", or „extralocality", or „other logic". „*Outsideness*" is the most popular and the most precise word of all, „*exotopy*" was apparently preferred by the late Professor Paul De Man (in: De Man, Paul, *Blindness and Insight: Essays in the Rhetoric of Contemporary Criticism*, Oxford University Press, 1971), whilst „*extralocality*" was proposed by Mathew Roberts (a colleague of Morson's and Emerson's from the Northwestern University, USA). Cf *Rethinking Bakhtin. Extensions and Challenges*, /eds./ Morson, Gary Saul & Emerson, Caryl (Northwestern University Press, Evanston, Illinois, 1989), pp. 54, 125.

in respect of another man. Death is the most immediate and authentic example of a hermeneutic situation, since the observation of an instance of Death invokes the strongest emotions yet the Observer should keep his/her distance. There is no possibility of eliminating the distance between the Dead man and the Survivor and that is precisely what requires of the Survivor the greatest effort to empathize – without being able to experience in practice and so to verify or to solve the problem (Cf Nikitaev, Vladimir, /in Russian/ „Germenevtika Smerti". Filosofsko-literaturnij zurnal Logos. Moskva. 2/47/2005, p. 203). In this sense, **altruism** is most essentially perceived in an individual's power to terminate *an Other's* suffering and pain by making the knowledge of the forthcoming Death easier and less threatening[32]. *The Other*, albeit final, is nonetheless the <u>sole objectifier of one's Being</u>. Bakhtin's phenomenology has its roots in Christian ethics, yet it puts the greater emphasis on the responsibility of the externally situated individual, on the Survivor rather than on the omnipotence of the *no-longer-alive*. A defective approach to Life would then clearly be one that lacks (or refuses to gain) awareness of *Otherness* (Cf Orlov in: Bakhtin, *Pro et Contra...* 2002, p. 351).

The act of *Einfühlung*, Bakhtin argues, alters both the subject and the object that relate to it. Being is always Co-Being (*„sobytijé"*), with no other alternative (CF Bakhtin, KFP, 2003, p. 18). In Art this act of Co-Being can be seen in that the viewing consciousness is always that of the Author, and never that of the Hero, whom the viewer (the Author) always precedes and completes (Cf Bakhtin 2003, AIG, p. 180). <u>One cannot complete one's own self, cannot own one's fate, cannot confirm the terminus of one's development for a fact – *the Other* is needed for that.</u> There exists no possibility to verify Co-Being as a Task: what could be verified is Co-Being as an event which has already happened (this includes the Past and the Present), and the Task, the Duty of Co-Being is what is forthcoming, what is set as the Task (Cf Shtitzova, T., 2002, p. 61). Death is in the Future – it is

---

[32] Cf Clark, K. in: Bakhtin, *Pro et Contra. Tvortchestvo I nasledie M. M. Bakhtina v kontekste mirovoi kul'turij., Antologia, Tom 2. Sankt-Peterburg. Izdatel'stvo Rossiiskogo gumanitarnogo instituta.* 2002, p. 54. Altruism implies unconditional, spontaneous and sincere donation, it is the free bestowal of the best of one's potential upon another person. Such attitude is also discovered in the following pairs: *gift–need, forgiveness–crime, benevolence–sin* etc. (Cf Bakhtin 2003, AIG, p. 165).

always forthcoming, yet it cannot be the task of Man's Being. An instance of Death confirms man's temporality, which in itself should activate and intensify (exactly because Time is limited for one) man's desire to transform living into Being for the sake of an Other, to insert new meaning into it through partaking of the Other's pain and happiness. Co-Being is profitable: the fact that one is never complete in the Present, but always looks forward to the Future (which is a Future shared with Others), which notably promises Death, is a positive feature of man's existence. The paradox of One non-coinciding with Oneself Now and in fact of Never hoping for completion should be seen as a blessing rather than as a curse (Cf Shtitzova, ibid., pp. 65, 69–70, 73). Time unfolds as the paradox of the continuum of the events of Co-Being.

In the Romantic context, the Author's „outsideness" in respect of a Hero (in this case the Poet's „outsideness" in respect of a Lyrical Persona) is rather weak. It is not at all uncommon for the lyrical persona to usurp the Author's right to finalize Life. The structure of the contents of a work of lyric poetry is more prone to yield to the irregularities, the fluctuations and modulations of the Lyrical Persona's own lifetime (Cf Bakhtin, 2003, AIG, p. 240). Death is most successfully employed a technique for capturing the fragmentarity of Life in which the essence of the Romantic persona is contained in the continuous alternation of appearances/disappearances, or birth/expiration, or revival/denial. Romanticism, Bakhtin argues, is a personification of the endlessness of a Hero (Ibid. p. 240). What Bakhtin highlights in *Author and Hero…*, is that the Romantic poet seems himself incapable of mastering the nature of such a deviant lyrical persona which also acts, apparently, as a receptacle for the Poet's own spiritual unrest and desire to confess. Such a „literary conqueror" is, for instance, A.G.A. – Emily Brontë's main lyrical persona. The structure of the Gondal poetic cycle appears to have been subjugated by Augusta's ambiguousness, to her murderous instincts – I believe these regulate the dramatic action of Gondal[33]. Gondal, as a whole, appears incomplete: in it Death represents

---

[33] At this point the critic would best remember Bakhtin's view that the literary form (in the case of Emily Brontë's *Gondal* – a compilation of lyrical fragments, ballads and confessional pieces) is the author's choice, yet it is the result of the interaction between the author and the hero and must be an adequate reflection of the specificity of the hero's character, if it were to give shape to the latter (Cf Bakhtin, 2003, p. 156). In this sense, the fragmented narrative about A.G.A.'s life is Emily's decision,

the constant search for meaning – both on behalf of the Poet and on behalf of the main lyrical persona. In it the dialogic principle of Co-Being remains a goal, it is never fully and unequivocally accomplished. The abundance of ballads in Emily Brontë's poetry hints at her wish to make some room for *dialogism*: i.e. to make room for *the Other*; to accumulate evidence for her belief in Life as unarguably based on the interaction between at least two individuals whose interdependence her ballads reflect. In this sense, Gondal could be defined as Emily's search for a stable and reliable *external/outside point of reference* that could master Death[34]. This search is noticeable even in Emily's landscape lyric pieces where Empathy is implied in the idea of Nature's generosity, as discovered in the principle of relentless death/revival.

Bakhtin argues that *the gift of the „surplus of vision" („izbytok videnia" – Cf Morson & Emerson, 1989, p. 154)* stretches as far as the awareness that it is within one's capacity to complete Life not only aesthetically. One owns another man's life in outliving him/her, but also, literally, – one man's life could be abbreviated by another man in the physical sense of the word. The Other is therefore extremely vulnerable in his/her dependence on „You". And so man's access to Death is valuable in so far as it is perceived as an impetus to activate man's conscience which ought, at all times, to make every effort to preserve Life. A refusal to protect the vital Other – weakness or unwillingness to do so, is a *crisis of authorship* – both in Art and in real Life, a crisis of the responsible position of „outsideness" as the true life-prolonging mechanism. As mentioned earlier, one example of the latter Bakhtin finds in the relationship between the lyrical persona and the Poet in the period of Romanticism (CF Bakhtin, 2003, AIG, pp. 258–259).

An important point Bakhtin argues is that Death cannot be verified

---

yet A.G.A.'s attitude to life is „fragmented" in its urge to destroy in order to defeat destructiveness in Nature, and to murder in order to curtail unexpectedness as ingrained in *Fate*.

[34] Charlotte Brontë's female characters are particularly susceptible to Other individuals who provide the essential feedback about their nature. Jane Eyre says: „*I know I should think well of myself; but that is not enough: if others don't love me, I would rather die than live*" (as quoted by Kathleen Blake in: McNees, Eleanor, /ed./ *The Brontë Sisters. Critical Assessments* /Helm Information LTD, 1996/, p. 707). Anne Brontë goes through the same mental trial in those of her poems which deal in particular with orphanhood, with the theme of the loss of the Mother, or those which investigate the image of Christ (especially in Anne's poetic period 1840–1842, e.g. *Retirement* – 1840, and *An Orphan's Lament* – 1841).

for a fact by the dying man: one's own Death one can never endorse and the Death that can be endorsed is always *the Other's Death.* In fact, the specificity of man's consciousness is in that it has no capacity to endorse not only its own Death, but also its own Birth – the other crucial moment (the beginning) only verifiable by *the Other* (Cf Bakhtin, [in Russian] *Sobranie sotchinenij. Tom 5.* Moskva. Russkie slovari. 1996, pp. 347–348). One could never estimate the emotional weight and value of one's own Life – only *the Other* can (Cf Bakhtin, 2003, AIG, pp. 179–180). Compared to the fear of the Death of *the Other,* the fear of one's own Death lacks a most significant ingredient – the moment of loss, of deprivation that only *the Other's Death* leaves behind (ibid, p. 179). It is obvious that the point of the present argument is the process of self-definition and self-cognition through the ethical values inherent for one in one's Co-Being with other people. This process starts as early as one's birth, and *the first Other,* through whose eyes the child begins to know the world, is *the MOTHER* (Cf Clark & Holquist, in: Mikhail Bakhtin, *Pro et Contra...* 2002, p. 48). An instant of Death which causes the lack of this primary Other (the mother) shatters the chances for one to foster and develop a compassionate, an empathetic attitude to Life as the only attitude which interprets and sculptures reality without crippling it. In the Brontë sisters works (both the poetry and the novels) *the Mother,* as a concept, is in a rather diffused state – it is missing, sought after, which is why the moral system of the Brontë sisters' characters/ lyrical personae is riddled with doubt and self-negating hesitation. In Emily Brontë's case this maternal deficiency is brought to a peak in the presentation of the character of A.G.A. who performs infanticide (see especially the poem *A Farewell to Alexandria,* 1839)[35]. In the lack of an *Other* living degenerates to the practice of sheer survival – stripped of any values and directed towards

---

[35] Two other poems particularly relevant to *the motif of orphanhood* are Emily's *O mother, I am not regretting* – 1837 and *A.G.A.* – 1839. The majority of Emily Brontë's poems dealing with *orphanhood* date back to 1839, and there is a subsequent rise in her interest in the role of Death in the family context around 1845. In *A Farewell to Alexandria (1839)* the elimination of Alexandria – A.G.A.'s child – could be interpreted as resulting from the mother's ominous desire to eliminate any possibility for future reduplication of the villainous A.G.A. The act of infanticide, as a route of achieving that, is the most violent breach of the moral code. Further on, Emily tries to compensate for the lack of a Mother by chiseling a corporate image of the native land and of one's comrades, who share the Lyrical Self's philosophy of „*the world within*" – the soul's abode and man's true home.

survival – stripped of any values and directed towards merely disentangling the knot of the internal havoc of self-sustenance (Cf Bakhtin, 2003, *AIG*, p. 128). The latter argument is well illustrated in Charlotte Brontë's poetry of the period 1836–1837 and around 1846 (see especially the poem *Reason*, 1836). Whilst persistently and conscientiously carving out the image of the missing/ dead authority in her poetry, Charlotte Brontë demonstrates a deepening conviction on the reliability of, and faith in, the <u>Past – as a moral informant to, and source of, the Present.</u> The Past – the time of *the No-Longer-Alive* – is the time which provides insight into the future (see the poem *The Teacher's Monologue* – 1837, *Gilbert* – around 1843, as well as Branwell Brontë's poem *Harriet* II 1838). The life-defining status of *the missing Other/ the missing authority* is also a main motif in Charlotte Brontë's novels *Jane Eyre* and *Villette*.

To know that „You, too, will die" is terrifying, yet practice shows that that would inevitably happen at some point, which is why man feels a natural urge to plan Life, to project in advance the development of some events – in temporal perspective. <u>The knowledge of the certainty of one's own Death could be reassuring in that provides one with a temporal framework in which one's creativity and genius could unfold, but without *an Other* to refer to, this knowledge unsettles one's mind, it feels uneasy, to say the least.</u> In this sense, *the Other* defines the limits and draws the outermost boundary of man's Presence in the World (Cf Orlov in: Bakhtin, *Pro et Contra*, 2002, pp. 349–350). Or, following Heidegger, *Otherness* always and unarguably precedes every Subject and is a condition of *Being-in-the-World*. To Charlotte Brontë such *Otherness* is contained in the image of the ghost of Nun/ the deceased female beloved: a recurrent emanation of unsurpassed goodness and benevolence which stir the lyrical-speaker's long-lost sense of guilt towards the *Dead Other* who he once neglected (see esp. the poems: *Matin* – 1830 and *Gilbert* – 1843). The Brontë sisters' mature works appear to agree on what Bakhtin would call *the condition of Being.* In his claim that every individual is the condition, but not the main participant, of one's own life, Bakhtin argues that in order for one to *Be*, one should at all times be incomplete, should be „forthcoming", so to speak, should never coincide with what one represents at given moment, should always *be prepared to be defined once again so long as the Other lives* (Cf Bakhtin, 2003, AIG, p. 95, pp.

180–181). Michael Holquist clarifies: „/.../ self for Bakhtin is a cognitive necessity, not a mystified privilege"; „the drive to meaning" is a process which should verify living (Cf Holquist. 1991, pp. 22–23). Every *Other* is limited, is mortal, but is the true condition of the **dialogic** vision of Being where no one is ever complete in himself/ herself. That is why Consciousness is Co-consciousness (Cf Clark & Holquist in: Bakhtin: *Pro et Contra...*, 2002, pp. 39, 52). The elimination of this „Co-" by Death shakes the props of consciousness. Particularly poignant examples of the above statement are Emily Brontë's poems *A.S. to G.S.* (1841) and *Julian M. and A.G Rochelle* (*Silent is the house – all are laid asleep* 1845). Only a spontaneous act of benevolence towards *an Other* (e.g. of Julian's act of benevolence when he decides to liberate and share his life with the ambiguous, incriminatingly mysterious Rochelle) could compensate for the internal deprivation an individual feels at the loss of *a primary Other* (the parent/the beloved/the friend). Rochelle addresses Julian, asks for help, but even before that request for help Julian appears ready to listen and to partake of her fate. „(...) if existence is shared, it will manifest itself as the condition of being addressed" (*„obrashchënnost'"*, *„обращенность"*, or *„addressivnost'"*, *„аддрессивность"*). Existence is not only an event, it is an utterance. The event of existence has the nature of dialogue in this sense; there is no word directed to no one. [...] The world addresses us and we are alive and human to the degree we are answerable, i.e. to the degree that we can respond to *addressivity*. We are responsible in the sense that we are compelled to respond, we cannot choose but give the world an answer" (Cf Holquist, 1991, pp. 27, 30).

To sum up, *Mortality* is that very ingredient of Being which r `:es the emotional background composed of various fragments of Time matter. The division of Time into: „*earlier v/s later, already v/s not yet, now v/s then* and *always v/s never*" follows man's life and man's measurement of chronology in accordance with *eventness* (Bakhtin uses in Russian the term *„sobytijnost"*, *„событийность"*) of one's life (Cf Bakhtin, *AIG*, 2003, p. 70). From an ethical point of view, Christ's Death has proved to be the first significant event in Man's culture. The peak of self-denial, it is the Death after which nothing appears the same any more (Cf Bakhtin, *KFP*, 2003, pp. 19–20). Further on, in space there are certain *points of reference* which prove that every Death leaves a gap in man's history.

Following Bakhtin, these could be called *chronotope markers*: they „**condense Time**", so to speak. They bear recurrent traces of the Past and those traces are, in effect, man's link to man's origin, to the origin of his consciousness and therefore conscience. At the same time, those markers contain the Future in that they promise certainty: some repetition of man's fate which makes man *one of the many*. Such an item of „concentrated Time" can be, for instance, *the castle* in the Gothic novel (Cf Bakhtin, [in Bulgarian] *Vaprosi na literatourata i estetikata*, Sofia, 1983, pp. 442, 446–447). The Brontë sisters take a deep interest in *the grave* as one such particular container of Time. *The grave* is the strongest „coagulant" of Time: in it man could hope to find Past, Present and Future united. *The grave*, or *the tomb*, whose symptomatic persistence is also seen in the vastness, immeasurability and ambiguous storage capacity of other natural phenomena (the sea, the wind, the night, the Earth), is the „proprietor", so to speak, of *the dead Other* who yields existential revelations upon man. To the Brontë sisters *the grave/tomb* is that component of Life which „opposes" man, which questions man's self-content and self-confidence and requires an answer concerning one's past deeds. The *grave/tomb* ignites man's cognitive urge and raises one's awareness of ethics (and thus one's self-awareness). The presence of *the grave/tomb* suggests that Being should happen as Co-Being, which is not merely available to one (not like, for example, the Past, which is always *'given'* to One – *dano /„дано"/*): Being as Co-being is given as a task to achieve (Cf Bakhtin, AIG, 2003, p. 173)[36].

Man's consciousness only exists as long as it partakes of *the Architectonics /„arhitektonica"* – *„архитектоника"/* of responsibility, which must unfold as *Eventness /„sobytijnost"* – *„событийность"/*, as Co-Being, as the recognition and application of the duty to always respond to, and *act /„postupat"* – *„поступать"/*

---

[36] In a near dozen of Emily's poems *'tomb'* rhymes with, is interpreted as, *'home'*. There is a Romantic yearning for the Past as for something capable of terminating a Present void of meaning, void of a soul-mate and a parent (see especially Emily's poems H 9, 14, 28, 34, 43, 56, 63, 133, 136, 143, 156, 158, 163, 184 in Hatfield's 1941 edition of her poems). Initially, one may observe Emily Brontë's hope that *the grave/tomb* provides the ultimate escape from the alienating Present; later, it appears that the grave is more of a representation of her quest for an „outsideness", for a „surplus of vision", which she portrays and imagines as non-subject to temporal definitions and restrictions (as, for instance in *No Coward Soul Is Mine*, 1846).

with the hope to be of some use to, an Other (Cf Bakhtin, KFP, 2003, pp. 7–8, p. 14, p. 68). This is the only truth that knows no temporal boundaries – as opposed to the finality of each individual, of each concrete Being, of each mind as a physical unit. The Romantics' readiness to yield to the euthanatic idea of the voluntary retreat from the World seems, in the light of the above reflections, ludicrous, but it also speaks of a fear to recognize the importance of the principle of addressivity and therefore of the *Architectonics of Eventness* as an achievable task. Self-recognition and self-appraisal, as it becomes evident in the mature works of the Brontë sisters (both poetic and prose fiction), and in the mature works of most of the English Romantics and further Victorian poets, is not something freely acquirable through perfection in Art, through real Love, or through early Death. What guarantees uniqueness is the act of Co-Being which each individual should accomplish *in practice*, in one's own lifetime, but the success of which undertaking is not something one knows of ever (i.e. it may only be the privilege of the Survivor). *The Deed of Co-Being* is redemptive, purgatorial, it *is* taking the Eucharist (Cf Bakhtin, *KFP*, 2003, pp. 16–17). Uniqueness is not something one could imagine: really, it is something one could only experience whilst participating in the Event of Co-being. Therefore thinking ought never to be impartial – it ought to constantly overcome its givenness /„*dannost*" – „*данность*"/ for the sake of the element of duty/task in it /„*zadannost*'" – „*заданность*"/ – *to act*, and so to live in penitence (ibid.).

An extended reflection on the above arguments would be that a lifetime is valuable, is able to „defeat" Death, if, and only if, it is a lifetime of partiality towards the fate of *the Other*, a lifetime of openness towards the Other's complexity. One man's uniqueness lies in his/ her unique *duty* of responsibility towards another man. The uniqueness of Being understood as *Duty towards the Other* is imposed on man, is not optional, and is something without which man has *No-Alibi-in-Being*. **It is „My" compulsory *duty* to partake of every single instant of Life and of reality** – if not always in practice, then at least in one's mind (which, in its turn, may lead to further actions which may prove equally fatal and categorical an act of encroachment upon one's right to be; Cf Bakhtin, KFP, 2003, pp. 39–40). Without a conscientious recognition and application of this principle of *duty towards the Other* one's lifetime looks like a „*rough* paper," like „*a draft of real life*". Only Partiality-in-Being, only *the Deed of Co-Being* has the capacity to transform this „rough paper" of a lifetime into *a „fair copy"*, into a real lifetime. An indifferent attitude to *the Other* is like a declaration that all types and instances of Death are all the same, are equally distant to „Me", or that Death has no emotional or moral impact on „Me". Hence Bakhtin's claims that the philosophy of Being could only be a moral philosophy, a philosophy of care and love: the philosophy of *the Deed*, and not some kind of incidental and rootless philosophy of indifference and detachment (Cf Bakhtin, KFP, 2003, pp. 41–42, p. 51). Love and altruism amalgamated form the strongest antidote against Death – they are the remedy against Death's tendency „to disperse the essence of Being into a myriad of elusive events". Only true altruism could sustain Being without impoverishing it and „schematizing" it. The architectonics of being human is therefore the architectonics of the opportunity for each mortal individual *to Be in the Deed/Act of Co-Being* (ibid. pp. 58–59). Co-Being is an axiom, a theoretical availability, ingrained in the essence of Life, but as such it is conditional upon man's conscientious decision to use it. It is undeniably interwoven in the texture of Life, which is exactly why Death can never interrupt this „line of the repeated opportunities": to Act for the sake of *the Other* (Cf Bakhtin, AIG, 2003, p. 182). The extinction of humaneness is implied in every instance of man denying this duty *to Co-Be, to Co-Exist*. The phenomenon of Death could not at all be regulated by whether man is aware of it, or else is oblivious of it (an obvious point of Bakhtin's debate with Derrida). Even within the boundaries of one single life Death is implied in every instance of doubt, in every moment of hesitation whether to consider/not to consider *the Other*. And each time, having made a decision, one enters a new phase of Life – not always the desired, or the one marked by the imagined personal success, but always one which contains *the ultimate opportunity to Be – as a Co-Participant*[37].

---

[37] Emily Brontë's confessional poem *R. Alcona to J. Brenzaida* (*Cold in the earth, and the deep snow piled above thee!* 1845), as well as her last ballad extant, *Why ask to know the date – the clime?* (1846) provide a very thorough illustration to the above reflections. A.G.A.'s own lifetime is a brilliant example: it is a mixture of both denied invitations to Co-Be, as well as of supposed chances to Co-Be which have been crossed out by other people's intervention in her life (as, for instance, in the poem *The Death of A.G.A.*, 1841–1844).

NOTES:

[i] Cf Freud, Sigmund (in Bulgarian): *Estetika, Izkustvo, Literatura*, sastavitel Isaak Passi. Sofia. Universitetsko izdatelstvo „Sv. Kliment Ohridski". 1991, pp. 45–46.

[ii] Georgiev, Nicola. (in Bulgarian) *Analiz na liritcheskata tvorba*. Sofia. DI „Narodna prosveta". 1985.

[iii] Cf Demichev, 1997, pp. 23–24.

[iv] Cf Gadamer, Hans-Georg, *Wahrheit Und Methode*, in Russian: *Istina I Metod. Osnovij filosofskoi germenevtiki*. Moskva. „Progress". 1988, pp. 343–344. My translation of this particular excerpt.

[v] Cf Gadamer, ibid., pp. 170, 188, 351, 360.

[vi] Cf Gadamer, ibid., p. 213.

[vii] Cf Demichev, 1997, p. 126.

[viii] Cf Ricoeur, Paul, *La mémoire, l'histoire, l'oubli*, Editions du Seuil, 2000 (in Russian) *Pamiat', istoria, zabvenie*. Moskva. Izdatel'stvo gumanitarnoi literaturij. 2004, pp. 493–494.

[ix] In criticizing Heidegger, Paul Ricoeur re-iterates Bakhtin: the art of Dying is counterbalanced by the art of Living in which the notion of Death plays an equally important role (Cf Ricoeur, *La mémoire…*, 2004, p. 499).

[x] Cf Ricoeur, *La mémoire…*, 2004, pp. 499–500. Ricoeur quotes Michel Montaigne's *Essays*, in which Montaigne argues that „*readiness to die sets us free from any submission and constraint whatsoever*" (ibid.).

[xi] Cf Gurko, Yelena. [in Russian] *Jacques Derrida: Dekonstruktzia*. Minsk. Ekonompress. 2001. p. 161.

[xii] Cf Demichev, 1997, p. 108.

[xiii] Cf Levinas, E. *Totalité et Infini*, 2000, p. 81.

[xiv] Cf Levinas, E. [in Russian] *Vremia I Drougoi*. Visshaya Religiozno-Filsofskaya shkola, Sankt-Peterburg. 1998, pp. 68, 79.

[xv] Cf Levinas, *Totalité…* 2000, p. 269.

[xvi] Cf Blanchot, Maurice. *L'Espace Littéraire*, [in Bulgarian] Literaturnoto prostranstvo. Sofia. LIK 2000, p. 161.

[xvii] Cf Derrida, *Apories* 1998, pp. 40–41.

[xviii] Cf Buchkov, A. *Aporiite…*, 2003.

[xixxix] Cf Morson & Emerson, 1989, pp. 154, 164.

PART I

A Survey of Critical Sources

A critically thorough investigation of the *theme of Mortality in the poetic works of the Brontë sisters* requires some clarifications to be made about its analytical context. To „skip" it would mean to deprive the research project of its proper critical background. It would also mean to neglect the main philosophy which underpins the present study – **dialogism,** or the faith in *Otherness,* the implied consideration of an ever present „someone Other than You", who could challenge „Your firm beliefs". Preceded by a general review of major critical sources on the matter, each sister's works are then highlighted through a specific range of critical texts. These are inevitably put in the broader context of English literature of the late 18th–mid 19th centuries, and some critical sources immerse the Brontë sisters' interest in *Mortality* into a wider European context.

Although the critic can rest assured in view of the thorough and scrupulously laid out editions of the Brontë sisters' poetry available nowadays, yet all of those position the poetic heritage of Emily, Charlotte, Anne, and even Branwell, within a certain range of critical debates about the structural specificities of the poems, as well as the route of acquisition of the extant manuscripts of the Brontë sisters' poems. None of the major Brontëists (i.e. Edward Chitham, Tom Winnifrith, Fannie Ratchford, Clement Shorter, Barbara Lloyd-Evans, Dorothy Van Ghent, Jacques Blondel, Winifred Gerin, Herbert Dingle, Lyndall Gordon, Patricia Ingham, James Kavanagh, W. D. Paden, M. Peters, Sally Shuttleworth, Victor Newfeldt, Jill Dix Ghnassia) have specifically and independently attempted to analyse the theme of *Mortality* in the Brontë sisters' poetry. Whilst the literary constructs *Angria* and *Gondal* have been discussed in detail (whenever links have been sought between the poetry and the Brontë sisters' novels), yet no agreement has been reached as to whether one specific philosophic field of creativity could be defined for each of the four Brontës in respect of their poetry[1]. And develop such a field they did, as the

---

[1] Hatfield's 1941 edition of Emily Brontë's poems is the only complete edition based on the hypothesis that, if A.G.A.' life and death were taken as the organizing centre of Emily's poetry, then the most obviously recurrent motif would appear to be that of Death. The arrangement of the poems – so that they form a meaningful thematic entity named *Gondal* – is one proof for the latter idea. An additional element is Hatfield's open respect for **Fannie Ratchford's study**, in which A.G.A., Queen of Gondal, is proposed as the axis of the course of events in Gondal (see Hatfield's

present study argues: **Mortality** – both the structural and the thematic centre of their works. What does exist, however, are some respectable studies on the theme of *Mortality* as developed in the Brontë sisters' novels. Those will be mentioned if/where appropriate.

As might be expected, the first in depth studies of the Brontës (and, in this sense, on the theme of *Mortality* in the works of the Brontës) were biographical. The first major such was <u>Elizabeth Gaskell's *The Life of Charlotte Brontë* (1857</u>, the edition quoted here is: New York: J. M. Dent & Sons LTD, 1928). Elizabeth Gaskell – the well-known Victorian novelist who did visit Haworth parsonage and met on a few occasions with Charlotte, accentuates what would certainly have contributed to occasions of Death in Haworth. Namely: the unsanitary position of the graveyard of the parsonage, as well as the still ongoing at the time interments inside the church; there was a serious threat to the local population who had to face infectious diseases through water poisoning, for instance. Gaskell also emphasizes the very early average age of Death of the inhabitants of Haworth, and their callous attitude to the value of human life (one prototypal locus of Death is *The Cowan Bridge Clergy Daughters' School* in Yorkshire – the *Lowood School* of Charlotte's *Jane Eyre /1847/ –* a novel which demonstrates its author's particular interest in the issue of infant death).

Another recent intriguing biographical study on the Brontës that the critic cannot pass by is <u>Eddie Flintoff's</u> guide to the prototypal places in the Brontë sisters' novels: <u>*In the Steps of the Brontës* 1993 (Newbury Berkshire, Countryside Books, 1993).</u> This is an extensive survey of the factual specificities of the various Halls, farms and Estates – half ruined and mysteriously implying Death – that the Brontës would have visited during their lives and careers as governesses, and later – used in their works (e.g. *the Cowan Bridge School* as *the Lowood* in *Jane Eyre*, or *High Sunderland Hall* and *Top Withens* – the possible prototypes of *Wuthering Heights*).

<u>Juliet Barker's</u> scrupulous monographic investigation of the Brontë family (*The Brontës*, London: Weidenfeld & Nicholson, 1994), as well as her editorial work in *The Brontës. A Life in Letters* (Viking at Penguin

---

introduction as well as: **Ratchford, Fannie, (ed.)** *Gondal's Queen. A Novel in Verse by Emily Jane Brontë* /University of Texas Press, 1955/).

Books LTD, 1997) emphasise the Rev. Patrick Brontë's ministry and daily involvement with mortality and the funeral practice as a solid basis for the Brontë children's interest in the given theme. Charlotte Brontë's confessional letters occupy a significant portion of the second book and they clearly demonstrate her continuous sensation of the destitution, the agony and the alienation that she experienced with the loss of each of her dear sisters and her brother (see in particular: Barker, J., 1997, pp. 218–351). Lamonica Drew's „We Are Three Sisters": Self and Family in the Writing of the Brontës (Columbia & London: University of Missouri Press, 2003) is one good recent study of Anne, Charlotte and Emily Brontë, which examines the Brontë children's involvement with the theme of Death in various contexts. The unnecessarily early loss of the „maternal element" is seen to have shaken the props of familial unity for the Brontë children, who were further educated and instructed to hope for a union with their Creator through frequent encounters with, and contemplation of, Death (ibid. chapter I, pp. 11, 15).

Of all the other general studies on the Brontës, I think it is worth mentioning Daphne Du Maurier's The Infernal World of Branwell Brontë (Penguin Books, 1960; the 1987 reprint quoted here), which draws a comparative analysis between the chthonian elements in Branwell Brontë's poetry and in Emily Brontë's poetry. Naturally, the author pays special attention to Emily's novel, Wuthering Heights.

In the 1960s, 1970s–1990s, there could be observed an expected critical urge to rediscover Romantic and Victorian literature through the investigative apparatuses of various modern schools such as: cultural theory, psychoanalysis, deconstruction, feminism etc. Although not exclusively dedicated to the Brontë sisters works, Philip Aries' L'Homme Devant La Mort, 1977 (the edition quoted here is: [in Bulgarian] Tchovekat pred Smartta. Sofia. LIK, 2004) inserts his impressions on the Brontës in a massive diachronic study of the cultural phenomenon of Death in a broader European context. Aries traces the rise, and the subsequent decline, of the motif of the yearning for the World Beyond in the works of Emily and Charlotte Brontë, as well as Charlotte Brontë's preoccupation with the concept of the afterlife in her quest to find a surrogate mother (mainly in her novel Jane Eyre, Cf Aries, 2004, vol. II – pp. 211–234). There is a focus on Emily Brontë's devotional lyrics (where Death is seen

31.

as the moment of transition into a coveted and firm reunion with *the Other*), on her obsession with the grave (the ultimate abode for prayer and the last abode of the Lyrical Self's many dead friends, ibid. vol. II, pp. 184–194). Aries also discerns a growing Victorian tendency to refuse to face the true, horrible, physical face of Death, which the listless mourner avoids by talking of the World Beyond only.

Sandra Gilbert and Susan Gubar's *The Madwoman in the Attic* (New Haven & London: Yale University Press, 1984) is the first major *feminist* study to position the Brontë sisters within the feminine psychological context of Victorian England. The Brontë sisters are perceived as Milton's descendants. Their interest in the controversies over the essence of the *daemonic* (particularly obvious in their female characters/ lyrical personae) places them amongst such other major women poets and novelists of the 19th century as: Mary Elisabeth Coleridge, Christina Rossetti, Emily Dickinson and Jane Austen. One merit of this book is the two authors' attempt to track down the development of *the female daemon*, as they provide evidence from earlier literary works, including the Biblical context, as well as Renaissance literature (e.g. Edmund Spenser's *The Faerie Queene* is mentioned).

The Brontës have not remained unnoticed by *psychoanalysis* either. I have found particularly useful Bettina Knapp's monograph *The Brontës 1992* (New York: A Frederick Ungar Book, Continuum, 1992). Knapp juxtaposes the traditional patriarchal benevolence of Christianity (epitomised by God as the male progenitor) to the Daemonic component in man's psyche in the face of Lucifer – a lethal mixture found in characters like Emily Brontë's Heathcliff, as well as in the violent and cruel images, in which her poetry abounds (ibid., pp. 102, 132). Another important psychoanalytical study of the Brontës is to be found in Elisabeth Bronfen and Sarah Webster Goodwin's editorial collection of essays *Death and Representation* (Baltimore & London: The Johns Hopkins University Press, 1993). Chapter I of the latter presents Garret Stewart's intriguing argument that Death is the most essential and furthermost „limit of representation." According to this „limit", the development of the typical Victorian character/ lyrical persona is positioned within the liminal space of „non-life" (and not „not-life") – the state of the active denial of representation – something the author manages to detect in Charlotte Brontë's female character (e.g. Lucy Snowe, from *Villette*).

The Brontës are known to have been not only brilliant poets and novelists, but they have also left some evidence of their talents as artists – a fact recognized by Christine Alexander and Jane Sellars in their book *The Art of the Brontës* (Cambridge University Press, 1995). Alexander and Sellars believe that the Brontë children's preoccupation (particularly Emily's and Branwell's) with images of Death and destruction in their art of drawing (half-ruined houses, bared trees, children being punished mercilessly, macabre Death-visitations and Biblical treatments of the theme of Justice) could be linked to certain Angrian and Gondalian personae who also have equivalents in the Brontë sisters' novels.

One PhD research work on the three Brontë sisters that I consider particularly valuable is Lisa Wang's *The Use of Theological Discourse in the Novels of the Brontë Sisters* (1998, a graduate of Birkbeck College, *University of London*). Lisa Wang analyses in detail the Biblical references in the Brontë sisters' novels. Thus, she sees *the wind* in Emily's poetry to be a recurrent symbolic pneumatological representation of the Holy Spirit (the history of which she traces back to its Hebrew origin, as well as to *Hegel's Phenomenology of the Spirit*, of the *Geist*, which is at the centre of German Romantic theory).

Of the less awe-inspiring studies of the Brontës I should like to mention two, both of which read as rather extreme viewpoints. The first one is Diane Long Hoeveler's *Gothic Femnisim. The Professionalisation of Gender from Charlotte Smith to the Brontës* (The Pennsylvania State University Press, 1998). The author's preoccupation with the subject of *the body*, as such, perceives the Brontë sisters' heroines as undeniably relying on „fate and chance": they are seen as striving to escape from their bodies which are, in the author's vision, authoritatively abused by the male subject in the corporally limited human world (pp. 188–198). I think this study misses out on in depth analysis of the ontological value of the body in the Brontë sisters' philosophy of Being, which would treat it as a part of man's identity which evolves through, and for the sake of, *someone Other*. Another rather extreme viewpoint based on non-benign literary speculations is that of James Tully, who makes a mystery of the Brontë sisters' life in his *Charlotte Brontë's Crimes* 1999 ([in Bulgarian]

32.

Prestapleniata na Charlotte Bronte, Sofia: Epsilon 2000). Tully draws an image of a callous and monstrous Charlotte, whose oppression of Emily and Anne, he claims, was in unison with her deep desire to annihilate the literary rivalry in the face of her two sisters. Charlotte is said to have destroyed the manuscripts of Emily Brontë's unpublished and long-lost works. With an ambiguous and factually unsupported determination, Tully pronounces Charlotte to have quickened the death of both Emily and Anne, so that, in the long run, the benefactor of her crimes would have been Arthur Bell Nicholls (Charlotte Brontë's husband and last curate of the Rev. Patrick Brontë). Tully explains how Arthur Bell Nicholls made quite a profit out of selling the Brontë sisters' manuscripts after Charlotte's death. In the context of the methodology of research defined as „*ontophilosophy/ dialogism*", such statements appear not merely rather authoritarian, indeed non-dialogic. I should have thought, that is an example of someone who dares interpret and sometimes thwart – for the reasons of originality, self-content, or simply in order to produce a stunning effect on the reading audience – facts of a lifetime which is no more Present, but is Past, and as such could be responsibly owned, rather than selfishly possessed and „fiddled with", or „complemented".

* * *

Little, if almost nothing, has been accomplished in researching the theme of *Mortality* in **Anne Brontë's works**. Most of the critical sources mentioned here are contemporary and they tend to emphasise Anne Brontë's philosophic input through her novels, rather than through her poetry. To the critic, Anne appears to be the least known of the three Brontë sisters, but certainly not the least important one, particularly in view of her apocalyptic ideas and her aptitude for interpreting *Mortality* in the religious context of Christianity. Otherwise, there certainly exist some good biographical studies of Anne's life.

The critic should not miss <u>Edward Chitham's *The Poems of Anne Brontë* (Macmillan, 1979)</u> – the first complete edition of her poetry. In the introduction to the latter, Chitham stresses Anne's ability to face and examine facts of Life in detail whilst being „analytical" and stoical, one such major fact being Death (he quotes one of Anne Brontë's last and best known poems: *Self-Communion*, 1847–1848). Anne's disagreement with

Calvinism (to which she certainly would have been exposed during her education – in Haworth, as a resident student, and during her won professional career) is counterbalanced by her growing Methodist conviction in God's undeniable _universal love and pardon_ (ibid. pp. 19–20). Another significant and fairly recent study of Chitham's that I cherish is _A Life of Anne Brontë_ (Oxford: Basil Blackwell, 1997). Chitham quotes some poems of Anne's poems in support of his belief in her sensitive perception of a World of growing alienation among individuals during the Victorian age. Chitham quite logically and reasonably chooses two poems that speak clearly of Anne's estrangement from Life during her Thorp Green period as a governess (i.e. _Retirement_ – 1840, and „_Call me away; there's nothing here_" – 1845). Again, Anne's Evangelical introspection and her love for humanity are underlined when Chitham talks about her faith in universal salvation. Winifred Gerin's significant contribution, her biographical book _Anne Brontë_ (Thomas Nelson & Sons LTD, 1959), reveals that Anne's Methodist upbringing would have underpinned Anne's orientation towards the theological discourse while developing her poetic vision. Gerin sees reflections on matters apocalyptic in Anne's preoccupation with the motifs of universal salvation and of sudden redemption, but also in Anne's unceasing self-vigilance and self-criticism. Gerin quotes in full the texts of such poems as: _Retirement_ (1840) and _Self-Congratulation_ (1840). She also argues that Anne Brontë's confessional lyrics suggest the poet's early exhaustion from Life's demands, and her unquenchable grief over the loss of childhood innocence and optimism. Another monograph on Anne Brontë, which appeared in the same year, is: _Anne Brontë. Her Life and Work, by Ada Harrison and Derek Stanford_ (London: Methuen & Co. LTD, 1959). The book could be described as a biographical study, but it is invaluable in that the two authors notice the relevance of the motif of _transitoriness_ (in a poem like _Self-Communion_, 1847–1848). A mature character of Anne's, whose philosophy of Life treats the above motif, is Helen Graham (from Anne's novel _The Tenant of Wildfell Hall_, 1848). Helen Graham's life is an incessant „internal debates" over the established belief in, and value of, the purgatorial functions of _Hell_ (one of the two abodes, people believed, which the soul of an expired body might be destined to and accommodated by). The focus of Ernest Raymond's _Exiled and Harassed Anne_ (in the

33.

1949 edition of the Brontë Society Transactions, quoted here from: /ed./ McNees, E., *The Brontë Sisters. Critical Assessments* /Helm Information LTD, 1996/) is very similar to the above study in it subject matter (Cf McNees, 1996, pp. 103, 110).

Overall, I would argue that the interest in the themes of *Mortality* in Anne Brontë's works has so far been somewhat haphazard. The works quoted above mainly recognize Anne Brontë's inclination towards apocalyptic thinking and her religious hesitation over the justification of the system of Heavenly judgement as a regulative mechanism in the temporally limited human world. They somehow fail to acknowledge Anne Brontë's broader ontological search, evident, for example, in such motifs in her poetry as _orphanhood, or euthanasia_ (which are given, I should like to hope, a detailed consideration in the present study).

Although more has been written about **Charlotte Brontë**, yet credits have been mainly given to Charlotte's achievements as a novelist. Very few are the references to Charlotte Brontë's poetic interest in the themes of *Mortality* and *Death*. As with Emily, the critics have so far been concerned with the factual specificities of the creation of her imaginary world of Angria (emphasis has been put on Branwell's contribution), on the structural arrangement of the poems, on the elimination and resuscitation of Angria's main lyrical personae, and, naturally, on Charlotte Brontë's severe personal conflict with Death throughout her life.

No doubt, among _the biographical studies,_ Elizabeth Gaskell's _The Life of Charlotte Brontë_ (1857) is the pioneering one. Mrs. Gaskell considers in detail Charlotte's whole life and literary career were burdened with the memories of the early death of her mother, and subsequently with the vivid memories of the deaths of her sisters and her one brother. Mrs Gaskell's confessional conversations with Charlotte at Haworth parsonage reveal Charlotte's intentions to commemorate her beloved dead sisters through her literary heroines (e.g. the devout Maria – Charlotte's eldest sister, could have been the model for Helen Burns, from *Jane Eyre,* ibid. pp. 385–387). Another rather early biographical study of Charlotte Brontë is _May Sinclair's The Three Brontës_ (London: Hutchinson & Co., 1912), in which the author, similarly, believes that the late Emily Brontë may have become the prototype for Shirley (in Charlotte's novel Shirley, 1849). Charlotte Brontë seems to be the only one of the Brontës who, apparently, had the chance to share – in her personal correspondence and in her diary – how the Death in her family eventually and quite literally destroyed not only „a lifelong writing partnership“, but also affected terminally her own spiritual Self (see Drew, Lamonica, 2003, p. 180). Innovative appears Rosamond Langbridge's _Charlotte Brontë. A Psychological Study_ (London: William Heinemann LTD, 1929). Chapters I, II and III are exclusively dedicated to Charlotte Brontë's daily encounter with Death – an event which formed (physically, but also intellectually) a great portion of her father's professional duties at the parsonage. The latter fact must have aggravated Charlotte's observations and feeling that, in her own lifetime, she was to become the witness of her sisters' and her brother's early and unnecessary deaths. Lyndall Gordon's _Charlotte Brontë. A Passionate Life_ (London: Chatto & Windus, 1994) is an intriguing contemporary study, in which Charlotte's numerous encounters with Death are analysed through the perception that Charlotte Brontë's life was one which unfolded as a pilgrimage towards maturation and independence – both literary and existential. The author discerns Charlotte's early isolation from life during her Roe Head poetic period (1831–1832); she tries to link the latter to certain states and spaces of confinement in which her works abound. Indeed, a very recent research on Charlotte Brontë is Heather Glen's _Charlotte Brontë. The Imagination in History_ (Oxford University Press, 2002, the 2004 reprint quoted throughout). Heather Glen places Charlotte's preoccupation with Death in the cultural context of 19th-century Evangelical England, an obvious and extreme representative of which was, to Charlotte and Emily, the Rev. William Carus Wilson – the patron of the _Cowan Bridge Clergy Daughters School_. In three regularly published magazines (_The Children's Friend, The Child's Magazine_ and _The Sunday School Companion_) the Rev. Wilson generously provided the infant scholars with examples of Death (of infants' death), which were aimed at catechising the children's imagination into an undeniable acceptance of, and gratitude for, the moment of ultimate salvation – Death. Life as a solitary pilgrimage and as a preparation for Death, „_the constant threat of obliteration [of personality] in a world of awful danger_“, the incomplete (one would say „defective“) Self – these are all issues which Heather Glen discovers both in Charlotte's _Juvenilia_ and in her mature works (ibid. chapters I, IV and VIII).

Again, Eleanor McNees' collection of critical essays and articles on the Brontës contains an important piece of criticism on Charlotte Brontë, written in 1857 (and published first in the *Scribner's Monthly* of 2nd May 1887). In it Charlotte's lifelong friend and confessor, Ellen Nussey, remembers Charlotte's sensitive and impressionable nature, which held forever the legend of the ghostly nun that had been brooding over the boarding school at Roe Head (Cf Nussey in: McNees, 1996, pp. 98–105). Later, the supposed nun's mysterious and anguished death may very possibly have helped Charlotte create the basis of the presence of the *ghostly* in a novel like *Villette* (1853), but also in affirming the importance of the image of *the revenant nun/the female ghost*, which presides over her poetry.

I feel an obligation to mention Winifred Gerin's *Charlotte Brontë. The Evolution of Genius* (Oxford University Press, 1969). Although not exclusively dedicated to her poetry, it is a meticulous investigation of such a crucial thematic element relevant to *Mortality* as *Heaven* (and *the apocalyptic*). Chapter VII examines Charlotte's lifelong interest in matters religious, her open condemnation (as observed in her letters and confessional pieces) of the Calvinistic idea of election and reprobation, which the moment of Death was traditionally considered to endorse (until the late 19th-century). This study pays special attention to certain incidents in Charlotte's life (like her visitations of the Protestant cemetery in Brussels during her stay at Pensionnat Heger), which later fermented into the motif of *orphanhood* (exemplified through such character as, for instance, Frances Henri, from *The Professor,* published in 1857). The year 1969 boasted another monograph worth mentioning: Earl A. Knies' *The Art of Charlotte Brontë* (Ohio University Press, 1969). This structuralist study, I would argue, could be seen as the first more specifically thematic research of Charlotte Brontë's preoccupation with Death. Knies analyses how, from a formal and structural point of view, the phenomenon of Death is refracted through Charlotte's practice of eliminating – resuscitating some lyrical personae in Angria: a technique which binds the incidents of the saga together (i.e. Death is not a permanent phenomenological state – ibid. p. 78).

Helene Moglen's *Charlotte Brontë. The Self-Conceived* (New York: WW Norton and Company, 1976) stands out as perhaps the first monograph on Charlotte Brontë which deals properly with the thematic specificities of Death in her poetry. Moglen's psychoanalytical inclination leads her to the conclusion that Charlotte's female Angrian personae are tormented by insurmountable physical and psychological loss (ibid. p. 51–52), which is being aggravated by various instances of lethal fear (the female's fear of the male authority, man's fear of castration – variations of the same kind of fear of the loss of selfhood to the „other"). In historical perspective, Moglen proposes parallels between such fear of the „loss of selfhood" and the Byronic outcast's fear of self-alienation (p. 92). Another invaluable manual on the specificities of Charlotte Brontë's treatment of Death in both her poetry and her novels is Robert Keefe's *Charlotte Brontë's World of Death* (Austin: University of Texas Press, 1979). The Duke of Zamorna is positioned at the centre of Angria's distrustful and murderous atmosphere, in which all the ladies he is surrounded by perish (e.g. Marian Hume, Maria Henrietta Percy). Zamorna's own assassination is another grievous instance of Death to which Keefe pays close attention as to an organizing centre within Angria (ibid. pp. 47–54). Keefe traces the motif of the punitive Death in Charlotte Brontë's novels *Jane Eyre* and *Villette,* whilst he also highlights some major representations of the motif of *the missing female authority and protector (i.e. the missing mother/sister/companion).*

The *gender theory* takes pride in the already cited *The Madwoman in the Attic* (by Sandra Gilbert and Susan Gubar, 1984) – frankly feminist in its critical orientation. Again, Gilbert and Gubar fit in quite well with those of the literary critical guild who choose to discuss *the motif of the missing mother* as the thematic core of Charlotte's works. Gilbert and Gubar give a new lease of life to this motif by revealing Charlotte's engagement with the problem of „*the missing Past*", for which one always tries to find a substitute through a surrogate mother (evident in Charlotte Brontë's *Jane Eyre,* in *Villette,* and in her poetry – the poem *Frances* is quoted, as well as in Emily's *Wuthering Heights* – 1847). In chapter IV (*The Spectral Selves of Charlotte Brontë*) ghostliness is interpreted as that element which speaks of Charlotte's attempts to find a compensatory mechanism for the incomplete Past, seen as female. Additionally, the authors suggest that Death might be perceived as a male tool of objectification, of itemization of females in the Victorian atmosphere

35.

of the repression of the female Self (Cf chapter XII – on *Villette*). Elisabeth Bronfen's brilliant study of Charlotte Brontë's *Jane Eyre*, which she sieves through Lacan's perception of *gender*, occupies chapter X of her monograph, entitled *Over Her Dead Body. Death, Femininity and the Aesthetic* (Manchester University Press, 1992). Bronfen argues that the quality of being liminal, of being incomplete, never whole, is typical of the nature of the female body, indeed of the female creature as such. Despite being fragmented, never quite alive, the woman is pronounced to be the determinant of the wholeness of Culture (which is traditionally seen as male). In her capacity to reproduce, the reduplicate, the woman also potentially possesses the ability to return half-alive, as a revenant to the World of the living – a world where she is otherwise often present as *the orphan*. After a close ontological consideration of the validity of the above arguments, I find that they would be valuable and worth quoting, where appropriate, in discussing both Charlotte's novels and her poetry. Peculiarly enough, they could relate in an innovative manner to the problem of *the missing Other* (especially in Charlotte's poetry), which is indeed the missing female authority.

Feminism and elements of psychoanalysis meet in Sally Shuttleworth's *Charlotte Brontë & Victorian Psychology* (Cambridge University Press, 1996). The author endeavours to interpret Charlotte Brontë's heritage as linked to one common Victorian issue: Death, as caused by human madness. Professor Shuttleworth elaborates on female insanity, while she also suggests that the irregularities of the female menstrual cycle are at the bottom of human tragedies and misunderstanding. Related to the latter are the issues of the urge towards self-assertion, and also the fear of the body's intactness being threatened (chapters III, VI, VII & X). Sally Shuttleworth notices that, in Charlotte Brontë's works, what hurts internally (i.e. inside oneself) is being embodied by external phenomena (e.g. in *Villette* Lucy Snowe's disrupted mind and deranged imagination produce the daemonic performance of the actress Vashti). In another article on *Villette* („*The Surveillance of a Sleepless Eye*", in: /ed./ Ingham, Patricia, *The Brontës*, /Longman Pearson Education, 2003/), Sally Shuttleworth focuses on the link between the symbolic presence of the nun, the grave and the motifs of sin and sexual transgression. The Nun, it would appear by now, is a generic representation of the concept of enclosure which could also be discerned in Charlotte Brontë's interest in discussing chastity and wholeness, as directly linked to the experiential and existential development of the female individual in her novels, but also in her poetry. The analysis of the theme of Death in both Anne's and Charlotte's novels is in direct connection to the development of the female character. One point I hope to be able to prove is that the same is valid for the evolution of the major female lyrical personae in their poetic works, which is where the parallels with their novels would seem inevitable.

Finally, one perhaps extreme application of colonial/ post-colonial theory to the Brontës is <u>Carl Plasa's *Charlotte Brontë* (Critical Issues Series, Palgrave and Macmillan 2004)</u>. Forcing the historical context of Britain's colonial oppression in Africa and the West Indies, and emphasising the image of the Brontë children's hero – Sir Arthur Wellesley Wellington (1769–1852), Plasa examines Charlotte's juvenile *Ashanti Narratives (1829–1839)*, some of her poems (like the famous *The Missionary* – *1845)*, her mature novels and her Belgian essays (e.g. *„Sacrifice of an Indian Widow"*, 1842). He tries to reveal the importance of the theme of Death in the cultural context of colonial oppression and miscegenation as two sources of human misery. Plasa boldly maintains Charlotte's consideration of certain subsidiary themes related to the above, such as: war, orphanhood, holocaust, religious sacrifice and revenge. Although Charlotte Brontë was very much aware of the historical complexities of her own time, I would argue that there is not enough biographical evidence that Charlotte was that deeply involved in matters political so as to take an attitude so personal to them and so write all her works exclusively as a critique on Britain's colonial invasion.

No doubt, *Mortality* has been most researched with regard to **Emily Brontë's works**. It is an aspect of critical investigation which has been approached by literary critics of both genders, which, undoubtedly, broadens its philosophic dimensions and makes it more objective. As was suggested earlier, there could be observed a rise of the interest towards the theme in hand during the 1980s and 1990s – with the development of the schools of feminism and deconstruction. Understandably attracted to the imaginary world of Gondal, literary critics tend to trace the development of the theme of mortality on the basis of a close study of Gondal's main female persona's life and deeds – A.G.A. The formation of her character is a crucial indicator of the poet's ontological growth. Unlike the biographical studies of Charlotte, or Anne, the ones dedicated to Emily are rather more explicitly related to thematic investigations of *Mortality* in both her poetry and her novel. As a result, the biographical studies are often hard to segregate from the ones with a categorical bias towards thematic research of Emily Brontë's works.

From first publication both Emily Brontë's novel *Wuthering Heights* and her poetry became a battlefield of critical ideas. The anonymous article on *Wuthering Heights* in the <u>North American Review</u> (October 1848) boldly compares Heathcliff to such literary giants like Goethe's Mephistopheles, Milton's Satan and to some characters from Dante's burning pitch – for all of whom Death appears a way out of ordinariness and of the routine existence of common mortals (CF McNees, 1996, p. 155). <u>Currer Bell</u> (Charlotte Brontë's poetic pen-name) herself did not linger to share her views on her sister's creative potential, as she claimed that for Emily Death represented „yoke", from which she „never quite freed herself" (from *The Hogg's Instructor* – 1855, quoted from: McNees, 1996, p. 180). For the first time Emily's works were officially included in the <u>1916</u> edition of the <u>Cambridge History of English Literature</u> (edited by <u>Sir A. W. Ward & A.R. Waller, *The Cambridge History of English Literature*, vol. 13 – the 19th century, Cambridge University, 1912</u>). Chapter 12 of the latter allots Emily's genius a taste for the diabolical and examines the symbolic significance of the moors and the grave in her poetry.

<u>Lord David Cecil's</u> monograph <u>Early Victorian Novelists</u> (London: <u>Constable & Co. LTD, 1948)</u> could be seen as a breakthrough in Brontë studies. *Good* and *Evil* are pronounced to be two ingredients intertwined and ingrained in Life – a motif Emily developed assiduously in her works. The non-differentiation of Good/Evil is a prerequisite for coming to terms with Life's complex experiential authenticity. Death, in that sense, is as much an ingredient of Being as birth, or love, or friendship is, and so cannot be viewed as inherently destructive. Cecil argues that in *Wuthering Heights* destruction appears lethal because it results from passion being diverted from its natural course. Similar is <u>Martin Turnell's</u> interpretation of Emily's works in the journal *The Wind and the Rain* (summer 1949).

He sees Emily's interest in *Death* as prompted by her metaphysical strife to reach „ultimate fulfilment", and he quotes the poem „*Silent is the house*" (*Julian M. And A. G. Rochelle* – 1845; Cf Turnell in: McNees 1996, p. 533). Considerably later, <u>Barbara Hardy's *Forms of Feeling in Victorian Fiction* (London: Peter Owen, 1985)</u> was to make the controversial statement that Death „was to Emily a worked-for, waited-for goal" (in her analysis of the poems *Julian M. and A. G. Rochelle* – 1845, and *No Coward Soul Is Mine* – 1846).

    <u>Dorothy Van Ghent</u> looks into Emily Brontë's novel and her poetic works through the contextual prism of *the Gothic trend*, which was a fact in English literature of the first half of the 19th century. In her monograph *The English Novel. Form and Function* (New York: Rineheart & Company, INC., 1953) In this psychoanalytical investigation, Van Ghent pays special tribute to the chthonian elements in *Wuthering Heights* (coffin-like spaces and closets, burial places) in order to reveal how they function in the formation of the main characters' psyche. Van Ghent also investigates how chthonian elements contribute to the development of some early prototypes of *Wuthering Height's* main characters as found in her poetry (as in the poem *H.A. and A.S.* – 1842). Demonism is interpreted as the ominous mergence of both the productive urge (through love) and the destructive impulse (through love unrecognised, unrequited); i.e. the daemonic arises from the darkest depths and recesses of the human soul which thus bears the seed of Death (see also: Van Ghent in: ed. Allott, M., *Emily Jane Brontë. A Selection of Critical Essays*, /Macmillan, 1994/).

    <u>The school of *deconstruction* reaches Emily Brontë first in the face of Hillis-Miller, J. (chapter IV of *The Disappearance of God, Five Nineteenth-Century Writers*, /Cambridge Massachusetts: The Belknap Press of Harvard University Press & London: Oxford University Press, 1963/).</u> I would define the latter study as an absolute must in exploring Emily Brontë's religious interest in *Mortality*. *Gondal* is perceived as Emily's poetic attempt to create a Heaven of her own by way of utilising the opportunities that the voluntarily chosen Death implies. Hillis-Miller was also the first critic to conscientiously draw the reader's attention to the intriguing substance of Emily's *Belgian Devoirs*, in particular to her essay *The Butterfly (1842)*, in which she fights and topples the conventional coherence and credibility of the moral judgement provided for the

individual upon his/her expiration by God. The latter argument is set in the context of Methodism – a religious movement whose influence Emily certainly experienced (particularly the idea of *universal salvation*). On the other hand, Hillis-Miller condemns Death as a mere act of will – which is what A.G.A. performs through infanticide, as she wishes to terminate the endless chain of Life in which every new generation replaces, repeats, and in effect ousts, the old one.

Peculiarly enough, Denis Donoghue's psychoanalytical reception of Emily Brontë in his 1970 study of her poems (see Donoghue in: Petit, J.-P. – *Emily Brontë. A Critical Anthology* /Penguin, 1973/) argues that Emily's preoccupation with Death springs from her desire to define the limits and the existential capacities of the actual Self that interprets the world (the same Self which reads meaning in Life, whilst striving to accomplishing sexual union). Similarly, Lawrence J. Starzyk notices such a striving for unity – of the Self and cosmically – in Emily's poetry (see *Criticism*, spring 1972 in: McNees, 1996, pp. 559–570). The Death-urge that commands so many of Emily's poems is read as the poet's attempt to refute the fragmentarity of being, inherent in Life and in Nature's terrifying randomness. Quite a few critics agree that Emily Brontë's works create the image of a character/ persona, who wishes to merge with *the dead Other* in actual life in order to erase the boundary between living and non-living matter, and thus to make the threat of Death irrelevant. One such critic is Geoffrey Tillotson, who assures the reader in the above through a close study of Heathcliff (from *Wuthering Heights*) – Emily Brontë's most explicit attempt to create a character who would like to master temporality (Cf Tillotson, G., *A View of Victorian Literature* /Oxford: Clarendon Press, 1978, Cf p. 214/).

I would argue that the first significant formal analysis of Emily's poetry is to be found in Rosalind Miles' guide to Emily Brontë's apocalyptic imagery (Cf Miles, R., in: /ed./ Smith, Anne, *The Art of Emily Brontë* /Vision and Barnes & Noble, 1976/). Miles notices that Emily Brontë is particularly prone to create and use such metaphors which bear certain references towards *Space* – and many of those imply Death. For example: „*the sea of death's eternity*", „*child of dust*", „*the portals of futurity*", „(…) *every star/ Stared like a dying memory*" and others. The *grave* is seen as the symbol of the paradox of Life, according to which the active persona, the Survivor's mentor, is a revenant (as in the visionary poem *Julian M. and A. G. Rochelle* – 1845).

Margaret Homans' *Transcending the Problem of Sexual Identity* (1980, in: Allott, 1994) is an important step forward. In it the author maintains that for Emily Nature is non-maternal, but alienating and terrifying so that transcendence of the earthly selfhood is needed in order to survive (as in the poems: *Stars* – *1845; I see around me tombstones grey* – *1841; Silent is the house* – *all are laid asleep* – *1845*, and also in Emily's novel *Wuthering Heights*). What the latter study really investigates is, in my opinion, *orphanhood* and *infanticide* in Emily Brontë's poetry – two crucial motifs which I have tried to do justice to in my research. Another intriguing study is Camille Paglia's *Romantic Shadows. Emily Brontë* (chapter 17 of Paglia's *Sexual Personae. Art and Decadence from Nefertiti to Emily Dickinson* /London and New Haven: Yale University Press, 2001/). This one interprets the motif of the dead/ the missing mother in Emily's works as one example of an author's deviation from High Romanticism in England, and as a swerve towards digging in the theme of Nature's daemonicity (something which the poet Samuel Taylor Coleridge did openly and very successfully). Marginally, David Holbrook notices that some mature poems of Emily's (he quotes „*How beautiful the earth is still*", „*Enough of thought, philosopher*", and „*Cold in the earth, and the deep snow piled above thee*", all written in 1845) illustrate Emily's involvement with the theme of *Death* (through the symbol of the grave) as related to the problem of *the missing/ dead mother*. Interestingly enough, in an appendix to his study *Wuthering Heights. A Drama of Being* (Sheffield Academic Press, 1997), David Holbrook subtly provides some details about the tragic events in the Rev. Patrick Brontë's own biography. Apparently, the unfortunate and controversial lot that Welsh – the adopted son of Patrick's great-grandfather (and the foster father to Hugh – Patrick's own father) played in their family history, may account, quite enigmatically, for the Brontë children's early awareness of the significance of loss within the structure of a family unit.

A turning point from the non-systematic interest towards the theme of *Mortality* in Emily Brontë's works appears to be Richard Benvenuto's massive research *Emily Brontë* (Boston: Twayne Publishers, 1982). Chapter III of the latter is entirely devoted to Emily's lyric poetry, in which

38.

the author discerns the soul's pilgrimage into liberty and away from the prison of the mind. The mind, single and unchallenged as it exists, is declared to distort and mortify reality for the individual. Benvenuto quotes Emily's early poem *Coldly, bleakly, drearily* (1838) and others within the H65–H74 sequence of poems in Hatfield's 1941 edition, which, he thinks, demonstrate Emily's desire to mould her poetry as a whole composed of clusters of thematically linked pieces that read like *a stream-of-consciousness novel* (see also the poems *Julian M. and A.G. Rochelle* – 1845, *Gleneden's Dream* – 1838, and *The Death of A.G.A.*, 1841–1844). This work was followed by another invaluable collection of essays: *Brontë Facts and Brontë Problems,* by **Edward Chitham and Tom Winnifrith** (Macmillan, 1983). The two renowned Bronteists touch upon major issues in Emily Brontë's poetry, such as Emily Brontë's platonically understood symbol of *the wind* – the agent which enables an individual to transcend the Present and step into the coveted mergence with the lost beloved (in comparison, they mention Shelley's *Epipsychidion* – 1821 – and also his *Ode to the West Wind*). Chitham and Winnifrith draw parallels between Coleridge and Emily Brontë: A. G. A., Emily's mystic ambivalent female personae of the succubus type, is compared to Geraldine, from Coleridge's *Christabel* (1816).

The 1980s proved a period of open surge of interest towards the motifs of female demonism (and infanticide) in Emily's works. James Kavanagh makes his significant contribution in his monograph *Emily Brontë* (Basil Blackwell, 1985). Although *Wuthering Heights* is at its centre, this study nonetheless comments on Emily's overall interest in such issues as: sadism, control, sexual tension and destructiveness. Strictly psychoanalytical in his approach, Kavanagh delves into one of the most crucial dilemmas which Emily's works present to the critic: how is it possible to combine in one persona (A.G.A.) the ultimate and so experientially complete image of the beloved, on the one hand, and the murderous urge towards your own child – on the other.

Although biographical in its essence, Muriel Spark's and Derek Stanford's *Emily Brontë – Her Life and Work* (Arrow Books LTD, 1985) is an indispensable modern critique on Emily's poetry. Spark and Stanford see Emily at once as a stoic, quietist, pantheist and mystic. They underline the poet's intention to transcend all natural phenomena through the agency of *the wind* – the most frequently discussed symbol in Emily's poetry. The wind is seen as capable of sweeping away memory's „cribbing and confining effects" (they quote the poem *I'm happiest when most away* – undated, probably written in 1838). Emily's mystic, night-dominated and ghost-visited Nature is juxtaposed to Wordsworth's meditative, didactic, mild and maternal appearance of Nature. The authors defend the thesis that Emily prefers the temporally limited through a verifiable Present to a dubious Christian promise of an ameliorated existence in the World Beyond (the poems quoted include: *Ah, why, because the dazzling sun* – 1845, and *Death, that struck when I was most confiding*, 1845). I find particularly fascinating another study with a similar subject of research. Namely, <u>Maureen Peeck-O'Toole's *Aspects of Lyric in the Poetry of Emily Brontë* (Costerus New Series, Volume 70 /Rodopi, Amsterdam, 1988/)</u>. O'Toole, for the first time, defines a variation of the main lyrical personae of Emily's poetry – that of *the woman mourning over her dead beloved*. She directs the reader's attention to Emily's confessional lyrics, in which *the wind* – for the umpteenth time – is seen as the mediator between the soul's daily confines and its future realm of freedom *within* (Emily's term). Again, Emily's preference for the earthly bliss shared with *the Other* – *here and now* – is seen to dominate over the unfeasible heaven of the World Beyond (the poem accentuated is *I see around me tombstones grey*, 1841).

George E. Haggerty's *Gothic Fiction. Gothic Form* (The Pennsylvania State University Press, 1989) interprets Emily's intention to present the metaphor of *Death* as the privacy of meaning of individual experience (indeed as the privacy of Life). Reciprocally, <u>Ashok Celly's comparative analysis of Emily Brontë and D. H. Lawrence</u> sees such „preservation of individual experience" as the preservation of the Past, in effect the preservation of childhood (Cf Celly, <u>*Emily Brontë, D. H. Lawrence and the Black Horse*</u> /Delhi: Pragati Publications, 1997/). Celly believes that the presence of violence in Emily's works could be explained with the individual's uncontrollable desire to find a remedy against the irrevocability of the „dead Past" of childhood.

Another avid Bronteist, <u>Lyn Pykett</u>, dedicates her biographical work, entitled <u>*Emily Brontë* (Macmillan, 1989)</u> to the investigation of the formation of the diabolical type of hero, whose destructiveness is but a replica of the principle of Mutability latent in Nature. Death is seen as that state created by the mind which comes to substitute a life of denial, betrayal and exile. Pykett argues that, the easeful Death Emily's poetry lures the reader with implies an imagined state in which an individual's Self and Nature would be amalgamated (Shelley's *Epipsychidion*, 1821, is reminiscent again, ibid. pp. 68–69). The two poems quoted throughout this study are: *I see around me tombstones grey* and *Death that struck when I was most confiding*.

By now, it would appear that there is a group of scholars (like Chitham, Spark & Stanford, Pykett), whose approach to Emily Brontë's works involves a purposeful attempt to trace parallels between her and the Romantic poets (chiefly Shelley, but also Wordsworth and Coleridge). Those parallels, it seems, were drawn on the basis of the observation of the following motifs, which may be perceived as subsidiary to the more general theme of *Mortality: Mutability, Freedom,* and *Love*. In this respect, it would appear inevitable to mention <u>Irene Tayler's monograph *Holy Ghosts. The Male Muses of Emily and Charlotte Brontë* (New York: Columbia University Press, 1990)</u> – a study of the supernatural and of *Death* in English poetry of the 19th century (see esp. pages 30–56). Tayler draws the reader's attention to such poems of Emily's as: *No Coward Soul is mine (1846); Cold in the earth, and the deep snow piled above thee (1845); Enough of thought, philosopher (1845); Death that struck when I was most confiding* and *Julian M. and A. G. Rochelle*. She argues that Emily's chief concern is the theme of <u>Mourning</u>: mourning over the dead mother, but also mourning over the temporality of a paternally governed life. The poet wishes to be harboured into the bosom of Nature, which possesses maternal qualities.

One should in no case pass by <u>Stevie Davies' *Emily Brontë* (Harvester Wheatsheaf, 1988)</u>, where Emily Brontë's faithfulness to the values of Protestantism is seen as made explicit in her neglect towards the external and so in her focus on the internal, on the private Self „*as sacred inner space, the sanctuary of illumination*". In the <u>*feminist mode of thinking*</u>, Davies argues that Mother Nature is sought as „*the tumultuous peace of insentient growth – a sanctuary from the Creator*" (she quotes Emily's poem „*In the earth, the earth, thou shalt be laid*", 1843). Elaborating on the functions of Nelly Dean in Emily's novel *Wuthering*

Heights, Stevie Davies concludes that the Mother – so desperately sought for – has „*taken up the abode of the underworld*". Cathy Earnshaw's grave/deathbed is presented in a way so as to suggest that „dissolution, decomposition and undoing" are seen as beneficent, as a „transformation into a new mode of life more abundant". Emily's preoccupation with *sleep* in her poetry speaks of nocturnal journeys, accompanied by change and by creative transactions, which „disclose an alternative dimension of vision". „Death and consummation are intrinsically related" (CF Davies, 1988, pp. 19, 87–88, 150–152, 155, 159–160).

Mimicking the title of Umberto Eco's masterpiece *The Name of the Rose*, the famous American feminist Margaret Homans entitles one of her essays *The Name of the Mother in Wuthering Heights* (see Homans, in: /ed./ Peterson, Linda, *Wuthering Heights*, with biographical and historical contexts, and critical history /Boston New York: Bedford Books of St. Martin's Press, 1992/). The essay interprets the image of the female persona in Emily's novel as a victim of spiritual and physical incarceration in a male dominated world. The female body – designed to bear, but also to get rid of, another life – parallels Cathy's row of books (marked by the enigmatic variation of names/surnames: Earnshaw, Linton, Heathcliff) and, generally, the story's many narratives – „locked" in closets and chambers and forced out by the circumstances of Nelly Dean looking after a sick male master (Mr Lockwood). The sole escape for the female individual is through *ghostliness* – *the other*, the threatening side of Nature, which horrifies Lockwood. Lockwood's fear of the literal – of Nature – is his fear of the possibility of meaning and language (essentially male) being brought to a close. Another study on the same aspect of Emily's novel could be found in Katherine Kearns' *19th-Century Literary Realism. Through the Looking Glass* (Cambridge University Press, 1996). Chapter 5 of the latter examines Emily Brontë's hermetically sealed environment of *sarcophagi* (coffin-like beds, closets, corpses of books), where one decays and others live – just like language evolving. Following Roland Barthes, Kearns sees that Death is ingrained in language in a way which gives power to one when another is ill (e.g. Lockwood's temporary illness unleashes and authorizes Nelly Dean's story). *Death* symbolizes openness – of meaning and of sexual interpretations (just like dead Heathcliff's eyes, which, by refusing to close, provide food for thought). Although set rather further away from the critical approach of the present research, the latter two studies contain a lot of substantial ideas which, if applied to Emily's poetry, may yield good crops in relation to, mostly, the investigation of A.G.A. (whose personal experience sustains Death as the tool which regulates the progress of *Gondal* and of Life in general).

It is my strong belief that **Jill Dix Ghnassia's _Metaphysical Rebellion in the Works of Emily Brontë_ (New York: St. Martin's Press, 1994)** is the most comprehensive research of Emily Brontë's poetry so far. It focuses on some major issues, which reveal the poet's undeniable interest in matters ontological, and therefore in Death. Those include: Emily's metaphysical rebellion (in her early, and then in her mature lyric poetry); Emily's persistence in exploring critically the grounds of man's trust in the principle of Divine creation; the *memento mori* theme. Ghnassia also notices Emily's obvious tendency to draw parallels between Human Death and Death in external Nature (both of which are very relevant). Consideration is given to Emily's *anti*-Theistic (rather than *a*theistic) beliefs and to her doubts about the concept of justified redemptive suffering upon the individual's expiration. Finally, the author declares Emily's perception of the inescapable „*ontological vice*", created by man's awareness of *Time* and *Space* – both dominated by, and justified only through, another individual – through *the Other*.

Edward Chitham's recent book, _The Birth of Wuthering Heights. Emily Brontë at Work_ (St. Martin's Press, 1998), tries to present Emily's works as a mosaic of recurrent images and symbols which have their roots in some of the most memorable masterpieces of world drama. It is interesting that Chitham compares A.G.A. and Catherine Earnshaw to Shakespeare's King Lear – for all the three Death represents a tragic way out of the state of being misinterpreted and misunderstood in Life. On the other hand, **Marianne Thormählen's _The Brontës and Religion_ (Cambridge University Press, 1999)** delves in Emily's symbolic and formulaic meaning of the trope of *Death*: for instance, Death understood as the achieved state of Peace which is to repair a fragmented and suffering Survivor. Thormählen emphasises the role of Death within the close family relations as professed by Evangelicals. Emily's interest in Death is also positioned in the context of the then growingly popular idea of Hell as a state of the mind. The author accentuates the poet's vision of the moment of Death as for the ultimate call for forgiveness/revenge (there is a discussion of two characters: Charlotte Brontë's Helen Burns /*Jane Eyre*/ is juxtaposed to Emily's Heathcliff /*Wuthering Heights*/).

Sadly enough, Emily Brontë is the only one of the three Brontë sisters who has so far openly gained some critical appreciation by the Bulgarian guild of literary critics. Professor Marco Mincoff's two-volume *A History of English Literature, 1970* (Sofia: Naouka I izkoustvo, the edition quoted in this thesis is the 1976 reprint) reaches only as far as Jane Austen. After the first appearance of that comprehensive textbook there is a period of about 30 years before one opens Professor Kleo Protohristova's textbook, entitled *Western European Literature* (in Bulgarian: *Zapadnoevropeiska literatoura*. IK „Hermes", 2000). In it, Professor Protohristova reads the symbolic meaning of the locus *Wuthering Heights* as the individual's utmost private abode – wild, irrational, suggestive of the *older* side of man's psyche. The tragic events in Emily Brontë's novel are explained with the fact that the senses, whenever suppressed, burst out in a violent way, which damages, and may annihilate, the family unit.

Finally, I would like to draw the following conclusions about certain characteristics of the critical investigation of the themes of *Mortality* in the poetry of the Brontë sisters. Naturally, the first leading research works in this direction appear to be biographical, chiefly due to the three poets' own intense and painful personal involvement with Death. Gradually, the critics begin to search for reflections of the latter fact in Emily's *Gondal* and in Charlotte's *Angria* – the two imaginary poetic worlds. Even the assuredly formal analysis of Gondal's and Angria's somewhat coded chronological sequence would reveal a poetic intention to present *Mortality* as harboured in the core of the Brontë sisters' ontological search (the search for meaning in Life through an idealised *Other* – the mother/ the close friend/ the beloved). The period of properly thematic studies of the Brontë sisters' poetry could be defined to have started in the 1960s and is still ongoing. Nowadays, in a situation of post-modern critical license, it has become harder to arrive at clear differentiation of this to that critical school's interest in the Brontës, yet it is more than obvious that the American scholars' involvement with Brontë studies is as strong as, if not stronger than, the English critics' dedication to the research of the works of these three unique women poets. I believe that the Brontë sisters' poetic and prose fiction heritage should be seen as one entity created conscientiously within *the philosophic discourse of Death* – the ultimate lifetime experience, the kernel element in an individual's practice of gaining ontological awareness – the theme of Mortality as the basis of man's cognitive development.

All the same, if one were to make some differentiation between various critical inclinations, then here is a picture of what one would meet:

a/ <u>Cultural history</u>: Philip Aries;

b/ <u>Psychoanalytical studies</u>: Bettina Knapp, Dorothy Van Ghent, Dennis Donoghue and James Kavanagh, and probably Helene Moglen, Elisabeth Bronfen (who may be perceived to cling to the gender theory too);

c/ <u>Studies based on gender theories</u>: Sandra Gilbert & Susan Gubar, Margaret Homans, Stevie Davies, Elisabeth Bronfen, Rosamond Langbridge, Sally Shuttleworth (who does not deny certain psychoanalytical concepts), Katherine Kearns, Irene Tayler, Diane L. Hoeveler;

d/ <u>Studies with a bias towards the theological discourse</u>: Lisa Wang, Marianne Thormählen;

e/ <u>Deconstruction</u>: J. Hillis-Miller, Katherine Kearns (whose study contains feminist ideas too);

I would have thought that the most comprehensive biographical studies of the Brontë sisters were written by: Elisabeth Gaskell, Daphne Du Maurier, Eddie Flintoff, Juliet Barker, Winifred Gerin, Derek Stanford, May Sinclair, Inga-Stina Ewbank, Norman Sherry and Muriel Spark.

There is a certain range of critics who are openly and persistently interested in elements of the Gothic in the Brontë sisters' works. These include: Earl A. Knies, Robert Keefe, Eve K. Sedgwick, Dorothy Van Ghent, George E. Haggerty and Lynn Pykett. Certain major critics' works reviewed in this chapter cannot be unequivocally ascribed the features of any of the above. Those are: C. W. Hatfield, Fannie E. Ratchford, Edward Chitham and Tom Winnifrith (the four being the best trained scholars and most convincing editors of the Brontë sisters' poetic works), Eleanor McNees' (whose voluminous collection of criticism on the Brontës is presented in a diachronic manner), Rosalind Miles, Richard Benvenuto and Maureen Peeck-O'Toole. Jill Dix Ghnassia's undisguised interest in Emily's metaphysical treatment of Death produced an invaluable ontological study of Emily's poetry. That is, *ontology* in the sense which Heidegger and Bakhtin mean (as they accentuate the idea of *Otherness* and of one's duty towards *the Other*). Apart from that, the dialogic mode of criticism is a field yet unploughed by Brontëists, which was one good reason for me to try and reveal the depth of that field in the present research.

42.

PART II

Section I

The Literary Context

I should like to imagine that, by now, the need has sprung up to clarify – briefly and systematically – the main specificities of the treatment of the themes of *Mortality* in <u>the period mid-18th–mid 19th centuries in English poetry</u>. A thorough research of *Mortality/Death* in the Brontë sisters' poetic heritage should more than benefit from such a thematic introduction, which would help the poetic genius of each stand out and emerge as unique within the more general philosophic discourse of *Mortality* (which the given period investigates assiduously).

English mid-18th–19th-century poetry demonstrates a surge of interest towards the theme of *Mortality*. This could be explained with man's growing need to re-evaluate *the Past*. Mortality becomes a dominant issue in literature, religion and politics; the Poetic Self confesses openly into being spiritually dependent on the Past. From a theological point of view, the above named period was a time of warring „enthusiastic religious movements of the feeling": i.e. Evangelicalism (which emphasized the sin-begotten nature of the child), on the one hand, and the redemptive and communal universal altruism practised by Methodism, on the other (Cf Gregory, Alan, in: Roe, Nicholas, *Romanticism. An Oxford Guide* /Oxford University Press, 2005/ p. 110). Evangelicalism and Methodism, each with a particular bias, probed into the question of what followed after Man's „Earthly existence": a prolongation of daily toil, or complete absolution (despite, say, a lifetime of wrongdoing). In Art, Nature was seen as the fathomless source of poetic inspiration, and a strong bonding between Nature and Man provided the individual with the hope that, after its earthly existence, the soul would transcend into the immortal realm of a just and omnipotent Deity. For the 19th-century individual, however, Life was to be characterized by a stably growing feeling (not rarely aggravated by actual experiences of Death/deathbed scenes as forced upon the person with a didactic purposeⁱ) of orphanhood and of alienating intellectualism. Death would then be gladly welcomed as bringing the anticipated spiritual completeness.

For the purpose of greater clarity and concreteness, it would be worth summarizing some major specificities of the period in hand, which provide evidence that in literature *Mortality* was a thematic field extensively explored and more than preferred:

44.

A/ There could be observed man's insurmountable yearning to re-establish a lost spiritual relationship with Nature. From a historical perspective, the 18th-century enclosure acts, accompanied by the steadily progressing industrialisation (a fact of English economy which, thematically, found its place in Art), brought about the individual's forced and sudden search for a „habitat" outside Nature – in the CITY – a true dungeon for the spontaneity of sensibility. The Romantics project the irregularities of man's „spiritual composition" and of his non-linear thought in externalised images of ruin and fragmentation. Broken trees, killed birds and animals, deserted landscapes – all of those dark images gradually oust the fair images of Nature's regularity that Classicism tends to maintain[ii]. As a contrast, the continuity and coherence of „free" elemental forces that both consume and replenish existence (water, wind, the night) begin to dominate the landscape. The poetic genre *„lyrical fragment"* reflects the Romantic malady of the „dispersed-dialogue"[iii].

B/ The Romantic individual tends to assume that premature Death (whether self-inflicted or caused by circumstances) could make a lifetime more readily recognised by others, than if Death were to overcome man as his natural end (Cf Vernant, 2004, p. 94). Such attitude to the notion of Death excludes a possible *Other* who would outlive and, as a Survivor, could be the bearer of the effects of one's suicide. This type of Death lacks the „communal", the Eucharistic element and so is not redemptive (to remember Bakhtin, AIG). For the Romantics, however, this appeared to be an aesthetic „tool for individuation" against the falseness and superficiality of the Present. Interpreted in the logic of Bakhtin's ontophilosophy, even such proneness to *monologism*, which characterizes the Romantic utterance, wishes to be aided by a Someone, wishes to be responded to. *„/.../ even language deliberately employed „monologically" – in ultimatums, categorical farewells, suicide notes, military commands – in fact wants to be answered. It wants to be taken as only the penultimate word, and the person who utters such bits of monologic speech is always hoping that the person who hears it will care enough (against all odds and linguistic cues) to answer back. Within such heightened fields of expectation, a failure to respond is itself a response, giving rise to its own fully voiced anguish. As long as we are alive, we have no right to pull out on another person who addresses us* *in need – and no right, apparently, to be left alone"* (Emerson, Caryl, *The First Hundred Years of Mikhail Bakhtin* /Princeton, New Jersey: Princeton University Press, 1997/, p. 157).

C/ The state of orphanhood emerges as an issue particularly relevant for the pre-Romantics, for Blake, for the Wordsworth (as one of the „older" Romantics), as well as for Byron. It could be broadly understood as the state of parental and therefore spiritual deprivation: in Bakhtin's terms, the early and irrevocable loss of an *Author* (Bakhtin). This „*missing–authority"* syndrome yields further on such lyrical persona as **the missing beloved/friend/soul-mate**. On a larger scale, the idealisation of the Past, and the simultaneous belittlement of the Present, could be discerned immediately in images of negation, such as *the voicelessness of the night, the ominous shadow of tress and mountains, the stillness and meditativeness of the grave* etc[iv].

D/ The tone of voice of lyric poetry is rather often confessional. The **confession** implies a Self's thoughts and remembrances of a Past blessed by the presence of an *Other*, whose disappearance has now left a mesh in the lyrical speaker's mind. The literary species of *Poetry* provides the Romantics with a better *literary mould*, by virtue of which they could declare their involvement with *Death* and *Mortality*. Poetry implies the momentous glimpse into the confessor's inner world, which overall, weighs more than the wholeness of the World (which to the Romantic is seen as defective and exists mainly through images, symbols, fragments, recollections and visions). The Romantic's recognition of *Mortality* is evident in a certain neglect of the genre of the novel, which (as one genre of the species of prose fiction) presupposes a desire to present a lifetime in continuity, within some definite and meaningful boundaries and limits (something which happened later, as the tradition of the Victorian 19th-century novel demonstrates). Lyric poetry gives the poet the chance to present the whole of man's life in a „snapshot", to emphasise life as a chain of intricately interrelated incompletions (Cf Bakhtin, AIG, 2003, p. 230). Death abbreviates, but does not complete existence. The episodicity, incompleteness and openness of the lyrical persona allow the „author" to penetrate into his being to the point of mere „internal transgredience/outsideness" (ibid.).

E/ The elegy establishes itself as one of the favourite poetic genres. It is the best stylistic „mould" for the *Mourner* (the self-chastising and conscience-stricken solitary genius). Ironically, *the Other's* death proves exclusively fruitful for the Mourner, whose fate to outlive presupposes deeper self-research and thus – self-validation through the lack of *the Other*. For the Romantics, the loss of this Other (present, as was explained earlier, as *the missing lyrical persona*) signifies an existential crisis. The „author" is so close to the mourning Lyrical Self that he/ she tends to merge with him/ her, which deepens the state of total gloom: there is no external/outside point of reference to rescue the Mourner, no aesthetic distance between Poet and Lyrical Self/Lyrical Persona, nothing to reassure the reader (Cf Bakhtin, AIG, 2003, pp. 158–160). This is one structural feature of poetry in support of the argument that the nature of the Romantic tone of voice is *non-dialogic*, indeed *monologic*.

F/ The nineteenth-century's thematic insistence on the death of the child is one way to phrase the perception of *Time deprived of a Future*. Certain poets cling more openly to social criticism, as they frown upon the fact of the high infants' death rate (e.g. Blake and Wordsworth); others (like the Brontë sisters) are more private. Emily Brontë's obvious contribution is her range of *Gondal* poems which deal with the problem of *infanticide* and with *the missing-mother syndrome* (illustrated best by the poem *A Farewell to Alexandria, 1839*). The Romantics' mourning over the death of the child could also be seen as a reaction against the established Evangelical belief in the sin-begotten nature of the child. Romanticism perceives the child as the perfect exemplification of innocence, as opposed to the particularly powerful during the 18th- and 19th-centuries Evangelical urge to preach morality amongst the young through constant references to Death (Cf Drew, Lamonica, 2003, p. 14). One interesting and probably quite well known fact is that during the Victorian Era, the bed, in which a woman would have given birth, might (as society was then less mobile) have been that very family heirloom in which she herself had been conceived and born. It was not unusual, but supposedly quite instructive, to invite children around the deathbed of a man – a practice which even then became the subject of much adverse criticism (Cf Wheeler, 1990, pp. 32, 43).

G/ The investigation of the theme of *Mortality* would profit immeasurably if carried out on the basis of a study of the subsidiary motifs of _redemption_ and _forgiveness_ (as two Eucharistic, i.e. _dialogic practices)_, posterior to that of _murder_. Readily available in Byron and Coleridge, the motif of *murder* implies, firstly, the notion of utmost alienation from society, and on a deeper level – the irrevocable „demythologisation of Nature"[iv] under man's basest instincts. At this point, the research will have to reveal certain specificities of the poetic works of Emily and Charlotte Brontë (and to mention some other relevant works by such women poets as Mary Robinson and Felicia Hemans[vi]).

H/ The literary representation of the sensation of the brevity of human life could be seen in the poets' preference for the motif of *parting*. In this link, the psychology of the late 18th-century emphatically makes **the grave**[2] the perfect place for meditation (as, for instance, in the works of *the graveyard school of poetry*). Gradually, the dominance of the theme of *parting* in art begins to suggest a late 18th–19th-centuries' tragic view of Existence[vii]. Death begins to signify the moment of final farewell, which damages Life's experiential and verbal coherence as it abbreviates one's possibility to objectify one's devotedness to *the Other*. Philippe Ariès notices that this period is also marked by the tendency to equalize *the Other's Death* with „My"/the Survivor's own (possible/future) death (Cf Ariès, Ph., *L'Homme Devant La Mort*, translated in Bulgarian as: *Tchovekat pred Smartta*. Sofia. IK „LIK". 2004, book II, p. 279). Roughly and simplistically speaking, the Victorian age is somewhat of a repetition – but with greater force – of mid-18th-century's European taste for necromancy – an aesthetic and a philosophic breach of the Christian understanding that *the dead* should be left to rest in peace... To remember Walter Benjamin, even the poorest and the most unrecognized

---

[2] Michael Wheeler defines *the grave* as one of the two loci, which speak of the Victorian cult for Death (the other is the deathbed). The rigidity and ceremoniousness of the dying man's last hours (i.e. the doctor's and/or the priest's visit, the presence of a loving attendant/confessor, the laying of the corpse in a darkened room, the last visit paid by the bereaved and the closing of the coffin), as well as of the body's journey to its last abode (namely: the funeral procession, the actual funeral, the erection of a memorial stone and the bereaved people's subsequent visits to the grave) hint that there existed a certain measure of „social and intellectual homogeneity". In art, the latter could be seen in the popular at that time anthologies of poems for mourners (Cf Wheeler, 1990, pp. 25, 27, 30).

pauper, when dying, possesses authority over the Survivor, who is destined to carry this death-scene in his/her memory. At the basis of storytelling lays this very authority – *the authority of „the One Before Me"* (Cf Benjamin, Walter, [in Bulgarian] *Razkazvatchat*, v: spisanie „Stranitza", 2-1999, p. 46; Walter Benjamin's original from 1936). Death sanctions everything which a storyteller may have said/written. In a broader sense, the Author's/Poet's creativity and authority springs up from Death (ibid.).

I/ The <u>re-actualisation of the notions of Heaven v/s Hell</u> (in the logic of the concept of the human being's further existence beyond earthly life) is seen in the fact that *the poetic genre of the prayer for the soul* becomes popular (a speciality of Byron's, Tennyson's, Browning's, Rossetti's and Morris'). In this respect, Anne Brontë's confessional lyric pieces make a particular contribution. Earlier, *the graveyard poets* have already interpreted the communal meaning of the grave (Cf Wheeler, 1994, p. 61). The locus of the grave and the genre of prayer contain an opportunity to re-establish the ontological link with the dead as with *the true Other*: the survivor's spiritual mentor, patron and, hopefully, a regulator of man's impoverished Present.

As might have become clear by now, in the present chapter the emphasis will be the <u>specificities of the Romantic vision of the theme of Mortality. The poetic works chosen contain the theme of Death in a most obvious and „concentrated" state. They therefore offer a secure ideological field on which *the issue of the Other and the Other's Death unfold.*</u> Parallels are drawn between the variety of poetic works of the given period and the Brontë sisters' perception of Death so that both parties may benefit from such comparative analyses. Most of the arguments would have been suggested by now, so that they only need to be summarised. To begin with, both the Brontë sisters and the Romantics seem to be keen on elements like the wind, the water (the sea), and on the symbolic properties of the night. Logically, man was trying to redress the balance between himself and Nature, from whose omniscient, vigilant and instructive protection he had drifted away. Having uprooted himself from the bosom of Nature, man felt to have fallen into a state of vacuum. This state yielded a series of images of fragmentation (ruins, deserted landscapes etc.), which found their place in the Art of the period. One formal proof for that is the poetic preference for *the lyrical fragment* (stronger with the Romantics, and less obvious with the Brontës, where *Angria* and *Gondal* seem to be structured like wholes of interrelated ballads). More often than not, the tone of voice of the lyrical pieces is confessional – it discloses the poet's meditative and melancholic attitude to Life. The other genre, which speaks of the same perception of Life, but is more specifically focused on the life and death of one individual, is *the elegy*. One definite similarity between the Brontës and the Romantics is that the poet's voice and the voice of the lyrical persona more than frequently merge – a phenomenon which Bakhtin terms *„crisis of authorship"*. The Romantics' tendency to mix up Poet and Lyrical Persona aggravates the feeling of fatality, because there is no external point of reference to judge, but also to save, the individual: there is no distance between action and reflection on that action, no „dialogic shelter". The romantic lyrical persona appropriates the poet's position of outsideness (of authority) and so overcomes it (Cf Bakhtin, *AIG*, 2003, pp. 80, 95, 101). Yet in lyric poetry, as opposed to the other literary species, the phenomenon of *„crisis of authorship"* appears to be least damaging, since Life is always explained in poetry only from *within*, Life is an attitude towards „My" own Self. Sadly, the unstable Spirit trusts not the benevolence of an externally acting power. There is an emphasis on the contradiction between the boundlessness of contents and the limitedness of embodiment of contents in a physical world (Cf Bakhtin, *AIG*, 2003, pp. 258–260). The missing-authority syndrome, which has to do with the latter practice, is much more painfully experienced by the Brontës, and less so by the Romantics. In *Gondal* the well being of its central lyrical persona – A.G.A. – is threatened as she exists in the climate of **orphanhood,** understood as a recurring metaphor for spiritual and physical deprivation (partly caused by A.G.A.'s own destructive negation of good, and therefore of Life). The individual's attraction to the Past is stronger in the works of the Brontë sisters because they admit to the necessity to recognize and to join a revered Dead Other in the World Beyond. The Nature of this Dead Other is undeniably superior to that of the Survivor whom He/She *precedes* and over whom He/She possesses authorial superiority (the capacity to define the individual in ontological terms).

The Romantics perceived an early and voluntary retreat from Life (i.e. the euthatanic availability of Death) to be one successful route of declaring one's *presence* and of defending one's uniqueness. For the

Brontës (as their mature works testify), the moment of Death bears the idea of taking the Eucharist: Death is communal, non-aesthetic, the awareness of it summons one towards reconsidering living as *Co-Being*, as Being in Dialogue, as sustaining *the Self* only and always through the formula *„I-for-another"* (see esp. Morson & Emerson, 1989, p. 159), as *Being-in-the-world* – trough Care (to paraphrase Heidegger). The phenomenon of Death leaves man's conscience with no chance to have an *alibi-in-being-just-for-the-sake-of-being*, because every instance of Death suggests that the relationship between two individuals is limitative, but also *definitive* (as to the meaning of Time and Space in an ontological framework). Death is most painfully and irrevocably defining in the case of *infanticide* (a motif available in the works of Blake and Wordsworth, but much more so in Emily Brontë's poetry). The motif of *infanticide* (or, in the broader sense, *the theme of the child's death*) is in direct connection with two other motifs hidden within the theme of *Mortality*. Those are *redemption* and *forgiveness* – two dialogic practices over which the 19th-century individual definitely stumbled, as he tried to tackle them (something which was reflected both in the prose fiction and in the poetry of the given period). The Brontë sisters' mature ballads (from around 1842 and onwards) depict a rare example of an individual, whose obvious characteristic is somewhat of a non-Romantic readiness to take the guilt upon oneself and to correct the world through self-inflicted chastisement and self-interrogation. For the Brontës, the ontologically positive value of the relationship *„I–Other"* seems to have been eclipsed by the awareness that it was this very relationship which inherently contained the sureness of the limited time span one was granted to achieve anything at all.

How much the Brontë sisters really knew of the Romantics (or whether they did have any contacts with them) is often conjectural, not always supported by biographical evidence. Yet a closer investigation of the theme of *Mortality* in the works of the major Romantic poets seems valuable both in a diachronic perspective and as the most appropriate thematic background to the subject of the present research. In my opinion, the subject area of *Mortality/Death* appears to be a thematic crossroads where the Brontë sisters' poetic freedom and confidence in interpreting Life intersects with *the literary history* of interpreting Life through the thematic prism of the more general notion of *the End* (which has been ever-relevant). In this sense, the Brontë sisters continue a major _tradition_. The consciousness of a hermeneutically vigilant interpreter must, from the very start, be open to, and receptive of, _a text's otherness and individuality_ (i.e. the Brontë sisters' thematic preferences, which also include other themes beyond Mortality/Death, ought to be acknowledged). However, such openness does not presuppose either neutrality toward the essence of the matter discussed, nor in fact self-denial, but it ought to include assimilation of one's own primary opinion and reflections. Naturally, the process during which the critic's own anticipations unfold, should happen within the atmosphere of methodological conscience: the critical license must at all times be bridled up through adherence to true facts. I should like to hope that „sieving" the poetic works of the Brontë sisters through exclusively interpreting Mortality/Death as the dominant thematic area would not be seen as a literary defect of this research, but as the necessary critical bias which, for the umpteenth time, would confirm the philosophical value and broad-mindedness of these three unique poets of 19th-century English literature – hopefully, in an innovative way[viii].

* * *

English poetry of the mid- and late 18th-century perceives the moment of Death as the ultimate liberation from human vanity and from the transitoriness that broods over daily troubles. Some early examples are found in the works of the **_graveyard school of poetry_ (Young, Blair) and in Gray's works.** For those poets Death is the ultimate gate into eternity in the World Beyond, where the carnal definitions of man's composition become irrelevant. Ostensibly, ruins, tombs and nocturnal gloom extend Space: they may be perceived to act as a frontier beyond which there may follow an after-life of infinite bliss (Cf Botting, Fred, _Gothic_ /London & New York: Routledge, 2001/, pp. 23–24). On a deeper level, however, the _graveyard school_ show a negative attitude to Death, because from the spiritual point of view it deprives, rather than completes, the human being. Although the graveyard and the grave were held as favourite spots for meditation and for self-contemplation[3], the late 18th, and

---

[3] Philip Aries notes that during the Middle Ages and until the end of the 17th century the graveyard functioned as a shelter – for paupers and victims during feuds and war. Some went further, using the graveyard as a building spot, despite the official prohibitions to do that (Cf Aries 2004, b. I, pp.

particularly the 19th centuries, had already drifted far from the medieval understanding of Death as „intra-vital". There was no more the former mergence of the two sides of man's spiritual experience, in which the eternal and the transitory complete, and do not oppose, each other (Cf Aries 2004, b. I, pp. 176–177, p. 283).

In his long poem *Night Thoughts* (1742) **Edward Young** describes Death as *„tired Nature's sweet restorer"*. At first, the poet envies the dead who *„wake no more"* to bear the misery of this world[4]. The *„primaeval silence"* of the night and the *„populous"* and *„vital"* grave are but a momentary respite from the life of constant change and dissolution that the living individual is burdened with in his „fathomless abyss" of „empty shades". There also shows the individual's doomed state of mind, which craves for the grave as for Immortality, yet „legions of angels can't confine me there". Another major poetic work, which that analyses the significance of the tomb and of the world beyond, is **Thomas Gray's** *Elegy Written in a Country Churchyard (1750)*. The elegy carries a premature feeling of calmness and bliss, which is soon ousted by the realisation that death is inevitable, rather than desirable (the negative particle *„no"* in certain negations /e.g. *„no more"*, *„no children"*/ in stanzas 5 & 6 suggests how a family – its warmth, unanimity and its achievements, have been swallowed by the Past). No human-made memorial has the capacity to restore what has been lost forever, yet the function of the tomb is to teach the living to cherish existence whilst reminding man of Heavenly forgiveness and love. All the same, the

---

91–92, b. II, p. 306). In England, the 17th and 18th- century graveyard was represented a vast lawn, where the parson's sheep would have been noticed to graze peacefully (ibid. b. II, p. 61).

[4] The latter is obviously comparable to Charlotte Smith's more dramatic envy for *the grave* in her *Sonnet XLIV (1784)*: *„(...)/ The wild blast, rising from the Western cave/ Drives the huge billows from their heaving bed, / Tears from their grassy tombs the village dead, / And breaks the silent Sabbath of the grave! / (...) While I am doom'd – by life's long storm opprest, / To gaze with envy, on their gloomy rest"*. – Cf Charlotte Smith in: (ed.) Feldman 2000, pp. 686–687. There is a group of early poetic works of Anne Brontë's that see *the grave* as the craved-for „container" of stolen bliss – the family, now destroyed by the death of the parent/ the closest relative (see for instance *Verses by Lady Geralda* – 1836, *A Voice From the Dungeon* – 1837, or *Lady of Alzerno's Hall* – 1838).

communal meaning of the grave[ix] in Grey's elegy is no recompense for the sense of loss the Survivor experiences[5].

Contrary to the 18th-century's taste for „dissecting" Nature and arranging the pieces as „trapped natural specimens for observation", **William Blake's** Nature is a coil of elemental forces which yield not to human power. It seems that Blake's perception of Death echoes privately the medieval understanding of „the revitalising Death". To Blake, Death does not negate Life, but appears to be a necessary ingredient in Life's complex structure. In an ambivalent manner, Death contains the idea of birth, or rather, of *palingenesis*: there is an exchange of lives in which one living organism is substituted by another and so no energy is wasted (Cf Bakhtin's reflections on Rabelais' works in: Demichev, A. V., [in Russian] *Diskoursij Smerti. Vvedenie v filosofskuiu tanatologiu.* Sankt – Peterburg. Inopress. 1997, p. 19; p. 331). Blake's works also give the critic the chance to observe two major motifs which are implied in the investigation of *Death.* Those are: *sin* and *the orphaned individual.* For example, some poems in Blake's diptych-like poetic compilations *Songs of Innocence (1789) & Songs of Experience (1794)* could be seen as the poet's reaction against the traditional for the late 18th–19th centuries' Evangelical perception of the infant as sin-begotten and doomed to eternal purgation. Poems like *Holy Thursday* and *London* argue that the greatest evil is not supernatural, but is human-born, and therefore not impossible to eradicate. Wild Nature only is immune to criticism, as it contains the grains of good and evil simultaneously (Cf *The Tiger*) and in every one instant, which is why no one life gets completely lost, but energy is transmuted on and on (as in *The Clod and the Pebble*). Another specificity of Blake's treatment of *Mortality* is its preoccupation with the motif of *infanticide.* He shares that with Emily Brontë, in whose poetry this same motif could be traced as originating from, and alongside the investigation of, the A.G.A. lyrical persona[6]. One weakness of society Blake condemns,

---

[5] In Emily Brontë's poetry the One and *the Other* appear always to be on two opposite sides, are divided by death. Her vision of the grave is both of home (in about a dozen poems „tomb" rhymes with „home"), but also of a false path towards Heavenly bliss (see for instance the poems *To A.S. – 1843*, and *In the earth, the earth, thou shalt be laid – 1843*).

[6] Augusta leaves her babe, Alexandria, to die in the snow in her desire to prevent multiplication of her own evil in the next generation (see *A Farewell to Alexandria, 1839*). It is with critical curiosity

which is declared vividly in *London* (*"the youthful harlot's curse/ Blasts the new-born infant's tear, / And blights with plagues the marriage hearse"*), but particularly awesomely in the poem **The Mental Traveller**, is that the child appears to be victimized by a pseudo-mother: a *"Woman Old" "binds iron thorns"* around the baby's head, piercing its hands and feet, and cutting his heart out to make it feel both cold and hot. This image is somewhat of an extreme macabre transmutation of the biblical scene of Christ's crucifixion.

One of Blake's prophetic books, **The Book of Thel (1789)** illustrates the above mentioned argument that every physically limited creature in fact comes to reiterate the immortal principle of existence that stands behind life. Death's omen is diminished when there is sure evidence that a Self serves, and lives whilst caring about, another Self[7]. The Cloud persuades timid Thel that one is likely to *"pass away into tenfold life"* only if his life is to the use of others (as the body becomes food for worms which then feed the higher creatures in the chain of life, and so on). With a hint to English metaphysical poetry, Blake's imagery amalgamates Death and Life in a productive, but also in a hermaphroditic[x] manner – any one's death becomes the source of another life (counter to the traditionally Christian vision of birth as mainly to do with the mother). Dissolution is a prerequisite for Life's prolongation and continuation (Cf Welburn, Andrew, *The Truth of Imagination. An Introduction to Visionary Poetry* /Macmillan, 1989/, pp. 106–113). That is why *the night* (as a complex image of Death and Evil) is seen by Blake as more productive. For Blake, the millennial significance of the night is interwoven in his revolutionary conviction that the positive is yet to be born. Similarly, Blake's Devil from **The Marriage of Heaven and Hell (engraved 1790)** is that *"contrary"* element whose discovery unlocks positive energy which is formative and which could master Death. Albeit radical and reactionary in his beliefs, Blake is yet another poet who considers man's existence threatened because of the corruption and ills that human psyche holds

---

that we find in one of Blake's *Proverbs of Hell (No 67)* the following statement: *"Sooner murder an infant in its cradle than nurse unacted desires"*.
[7] This notion is reiterated in proverb 17 of *The Marriage of Heaven and Hell*.

within. The idea that Evil contains the source of light is really true only on the level of external Nature, where no energy gets lost.

Of all the Romantics and later Victorian poets, **William Wordsworth's** treatment of Mortality is the most religious, the most (though not fully) Orthodox one[xi]. Wordsworth's account for his first-hand autobiographical encounters with, and remembrances of, Death appears to be far from the supernatural, cosmic or revolutionary dimensions Blake or Shelly would impart to it. His focus is on the significance of Death in the life of the child, as well as on infants' death in the lives of parents. *The infant's death* gains ontological status as early as his literary participation in the *Lyrical Ballads* (Wordsworth's and Coleridge's joined poetic project of 1798). It puts the Survivor in a position in which he/she struggles to validate his/ her significance after that *Other little individual,* on whom one could naturally bestow one's love, care and spiritual achievements, has been lost. The poem *We are Seven (1798)* may serve as one example. Here, the little cottage girl relentlessly assures the dismayed poet in the macabre presence and relevance of her dead sister and brother, as if trying to bring them back to life and recompense for their broken family unit[8]. Another relevant poem may be *Vadracour and Julia (1820)*, where the rejected out-of-wedlock child dies to some „indiscretion of the Father". To Wordsworth the loss of an infant's life equals an interrupted link to real Life and threatens to destroy the wholeness of one's memory and sanity. The specific **spiritual state of orphanhood** that the dead child „leaves behind" for the parent has its reverse counterpart – the child's own state of orphanhood upon the loss of a parent (which Wordsworth elaborates on whilst rending the story of his own father's death in book XII of *The Prelude /1799–1850/).* In Wordsworth's works the Survivor bows to God as to a surrogate Father and a sure spiritual guide. Of all the poets of the Victorian Age, Wordsworth is the first one to suggest the concept that

---

[8] Jumbling up the common-sense approach of the interlocutor (an adult), the little girl describes first the short distance, at which the graves of her brothers and sisters are situated in the graveyard, then how she sings songs to her buried brothers and sisters, then she goes on to admit that she eats her dinner near their graves. On a formal level, the little girl's resistance to come to terms with the fact of her siblings' deaths could be seen in her insistence on the first person plural personal pronoun („we"), as well as on the use of the present tense („dwell", „lie"), rather than on the expected past tense simple (for an accomplished event). Towards the end of the poem the adult's confidence in the girl's naivety is shaken and he is completely bemused.

the Other's death (here – the child's/the parent's death, or as with poets after Wordsworth – the friend's/comrade's death) equals the Self's own death (Cf Jankelevitch, 1999, p. 31).

Wordsworth's interpretation of Mortality involves a focus on discovering Death as inherent in all grand and awesome Natural phenomena/objects[9], which may alternatively harm/aid Man. Wordsworth clearly demonstrates his awareness of the theory of the Sublime and the Beautiful. He trusts that Nature contains the exterminable wise and protective Holy Spirit (i.e. God, as in ***Tintern Abbey, 1798***), which masters Temporality and whose presence *"disturbs [him] with the joy/ Of elevated thoughts"*. The mind *"feeds upon infinity"*, as it exists in the bosom of Nature's harmonious wholeness, which allows for an *"interchangeable supremacy"* between all natural phenomena/objects and their Creator (see *The Prelude, Book Fourteenth – Conclusion:* ll. 65–90, 160–175, 245–262, 430–454)[10]. On the other hand, Wordsworth seems rather unwilling to come to terms with any one single instance of Death. To him, the World dies over and again with the death of each one man (*The Excursion: Book I-ll..* 470–474)[11]. Of the three Brontë sisters,

---

[9] Those are enumerated in ***Descriptive Sketches (1793)***: „gigantic floods", „drizzling and vibrating crags", „desolate steeps", „the Demon of the snow (i.e. avalanches)", and among those – „crosses reared to commemorate travellers' incidental death".

[10] Cf „(...)/ *Dust as we are, the immortal spirit grows/ Like harmony in music; there is a dark/ Inscrutable workmanship that reconciles/ Discordant elements, makes them cling together/ In one society. (...)"* Towards the end of *The Grassmere Journals*, Wordsworth's sister, Dorothy, writes that *„it would be as sweet thus to lie so in the grave to hear the peaceful sounds of the earth and just to know that our dear friends were near"* (as quoted in: Alexander, Meena, *Women in Romanticism* /Macmillan, 1989/, p. 107). Emily Brontë's poem *Shall Earth no more inspire thee (1841)* revolves around the same issue.

[11] In his *„Essay upon Epitaphs"* (1810) Wordsworth describes the contemporary burial grounds, as he compares them to the old Greek/Roman tradition of interring the body by the wayside („death as a sleep overcoming the tired wayfarer"). Seemingly, there is the Victorian cult for the rural burial site, „in the country churchyard or tree-lined suburban cemetery" – an attempt to build „the memorial stone in a context which is redolent of the 'soothing influences of nature' (Cf Wheeler, 1990, p. 47–48). At the same time Wordsworth managed to capture the Victorian Era's equivocal attitude to the „benevolence" of the grave in *The Excursion*. Thus, for the skeptical Solitary the graveyard/grave represents *„a subterranean magazine of bones"*; for the Poet, it is a *„pregnant spot of ground"* (about which he has mixed thoughts and emotions); for the Pastor it reminds one of Christ's sacrifice for humanity and bears the idea of solidarity (both the living and the dead are covered with *„motherly humanity"* (as quoted in: Wheeler, 1990, p. 49). Interestingly enough, for the poet the graveyard is a *„capacious bed"*, *„a communal resting-place"*, rather than the

the motif of *irrevocability* is particularly strongly felt when off reads Emily Brontë's poetry, which argues the existence of an ever-present but inaccessible Friend whose life the Survivor is trying to retrieve and „print out" onto what is left of Life. Wordsworth's *memento-mori appeal* is his invitation towards a conscientious preparation for Death („/.../ *death to be/ Foretasted, immortality conceived/ By all /.../")*, which appropriates the Divine principle as a benevolent and altruistic approach to Others (*The Excursion*, Book IX – Cf ll. 220–290). To Wordsworth, nonetheless, Death is of a „chameleon nature" – its physical verifiability proves a restriction on Life in the general sense of the word. On the other hand, Death seems philosophically fruitful (Cf Wheeler, Michael, *Heaven, hell and the Victorians* /Cambridge University Press/, 1994, p. 28). Another interesting thought, suggested by Guinn Batten, critic of Victorian literature, is that Wordsworth's poetic works are an example of *writing as postponement of dying*. Namely, that even the most undeniably physical descriptions (and these would include the places and „fetishes" that commemorate death in some poems of the *Lyrical Ballads*, the *Prelude* and particularly *the Excursion*) resist, so to speak, „*interment*", as they are in effect highly verbal and so evade the physically proven idea of temporality (Cf Batten 1998, pp. 189–190).

Samuel Taylor Coleridge's taste for *Mortality* is flavoured with a kind of idealism, which could be defined as *not fully orthodox*, because when Coleridge is concerned with the issue of the transcendence of the spirit, he does not always make allowances for the idea of Heavenly bliss with which man usually associates the ultimate gift bestowed upon the righteous. Influenced by German Idealism (mostly by Kant), he argues that Nature breathes eternally: it represents a collection of „organic Harps", played by „*one Intellectual Breeze, / At once the Soul of each, and God of all" (The Eolian Harp – 1795)*, „*the omnipresent Mind,/ Omnific /.../"*, „*Nature's Essence, Mind, and Energy!" (Religious Musings, 1794–1796)*. This purposeful Mind (without which „*the moral world's cohesion*" would turn into an „*Anarchy of Spirits" – Religious Musings, ll. 159–160)* ensures eternity through Love[12]. Love is seen as the capacity to

---

orthodox 'God's acre' of individual 'narrow beds': the '*pall*' chills the turf no more: this meadow is a „*carpet for the dancing hours*" (ibid., pp. 49–50).

[12] „/.../ Lovely was the Death/ Of Him, whose Life was Love! /.../" – Religious Musings, ll. 33–34.

combine contraries, to summarise all representations of Nature (negative and positive) into one harmonious whole: *„the Throne of God/Forth flashing an imaginable day/ Wraps in one blaze earth, heaven and deepest hell"* (as in *Religious Musings – 1794–1796*, ll. 115–125; ll. 412–420). Like Blake, Coleridge assumes that Heaven and Hell coexist as states of the mind, rather that as topographically or temporally verifiable realms. Even though millennial hopes are weak with Coleridge, there lurks in his works the image of the corrupt mind, which deforms reality, and then suffers a lack of source of inspiration, condemning itself and asking for heavenly forgiveness, which is never granted it. The *„Destruction"*, with which Angels threaten the human race towards the end of *Religious Musings*, is counterbalanced by the chance ingrained in each one Life – to breathe *„the empyreal air of Love, omnific, omnipresent"*, which swells in the poet's soul like a day-spring and promises continuity, harmony and benevolent wisdom.

Coleridge, and later Byron, interpret *dying as a dreamed-for unachievable state of quiescence, of internal peace, and of harmony with external Nature and with God*. In *The Wanderings of Cain (1797–1798)* *„mighty Cain"* is *„perishing with thirst and hunger,"* his form wastes away, yet he never quite dies and never gains peace after a sinful life. *Immortality is hell*: it is a punishment for man's outreaching Thought, which once durst divide the dead from the living (claiming the autonomy of each of those categories, which are in fact two halves of one dichotomy). As in his best known ballad, ***The Rime of the Ancient Mariner (1797–1816)***, Coleridge's individual often seems incapacitated, because he is unable to ask for forgiveness; instead there is just the „wicked whisper" that dries man's heart to „dust" (ibid. part IV). In this cataleptic state the spirit is locked within itself, unable to correct his misdoings, or to help others. The moment of liberation comes when the individual gains the capacity to pray, which is when the Ancient Mariner himself re-gains mobility. Both literally and figuratively, the curse of the dead Albatross drops down from the Mariner's neck, and the numb bodies of the crew are re-inspired[13].

---

[13] *„The cold sweat melted from their limbs,/ Nor rot nor reek did they:/ The look with which they looked on me/ Had never passed away.// An orphan's curse would drag to hell/ A spirit from on high;/ But oh! More horrible than that/ Is the curse in a dead man's eye!/ Seven days, seven*

An interesting peculiarity of Coleridge's vision of the human mind as containing the grain of the daemonic and of the destructive is observed in some of his female images of negation. The image of *Life-in-Death* (who dices together with Death, but wins the ship's crew and the Mariner), or *the stepmother, or the witch-woman* – they all deny the eternal/God; the step-mother is also capable of terminating life by cursing her own child[14]. In part II of *The Rime of the Ancient Mariner the Spectre-Woman* is irresistibly attractive, yet snake-like she has a stupefying effect upon the Mariner. Geraldine (in **Christabel – Part I 1797, Part II 1800– 1801**) is another reiteration of this Life-in-Death woman. The „frightfully and exceedingly" richly dressed woman that writhes beneath the oak and attracts the maid is somewhat of a revenant step-mother, whose „unsettled eye and hollow voice" marginalize Life for Christabel. Geraldine casts a deadly spell on the orphaned maid and then exposes her to her own evil mind by urging her to undress. Coleridge's understanding of *magic* is that it is like a sleep of Death. Initially, Geraldine is in a cataleptic state – typical for the witch, whose body and self are only figuratively one[xii]. Later on, this state is transferred onto Christabel (the maid starts a „dizzy dance", at which the „dove" is smothered by the „snake"). Geraldine is No one; she represents the ungovernable, immeasurable, and not clearly definable. On the one hand, this female persona absorbs Evil which springs from nowhere and is immediately lost[xiii]. On the other, Geraldine herself projects evil around – and that idea appears (bearing in mind Coleridge's overall literary heritage) more justified than the claim that man's mind is a replica of Life-negating powers which attack it from without.

Although Coleridge believes that unknown external negative challenges threaten the integrity of the human mind, yet sinfulness (resulting in a most violent manifestation after an act of murder) seems to be more of defect of man's own mind. In this sense, the Mariner's own negative and impartial attitude to Life leads him into committing the

---

nights, I saw that curse,/ And yet I could not die" (Cf *The Rime of the Ancient Mariner*, ll. 253– 262).
[14] For instance, in Coleridge's ballad *The Three Graves (1797–1809)*, the mother casts a spell on her daughter, Mary, who dies on her wedding-day. Again, one tends to remember Emily Brontë's preoccupation with the theme of infanticide in the image of A.G.A.

murder that he does in respect of the Albatross[15]. It would be also interesting to note that Coleridge's understanding of the prayer for the soul departs from the institutionalised regular request for forgiveness – it has to do with a spontaneous act of gratitude, prompted by man's capacity to Love *„all things both great and small" (The Rime of The Ancient Mariner)*[16]. *„The unfathomable hell within"* at the sight of men's sinfulness that torments the Lyrical Self in *The Pains of Sleep (1803)* is quelled by his admittance that the greatest threat to Life is *„positive Negation"* (see also the poem *Limbo, 1811*). In other words, the success of the quest for Truth in Life depends on the acceptance and reverence of other Beings and living creatures[xiv].

Of all the Romantic poets, **Lord Byron's** treatment of Mortality is the one most deeply situated within the context of *the family*. In his *Oriental tales* Byron illustrates how the theme of adultery/treachery directly relates to the theme of murder. The theme of adultery/treachery is a good opportunity for Byron to develop his belief in the incidental quality of Death, which, ironically, also seems to rescue the Survivor from „a life of lingering woes". In **The Giaour, 1813,** the Giaour's decision to murder Leila's husband is dictated by his passion for her, but also by his own feeling of oppression under Hassan's rule. Sadly, the Giaour's attempt to build a happy life for himself and his beloved Leila is thwarted by the incident, in which Leila drowns in the sea. This momentary and unexpected disaster overshadows the Giaour's self-confidence and, in effect, has a punitive effect on the Giaour's conscience as a Survivor. The Giaour's sensation about the roots of Evil in his own mind is evident in his own delirious vision of a *„serpent round [his] heart wreathed"* that stings his every thought (like the albatross that „strangles" Coleridge's Mariner). His feeling of relief in „giving his foe a grave" is counterbalanced by the memory of his beloved Leila, whose unfortunate fate he is in effect responsible for. Like Coleridge's Mariner, the Giaour craves not for

---

[15] The Mariner's general inability to speak and act reasonably is suggested in the episode where he bites his own arm and, vampire-like, sucks his own blood (before he is able to cry: „A sail!").

[16] The same reflections would apply to Julian's act of benevolence towards the dark-natured Rochelle in Emily Brontë's poem *Julian M. and A.G.Rochelle* (1845).

Heaven, but for rest from the ontological vice in which he has fallen with his act of murder[17].

In a Bunyanesque manner, Byron takes the chance to prove that true maturation for man is achieved through the awareness of Death. And the journey towards spiritual elevation is the more toilsome and aggravating in the case of the individual's state of orphanhood, i.e. when the protective authority of the parent/ the friend/ the native land is unavailable. This broadly understood state of orphanhood is one motif behind the Byronic hero's inclination towards introspection and behind his proud withdrawal from what J. R. Watson calls „*the anaesthetizing confines of society*" (Cf Watson, J. R., *English Poetry of the Romantic Period: 1789–1839* /Longman, 1992/, p. 263). Appropriate examples of lyrical personae who could support the above statements would be: Childe Harold */Childe Harold, 1812/,* Don Juan */Don Juan, 1819–1824/,* and even Manfred */Manfred, 1817/* and Cain */Cain, 1821/.* These characters' voluntary and self-imposed alienation from the social environment of Other human beings springs from a desire to explore the dimensions of the Human Spirit, which in fact expires with thirst to see home again (as with *Don Juan – Canto II–XVIII*), or to regain its erstwhile innocence. All these *outcasts* are endowed with an excess of knowledge, yet none of them (except for Cain) leaves behind a next generation, or something meaningful for *Others* (see also *Childe Harold, Canto I–XIII*)[18]. Their „unspecified sorrow" is down to an excessive urge for cognitive growth, which almost always proves fatal in the Christian world, where *the Other* always comes first, is ontologically superior and has an instructive influence over the Self[19]. Manfred's grievous realisation is that „*the Tree of*

---

[17] Byron, more than any other of the Romantics, emphasises the role of *fate*, of *accident*, due to which Life swerves from its expected course and into an undesirable and irreparable direction. In *The Bride of Abydos (1813)* Zuleika's accidental discovery of Selim's true relation to her (that he is not her brother, but her cousin, whose father was murdered by his own brother – Giaffir, Zuleika's father) deepens their love, but eventually brings about Giaffir's murder of Selim, whereupon Zuleika dies of a broken heart.

[18] „/.../ For pleasures past I do not grieve,/ Nor perils gathering near,/ My greatest grief is that I leave/ No thing that claims a tear.// 'And now I'm in the world alone,/ Upon the wide, wide sea:/ But why should I for others groan,/ When none will sigh for me?" (*Childe Harold*, Canto I–XIII, ll. 70–77).

[19] The desire to overcome one's carnal frets and to be able to see beyond ordinary Life is also the thematic focus of Charlotte Brontë's poem „*But once again, but once again*" *(1836)*. In *Frances*

Knowledge is not that of Life" (Act I). The blissful madness he craves for is denied him (*„I dwell in my despair – / And live – and live forever."* *Act II, Scene II*). He yearns for Death as for a longed for cessation of his mental activity that always analyses – i.e. fragments, destroys – and never re-constructs meanings in Life (*„/.../ I dived./ In my lone wanderings, to the caves of death,/ Searching its cause in its effect; and drew/ From wither'd bones, and skulls, and heap'd up dust,/ Conclusions most forbidden /.../"* – *Act II, Scene II*). Yet even when Death is granted him, it is a replica of his life – he is left alone and to his own exhausted imagination and degenerated mind (Act II, sc. IV). The Byronic type is prone to spiritual expiration because he lacks what Heidegger would call *„Care"* (*a caring attitude towards Life*), and Bakhtin – *responsibility/ duty-towards-Another*, without which one has *No-Alibi-in-Being* in this world (Cf Bakhtin, KFP, 2003 pp. 41, 51, 67–68). This type of man finds fault with God in the factual impossibility to verify the event of Death, to penetrate beyond it – a defect, as it were, of God's creation (*Cain, Act I*)[20]. Another interesting argument in this regard would be that for Manfred and Cain Death is a rescue because it is seen as final – and *finality* is something the concept *Heaven: Hell* lacks (Cf Eagleton, Terry, *Sweet Violence: The Idea of the Tragic* /Blackwell Publishing, 2003/, p. 256). The desire to expire physically is a desire to leave the semiotics of *Being*, which the body supports so long as it is a physical definition of the Spirit (Cf Shuttleworth, Sally, *Charlotte Brontë and Victorian Psychology* /Cambridge University Press, 1996/, p. 293).

In his treatment of the themes of *Mortality* Byron seems to be intimately involved with the motif of *forgiveness*. In *Cain* Byron demonstrates an example of what Derrida would have considered *„true*

(1846) she describes her own mind as a *„narrow cell, (…) a living tomb"*. In the poems *„Call me away"* (*1845*) and *Self-Communion* (*1847–1848*) Anne Brontë rather frankly admits to the corruptness and destructiveness of a mind that feeds solely upon its own internal strength. Emily Brontë feels in the same way in *Lines (1839)* and in *The Philosopher (1845)*.

[20] Cain agonizes over that fact that, as a common mortal, he too, must die: *„Thoughts unspeakable/ Crowd in my breast to burning, when I hear/ Of this almighty Death, who is, it seems,/ Inevitable. Could I wrestle with him?"* – *Cain, Act I, Scene I*. Cain would lie to know, to be conscious of, the time when he is actually resolved into the earth. See also Emily Brontë's poem *„Death, that struck when I was most confiding"* (*1845*), her Belgian essay *The Butterfly (1842* and Anne Brontë's poem *A Hymn (1843)*.

pardon". Abel finds the physical and spiritual potential to pray for Cain's soul immediately after Cain has dealt him a lethal blow with a brand on his temples (there is a powerful description of this act of fratricide – an example of a crime particularly anti-Christian). Abel is an epitome of the Redeemer – he is the only absolute victim who, and only who, has the right to absolve the murderer of his/her sin (Cf Derrida, Jacques, [in Bulgarian], *Viara I Znanie.* Sofia. LIK. 2001, p. 118). Forgiveness – for everyone and on all occasions – has the capacity to defeat Evil whilst it stirs man's conscience. Adah's unique act of charity is in her determination to share Cain's „burden" and follow him, with her child. Ironically, Abel's death activates Adah's humanity and devotion to her Cain[21]. As Paul Ricoeur would argue, Adah's act of forgiveness is real, because it is unconditional; it is born spontaneously, without being sought, and is her true Eucharist, as well as Cain's (Cf Eagleton, 2003, p. 58 & Ricoeur, 2004, pp. 646, 661–662).

In some of his early poetic works **Percy Bysshe Shelley's** views on Mortality bear the marks of his infatuation with Deism and Necessitarianism. In *Queen Mab (1813)* the poet glorifies the „*imperishable Spirit of Nature*"[22], which is good because it maintains Life's wholeness and harmony. „*Each heart contains perfection's germ*" (ibid. V), which is exactly why Life continues. Shelley evades from prohibiting Death as punishment for misdemeanour[23]. Regular seasonal changes and natural disasters are equally constructive in a universe regulated not by the usual Christian God, but by Nature's exterminable spirit. Shelley's early adherence to ideas Deistic does away with the solemnity and meditativeness Mortality stimulates in man's mind in traditional Christian ethics. Ostensibly a vindication of inextricable Evil, the

---

[21] Cf Jankelevitch, 1999, p. 127 & Bakhtin, M., *KFP, 2003, p. 39.* Compare also Anne Brontë's poem *The Power of Love (1846),* and Emily Brontë's poem „*Why ask to know the date – the clime?*" (1846).

[22] Cf „(...)/ *There is no God! / Nature confirms the faith his death-groan sealed: / (...) / infinity within, / Infinity without, (...) /The exterminable spirit it contains/ Is nature's only God; (...)*" (*Queen Mab, VI*).

[23] Natural order, in which Mortality is a part of harmony, is superior to social order, in which Mortality may appear a defect, a drawback brought about by man's own imperfection, helplessness and inability to maintain Life („*commerce /.../, poverty and wealth /.../ unfold the doors of premature and violent death /.../; „even love is sold*" – *Queen Mab,* V). That is why natural death (caused by, say, elemental forces) often regulates „socially constructed death".

cyclical re-appearance of Death confirms, and does not oppose, Creation and Eternity: each time there comes the longed-for renovation[24]. The wind is the „*messenger of hope*" (as Emily Brontë would call it) of this necessitarian concept of the link between Mutability and Death. In *Ode to the West Wind (1819)* it is both „*destroyer and preserver*" (stanza I). As a symbol, it is doubly constructive. First, it heralds the arrival of the „*trumpet of prophecy*" of Spring. And secondly, it spreads the poet's „*dead thoughts over the universe*", which, like „*withered leaves*", are to germinate among other human beings (ibid. stanza V).[25]

In his later poetry, Shelley grows more convinced that with Death the life of an ordinary person reaches its limit; reaches a boundary at which there exists no possibility of returning to erstwhile bliss and happiness[26]. For Shelley there appear to be three ways of overcoming the terminal irrevocability Death incurs on one's Life. The three also summarize in a general manner the overall view on the Life-Death relation during the Romantic Era. The first one has already been suggested during the discussion of Shelley's Deistic attitude towards the spirit of Nature. The second route to master Death is through Art: through „the spirit of poetry." In *Adonais (1821)*, the brilliant elegy over the death of the poet John Keats, Shelley pays tribute to Adonais' „*immortal [poetic] strain*", which braves Life's evils (e.g. „lust" and „corruption" – stanzas IV and V) and carries the poet valiantly into „*the gulf of death*". Shelley the poet seems almost stupefied by Adonais' talent: Adonais' spiritual power makes the

---

[24] At this point I could almost hear Jean-Pierre Vernant saying that *Death is hidden in every instant of Life like the hidden face of the condition to Be* (Cf Vernant, 2004, pp. 22–23).

[25] For Emily Brontë **the wind** has the capacity to carry the soul to its home – always the Earth (and not Heaven). The wind is the power which exceeds Mortality, i.e. it exceeds Time. The wind immortalises the Lyrical Self's soul, as well as the much revered and longed-for Dead Other's soul (Cf „*Loud without the wind was roaring*" – *1838* and „*Aye, there it is! It wakes tonight*" – *1841*). As a contrast, both Anne's and Charlotte's poetry lack such an ingredient of immortality. For them there is a clear division into: Earth (as the abode of humans), and Heaven (as the abode of God) and there is no natural agent which could always travel freely between the two.

[26] Cf *Adonais – LII*: „(…)/ *Life, like a dome of many-coloured glass,/ Stains the white radiance of Eternity,/ **Until death tramples it to fragments**. /.../*" The bold type in the last line is mine. Compare also **Shelley's poem *Death*: „*Death is here, and death is there/ Death is busy everywhere./ All around, within, beneath,/ Above is death – and we are death.// Death has set his mark and seal/ On all we are and all we feel,/ On all we know and all we fear,/ First our pleasures die – and then/ Our hopes, and then our fears – and when/ These are dead, the debt is due,/ Dust claims dust – and we die too.//…*"

dead body „*exhale itself in flowers of gentle breath*". Whilst ordinary people „*decay [with] fear and grief like vulnerable nothings*", Adonais' „*spirit tender (...) mocks the merry worm that wakes beneath*": it mocks Death's degenerative agency over man (stanzas XX & XXXIX). Adonais' poetic might, which is impervious to Mortality, is finally juxtaposed to Shelley's feeling of his own mediocrity: he is „*chained to Time, and cannot thence depart*" to follow Adonais (stanza XXVI). The only consolation for Shelley is that he has caught a glimpse of „*the fire for which we all thirst*" and that „*Adonais, like a star, / Beacons form the abode where the Eternal are*" (stanza LV) – i.e. he is in Heaven.

Yet another remedy against Mortality is contained in the power of true Love. In **Epipsychidion** (**1821**) Shelley relates the melancholic story of a poetic soul, which pines after his imprisoned beloved – Emily. The „*adored Nightingale*" is here the typically Romantic mediator: its divine singing establishes the link between Earthly existence and Heavenly bliss; it represents the female beloved's „*spirit-winged Heart*"! The poet's love for his dead beloved transfigures his sorrow into an ecstatic feeling of relatedness to a being spiritually superior to him, who is obviously capable of „*blotting*" Mortality from his „*sad song*". Even though his beloved is now gone, the poet is still under the spell of this heavenly „*serene Omnipresence*", which „*diffuses*" good and bad, light and dark – into an unvanquished sensation of peace. The image of the poet's beloved is then elevated to a higher level – she seems to merge with the planet Moon, whose „*silver voice*" marries Death and Life, which seem like „*twin babes*". It is Shelley's belief that, even if the One is gone, true Love still keeps the Survivor in an intermediary state of non-Death/non-Life, in which he receives positive charges from this eternal epitome of beauty and harmony. Love has more strength than Death, who „(...) *rides upon a thought, and makes his way/ Through temple, tower, and palace*". Love seems to amalgamate the two souls into one positively charged whole: „*one spirit within two frames*". The mourner is expected to merge with his beloved into one common „*life, one death, / One Heaven, one Hell, one immortality, / and one annihilation*". As was stated earlier in this chapter, for the 19th-century individual, the Other's Death begins to signify „My Own Death", at which point Death's euthanatic attraction surges. I think this mature work of Shelley's is a good illustration of the latter. And in his last major poem, *The Triumph of Life* (unfinished), Love appears to be the only antidote to magic, the most extreme manifestation of which is Death. Here, Rousseau's story of true Love confirms that Love, and only Love, is capable of curing the manic dancers, who know not what to do with Life. Love – the only phenomenon which withstands mutability – makes „*the night a dream*": it embalms the World with „silver music". Shelley's devotion to the senses is particularly obvious in this synaesthetic epithet.

With **John Keats,** the theme of Mortality receives a new, even more sensuous, treatment. Again, there is a tendency to resort to the power of Art /Poetry/ and to true Love as to Death's two strongest opponents. For one thing, Keats searches Greek culture and mythology through and through in order to provide a rich cultural and historical background for the theme of the unfortunate/impossible love, which can only be consummated through Death. One motif behind such fascination with classical art is that certain *objects of art seem to be impervious to temporal decay*. It would also appear possible to argue that in Keats' works there is an intricate interplay between the motifs of *marriage and sleep, or marriage and death*[27] – something the Pre-Raphaelites would take on board later.

In *Ode to a Nightingale* (1819) Keats admits to his poetic soul's vulnerability. As he is incapable of handling man's lot („*the weariness*" of mundane existence; physical diseases – „*the palsy that shakes a few*", the melancholic feeling of growing old), he wishes to „*leave the world unseen*" and „*to fade away into the forest dim*", as he gets inebriated and numb with the nightingale's song. An epitome of natural perfection, this little bird's presence is also linked to the art of poetry. The poet is hoping that he would be able to pass into eternity and, in fact, into blissful noneity on the „*viewless wings of Poesy*", as he is being carried away by the nightingale's singing[28]. Yet, whilst in the first half of the poem the bird's

---

[27] It is in a state of dreaming during the night that Isabella sees the vision of her dead beloved, who relates the story of his hideous murder (which Isabella's two brothers committed against him) and suggests the place where his body rests now (Cf *Isabella – 1819, stanzas XXXIV–XLI*). The state of sleep presupposes the dominance of feelings, of the sub-conscious, of the irrational, which is free form social conventions. Sleep is for man liminal: it is that cataleptic state, which implies crossing over a boundary – the boundary between Being and Non-Being (Cf Passi, I., 1991, p. 9).

[28] For Emily Brontë the eternal is reached through cataleptic contemplation, but of *the world within*. This world opens for the poet new spatial dimensions where the wind „*bears the poet's soul away*"

song seems to nourish the poet's talent, and self-sufficiency, in the second half the poet is thrust back into a sensation of inescapability from his mortal and imperfect world – the world where he rightly belongs. To the poet „*it seems rich to die*"[29] at the peak of this beautiful natural melody, yet when that peak is reached he realises that in order for him to preserve this sensation of achieved perfection, he must be „*tolled back to [his] sole self*". Death is a dreamed for goal, an unachievable state of exemption from the ontological burden to be one of the many and to experience this temporally definable world of humans.

The striving to reach eternity and so to master the daemonic grip of Time is evident in another brilliant ode of Keats' – ***Ode on a Grecian Urn* (1819)**. This time, the typical for the Romantics near-cataleptic state of abandonment of reality is achieved through the contemplation of an object of art – the Grecian urn. The perfection of this piece of art implies its capacity to preserve the Past – to withstand the ravages of Time, to which the human being himself is readily susceptible. The memorable images of the „*unravish'd bride*", the „*sylvan historian*", the „*maidens loth*", „*the pipes and timbrels*" mystically decorate this object, which evades categorisation because it is neither of the human world, nor of a purely supernatural quality. Again, it is a mediator between Time and non-Time. The urn is *a*-temporal, yet its eternal impact is evident as it is being contemplated only for a short time by a special type of mortal – the poet. Quite ominously, the poet seems fascinated with the fact that Nature on this urn seems stagnant[iv] („*the happy boughs*" cannot „*shed [their] leaves*"). The procession, which is heading towards the „*green altar*" (and towards sacrifice), appears disconcertingly alive, yet this „*cold pastoral*" must remain silent, marble-like, must step back into oblivion, because it has been called forth by a poetic fancy. This poetic fancy is an expression of the poet's striving for eternal happiness – a striving temporally limited and, as

---

from its *home of clay*" and eventually draws her near „*infinite immensity*" and freedom (Cf Emily Brontë's poems „*I'm happiest when most away*" *[?1838]* and *To Imagination – 1844*). See also McKusick, J. in: Roe, 2005, p. 207.

[29] In Keats' last sonnet, ***Bright Star***, the lyrical self's wish to keep forever the sensation of „*sweet unrest*" (i.e. of being close to his beloved) is a variation of the same delirious state of perfection (this time of matrimonial bliss), whose only alternative would be to „*swoon to death*".

such, unconsciously failing to recognize this piece of art's autonomy[30]. The finale re-phrases the opening lines of *Endymion*: „*beauty is truth, truth beauty*" – all the knowledge one needs on earth. That is, true beauty remains forever, and remains intact. And despite the fact that each such realisation of Art's eternal might faces the sad expiration of the viewer, yet the dimensions of this preserved Past are greater than the instantaneousness of each occasion of Death, which the Past, ironically, also contains. Generally speaking, it seems that to Keats, the peak of the striving towards a physical sensation of happiness/ perfection almost always crashes against the sensation of physical loss, of the loss of Life[xvi].

In later Victorian poetry the motifs of *orphanhood* and *alienation* (as subject to the wider philosophic discourse of *Mortality*) tend to be laid out onto the fabric of English folklore and medieval legends (rather than Old Greek culture exclusively). In **Alfred Tennyson's *The Lady of Shalott (1832)*** Art appears to be the hermetically sealed environment, which shields the lady off from the real world. The lady could only watch what is reflected of real Life in a mirror in her room, where she is busy weaving her „*magic web of colours*". She finally chooses to come to contact with the Present that is happening below her „grey towers", but when she looks down to Camelot, her mirror cracks down and she dies. In comparison, Keats' voluntary „burial" into Art, and Emily's retreat „into the world within" are conscientiously employed techniques by means of which the poet hopes to achieve consummation of physical existence. To Tennyson, the individual's apathetic non-resistance to the general course of Life-towards-Death is in unison with the escalating Victorian fear of loosing the skill to communicate to *Others*. The magical abode of delirious forgetfulness in his poem *The Lotos-Eaters (1832)* is so appealing because there man is required to apply no efforts: there is no combat with daily toil and no threat of Life's unpredictability (stanza IV). The individual is no longer a knight: he cannot live with the idea of pledging to someone, of spontaneously sacrificing his/her life for the sake of *an Other* (see *Morte D'Arthur – 1842*). Life, which oozes through one's fingers, is no

---

[30] In some lines of the poem *Winter Stores* (around 1837), which were omitted in its final version, Charlotte Brontë sees that there are „*dying dreams of light*" which are „*sealed in marble urns, to be/ No more to ear or eye revealed/ Save, Memory, by thee*" – *Cf* Winnifrith, 1984, p. 362.

different to Death, which whilst happening, snatches away its own chance for completion, because the bearer of its effects cannot register it for a fact. In Tennyson's work the latter perception is appears to be an approach to Life, rather than just a consequential reflection on it. His very early poem *Mariana* (**1830**) depicts a lyrical self who is „*aweary, aweary, / I would that I were dead!*" In *Maud (1855)* the lyrical speaker declares that his heart is „*a handful of dust*". The feeling of wretchedness that creeps upon the individual is aggravated by the feeling of loss of faith (Tennyson holds the failing spirit of the institution of the Church partly responsible for that: „*they cannot even bury a man*" – Cf *Maud*, Part II, section V, stanzas I & II).

Tennyson's personal and very painful involvement with Death reached a peak with two events. Firstly, he lost his close university friend Arthur Hallam (1833), to whom he dedicated *In Memoriam – 1834– 1850*; and in the spring of 1851 he had his first son born dead. In his poetry Tennyson shows that, bereaved of the dearest people around him, the individual begins to work out a form of escapist subjectivism, in which the mind is thought to nourish reality. As the mind is empty, Nature is empty too, because it is „*a hollow echo of my own*" (*In Memoriam*)[31]. As such, Nature could easily be „*crushed like a vice of blood, / Upon the threshold of the mind*" (*In Memoriam* – stanza III). Yet both *In Memoriam*, and *Maud* condemn this very mind, because of which „*the spirit of murder works in the very means of life*" (*Maud*). One could also perceive Tennyson's treatment of Mortality as a revision of certain specificities of Blake's and Wordsworth's poetic heritage: they both demonstrate an avid interest in Death as an illness of a defective society. In *Maud* poverty is seen as the misery which shortens man's life. The Lyrical Self's's suicidal thoughts in *Maud* are a form of protest against a reality where inequality limits and models the World, in which both his parents have been snatched away by Death. He wants to „*bury [himself] in [himself]*", so that „*the man I am may cease to be*" (Cf *Maud*, Part I – I-I, ix; – X-vi). Tennyson's Lyrical Self seems to be lingering between Life and Death, he exists in Non-Life/Non-Death and is reluctant to make any further

---

[31] Charlotte Brontë would have said that the fire of her life is „self-kindled, self-consumed" (*Reason – 1836*), and her brother Branwell feels „*confounded to inward thought*" (*Harriet II – 1838*).

step in order to define his status in a way so as to relate to Others ^{not} without any regret or sense of guilt.

As with all Victorian poets, who realised Death's ironic sneer over man's desire to make most of Life, Tennyson's route was one towards embracing the idea that <u>it is only faith that outlives man</u>. The faith, which the poet hopes to find impersonated by one higher Being (trustworthy and benevolent), in effect leads to God (Cf *In Memoriam*, LXXII) – the *„one law, one element/ And one far-off divine event, / To which the whole creation moves"* (ibid, Conclusion). That longed-for deity appears to be the ultimate antidote to Life's finality and fragmentarity. As the image of God tends to merge with that of his late friend, it naturally receives the providential status of *the missing Other*, who shall *„look me thro' and thro"* (*In Memoriam* – L). The contact with the dead (at the tombstone, in the graveyard etc) qualifies as the communal practice of taking the Holy Eucharist (ibid XCIII). An occasion of Death aids the Survivor when he needs to recognize the role of *Otherness* in his/her own individuation[32]. In Emmanuel Levinas' terms, Death challenges destabilizes the grounds and values of the Survivor's existence, yet it is only thanks to such challenge that the individual could make the ontological leap forward – to grow more knowledgeable and more sensitive to Life[xvii]. Hence the narrator's words: *„So dark a mind within me dwells,/ And I make myself such evil cheer, That if I be dear to some one else,/ Then some one else may have much to fear;/ But if I be dear to someone else,/ Then I should be to myself more dear. /.../ If I be dear, If I be dear to some one else"* (*Maud* – Part I – section XIV, stanza XV). That *Other* has the capacity to raise the lyrical speaker from the dead[33]. Tennyson's belief is that incompletion is a vital characteristic of one's Spirit. The awareness of one's own imminent Death strengthens one's dependence on one's completing *Otherness*[xviii], which in the long run always outlives/succeeds one.

---

[32] See also Charlotte Brontë's treatment of the theme of guilt in her poems: *Pilate's Wife's Dream* (1846), *The Rose* (1839) and *Gilbert* (1843).

[33] In *Maud (Part I – XXII – xi)* the narrator confesses his devotion to Maud: *„/.../ My heart would hear her and beat,/ Were it earth in an earthy bed;/ My dust would hear her and beat,/ Had I lain for a century dead;/ Would start and tremble under her feet,/ And blossom in purple and red"*.

*   *   *

The conclusion to this chapter comes with the hope that it has by now become clear that the theme of *Mortality* emerges as one central philosophic discourse in the **English poetry of the period: mid-18th century–mid-19th century**. It is my strong belief that that temporal frame provides also an adequate thematic context in which the specificities of the Brontë sisters' vision of Mortality should be sought. The gradual loss of contact with Nature, which has its socio-political dimensions within the process of industrialization, is felt to have opened an ontological gap. The 19th-century individual's striving towards singularity and spiritual independence crashes against his/her realisation that he/she is spiritually kinless. This individual's past seems to be divested of a wise and protective Deity, formerly found in the natural world. The 19th-century's interest in the themes of *Mortality* reveals man's emphatic interest in the Past – a receptacle of everything important the Present lacks (parents, brethren, spiritual companionship, regularity, and hope). From a theological point of view, *Mortality* in the above named period is the most densely populated contextual field of warring religious concepts and denominations within the Protestant tradition (some of which were mentioned in this chapter, while some further references are due to be made). The different views on the epistemology of Being presuppose different attitudes towards, and interpretations of, the (ir)relevance of the idea of the End (and consequently towards the notions of Justice and of Punishment).

The Bronte sisters' poetry shares certain characteristics of the treatment of Death with the poets of the period mid-18th–mid-19th centuries. The meditativeness of the graveyard and the informativeness of the grave (which gives one the hope for a respite from the brooding physical dissolution) are features of both the works of **the graveyard poets** and the young Brontë sisters. Further on, **Blake's** chthonian images of palingenetic rebirth blend good and evil into the belief that Death is the necessary condition for Life in the formation of every next ingredient in the chain of existence. Man is but a component like all others. Some of Emily Brontë's early poetic pieces, as well as her Belgian Devoir, *The Butterfly* (1842), respond to the latter opinion.

It is possible to establish certain links between the Brontë sisters' preoccupation with the theme of orphanhood and **Wordsworth's** interest in that. In the works of both Wordsworth and the Brontes the missing mother/the missing Authority is a major impetus for the individual to face his/her ontological duty to step into, and become a part of, the world around. The syndrome of *the missing parent* is alleviated through a gradual orthodox reintegration of the individual into Nature's protective benevolence, which is the only remedy against the feeling of being spiritually dead after the *Other's* death. As a contrast, **Coleridge's** exploration of the type of man who tends to project his own nature's irregularity and lack of compassion onto external reality (which thus becomes a replica of his mental state of „Life-in-Death") is comparable to Emily Brontë's struggle with the ambiguous nature of A.G.A. Coleridge's *daemonic woman-mother/ woman-lover* (as in *Christabel*, or in *The Rime of the Ancient Mariner*) is a direct opponent to Worsdworth's maternal vision of Nature. Charlotte and Branwell Brontë must have found it rather satisfying to exchange ideas with Hartley Coleridge (Coleridge's son), who made the effort to give Branwell some advice about his translations of Horace's *Odes*, and possibly to read one of Charlotte's tales (Cf Barker 1995, pp. 261–263; p. 331; pp. 337–338). In various biographic studies on the Brontes it is emphasized that the Brontë children definitely kept in their home library volumes of **Byron's** works. Byron's wilful images of Cain and Manfred would certainly have suggested some ideas about the Brontës's Augusta Geraldine Almeida (*Gondal*) or Alexander Percy, Earl of Northangerland (*Angria*). The motifs of the voluntary retreat from society and that of fratricide are what Lord Byron and the Brontë sisters have in common. The existential guilt in the works of both Byron and the Brontës could be seen as resulting from the proud individual's determination to own the World, to surpass the boundary of knowledge which Death draws before one, and to unravel the dichotomy *Heaven: Hell*, whilst trying to handle the impossible combination of both in one's own mind.

What brings the Brontë sisters' poetry and the works of **Shelley** and **Keats** together is one common Romantic belief in the power of Love as one sure way to master the dilemma of Death. Shelley's early Necessitarianism (the belief in a benevolent spirit which stands behind Life's progress) is further away from the works of the Brontës than is his mature belief in Death as a terminus. Yet both Shelley and Emily Brontë plead for a Heaven of their own, where the private union between two souls would be accomplished and immortalised. Shelley and Keats both agree that Death could be mastered through the Art of Poetry, the best products of which remain impervious to the ravages of Time. Keats is the poet furthest away from the Brontë sisters' vision of Death, yet his sensuousness and at times daemonicity of affection, which the Survivor shows towards *the Dead Other* (*Isabella*), does bring this finest of the Romantics nearer the Brontë sisters.

Certain peculiarities of the Brontë sisters' poetic treatment of Mortality are in concord with the later Victorian poets' perception of Mortality. That, however, becomes obvious only in a diachronic overview of 19th-century English poetry. In Anne and Emily's poetic works, the individual's early and faithless estrangement from life, the suicidal alienation from the parentless and companionless environment of the Present share **Tennyson's** mood in *The Lotos-Eaters, Mariana* and *The Lady of Shalott*. On the other hand, Emily's *Gondal* anticipates Tennyson's Eucharistic deification of *the (Dead) Other*, the communion with whom (as in *In Memoriam,* or in *Maud*) helps man overcome his introspective negation of the external world. How the Brontë sisters' works could be related to some later and late Victorian poets is one point which the conclusion of this thesis will briefly discuss – with the idea of how to possibly continue and broaden the scope of investigation of the themes of Mortality in 19th-century English literature.

In the period mid-18th–mid-19th centuries the literary interest in the theme of Mortality „undulates" between two visions of Death. According to the first one, Death is seen as non-negative and structurally valuable: it is an ingredient which confirms the constancy of Nature, which is perceived as wiser and more experienced than each concrete individual. According to the second one, Death curtails the Self's potential. Further on, there is the grievous realisation that Life, and therefore Nature, have in fact become predicates to a Self which is destructively avaricious in its urge to own the knowledge of Existence. Gradually but surely there creeps upon the 19th-century individual the feeling of deficiency in *Authorial Otherness*. The Past is cherished as a container of the now lost ontological balance of *Being* – something, which is evident in the poets' search for truth in the contextual background of classical literature and of English folk and medieval literature. As far as the poetic form is concerned, the internalisation of the theme of Death in the above named period shows in the poets' preference for the elegy, the ballad, the lyrical fragment and, generally speaking, in their clinging to confessional lyric poetry.

NOTES:

[i] Cf Wheeler, Michael, *Death and the Future Life in Victorian Literature and Theology* (Cambridge University Press, 1990), pp. 44–46.

[ii] Cf Thomas, Sophie in: Roe, Nicholas, *Romanticism. An Oxford Guide* (Oxford University Press, 2005), p. 504.

[iii] Cf Vainstein in: /ed./ Grintzer, I. A., [in Russian] *Istoritcheskaya poetika*. Moskva: „Nasledie", 1994, p. 418.

[iv] Cf Jauss, Hans Robert, *Kunst ALS Anti-Natur: Zur astetischen Wendenach*, (translated in Bulgarian and published in: /ed./ Anguelov, Angel, *Istoritcheski opit I literatourna hermenevtika*, Universitetsko izdatelstvo „Sv. Kliment Ohridski", 1998, p. 366).

[v] Cf Jauss, 1998, p. 360.

[vi] Cf Labbe, Jacqueline, M., *The Romantic paradox. Violence and the Uses of Romance: 1760–1830* (Macmillan, 2000).

[vii] Cf Jankélévitch, Vladimir, *La Mort*. [in Russian] Smert'. Moskva: Literatourniy institut imeni M. A. Gor'kogo. 1999. p. 312.

[viii] Cf Gadamer, Hans-Georg, *Wahrheit Und Methode*, 1988, pp. 321–322, p. 334.

[ix] Cf Wheeler 1994, p. 61.

[x] Cf Batten, Guinn, *The Orphaned Imagination: Melancholy and Commodity Culture in English Romanticism* (Durham and London: The Duke University Press, 1998), p. 81.

[xi] Cf Beach, Joseph Warren, *The Concept of Nature in Nineteenth-Century English Poetry* (New York: The Macmillan Company, 1936), p. 26.

[xii] Cf Boyadziev, 2000, pp. 223–224.

[xiii] Blanchot, as referred to in: Bronfen, E., 1992, p. 85.

[xiv] An allusion to Feuerbach, as quoted in: Panova, E. et al, [in Bulgarian] *Antologia: Evropeiska Filosofia 17–19 vek,* tchast II. Sofia. „Naouka I izkoustvo", 1988, p. 603.

[xv] Cf Cronin, Richard in: Roe, 2005, p. 270.

[xvi] Refer to Jean-Pierre Vernant's reflection of the image of the woman-daemon for the ancient Greeks (Cf Vernant, 2004, pp. 144–146), as well as J. R. Watson's interpretation of *Lamia* in: Watson, 1992, p. 360.

[xvii] Cf Levinas, *Totalité et Infini*, 2000, pp. 81, 88.

[xviii] Cf Bakhtin, AIG, 2003, p. 95.

Section II

Anne Brontë

One way to start the investigation of the themes of *Mortality* in Anne Brontë's poetry would be, first of all, to track down the main thematic specificities of Anne's vision of Death/Mortality in a way, which would accommodate those in Anne's literary context.

In both the religion and the literature of the period mid-18th–mid-19th centuries man's existence is seen as a solitary pilgrimage of the soul that yearns simultaneously for uniqueness and salvation. The poets' spontaneous retreat into an imaginary world of dreams that appear more wholesome than the actual Present, their striving for the World Beyond reflects, as was already explained, the individual's desire to make up for the irreparable feeling of loss that the departure of the dearest people leaves behind for one. Anne Brontë's early poetry suffers from a Romantic euthanatic urge – the wish to get exempt from the duty of carrying the „cross" of Co-Being (the non-optional need to acknowledge those who precede, co-exist with, and would succeed one).

Another common element between Anne Brontë and her literary environment is *an orphan's existential feeling of confusion and desertion*. The latter engenders an individual's quest to create an adequate image of the deceased parent/Author in order to have someone more experienced, wiser and protective to relate to. To Anne Brontë such lack is partly compensated for by man's reverence for the one supreme exemplary being – Christ – the ultimate omnipotent protector and Redeemer. Of the three Brontë sisters, Anne Brontë most openly and frequently clings to the common Evangelical understanding of Life as a „*constant vigilant preparation for death*". *The awareness of Death's communal dimensions (i.e. as a practice Eucharistic), Death humanized and integrated into man's moral code* (as **Philippe Ariès** maintains[1]) – this belief is earliest evident nowhere else in the Brontë sisters' works, but in Anne Brontë's poetry. Rather more toilsome appear to have been Charlotte's and Emily's (in particular) journeys towards accepting the latter philosophy. I believe that is one significant deviation

---

[1] Cf Ariès, 2004, Part I, chapter 1. It should be remembered that the images of Death Anne would have grown up with (under the strict Methodist upbringing carried out mostly by her Aunt Branwell and through her father's professional duties) would have been crude, at times fearsome and even vulgar. Yet those very images must have acted as a stimulant for her imagination (Cf W. G. G. James in: Gregor 1980, pp. 229–230).

from the individualistic approach to the idea of the End some Romantics may be seen to have taken in their works.

Millenarianism (in the sense of the radical apocalyptic social changes described and anticipated in Blake's, Worsdworth's and Shelley's works) is not a distinctive feature of Anne Brontë's poetry. For her, the anticipation of the End, of the Day of Doom and of Justice is rather more private and quietist. One cannot fail to notice, however, that Anne Brontë's model of Life postulates God to be the ultimate answer, the ultimate master of Nature and arbitrator of man's life. She believes in that God is what can never be limited: his ameliorative influence on humanity will never cease. Or, to paraphrase Paul Ricoeur, there is nothing which could undeniably be recognized for Good other than an essentially good Will[ii], which is What God appears to be in Anne's mature poetic works. The Brontë sisters' family background would have provided them with abundant religious resources necessary to form such an orthodox attitude towards existence[2]. In Anne Brontë's works there are few, if any, traces of the fear of Death as something unfamiliar and threatening. Anne's mature poetry defends the poet's strong belief in an emphatically sacrificial, devoutly Christian lifestyle, which should be embraced as the only right line of behaviour. The interiorization of God's image in Anne Brontë's poetry is evident in the Lyrical Speaker's belief that in order to *Be* in a wholesome manner, one must at all times be *answerable* (to use Bakhtin's term) for one's deeds to *someone Other than Oneself* [iii]. Penitence and Empathy form the truly ontological attitude, the execution of which urges one to embrace and personalise the idea of the End into an existence of Care and Love for *Others,* who simultaneously limit and justify one's time on Earth.

The originality of Anne Brontë's poetic works then lies in **her understanding that the ontology of human existence, the ethical dimensions of one's life, should be built on one's benevolent attitude toward Death and so toward the Past.** As one might expect, there is the poet's early readiness to take an escapist attitude to Life through voluntary Death. The poet now merges with her lyrical personae, now distances herself from them. It is the poet's intention to try and see

---

[2] The Brontë children were certainly familiar with some popular moral writings at the time like: Hannah More's *Moral Sketches (1818)*, the Bible and certainly John Bunyan's works (Cf Drew, Lamonica, 2003, p. 21).

whether she could experience the cognitive „thresholdness" of Death (in Derrida's terms, Cf Derrida, J., *Apories*, 1998). She would like to discover for herself whether empathy is possible towards a phenomenon of which man, whilst alive, has no personal experience. Anne Brontë's mature perception of Life sieves the idea of Mortality through the themes of Christ's/ the mother's death – the two events which instil Anne's Lyrical Self with a Methodist benevolence and a desire to forgive everyone and even the unforgivable. True *Being* involves a non-conditional feeling of gratitude for, and obligation towards, the Past, through which, and only through which, one's Future could be imagined and anticipated. Anne Brontë knows that the obligation towards the Past, which Death imposes on Man, is in effect the obligation to admit that one only gains social awareness through an Other human being who came first into the World (who came before „Me"). Reciprocally, the supposition that such an *Other* would necessarily succeed one, strengthens the hope that „My own death" would not be in vain (Cf, Bakhtin, AIG, 2003, p. 179).

I am strongly inclined to believe that Anne Brontë's philosophy and attitude towards Mortality must have absorbed and appropriated deeply some specificities of her religious milieu – much more so than any of her sisters did. Discernible in her works are traces of the didactic tone of voice dominant in the late 17th century and throughout the 18th century. Some major English treatises on human nature (written by Locke, Hume and Burke), the philosophic and political obsessions with the idea of self-improvement and self-study – those could not have been passed by Anne, even though her knowledge of them now seems somewhat more distant, fragmentary and less coherent than the critic would perhaps like it to be. Meanwhile, Jeremy Bentham's *deontology* (particularly influential in the 1820s) stimulated an attitude to Life analytical and observant (hence Protestant[iv]). The rejection of passivity, the urge towards building a private ethics, whose core ought to be the eradication of evil – these two elements Anne Brontë has in common with the above. On the other hand, the Brontës would have been initiated in the practices of self-examination and self-chastisement that Calvinism and Evangelicalism would stimulate. Anne Brontë's numerous hymns and prayers, particularly the ones obviously addressed to God, with their solemn and eulogist tone of voice, heavy and lengthy in syntactic patterns, are suggestive of the latter (Cf, Chitham,

Edward, *The Poems of Anne Brontë* /Macmillan, 1979/, p. 40). Considerations over the doctrines of *predestination, election and reprobation* are abundantly available in Anne Brontë's prose fiction and poetic works. While residing at the Misses Woolers' school at Roe Head (1836–1837), Anne Brontë is known to have been visited by a Moravian minister (the Rev. James La Trobe) of the Moravian church at Mirfield, who would have suggested to her ideas of silence and humbleness in expecting the Revelation, of salvation by faith (Cf Gerin, Winifred, *Anne Brontë* /London: Thomas Nelson & Sons LTD, 1959/, pp. 98–100).

It is a well-known fact that the Brontë children wrote from a very early age. They collaborated in developing their Juvenilia, the main products of which are now the literary constructs *Angria* and *Gondal*. It is unfortunate for the critic to discover that nothing of Anne's own Juvenilia seems to have survived. Anne's earliest poems are dated to 1836 (Cf Chitham, 1997, p. 5). Most probably, *Gondal* developed out of *Angria* around 1831–1832, when Anne and Emily were left to develop their own talents without Charlotte, who left for Roe Head (for the Misses Woolers' School). Apparently only in 1834 do the Bronte sisters' journals mention the existence of *Gondal* (Cf Chitham, 1979, p. 5). As mentioned earlier in the present research, *Gondal* formed, indeed, from the stories the Brontë children created about the 12 wooden toy soldiers, brought to them by their father, the Rev. Patrick Brontë, from Leeds in 1826'. To pioneering critics like Edward Chitham it must have seemed a toilsome job to compile and present Anne Brontë's poetry as one whole. One hypothesis is that Anne and Emily might well have decided to destroy the manuscripts of the *Gondal* saga when their partnership dissolved. Another immediate obstacle that the critics faced was that some additional pieces of the Brontë sisters' poetic heritage might have been lost as the Brontës' works (manuscripts, transcripts etc.) migrated and were being collected over the years. It nonetheless seems quite plain that Anne worked over her poems constantly and most probably revised them as she copied them in her copybooks of 1836–1848 (Cf Chitham, 1979, pp. 26–27, p. 31), demonstrating a respectable level of punctuation (which is something Emily's poetry boasts not; ibid. p. 46). There is but one significant factor, which frustrates the certainty about the authorship of some of Anne's poems. And that is, that Charlotte Brontë's perseverance in editing both Emily and Anne's poetry was accompanied by her at times rather authoritarian intervention in changing some words and structures of their poems (ibid. pp. 26–27).

Compared to Emily's and Charlotte's poetic heritage, Anne Brontë's occupies just over 110 printed pages in Edward Chitham's authoritative edition of 1979. Yet Anne's poems feel rather homogenous in their overall philosophic sounding and complexity. Anne explores and develops the themes of *Mortality* in a way, which reveals not an unhesitant, yet a gradual and consistent consideration of the phenomenon of Death as placed at the core of her philosophy of Life as Co-Being. The present study endeavours to follow the chronology of composition of the poems, and thus observe the development of the lyrical persona of the Survivor, keeping in mind, but not automatically and necessarily referring all arguments to, the context of the *Gondal* saga. There will be some thematic re-grouping of the poems with the purpose of discovering some common contents, which, in itself, however, will not eclipse the need for precision in referring to the dates and order of composition of those poems. One thing, which I hope such a combined investigative technique would reveal, is that in Anne's poetry, various speaking/confessing selves intersect, so to speak, in their partiality towards major philosophic issues: they complement one another and the poet herself in their uneasy journey towards ontological maturation. They do all finally come together in their acceptance of Death as a phenomenon prior to, and explanatory of, the phenomenon of Life. As might be expected, the range of genres includes: elegies, hymns, companion pieces and confessional private lyric pieces.

As in the chapters dedicated to Emily and Charlotte, this chapter is organized in such a way so as to present the themes of Mortality in some motion – as a sequence of sub-chapters, each of which focuses on one/more specific motifs/features, which comprise the theme of Death. In this way I hope to be able to provide substantial and more precisely arranged textual evidence in support of my main thesis (that Mortality, as a philosophic discourse, is also the central thematic concern of Anne's, Charlotte's and Emily's). As the Lyrical Self matures, so does the Poet herself (in terms of depth and originality of thought and technical skills). This could be observed well in Anne Brontë's poetry.

* * *

„*Ars de bene moriendi*": Anne Brontë's Thanato-Ethics[vi]

This first part of the study of the themes of *Mortality* in Anne Brontë's poetry deals with her earliest poetic works extant: 1836–1838 (stretching up to 1840). In this span of time the poet's mind is focused on the motifs of *solitude* and *alienation*. The Lyrical Speaker descends into the grave to look for familiar people/environment in the World Beyond, which is juxtaposed to the hostilely unknown world of the Present, which appears undecipherable and therefore distant and threatening. There is a wish to find a quick and painless way to leave the world, which the Lyrical self hopes, will be the way to compensate for the feelings of despair and self-pity. Many of the poems are obviously signed by personae of the Gondal saga. It is therefore logical to assume that Anne Brontë's preoccupation with Death is as old as her first juvenile attempts with Gondal. There is a striving to verify whether Death implies any thresholdness, and as such, whether it promises cessation or prolongation of one's existence. What happens here is that the Lyrical Self stumbles over the impossibility to experience her own death, which is dreamed for as she would like to join the departed family members in the after life (another element of the Evangelical perception of Life as centred around the family unit). The theme of Death gives the poet the chance to explore the limits of the individual's sense of reality and of his/ her consciousness (which matures, as she realises the need to continue to Be in the Act of Co-Being). The ballads of this period are strewn with confessional and reflexive digressions. From a biographical point of view, the years 1836–1837 proved for Anne Brontë's particularly lonely, as she had to stay at The Roe Head Boarding School in Mirfield (the time before she went to Blake Hall as a governess to the Inghams). The feelings of gloom and loneliness, indeed, dominate her poetry of the time.

The very first poem in Chitham's edition of Anne Brontë's verse, **Verses by Lady Geralda** (December 1836, Chitham, 1979, pp. 49–51), depicts a woman who has lost both her parents and has also been deserted by her brother. Eventually, she realises that keeping busy until self-oblivion and weariness seems to be the only way out of the gloom, in which she has been living since the loss of her closest people[3]. Yet even that remedy has limited power, because it, too, depends on feelings and thoughts definable only within a certain span of time. As she lies *„upon the pathless moor"*, she hears *„the wild wind rushing by/ With never ceasing roar"* (and sometimes the wind takes another tone – the *„melancholy moan"*) and ponders on her lonely life. Lying in the bosom of Nature, and in a state of total seclusion and privacy, Lady Geralda seems to be crossing mentally the margin between the two worlds: that of the living and that of the dead (a motif particularly common in the Brontës' poetic and prose fiction works in general[4]). She hopes to be able to restore the world of her childhood, and so to scramble up and out of the ontological abyss she has fallen into after the deaths of her parents. One proof that she discerns the ontological value of the phenomenon of Death is that she remembers how she cast a little flower to die and how later this occasion filled her heart with misery, and *„nature smiles no more"* (an occasion of someone else's Death reminds one of the certainty of one's own Death, which is always imminent to the Survivor).

It is most typical of Anne Brontë's to portray an individual who is both the victim and the instigator/initiator of the depressive state of striving for the grave, or for Death. In the poem *A Voice from the Dungeon* (October 1837, Chitham 1979, pp. 60–61) the woman (in Anne's poetry the Lyrical Self's voice seems to be exclusively female) perceives herself as a victim, as ontologically incomplete: she anticipates the grave as salvation, but she is also afraid of a lonely End (which would be her deserved punishment). Marina Sabia (most probably a persona pertaining to the

---

[3] *„./…/ There is still a cherished hope/ To cheer me on the way;/ It is burning in my heart/ With a feeble ray.// I will cheer the feeble spark/ And raise it to a flame;/ And it shall light me through the world,/ **And lead me on to fame**.//…/ From such a hopeless home to part/ Is happiness to me,/ For naught can charm my weary heart/ Except activity."* The lines I have typed in bold indicate of a certain dose of hubris. Typically for the young poet's vision of existence, Lady Geralda imagines that she would be able to heroically swallow the deaths of the people dearest to her, and that this would be treated as a noble act of stoicism, which would dutifully win her some fame among other Survivors. Such thoughts suggest philosophical closeness between Anne and the Romantics – the early *hubris* (surviving and standing out amongst others despite of/ thanks to loneliness) has not yet been ousted by Anne's mature feeling of existential guilt. The feeling of duty towards an Other is still dormant and non-developed in the Lyrical Self's mind.

[4] Compare especially Emily Brontë's poem *R. Alcona to J. Brenzaida („Cold in the earth, and the deep snow piled above thee!" – March, 1845).* In it Rosina dreams of descending into the grave of her beloved, which is how she hopes to achieveheaven after this *„divinest anguish".*

Gondal saga) voluntarily retreats into the grave. It may well be that she is literally kept prisoner, but the whole sounding and contents of the poem show that, she herself causes, or allows, to be buried. She is indifferent to Life. Marina Sabia's reveries of her beloved and her little boy are overshadowed by dreams of *fiends* all around. She has been deprived of both son and husband, so that now she is a mother and wife in name only, and her greatest hope is to deny Life completely *("I'm buried now; I've done with life;/ I've done with hate, revenge and strife;/ I've done with joy, and hope and love/ And all the bustling world above.// Long have I dwelt forgotten here/ In pining woe and dull despair;/ This place of solitude and gloom/ Must be my dungeon and my tomb")*. Marina Sabia is enigmatically suggestive of the guilt-ridden Augusta (the mother who murders her own babe, and the wife who brings about her beloved men's deaths) – Emily's most notable contribution to the Gondal saga. For Marina Sabia, the truth about Life has been restricted and limited by the death of her closest people. Life has ceased for her and she wants put an end altogether to her grievous existence. As a rather immature impersonation of the young poet herself, Marina Sabia fails to realise that the spiritual vacuum she has fallen into *("I dream of liberty, 'tis true/ But then I dream of sorrow too")* could be transformed into the opportunity of developing a new kind of responsibility towards Life even after the death of her family. A wish to disappear from Life, to be feasible and available No More to Others, contains a dose of self-centredness: it shows a desire to own one's own fate, the memory of which one cannot have (Cf Derrida, *Apories*, 1998, pp. 17–18).

The above poem also suggests Anne Brontë's interest in what Jacques Derrida would have termed „the dilemma of the thresholdness of Death". Namely, at the moment of Death, does one step over the boundary of something and thus get a chance to prolong Life by literally stepping into a new world, or is the boundary in fact a dead wall which puts an end to man's hopes for an existence *afterwards?* In other words, does Death preclude, interrupt movement, i.e. is Death static, or does it presuppose motion (Cf Derrida, *Apories*, 1998, pp. 20–22)? Can Death be categorised as salvation, if its status is non-defined? Anne Brontë must have considered the duality of *the grave*: its concreteness and tangibility, but also its morbid deficit of objectivity: as an item of the night, it threatens the

individual with depersonalization (it's it a construct in the formula „*Il y a*",
the „*Il y a*" of the Night). Marina Sabia amalgamates *dungeon* and *tomb* as
she searches for a symbol, which would comprise both prolongation and
cessation of activity (i.e. relief from earthly toil). *The grave*, as an item of
the impersonal realm of the Night, consumes the familiarity of objects, and
so any attempt to hide behind and amongst them is contravened by this
dark space's power to expose one to the irregularities of one's own Self
and universe, in effect – to Being, from which there is no escape (Cf,
Levinas, *Totalité...*, 2000, pp. 34–37).

In Anne Brontë's philosophy, the states of loneliness and deprivation
urge the individual to wish one's own death. In **Lady of Alzerno's Hall**
(10th July 1838, Chitham, 1979, pp. 66–68), signed by Alexandrina
Zenobia (another reminiscence of Anne's involvement with the Gondal
saga), a woman admits to the fact that the beloved person's death is such
an existential burden to her that she would rather he were confirmed dead.
In that way, at least the aggravating uncertainty about his actual fate would
be eliminated. Having waited for her husband to return for three years, she
rules:

> *(...)*
> *'I wish I knew the worst,' she said,*
> *'I wish I could despair.*
> *These fruitless hopes, this constant dread,*
> *Are more than I can bear!' –*
> *(...)*

Another important participant is present actively. The Lyrical
Speaker, who relates Eliza's grievous fate, is in fact Alexandrina Zenobia[5].
In the last stanza of this brilliant ballad of Anne's, Alexandrina discloses to
the listener/reader the fact that she knows „*so well/ The time and nature
of [Eliza's beloved's] death*": his head was „*pillowed on her knee*" and
she was with him until he departed from this world („*/.../ the look of a
dying man/ Can never be forgot*", she says).

---

[5] Alexandrina Zenobia was „*forcibly separated from her lover by civil war, imprisoned and
deserted by her friends*" (Barker, J., 1995, p. 983).

The idea of appropriating and of authenticating one's own death (to contrast the unpredictable and inescapable biological end each life is abbreviated by) is what lurks in the philosophy of early Anne Brontë. Although a last resort of man's, voluntary dying is felt to be dubious in its final result and impact on Life. Anne Brontë's lyrical personae are hesitant about whether the ownership of one's own death[6] *is* going to bring them a happier existence (Cf Eagleton 2003, p. 104, p. 269). Philippe Ariès would have classified the above desire as man's strong temptation to savour Life in loneliness. To savour the aesthetic pleasure of the idea of a self-controlled, decidedly quick and painless ending (without disturbing the convenient tranquillity of other people). One tends to smother one's grief with the reverie about euthanasia (Cf Ariès, Philippe, *Western Attitudes Towards Death*, [translation in Bulgarian], Sofia. BAN. „Literatourna misal", kniga 5, 1993, pp. 5, 34). Ariès argues that for the representative of the growingly self-alienating 19th-century society, who emerged as unprepared and scared to share one's grief with others, euthanasia would have been the ultimate solution to all earthly travail. In the poems analysed above the individual is in fact calling for help, for *empathy*, for a rescuing Other. There is a hidden fear that when dead, the Lyrical Self might deserve no one to mourn over her. The compassion, expected from the listener/ reader, has to go towards the process of the Lyrical Self's own coming to terms with her own death – the one event she will not witness[7] (Cf Ricoeur, *La Mémoire...*, 2004, p. 501). On the whole, the idealistic intuitive conviction in self-interpretation, the phenomenology of self-treatment, and not of the treatment of *the Other*, is what is easily discernible in Anne Brontë's early poetry. The concept of *After Life* as relevant through the concepts of *Empathy* and *Care* during one's own lifetime are still missing.

---

[6] Compare also Anne Brontë's poem *Lines Written at Thorp Green* (28th August 1840, Chitham 1979, p. 75).

[7] **Felicia Hemans (1793–1835)**, one of the best English women poets of the Romantic age, treats the availability of Death in a similar manner. The poet juxtaposes the temporal limitations of the finite world of the Present, and the threat of sinking into imperfection in one's own lifetime *to* an imminent World Beyond – perfect and peaceful. The dove symbolizes the woman's soul, whose beauty the World of the living could now truly appreciate and cherish. Compare, for instance, *The Voice of Spring* (1823) and *The Wings of the Dove* (1827) – all in: Feldman, Barbara, *British Women Poets of the Romantic Era. An Anthology* (Baltimore & London: The Johns Hopkins University Press, 2000), pp. 285–300.

Two events in Anne's own biography certainly found place in her earliest poetic works[8]. The first one was the death of William Weightman (Patrick Brontë's young curate at Haworth parsonage) in 1842. According to most biographical sources, William Weightman might have given Anne some hopes for shared future bliss. In the same year, this tragic event was followed by the death of the Brontë children's surrogate mother – Aunt Branwell (their own mother's sister, who had taken over the maternal responsibilities shortly after Maria's Brontë's death). Additionally, infant Anne might have retained some memories of her two older sisters, Maria and Elizabeth – the much loved older children in the Brontë family who both died of consumption. The family unity and intactness Evangelicalism cherished and encouraged was destroyed for Anne very early, as death settled down steadily in her personal life (Cf Thormählen, 1999, pp. 15, 20). According to a letter Charlotte Brontë wrote to William Smith Williams (Scarborough, 4th June 1849), Anne's life must have been a quietist and purposeful preparation for death, which her works could be seen to reflect[9]. Charlotte claimed that for Anne Death was not foreign, it bore no threat to Life.

At this point, it would be appropriate to remind the reader that for the Victorians, the words „grave", „deathbed" and „dream" seemed to contain an ambiguity, which resulted from the people's unequivocal attitude towards the notion of the End. On the one hand, those words implied the concept of intimacy, peace and hope, of continuity, and on the other – the concept of fatigue, of exhaustion from Life and of a terminus. In the funeral practice in the early 19th century they would „allow this ambiguity happen" by letting children be present at the deathbed and witness the lengthy funeral arrangements (Cf Wheeler, Michael, *Heaven, Hell and the Victorians* /Cambridge University Press, 1994/, pp. 31–40). Patrick Brontë's job would naturally have permitted the children to partake

---

[8] The fact that Anne considered the importance of Mortality could be supported with an example from her art of drawing too – for instance *Ruined Church – 10th February 1836* (reproduced with commentary in: Alexander, Christine & Sellars, Jane, *The Art of the Brontës* /Cambridge University Press, 1995/, p. 401).

[9] Charlotte Brontë wrote: „(...) *her quiet – Christian death did not rend my heart as Emily's stern, simple, undemonstrative end did – I let Anne go to God and felt He had a right to her. (...) – Anne, from her childhood seemed preparing for an early death –*" (quoted as in: Barker, 1997, p. 237).

of the holiness and morbidity of funeral practices (the Parsonage itself overlooks the graveyard and the parish church at Haworth). According to Eve Kosofsky Sedgwick, who looks into Death in the context of the Gothic tradition, *the deathbed* allows an enlargement of the sense of reality. The deathbed contains the possibility for an imaginary descent into the flexible space of the world beyond within the space of the Present, of the living world (Cf Sedgwick, E. K., *The Coherence of Gothic Conventions* /New York & London, Methuen, 1986/, pp. 3–4).

*   *   *

The Deserted Body: The Union with the Revered *Otherness*

Anne Brontë's further engagement with the theme of *Death* unfolds in the individual's search for a remedy against the carnal frets of man's body – a problem that man's Spirit, or man's Mind has to face. There is an urge towards self-observation, which reaches a peak when the Lyrical Self's soul abandons its material case, as the body is considered to be the less relevant part of the integrity of one's identity. The poet is hoping that the spirit would manage to document the moment of this transition towards a better life and towards a place where the Mourner could join the missing Other – the crucial component of his/ her disjoined self – the Mother, and later – Christ. From a biographical perspective, the years 1840–1842 were for Anne Brontë rather solitary. She would see her sisters only twice a year (in December and January, and then in June and July). In her new post as a governess to the Robinsons (1840–1845) she felt rather isolated (Cf Chitham, 1979, pp. 6, 11).

In her poems of the period 1840–1842 Anne Brontë strives towards liberation and towards achieving a spiritual form of being. Yet unlike, say, Shelley, she aims not at making the mind become „*one piece with the underlying reality of things*", she wishes not to „*merge with the spirit of Nature for a fuller existence*"[vii]. Sinisterly, the Lyrical Self in Anne Brontë's poem **Retirement** (13th December 1840, Chitham, 1979, p. 77) plans to rend her physical frets asunder, as she hopes for an existence with „*no human form nigh*":

O, let me be alone a while,
No human form is nigh.
And may I sing and muse aloud,
No mortal ear is by.

Away! Ye dreams of earthly bliss,
Ye earthly cares begone:
Depart! Ye restless wandering thoughts,
And let me be alone!

One hour, my spirit, stretch thy wings,
And quit this joyless sod,
Back in the sunshine of the sky,
And be alone with God!

Among the Brontës, this introspective practice of the spirit separating from the body has almost become a patent of Emily Brontë's, who goes further than both Anne and Charlotte. In Emily's poetic vision, the body surely feels like physical incarceration to the spirit[10]. Religious in its tone of voice, this hymn of Anne Brontë's delivers the idea of „rejection of the earthly bliss" as possibly „earthly love" (Cf Chitham 79, p. 172). It expresses the poet's disillusionment with the dim and dull existence on earth in a broader sense. The poem declares the Lyrical Self's reverence for the One Being – for God – the criterion against which man should „measure" his/her worthiness. The metaphor in the last stanza of the poem

---

[10] Compare Emily Brontë's poem *I am happiest when most away* (around 1838). In Emily Brontë's works the separation of the spirit from the body is usually accompanied by the certain natural phenomena, which complement the spirit, like, the WIND:

I am happiest when most away
I can bear my soul from its home of clay
On a windy night when the moon is bright
And the eye can wander through worlds of light –

When I am not and none beside –
Nor earth nor sea nor cloudless sky –
But only spirit wandering wide
Through infinite immensity.

(*„Bask in the sunshine of the sky,/ And be alone with God"*) suggests the ritual of ablution, of christening anew, of purification of spirit and body[11]. In Anne's further works, the individual continues dreaming about quitting the joyless World with the desire to restore the age of childhood, which is when the spirit was seen to partake of the altruism and benevolence that the family possessed and used as a shield against the hostile world outside[12].

In the already quoted poem *Retirement* one could also sense man's exhaustion with the constant efforts to try and adjust oneself to the ever changing, inconstant and therefore hostile life of the *here and now*. There is a desire to quit this life of unfinished thoughts and words, of frequent misinterpretations of one's character by someone else (whose task and privilege and curse it is to carry the memory of what one once was). The anticipation of Death is therefore the anticipation of the self's completion, of the self's uniqueness, which happens at the moment when one ceases to be, so that one's achievements and failures take shape. What William Hazlitt might have replied to the above is that *„(…) we are torn from ourselves piecemeal while living; (…) and death only consigns the last remnant of what we were to the grave"*[viii].

Anne Brontë perceives Death as an opportunity for subtler self-cognition, because if the planned separation of body and spirit is accomplished successfully, then the spirit is given the chance to observe the body's behaviour from outside. Such relationship between the spirit and the body mimics the relationship between one man and another man. The young poet is being lead by a kind of reductionism, which makes her dissect the whole in order to see the parts. It appears that the phenomenon

---

[11] Anne Brontë's determination to follow God through Death, to be reborn and rectified through accepting his benign influence invokes the following lines form John Donne's *Holy Sonnet #10*: *„Batter my heart, three-personed God; /…/ o'erthrow me, and bend/ Your force, to break, blow, burn, and make me new. /…/ But I am betrothed unto your enemy, / Divorce me, untie, or break that knot again ,/ Take me to you, imprison me, for I/ Except you enthrall me, never shall be free, / Nor ever chaste, except you ravish me"* (quoted from: Donne, John, *A Critical Edition of the Major Works*, edited by John Carey /Oxford & New York: Oxford University Press, 1990, pp. 177–178). In some of Anne's mature works the Lyrical Speaker appears to be more than ready to bear God's sentence, as she worships His omniscience and universal power (compare, for instance *Despondency – 1841, In Memory of a Happy Day in February – 1842, A Hymn – 1843, Confidence – 1845*).

[12] See especially Anne's poem *Memory* (May 29th 1844, Chitham, 1979, pp. 101–103).

of Death, quite like the phenomenon of language, could be extremely analytical (Cf Kearns, Katherine, *Nineteenth-Century Literary Realism. Through the Looking-Glass* /Cambridge University Press, 1996/, p. 159). Death analyses and may eliminate any remnant of the carnal case of the Self, everything that signified the link between physical nature and man's own physics. What Death cannot eliminate for sure is that aspect of the existence of the Self, which is secured by the *Otherness* man depends on (and carries within oneself whilst alive). Anne Brontë's young Lyrical Self hopes very much to be able to continue in a more devout and worthwhile way in the after life. As might be expected, she unconsciously ascribes the characteristics of a better and more perfect world of *here and now* to that longed for reality in heaven. And the *here and now* are only accessible through the body, whose proper functioning guarantees participation in reality. Ironically, Death is the one moment, which is not accessible to one as an experience of reality[ix]. And the reality man is hoping for in the after life does not guarantee the familiarity of physical substance (which is an element essential to the wholeness of man's consciousness).

The phenomenology of Death looks more complex in view of the fact that Death does not exist in a tangible way neither for the observer, i.e. for the Mourner, nor for the dying individual. In the first case, despite the ontological burden it lays upon the Mourner, Death remains external and distant because of the Mourner's capacity to perceive it as an objective fact through his/ her consciousness, which works so long as one is alive. And in the second case, Death is elusive because the capacity to perceive it physically and philosophically – i.e. through one's consciousness – vanishes at the moment the human being expires physically (Cf Bakhtin, M. M., *Sobranie sotchinenij. tom 5. Rabotij 1940 – natchala 1960 godov.* Moskva: „Rousskie slovari". 1996, pp. 347–348). Accordingly, instead of indulging in fanciful speculations about dying, Anne Brontë chooses to create one lyrical persona proper, whose task is to experience Death in truth. This central lyrical persona of Anne Brontë's poetry carries – in a responsive and responsible manner – the memory of the deceased, of the person who is no more, which is the only way the living one could become aesthetically complete (Bakhtin, AIG, 2003, pp. 179–181). In the pair *Mourner: Dead* **the Mourner** (the living one) is the central lyrical persona in Anne Brontë's aesthetics (traceable in her contribution to the

125

Gondal saga too). It is the Mourner who <u>projects in the future his/her own</u> <u>death, the one who outlives, mourns, and reveres the deceased one</u>. The <u>deceased one, respectively, could also be termed *the missing lyrical* *persona* (namely: the mother, the husband, Christ, the soul's companion)</u> <u>– or the so called *Other*</u>. <u>Anne Brontë's ethics can then be seen as</u> <u>contained in the *mourning for the Other*[13]</u>.

In this second period of Anne Brontë's poetic development, the most prominent motif is <u>the death of the individual's **Mother**</u>. In the poem *An Orphan's Lament* (January 1st 1841, Chitham, 1979, pp. 78–79), at first, the lyrical speaker (again most probably Alexandrina Zenobia Hybernia, whose initials – A. H. – appear after the poem to confirm its Gondal context, which is also seen in the use of the toponyms of the imaginary Angora and Exina) expresses her quiet joy at the fact that her mother's toils on earth are finally over. Yet she soon realizes that the loss of her mother is irreparable and so the world will always be an empty place for her. Alexandrina finds herself divested of her potential to bestow her love on another human being and thus to be a wholesome personality:

> *(…)*
> *And thou couldst feel for all my joys*
> *And all my childish cares*
> *And never weary of my play*
> *Or scorn my foolish fears.*
>
> *Beneath thy sweet maternal smile*
> *All pain and sorrow fled,*
> *And even the very tears were sweet*
> *Upon thy bosom shed.*
>
> *Thy loss can never be repaired;*
> *I shall not know again*

---

[13] In Bakhtin's aesthetics the relationship between *mourner* and *deceased* is projected in the relationship between *Author* and *Hero* (the Author being the one to outlive, to precede and succeed, to *own* the fate of the character, whose limited existence and fate become the subject matter of a work of fiction/ poetry).

While life remains, the peaceful joy
That filled my spirit then.

Where shall I find a heart like thine
While my life remains to me,
And where shall I bestow the love
I ever bore for thee.

The tears the Lyrical Self sheds here are not merely inspired by
„*childish grief*", which is „*only for a day*". In her refusal to forget her
mother, Alexandrina declares that the only way to live is to *share: to share
one's life* with an *Other*. Her life was blessed with her mother's omniscient
protective presence, love and generosity of soul, and there is the natural
wish to continue this positive relationship between Author/ Authority and
creation/ child in the after life. Alexandrina dreams of receiving the
Eucharist in building up, once more, the intimacy between herself and the
mother, who could bridge the gap between various portions of Time,
between familiar and the unfamiliar, between the obvious and the hidden,
and at last between the mighty (i.e. God) and the subjective (Cf Eagleton,
2003, pp. 58, 121). As stated earlier, in Anne Bronte's philosophy, <u>the
mother, being a most essential part of the dreamed-for after life, in fact
epitomises the sublime</u>[14]. The Lyrical Self's involvement with this *Other*
person's death is highly emotional, it contains a hidden task Anne Brontë
poses to the living. Namely: „*how can we redeem our own past, in order*

---

[14] In his analysis of the principle of Einfühlung (or empathy), Bakhtin argues that **the mother's
death** shutters the process of self-definition, which starts for one as early as the moment of birth.
From the moment of birth one gets initiated into the benevolent and unselfish care of the mother,
who is also the first Other, through whose eyes the child begins to get awareness of the world. The
mother's death is the moment of utter spiritual deprivation for one (Cf Bakhtin, AIG, 2003, p. 179;
Cf Clark & Holquist in: Clark & Holquist, *Pro et Contra…*, 2002, p. 48). There is another, more
immediate and readily available angle of looking at the above problem, which angle, however,
appears to me somehow superficial and less feasible within the complexity of Anne's philosophy of
the Other. And that would be to interpret the issue of the loss of the mother through the optics of
psychoanalysis, which reveals that for the Super-I to emerge, one needs to overcome, to forget the
feeling of childish dependence on the parent, whose behaviour the child tends to mimick. (Cf
Sigmund Feud, in: Passi, I., 1992, p. 177). Or, that the loss of the mother is a biological necessity:
„matricide is a condition sine qua non for one's individuation" (Kristeva, J., *Black Sun…*, 1999, p.
37).

to be more worthy of the future whose ethical basis should be the memory of the life of the deceased Other?". The poet's own ethical maturation shows in that the lyrical personae begin to more persistently evaluate the Present in comparison to, and *only in comparison* to the Past, which is what Christ's sacrificial presence dictates to the individual. In Heidegger's terms, Being is possible, is unlocked, is made open only through the analytics of Presence, which involves a positive appropriation of the Past, of recognizing one's duty to the memory of an *Other* (Cf Heidegger, SUZ, 1997, p. 21). In Levinas' terms, the *Other's Being* precedes any debate about the independence of one's mind. With no *Otherness* available, man's individuality appears absurd, the subject „looses its balance" and is no more (Cf Levinas, *Totalité et Infini*, 2000, p. 359; Levinas, [in Russian] *Vremia I Drugoi*, 1998, p. 69).

With the commencement of her new position as a governess to the Inghams at Blake Hall in 1839, Anne Brontë's religious convictions would have been exposed to the eye of the public. She was now expected to educate – in piety as well as in everything else – two rather difficult to handle young characters in the puritan family that happened to be her new employer (Cf Chitham, 1997, p. 58). The Rev. Patrick Brontë's adherence to Methodist ideas would have already poured into Anne's mind the notions of equality in the chances of happiness for each person, the desire to defend of the poor and a firm belief in following Christ's quietist and non-remonstrative lifestyle. Such upbringing rejected frailty of spirit and sacrilege, to which man would easily yield, if left to his/ her own devices[15]. In her poetry of 1841 and onwards Anne Brontë demonstrates that during the time she spent on her own and, most probably, in consideration of her own worthiness of being, there must have formed in her mind a feeling of awe of *the* supreme Being of Christ. The poet now believes that the awareness of Christ's lifetime example could serve as litmus, which could verify the strength of man's faith and could justify one's place amongst the many. There begins to lurk a kind of fear of Death, and the poet manoeuvres the current of her thought towards *the Sublime*[x] (in the sense of a thematic focus on the grandeur of Christ's miraculous life, rather than

---

[15] On 17th April 1837 the Rev. Patrick Brontë wrote to the editor of the *Leeds Intelligencer* (on the occasion of the Poor Law Amendment Bill): „(...) I see no plan better for us than that adopted by the Apostles, (...) to obey God, rather than man" (as quoted in: Barker, 1997, p. 51).

on a preoccupation with the sublime in Natural phenomena). Hence the increasing number of hymns in Anne's poetry.

The feeling of guilt arises in the Lyrical Self as she tends to remember more often the many sins, which accumulate – despite her attempts to uproot the deviant and the evil in her soul. Many times has she „*vowed to trample on [her] sins*", considering her future lot in the after life. She has no idea whether she would be granted any more power over Time, even if she did overcome the restrictions of her own body, which is doomed to expire at the moment of her actual death. Would she represent anything substantial after she expires physically?

(…)
And yet, alas! How many times
My feet have gone astray,
How oft have I forgot my God,
How greatly fallen away!

My sins increase, my love grows cold,
And Hope within me dies,
And Faith itself is wavering now,
O how shall I arise!

I cannot weep, but I can pray,
Then let me not despair;
Lord Jesus, save me lest I die,
And hear a wretch's prayer.

(From **Despondency** – 17th December 1841, Chitham, 1979, pp. 80–81.)

I think that the lines in bold type illustrate that at this stage the individual in Anne Brontë's poetry is still struggling to overcome her ego. This seems to be the reason why she tends to relate the idea of Death to the reward/pardon Christ the Redeemer may, or may not, bestow upon her personally. She has still not reached her mature interest in Christ as the ultimate source of humanity's well being taken as a whole. Nonetheless, there lurks the Evangelical vision of Life as a journey road towards self-formation and self-improvement, the last and innermost stage of which is the moment of Death, which confirms the individual's status by rewarding his/her merits/features accordingly. The plentitude of verbs of motion throughout the poem indicate at this image of traveling, of progressing, of evolving *(e.g. „gone backward", „rouse", „raised hands",/ „trample /on my sins/", „wander back again", „/my feet/ have gone astray", „fallen away", „/Faith itself/ is wavering", „/how shall/ I arise")*. In this regard, it would be appropriate to notice the abundance of verbs of motion in Anne's poetic heritage – even in the most reflexive and statically introspective poetic pieces of hers, which hints at the poet's vision of Life as something developing, evolving, whose ingredients actively relate to one another and dialogize.

In the next poem in Chitham's edition, ***In Memory of a Happy Day in February*** (February–November 10ᵗʰ 1842, Chitham, 1979, pp. 82–83), the Lyrical Self strives to appropriate and personalize Christ's image, again, by reflecting on his significance in relation to her own future death – the moment which would finally and unequivocally verify her own worthiness as a human being. She would have that knowledge sooner than she would belong a little more to the living lot, who would, ironically, be charged with the task to bear the memory of her life and death:

> *(…)*
> *And while I wondered and adored*
> *His wisdom so divine,*
> *I did not tremble at his power,*
> *I felt that God was mine.*
>
> *I knew that my Redeemer lived,*
> *I did not fear to die;*
> *I felt that I should rise again*
> *To immortality.*

Christ appears to be exclusively the One *Other* whom the Lyrical Self wishes to join in spirit (the second stanza specifies that she is an orphan). Certain taste for Calvinism is felt in the Lyrical Self's urge to discover marks of chosenness: that she belongs to the elect, whom God has praised with a

„glimpse of truths divine/ Unto my spirit given/ Illumined by a ray of light/ Than shone direct from Heaven!". Christ is that element in the concept of the Holy Trinity that Anne Brontë's poetry has explored most, which suggests her faith that the Holy Trinity has a human face.

It seems that in the above few poems discussed Anne Brontë is also trying to examine the idea of whether once suffering is acknowledged by an external referee redemption really becomes likelier. One's acknowledgement of one's own sinfulness is a good reason to strive for redemption. Professor Terry Eagleton's view of Christ's redemptive example poses an intriguing question mark over a categorical treatment of Anne Brontë's proneness to some Calvinism (observable in the poems above). In his book *Sweet Violence. The Idea of the Tragic* (Blackwell 2003) he argues that it is ironic that *„once suffering is conceived in this instrumental or consequentialist way, it ceases to be redemptive, (…) it ceases to be a gift when one is thinking of a return. This is another reason why Jesus's crucifixion is genuinely tragic. If his death was a mere device for rising again in glory (…) then it was no more than a cheap conjuring trick. It was because his death seemed to him a cul-de-sac, (…) that it could be fruitful"* (Cf Eagleton, 2003, p. 37). Anne Brontë's later poetry (especially from 1843 onwards) demonstrates a shift towards actually exploring the philosophical impact Christ's atoning death has had on man's conscience. What I mean is the conscious and actively responsive memory of the Past and therefore of *Others* (through the image of Christ) as an approach to Life Now. Anne Brontë's vision grows more apocalyptic as her inner doubts and self-criticism oust the earlier hubristic urge towards self-sufficient introspection[16]. On the whole, her mature works are dominated by more socially oriented overtones; the poet begins to question the Calvinist belief in the value of Death as the moment of dividing the human lot into *elect* versus *doomed/reprobate*.

---

[16] Rather useful and relevant here appears Northrop Frye's perception of the image of Christ as he offers us that in *The Great Code. The Bible and Literature* (London & Melbourney Henley: Routledge & Kegan Paul, 1982). Fry writes: *„the apocalyptic vision, in which the body of Christ is the metaphor holding together all categories of being in an identity, presents us with a world in which there is only one knower, for whom there is nothing outside of or objective to that knower, hence nothing dead or insensible. This knower is also the real consciousness in each of us"* (Cf Frye, 1982, p. 166).

* * *

The Doubt in Receiving Justified Pardon with Death

– What? In this universe,
Where the least control the greatest, where
The faintest breath that breathes can move a world;
What! Feel remorse, where, if a cat had sneezed,
A leaf had fallen, the thing had never been –
Whose very shadow gnaws us to our vitals?
*(*From William Wordsworth's *The Borderers – III, V. ll. 83–88.)*[xi]

From around 1843 Anne Brontë's poetry begins to demonstrate unhidden criticism for the idea of pre-destination as for a principle in accordance with which pardon at Death may be bestowed upon the sinner. She questions the foundations of the Heavenly institute, on whose doctrines Man's moral system is traditionally considered to be based. The poet finally acknowledges the defects of the individual's own doubting nature, his inability to categorise Death in a non-positivist, based-on-faith manner only. The Methodist beliefs Anne Brontë was brought up with surely had an impact on the poet's interest in the social dimensions of the image of God and of his power. Without frustrating the hypothesis about God's infinite potential to rescue and save, Anne Brontë examines purposefully the redemptive capacity of Death as a threshold to holiness[xii]. Anne Brontë's own biography abounds in examples of what one would categorize as an unjustified, or unnecessary, loss of people very dear to her. A major point of argument is that one might not have lived a devout life, from which it does not automatically follow that one's attitude to Life has been entirely unholy. Anne tries to accommodate the latter reflections within a broader, Universalist understanding of God's love for humanity[17]. Naturally, there is a

---

[17] On 30th December 1848, shortly after her sister Emily's death, Anne Brontë writes to the Rev. David Thorn of Edge Hill in Liverpool that she adheres to the doctrine of Universal Salvation: „(…) *I drew it secretly from my own heart not from the word of God that any other held it. And since then it has ever been a source of true delight to me to find the same views either timidly suggested or boldly advocated by benevolent and thoughtful minds; and I now believe there are many more believers than professors in that consoling creed. (…) We see (…) how little the dread of future punishment – how still less the promise of future reward can avail to make them*

swerve towards the religious context and considerations of treating the phenomenon of Death. Death is the one event in man's Life which Christianity sees as directly modified by social behaviour, the most immaculate and example of which appears to have been Christ's altruistic sacrificial attitude of *Care for the Other.*

In the poem *To Cowper*[18] (10th November 1842, in: Chitham, 1979, pp. 84–86) the Lyrical Self starts with a somewhat innocent confidence in God's just criterion, as he possesses the power to rescue those dearest to her. Yet even the phrases, which confirm God's benevolence, are moulded as questions, there is a hidden interrogation of the verity of his altruism: „*if God is love*", or „*Is He the source of every good, / The spring of purity?*". She is gradually seized by doubts as to the purpose of an avowal in piety and of striving for Heaven, as she realises that person dear to her and righteous has, like many others before, simply disappeared for good. And that she, too, may well be rejected by God, since she considers herself to be less than what Cowper was:

> *(…)*
> *Yet should the darkest fears be true,*
> *If Heaven is so severe*
> *That such a soul as thine is lost,*
> *O! how shall I appear?*[19]

The Lyrical Self's confidence is shattered, as she supposes that a Life of virtue, poetic perfection (Cowper) and Love may be treated in the same ruthless manner by God as He would treat a sinner's life, which may be abbreviated immediately. Reciprocally, the most categorically confirmed sinner deserves peace in the after life, which is why Helen Graham pleads

---

forbear and wait; and if so many thousands rush into destruction with (…) the prospect of Eternal Death before their eyes, – what might not the consequence be, (…)" – as quoted in: Barker, 1997, pp. 220–221. Anne Brontë expresses hereby her concern for people's misinterpretation of God's benevolence. She is genuinely frightened by the number of people who claim to believe, rather than profess, the principles of Christianity, and are thus left unharmed to impose their unrestrained free will on others.

[18] To Anne Brontë the poet William Cowper was a figure of poetic reverence as the author of some exemplary hymns (Cf Chitham, 1979, p. 175).

[19] Compare also Emily Brontë's poem *Death, that struck when I was most confiding* (10th April 1845, Hatfield, 1941, pp. 224–225).

for God to save her husband, Arthur Huntingdon, whose wretched character leads him to physical disease and spiritual dissolution (Cf *The Tenant of Wildfell Hall*). To Anne, the more significant proof of one's worthiness to receive divine mercy seems one's true faith in what Jesus' death means for humanity (rather than just an ostensibly and demonstratively pious lifestyle as the one criterion for receiving pardon at the moment of Death). She trusts that the Universalist belief in redemption would yield better results in developing human awareness than would the elitist philosophy of election, as encouraged by Calvinism. Other mature poetic examples in support of the above arguments include: *Confidence* (1st June 1845 – Chitham, 1979, p. 114), and *Song* (3rd September 1845 – Chitham 1979, p. 121). Universalism urges man to look ahead into the Future through the Past, which is a Past based first and foremost on Christ's lifetime example sealed by his own death. Only a sober and responsive awareness of the value of Christ's death could justify the existential burden that the Present lays on one. This awareness presupposes empathy towards what happened, as well as towards what may happen, but most importantly – towards what is happening Now, which is the only time each man actually possesses to prove his/ her worthiness as a human being:

> *(…)*
> *That none deserve eternal bliss I know:*
> *Unmerited the grace in mercy given,*
> *But none shall sink to everlasting woe*
> *That have not well deserved the wrath of Heaven*
> *(…)*
> *… when the cup of wrath is drained,*
> *The metal purified,*
> *They'll cling to what they once disdained*
> *And live by him that died.*

(From *A **Word** to the Calvinists* – 28th May 1843, *in:* Chitham, 1979, pp. 89–90.)[20]

---

[20] See especially Edward Chitham's views on the relation between the universalism in Anne Brontë's novel *The Tenant of Wildfell Hall* and the poem *A Word to the Elect* (same as *A Word to the Calvinists*) in: Chitham, 1979, p. 176.

Anne Brontë expresses her strong doubts as to the adequacy of a very early implantation of the sense of fear of death. She is also hesitant about the appropriateness of the notion of reprobation, which destines man to eternal punishment. To Anne, Death is the final point which verifies a lifetime's worthiness, yet during a lifetime the notion of the End ought to be embraced spontaneously and consciously – as a stimulant for assiduity in assisting unselfishly *Others,* rather than perceived unquestionably as the great threat decreed by the Almighty[21].

On the one hand, Anne's faithfulness to the Christian belief in universal salvation solidifies the image of Christ as the ultimate trustworthy friend and Authority, indeed, as the ultimate Author (as, for instance, in the poem *Music on Christmas Morning,* in: Chitham, 1979, pp. 96–97). Yet poems like „*I will not mourn thee, lovely one"* – *December 1842* (in: Chitham, 1979, pp. 87–88) give substance to the thought there lurks the uncertainty about the relevance of a fixed system of judgement on Life, particularly in view of the numerous examples of young and fruitful personalities unjustly deprived of their lives by „stern death". Really, though, what the Lyrical Self cannot overcome is only a natural uncertainty about the claim that living with the awareness of Christ's redemptive death is a sure guarantee for salvation at Death[22]. The collision between hubris and empathy in one's mind shows every time when one comes across another individual who is morally and spiritually superior. The relativity and uncertainty in one's attitude to *the Absolute* makes the absolute relative. Overall, however, Anne Brontë's interpretation of Christ's death

---

[21] To Ellen Nussey Anne Brontë writes: „*I long to do some good in the world before I leave it. I should not like to have lived to little purpose"* (Raymond, E. 1949, *Exiled and Harassed Anne,* quoted in: McNees, El. 1996, vol. IV, pp. 103–104, p. 110).
[22] In comparison, in her Belgian Essay *The Butterfly* (11th August 1842), Anne's sister Emily writes: „*It is true that there is a heaven for the saint, but the saint leaves enough misery here below to sadden him even before the throne of God"* (Lonoff, Sue, *Charlotte Brontë. Emily Brontë. Belgian Essays,* translated from French by Sue Lonoff /Yale University Press, 1996/, pp. 176–178). Similar is the sounding of Felicia Hemans' poem *The Coronation of Inez de Castro 1828* (in: Feldman 2000, pp. 303–305):

(…)
Death! Death! Canst thou be lovely
Unto the eye of Life?
Is not each pulse of the quick high breast
With thy cold mien at strife?
(…)

insists on his eternally valid and unconditional good and altruism[23]. Altruism *is* an attitude, which should, if possessed in earnest, reject negativity (which is what hubris in effect contains). This attitudinal good is only possible through a desire to bestow the positive potential of one's lifetime experience upon another human being. And the ultimate moment of drawing the aftermath, of evaluating the amount of good in a lifetime, really is Death (Cf Levinas, 2000, pp. 87–88) – the moment of non-optional transference of the personality of the deceased upon the Survivor. The task of each such Survivor, each such Successor, is to implant the memory of the deceased one into a responsible approach to the living *Others* who constitute one's space and time on earth.

The constant anticipation of Death in Anne Brontë's poetry raises the phenomenon of Death to the status of an integrative part of everyday life, and so Death is seen as possessing the capacity to put meaning in perspective (Cf Eagleton, 2003, pp. 269–270). There emerges the recognition of the need to appropriate Christ's sacrificial example in one's own limited lifespan, which accounts for a straightforward trust in the undeniable benevolence of heavenly bliss (*„A shield of safety o'er my head,/ A spring of comfort in my heart"*), which is expected to descend upon man at the moment of one's expiration. On the other hand, Anne's poetry exhibits the rationalist disbelief in the existence of an after life and of its redemptive rescuing power over the world of the living. In the *A Hymn* – 10th September 1843 (Chitham, 1979, pp. 91–92) the Lyrical Self is crying for Faith (*„O give me – give me Faith"* – stanza III), which, she is not sure she has. The contents of this poem amalgamates well both of the above mentioned tendencies to interpret the role and the image of God in examining the theme of Death:

(…)
If this be vain delusion all,
If death be an eternal sleep,
And none can hear my secret call,
Or see the silent tears I weep.

---

[23] That is why the poem *Music on Christmas Morning* expresses the hope that Christ's birth was expected to *„rescue Earth from Death and Hell"* and that there is the *„sinless God"* who descends to *„sinful men"* (Cf Chitham, 1979, p. 96).

(…)
O drive these cruel doubts away
And make me know that thou art God;
A Faith that shines by night and day
Will lighten every earthly load.

If I believe that Jesus died
And walking rose to reign above,
Then surely sorrow, sin and pride

Must yield to peace and hope and love[24].
(…)

What Anne Brontë is really concerned about in this poetic period is whether the liminal value of Death could be made tangible[25]; whether there is a vivid proof (and that could only be a material proof) that there exists this Absolute Being, who would meet the hopes and expectations of the believer/ sinner. The Lyrical Self falls into the ontological trap of looking into the issue of Death first from the perspective of her own future expiration. This causes internal turmoil, which is additionally exacerbated by the individual's feeling of loneliness. Approaching Death from the point of view of the horror one's own future Death instills one with leads one towards a limited and immature perception of the phenomenon of Death as such. As mentioned earlier in this research, <u>Birth and Death are the two moments that are owned not by the immediate bearer of their physical happening, but by the external witness, by the Other, by the Survivor, for whom, and only for whom, one's death can become a fact and who keeps the golden key for its interpretation (Cf Bakhtin, AIG, 2003, p. 179).</u>

---

[24] Compare John Donne's *Holy Sonnet #I*: „*As due by many titles I resign/ Myself to thee, O God, first I was made/ By thee, and for thee, and when I was decayed/ Thy blood bought that, the which before was thine, / I am thy son made with thyself to shine, / Thy servant, whose pains thou has still repaid, / Thy sheep, thine image, and, till I betrayed/ Myself, a temple of thy Spirit divine;/ Why doth the devil then usurp in me? / Why doth he steal, nay ravish that's thy right? / Except thou rise and for thine own work fight, / Oh I shall soon despair, when I do see/ That thou lov'st mankind well, yet wilt not choose me, / And Satan hates me, yet is loth to lose me.*" – Cf Donne, in: (ed.) Carey, J., 1990, pp. 173–174.

[25] Compare Van Gennep's study over the rites of passage of the soul at Death – for the dying person, for the mourner, for the soul itself and for Christ (in: Wheeler, M. 1994, pp. 69–70).

*   *   *

Death: Self-Completion and Self-Denial

(...)
(...) 'Tis better too
To die, as thou art, young, in the first grace
And full of beauty, and so be remembered
As one chosen from the earth to be an angel;
Not left to droop and wither, and be bourne
Down by the breath of time.
(Percy Bysshe Shelley, from *Adonais – V. iii. 117–121.*)

Anne Brontë's poetic period of 1845–1847 could be interpreted as the last major „portion" of time when the poet moulds her attitude to the opportunities the phenomenon of Death presents to the Self. Again, Death is both alleviation of, and eventually salvation from, earthly misery and toil. Factually, Death confirms the degree to which one man has utilized his/her faith in existence shared with, dedicated to, *Other* human beings. This period also demonstrates rather well how vague seems the promise of self-completion and of reaching the ultimate meaning which man is hoping to find through one's own Death (Cf Eagleton, 2003, p. 115). There is a predicable temptation to believe that dying is a condition for achieving immortality[xiii], which indicates a thematic return to Anne's earlier desire to flee from Life's care, vice, and sin. What is most aggravating is when one is forced to observe passively how friendship decays in the grip of Life's hostility (see for instance the poem *O God! if this be all*, 20th May 1845– Chitham, 1979, pp. 111–112)[26].

In Anne Brontë's ballad „*Call me away...*" (24th January 1845, Chitham, 1979, pp. 107–109) the Lyrical Speaker laments the atmosphere of spiritual perfection, which she has lost possibly after the death of a dear

---

[26] One could draw a parallel between this work of Anne's and Felicia Hemans' *The Painter's Last Work, 1832* (Cf Feldman 2000, pp. 321–322), where the painter Francesco feels that „*this bitter world /.../ hath no voice/ To greet the heavenly spirit – that drives back/ All Birds of Eden, which would sojourn here/ A little while – /.../*". The painter's only hope for achieving earthly perfection is through his beloved Teresa.

friend, yet this atmosphere seems likely to restore through introspective withdrawal from the fleeting Present and into the ideal world of imagination and thought:

Call me away; there's nothing here,
That wins my soul to stay;
Then let me have this prospect drear
And hasten far away.

To our beloved land I'll flee,
Our land of thought and soul,
Where I have roved so oft with thee,
Beyond the world's control.

There appears a feverish youth, who stands in the midst of the blast adamant and passionate (quite like Emily's Heathcliff, with whom he bears some physical resemblance), who mourns his beloved (until she finally returns to him as a ghost and consoles him that she would always be near him):

(...)
With none to comfort, none to guide
And none to strengthen me.
Since thou my only friend has died –
I've pined to follow thee![27]
(...)

What escapes the gaze of both the Lyrical Speaker and the Youth in their outpourings is the awareness that, although it is possible to indulge in thoughts of future bliss after one quits this joyless world, one cannot live in the same way in the same World after one's own death has already become a fact. So that one could not verify the supposed satisfaction with the fact that one has gone into a better place. Death, as *a possibility of the absolute impossibility of Being*[28], is the possibility for the human mind's

---

[27] The notes to this poem (in: Chitham, 1979, p. 182) suggest a Gondal context and setting.
[28] Cf Derrida, 1998, p. 7.

expiation at the prospect of Non-being, rather than as a planned avoidance of the unknown the Future stores for one.

In the poem *Confidence* – 1st June 1845 (Chitham, 1979, p. 114), in a very orthodox way, the Lyrical Self yearns to ascend to Heaven and be translated there as the lamb's bride[xiv]. She „gives [herself] to [Christ]" (stanza VI); she knows she is „*prone to every sin*", but that the „*holy spirit*" will „*shine/ For ever on my heart*".

> (...)
> **With this polluted heart**
> I **dare** to come to Thee
> Holy and mighty as thou art;
> For thou wilt pardon me.
> (...)

In this brilliant hymn of Anne's, the realisation of one's own imperfection is followed by a firm trust in God's assistance. This is a prayer: the Lyrical Self is calling for help, she wishes to correct her nature and to strengthen her spirit through her belief in God's magnanimity and unconditional altruism. The latter is not something the Lyrical Self in Anne's poetry arrives easily at. In *The Three Guides* – 11th August 1847 (Chitham, 1979, pp. 144–152) – the individual revolts against the „ruthless eye" of two spirits – that of the Earth and that of Pride, who both leave people to their own nature[29]. As a contrast, the spirit of Faith, which epitomises God's benevolence, could help one find one's way back home, and to one's true self. Meekness, assiduity, strength in faith and internal peace is what this last Spirit offers the lyrical speaker as a cure for the deficiencies of her own faulty judgement[30]. By choosing to be guided by God, she chooses to be aesthetically moulded and lead by an *Other*, who would gladly be accepted to justify and complete her, and thus provide her life with meaning (Cf Bakhtin, AIG, 2003, pp. 180–181). One's own power

---

[29] The spirit of the Earth forces the poet to have her eyes directed „earthward" solely – towards „*trampled weeds, and miry clay, / And sand, and flinty stone*". It screens her view of Heaven and of God's beneficial influence on man.

[30] This must have been the only poem of Anne's (apart from certain poems in the joint edition of the three Brontë sisters' poetry of 1846) published in Anne Brontë's own lifetime in the *Fraser's Magazine* (Vol. 38, No 224, pp. 193–195) in August 1848 (Cf Chitham, 1979, p. 193).

over the fact that one is alive must be directed towards self-perfection, which necessarily presupposes the recognition of the significance of God, and of an *Other*.

As was mentioned earlier, the three Brontë sisters' poetry elevates *the Other* (not always directly present as an interlocutor/ participant in the events in a poem) to the status of a lyrical persona proper. This persona is what the poet hopes to implant in the reader's mind as an element active and ever present for one. This *Other* lyrical persona, whose proto-image is God (with his unconditional altruism), is the true link between people's lives. In a very Christian way, Anne Brontë sees that this image imparts meaning to Death, which thus becomes a phenomenon voluntarily recognized, rather than felt as externally imposed. So, although Death is unarguably destructive in its direct physical effect upon the living, yet it does appear to be an impetus for man to use in the best wholesome way the little time one is granted on earth. The purpose of Life is then to prove one's usefulness to others – something Death cannot really deny man, since the effects of an act of good should, ideally, outlive the doer of this act:

(…)
Death comes our labour to destroy
To snatch th' untasted cup away,
For which we toiled so many a day.
What then remains for wretched man?
To use life's comforts while he can;
Enjoy the blessings God bestows,
Assist his friends, forgive his foes,
Trust God, and keep His statutes still
Upright and firm, through good and ill –
Thankful for all that God has given,
Fixing his firmest hopes on Heaven;
Knowing that earthly joys decay,
But hoping through the darkest day.

(From *Vanitas Vanitatis Etc* – 4th September 1845 – Chitham 1979, pp. 123–124.)[31]

The moment of the Spirit's complete self-revelation and voluntary self-crucifixion, so to speak, is reached in the poem *Self-Communion* (*November 1847*–17th April 1848, Chitham, 1979, pp. 152–161). The poem is built in the form of a loosely constructed parable, in which the „pilgrim"/the Sinner/Man/the Lyrical Self is left to ruminate his life and several times enters into dialogue with God, who discerns reads man's worries and suggests answers to some of the most frustrating questions, which have been haunting the Sinner[32]. The Lyrical Self discerns signs of decay in man's brain and spirit, which are the result not merely of Time's degenerative influence over Man, but also of the actual „*toil, and truth*", which „*can freeze the generous blood of youth,/ And steel full fast the tender heart*" (imagery based on physical sensations, particularly to do with touching, feeling etc. is very common among the Brontës, which makes their references to Death appear strikingly relevant and physically feasible). The „pilgrim" complains that, gradually, the Self is beginning to „harden up", to develop a crust against emotional damage and starts accumulating „*foes within*". Being scared lest his spirit should perish in the atmosphere of spiritual abandonment, the „pilgrim" is also aware of the futility and absurdity of mourning the departure of his own spirit. The revelation, which descends upon the „pilgrim" towards the end of the poem, contains the idea that one could never really lose one's own Self: not like one may lose in the physical sense of the word another human being – the only even that does shatter one's ontological stability (Cf Bakhtin, AIG, 2003, p. 179). The grief over the imminence of one's own death is just as absurd as a wistful contemplation of one's ageing face in the mirror. One possesses no power over either of these two things, yet one has the power

---

[31] Anne Brontë suggests the Methodist concept of life as toil and work for the sake of Others as the only true way of self-completion – something evident quite early – in the already discussed poem *Verses by Lady Geralda* (*December 1836*, Chitham, 1979, pp. 49–51, see esp. lines 81–100).
[32] Consideration is given to the following: the youth's relentless decay; the formation of Memory through toil and pains on Earth and amongst Others; the child's spontaneous trust in God's omnipotence and protection which allows not for grief on Earth; early friendship's decay and loneliness of spirit; the incessant alternation of „Hope's rainbow" and the gloomy „clouds of saddening hue"; the elusiveness of earthly joys, etc).

to acknowledge that existence well justified implies time spent with the thought of, and in favour of, an *Other*, to whom one always owes an explanation:

(…)
Lo, strength and wisdom spring from grief
And joys behind afflictions lurk!
(…)
And my worst enemies, I know
Are those within my breast;
(…)
'There is a rest beyond the grave,
A lasting rest from pain and sin,
Where dwell the fruitful and the brave;
But they must strive who seek to win.
Show me that rest – I ask no more.
(…)
May I but land and wander there,
With those that I have loved and lost;
With such a glorious hope in view,
I'll gladly toil and suffer too,
Rest without toil I would not ask;
I would not shun the hardest task:
If God's approval they obtain.
(…)

The pilgrim seems to have absorbed God's words (spoken to him earlier), that he „*has much to do; –/ To lighten woe, to trample sin,/ (…) Dost thou indeed lament?/ Let not thy weary spirit sink;*" – and in the light of the knowledge that one is granted only a limited time to complete this task, the Task seems even more relevant and responsible. This Task is the Duty in the way Bakhtin sees Life to be – a Duty to the Past, but also a Duty to the Present[33]. To sum up, meaning in life is not measured

---

[33] One ought to summon courage even in the most grievous moments of one's life: to not let nostalgia paralyze his/her potential, but to necessarily assume the burden of one's Duty towards the Here and Now, which no one else can do for one. This Duty towards the World is the Duty to those deprived of

against being or non-being after Death – being and living themselves are built upon the meaning one accomplishes in one's lifetime – through one's duty to the Other (Cf Levinas, Emmanuel, [translated in Bulgarian] *Drougoiatche ot Bitieto, ili otvad Sashtnostta.* SONM. 2002, p. 189).

* * *

Dassein's Options, or Ontology through Eschatology

„Talk as we will of immortality, there is an obstinate feeling
that we cannot master, that we end in death;
and that may be felt together
with the firmest belief of a resurrection.
Brethren, our faith tells us one thing,
and our sensations tell us another.
When we die, we are surrendering in truth
all that with which we have associated existence."
(From *Sermons, Preached at Trinity Chapel, Brighton,*
Third series – 1857, by Frederick W. Robertson)[xv]

A group of Anne Brontë's mature poems „rounds off" her interest in Death as the liminal phase through which the true image of one's Self is confirmed. Again, the focus is on the moral boundaries the phenomenon of Death creates for the Mourner, as Death appears to be the one moment, which verifies the value and quality of a lifetime. There is a revision of the idea of Death as the furthermost point in the penitent's journey within the Christian system of ethics as dominated by God the Redeemer. This is done with an inclination towards introspective self-analysis, reaching at times self-chastisement. Anne Brontë's last poems show how her ontological awareness evolves alongside the developing conviction that the limitedness of man's existence contains the hidden blessing of man's life too (as bound to the life of *Others*, who are the true basis of each individual's self-revelation).

Life, which Life still contains only thanks to our dedication to them, thanks to the power and depth of our thought (Cf Manchev, Boyan, [in Bulgarian], *Ruini. Posvestenie* – na Jacques Derrida. Vestnik „*Kultura*" – 40/41. 29th October 2004, p. 5.

In *Parting Address from Z. Z. to A.E.* – 1ˢᵗ October 1845 (Chitham, 1979, pp. 125–126), one poem pertaining most probably to the Gondal saga, the Lyrical Self notes that *Being* is a composite of openly and non-hesitantly executed responses to the needs of Others (the friends, the beloved etc). That one's life is affected by the lives of others to whom one relates.

> *(…)*
> *And do not droop! However drear*
> *The fate awaiting thee.*
> *For my sake, combat pain and care,*
> *And cherish life for me!*
> *(…)*
> *Fear not for me – I've steeled my mind*
> *Sorrow and strife to greet,*
> *Joy with my love I leave behind,*
> *Care with my friends I meet.*
> *(…)*
> *I love my mother, I revere*
> *My sire, but doubt not me.*
> ***Believe that Death alone** can tear*
> *This faithful heart from thee.*

There is no more the early poetic strife to reject Death as the sure imminent cessation of one's conscious life. The fear of Death seems to have been transformed into an impetus to act devotedly upon the realisation that such fear may only paralyses man's ability to empathise[xvi]. The fear of Death tends to unlock man's inclination towards self-pity and self-satisfaction, which in itself put frets on the personality's chances for self-expression and self-fulfilment. In this confessional poetic work of Anne's, the declaration of the woman's love and faithfulness to her beloved shall withstand the ravages of Time, as well as the parents' disapproval It is the beloved, *i.e. the Other*, who indeed justifies her Being as Co-Being: he makes her life an event.

At this stage, it is already clear that Anne Brontë is convinced in that the possibility of salvation, which Death carries for man's weary spirit, is granted one only after an unselfish projection of one's identity beyond one's own needs – whilst one serves *other people*, who represent Life for one (for instance see the poem *Power of Love* – 13th August 1846 – Chitham, 1979, pp. 134–135). It is those very *Others* who could help one „*burst [Despair's] bounds asunder*" and „*defy his deadliest frown*", and could aid one cast away pain and grief and hold „*mighty Death at bay*." It is only after the soul „*grasps the thorn*", that it is entitled to „*crave the rose*"; one „*crushes pride into the dust*", „*seeks not [his] treasure here*", but labours on, loves and endures. The soul that stumbles along the „*upward path*" does recognize that *Otherness* is the moral imperative each man should embrace, and the image of the *Other* is defined by *the First and Ultimate Other*, named God (see the poem „*Believe not those who say*" – 24th April 1848, Chitham, 1979, pp. 161–162). Further on, the poet professes that forgiveness in the first place, forgiveness as a preamble to any major undertaking in Life, acknowledges and solidifies one's bonding with the *Other*, who plays the main role in shaping up one's personality (whose confirmation and, so to speak, registration, is endorsed physically by Death).

Anne Brontë's last poem extant, „*A dreadful darkness closes in*" (7th January [1849] & 28th January 1849, Chitham, 1979, pp. 163–165), argues that one's life is evaluated by the earnestness, perseverance of faith and stoicism demonstrated by the person, who sadly, never lives long enough to see the fruit of one's efforts to maintain Life[34]. The „*dreadful darkness*" enshrouds the Lyrical Self's „*bewildered mind*", which anticipates Death, yet a prayer is born, in which she admits to her sinfulness and declares her desire to „*gather fortitude from pain*" (rather than to „*sin*" – Cf stanza I) and serve God, independent of the length of time allotted her:

(…)
Thus let me serve Thee from my heart
Whatever be my written fate,

---

[34] In a series of essays entitled *Table Talk* (1821–1824) William Hazlitt writes: „*If I had lived indeed, I should not care to die (…) I should like to leave some sterling work behind me*" (as quoted in: Priestman, Martin, *Romantic Atheism. Poetry and Freethought: 1780–1830* /Cambridge University Press, 1999/, pp. 247–251).

Whether thus early to depart
Or yet awhile to wait.

If thou shouldst bring me back to life
More humbled I should be;
More wise, more strengthened for the strife,
More apt to lean on Thee.

Should Death be standing at the gate
Thus should I keep my vow;
But, Lord, whate'er my future fate
So let me serve Thee now.

This is Anne's mature admission into the necessity of believing in God, which may be compared to Coleridge's claim that *„a world (…) in order to be a world (…) supposes a god – an infinite one – one not by participation, or union, but (…) absolutely infinite. – Now to conceive this is impossible – but to assume it is necessary*[cxvii]. Indeed, it is necessary to assume the existence of God, because one needs an impeccable example of moral perfection, of ontological props. God *is* for man the peak of imagined altruism and love – the only sure antidote against Death's ability to disperse Being into a myriad of elusive events (Cf Bakhtin, KFP, 2003, pp. 58–59). The awareness of God is for man a way of estimating the capacities and dimensions of one's identity, whose boundaries are physically determined by two moments: *natus est anno Domini…* (in Latin *„born in…"*) and *mortuus est anno Domini…* (in Latin *„died in…"*; Cf Bakhtin, AIG, 2003, p. 180). Anne Brontë maintains that from the aesthetic point of view, the awareness of Death encourages one to be magnanimous, to be an altruist. The physical dimensions of Death bear an ontological message too. For, each occasion of an individual's *Death* lays spiritual weight upon his/her life as an accomplished, finalized lifetime – because the latter is now open to be had by Others, by the Survivors, whose own being must actively contain the Past. And the availability of the Past is the basis for the ontological axiom of Co-Being, which is conditional upon man's conscientious decision to use it. Each Survivor's life partakes of this „line of repeated opportunities, in which to Act would mean to Act for the sake of an Other" (Cf Bakhtin, AIG, 2003, pp. 181–182).

* * *

By exploring the **themes of Mortality** Anne Brontë subjects man to an introspective analysis of the possibilities of a Self who is at first defined as solitary, alienated and spiritually repressed. Gradually, the perception of Being as Co-Being emerges upon the realization that the solitary and dejected individual must seek individuation through discovering the limits of existence as a Christian. Anne Bronte defends a conscientious acceptance of the Past, of the memory of Christ, whose lifetime example is indeed accessible to man as a rescue – through the knowledge of the purpose of his tragic death. In her early poetry Anne Brontë's interest in the theme of Death is linked to the theme of the decay of the mind – a problem exacerbated by the loss of a dear person. The later poetic works follow a more traditional analysis of the theme of Death in studying *„the purpose of man and of creation in the context of the Christian doctrine of temporal passage, of ethical meliorism"[35]* (Cf Ghnassia 1994, p. 212). It therefore seems quite natural that Anne Brontë would want to carry out a study of man's ontological development in relation to the study of Death as an ingredient of one's consciousness, of one's moral code, of one's ethos.

In Anne Brontë's early poetry the lyrical personae (Gondal)/ the Lyrical Self see Death as a kind of „aesthetic escape" from the ontologically burdening Present. Anne Brontë's mature verses sound rather more confessional, more devout: they cherish Death's redemptive imminence. Death provides a means to verify the level of fulfillment of one's Duty towards *the Other* – a Duty temporally defined, yet unavoidable. The emphatic presence of certain personae of the Gondal dramatic world in Anne's early poetry is gradually substituted by the more considerate confessional voice of a more experience individual, whose spiritual revelations and inner purgation the reader is invited to partake of.

---

[35] The word *meliorism* is understood as „*the belief that the world naturally tends to get better, and, especially, that this tendency can be furthered by human effort*" (Cf ed. Neufeldt, V. & Guralnik, D. B., *Webster's New World Dictionary* /Prentice Hall, 1989/, p. 845).

A thoughtful and sensitive individual is naturally afraid of being misinterpreted during one's Life. Here, this is evident in Anne's search for a spiritual authority that inhabits a world different to the world of the Present – a world that would follow on after an unbearable and spiritually impoverished Present, yet one that would retain certain features of the spiritually complete Past. This *world beyond*, or Life beyond, the reader is assured, contains those things most sacred to one – the family, and in particular, the mother, whose presence is sought as the props in the stability of one's own identity. One's desire to quit the boundaries of one's physicality, of one's own body, is meant as a step towards the longed for re-union with the deceased mother. The theme of the deceased beloved in Anne Brontë's poetry is not fully developed. Rather more powerfully versed and persuasive seems the yearning for a redemptive union with Christ.

The tone of voice of Anne Brontë's poetry from 1845 onwards becomes more self-analytical. The individual is increasingly tormented by the thought that the authenticity of one's nature, the feasibility of self-dependence become irrelevant in the absence of *an Other*, who imparts to the phenomenon of Death meaning, and in that way imparts meaning to the Survivor's own limited lifespan. There is readiness to fulfil one's duties to others diligently, and until the moment of Death, to sacrifice one's time and go through whatever toil life might make one face. Finally, the conclusion is reached that one's life does not yield to the temptation of self-validation, and that *the Other* is the only one with whom man may share happiness and misery and whose life, and therefore death, one can ascertain[36]. There is almost no trace of the Romantic taste for Death as hiding some possibilities for aesthetic perfection. Dying for the Romantic poet usually brings not redemption, it is not communal, because it lays emphasis on the doer in the act of departure from the world, rather than on the dialogic *Other* as the bearer of its effect. To the Romantics Death rather comfortably contains an opportunity for premature individuation, for becoming unique, which the individual is hoping to achieve whilst abandoning the falseness, fleetingness and superficiality of the world of the Present. To Anne Brontë, individuation is carried out with the thought of the moral and ethical limits, within which Death accommodates man's aspirations and ego[37]. The

[36] Cf Bakhtin, AIG, 2003, pp. 179–180.
[37] Cf Levinas, 2000, p. 81.

awareness of Death is a most crucial element in the formation of man's consciousness, which lasts until one's own physical death. However limited life it may have, man's consciousness is always and only supplied by, and ameliorated through, the awareness of the possibility of *the Other's* death. The knowledge that the Other's life has limits ought to teach the Survivor humbleness and forgiveness. Forgiveness inevitably crushes one's pride, as it presupposes solidarity with, and appreciation of, *the Other*, who for Anne Brontë reaches the level of canonization in the image of Christ. An interest in **Death,** which shows in the earnest consideration of the possibility of *someone else's death before your own death* (be that the mother's death – to be found in Anne Brontë's early poetry – or, at last Christ's death), is the key to a humane attitude to Life. This is what Anne Brontë's poetic heritage professes. The poetic genres *hymn, elegy* and *prayer* are the formal clothing to Anne's thematic preference for Mortality/Death.

NOTES:

[i] W. G. G. James in: Gregor, Ian, (ed.) *Reading the Victorian Novel: Detail into Form* (Vision, 1980), pp. 229–230.

[ii] Cf Ricoeur, Paul, *Soi-même...*, 2004, pp. 323–324.

[iii] Cf Gurko, Yelena, [in Russian] *Jacques Derrida. Dekonstruktzia.* Minsk. Ekonompress. 2001, p. 162.

[iv] Cf Hunter, J. P., *Before Novels: The Cultural Contexts of Eighteenth-Century English Fiction* (New York: W. W. Norton & Company, 1990), pp. 119–137.

[v] Cf Ousby, Ian, *Companion to Literature in English* (Wordsworth Reference, 1994), p. 118.

[vi] Cf Derrida, *Apories*, 1998, p. 87.

[vii] Cf Beach, Joseph Warren, *The Concept of Nature in Nineteenth-Century English Poetry* (New York: The Macmillan Company, 1936), p. 275.

[viii] McFarland, Thomas, *Romanticism and the Forms of Ruin. Wordsworth, Coleridge and Modalities of Fragmentation* (Princeton University Press, 1981), p. 16.

[ix] Cf Bolnoff, O.F., [translated in Russian], *Filosofia ekzistentzializma. Filosofia sustestvovania.* Sankt-Peterburg. Lan'. 1999, pp. 127–137.

[x] Cf Kiely, Robert, *The Romantic Novel in England* (Cambridge Massachusetts: Harvard University Press, 1972), p. 13.

[xi] As quoted in: Paley, Morton D., *Apocalypse and Millennium in English Romantic Poetry* (Oxford: Clarendon Press, 2003), p. 227.

[xii] Cf Harrison, G. E., *The Clue to the Brontës* (London: Methuen & Co. LTD, 1948), p. 13.

[xiii] Cf Kalchev, Ivan, *Metafizika na Smartta.* Sofia. Biblioteka „Nov Den" – 3, 1993, pp. 249 – 268.

[xiv] Cf Abrams, Meyer, *Natural Supernaturalism. Tradition and Revolution in Romantic Literature* (New York & London: W. W. Norton & Company, 1973), p. 46.

[xv] As quoted in: Wheeler, 1994, p. 30.

[xvi] Cf Ariès, 1993, p. 41.

[xvii] As quoted in: McFarland, Thomas, *Romanticism and the Forms of Ruin. Wordsworth, Coleridge and Modalities of Fragmentation* (Princeton University Press, 1981), p. 410.

Charlotte Brontë

We have our bodies in the Tomb,
Like dust to moulder and decay,
But, while they waste in coffined gloom,
Our parted spirits, where are they?
In endless night or endless day?

Buried as our bodies are
Beyond all earthly hope of fear?
Like them no more to reappear,
But festering fast away?
For future's but the shadow thrown
From present and, the substance gone,
Its shadow cannot stay![1]

The angle from which I have chosen to approach Charlotte Brontë's treatment of the theme of Mortality is one which challenges one firmly established understanding of her poetry as relevant solely within an Angrian context. The poet's attitude towards some of Angria's main personae is irregular, which could be observed in the specificities of the poet's attitude towards the life of some of Angria's main lyrical personae (like, for instance, Alexander Percy, Duke of Northangerland)[2]. Patrick Branwell Brontë's own zest, as a co-author, in creating Angria is known to have been one reason for the literary rivalry between brother and sister, in which certain personae would disappear and would subsequently be revived in accordance with one of the two co-author's efforts to establish his/ her philosophy of existence. It seems to me that this literary „flirtation" with the phenomenon of Death resulted in the characters' own perception of Life as an experiment, in which the Self's potentials are being formed continuously and incessantly subverted – somehow at the expense of evading the ontological duty towards *the Other*. At the same time, there is the Lyrical Self's constant self-chastisement, evident in the poet's preoccupation with

---

[1] Patrick Branwell Brontë: Lines (composed by Percy and transcribed and corrected on 11th March 1837) – Cf Winnifrith 1983, pp. 198–199.
[2] It should be remembered, that the format in which the Angrian poetic cycle is in possession of the reader nowadays (thanks to Tom Winnifrith's comprehensive 1984 edition of Charlotte Brontë's poetry) is only an extract of the whole of the dramatic prose cycle Charlotte and her brother Branwell called Angria. It is therefore just to note that the status of those 'lyrical personae' could be traced back to their origin as 'characters' in a prose fiction world, which was supplied with dramatic canvas.

the motif of *faith*. Charlotte Brontë's major prose fiction characters' frequent encounters with Death force them to embark very early (in the case of Jane Eyre and Lucy Snowe, as early as the age of childhood) on the inevitable journey towards ontological maturation. In her poetry, however, the Lyrical Self drags in pledging himself/ herself to another human being, through whom Life becomes meaningful. I think that the poet's authority over her lyrical personae is particularly easily detectable in the fact of the introduction of the so-called **ghost persona – the dead beloved/ „the silent Nun".** This persona seems to have been born out of the poet's feeling of necessity to spiritually „upgrade" an individual, who is exposed to the perilous superficiality of social equilibrium and mimicry, as well as to the destructive impact of the phenomenon of mutability and of the self-sufficiency of one's mind.

In Charlotte's poetry there are almost no traces of Anne Brontë's Evangelical piety or of Emily Brontë's stoical solitude in response to Death. Charlotte Brontë seems to have ceased composing verse earlier than her two younger sisters (by around 1844). On the one hand, the individual in Charlotte's poetry clings, it would appear, to God as to *the ultimate Other* (to His benevolence and altruism): there is a striving to achieve resurrection through spiritual perfection. Yet equally strong feels the individual's subjectivist urge to own Life exclusively through self-cognition, self-appraisal, through introspection during which the individual falls prey to the mortal trap of consciousness. The latter feeds the delusion that it is possible to enlarge the scope of a lifetime of self-content and self-admiration into an experimental existence beyond, based on separation from all and everything. The Lyrical Self emerges and is moulded not so much as subject to Fate, but as an Idea, as an embodiment of the poet's idea of the powerful Self. This Self evolves, continues, re-appears into the World anew and again: It is endless and indeterminable, which, according to Bakhtin's aesthetics, is typical for the Romantic lyrical persona (Cf Bakhtin, AIG, 2003, pp. 239–240). The Romantic persona, who acts „from within", in fact realises some necessary truth about Life, some proto-image of Man – somehow God's intention towards the human being. Charlotte Brontë's Survivor, the intellectual outcast, is a variation of the Romantic vagrant, strange, solitary genius. The moments of the life of such a Lyrical Persona, as well as his aspirations, find their transgredient definition in the form of symbolic stages, or phases, of the Author's/Poet's method of accomplishing his/ her major idea – in this case – the understanding that the Other (and the Other's Death) is the unarguable moral corrective for one. As a poet, Charlotte Brontë does yield to the romantic temptation to reflect upon the fate of her lyrical personae „from within". In the meantime, the lyrical persona seizes any definition of the Poet as being „transgredient", or „outside" the lyrical persona. Thus the Poet's own self-definition and evolution appears to be ongoing, endless (Cf Bakhtin, 2003, AIG, pp. 239–240).

The poet's insistence on the dominance of the *Ghost* above all other lyrical personae is one remedy against the individualistic tendency which I have chosen to explain above through Bakhtin's reflections on the „crisis of the Authorship" problem (one component of his discussion of the „*Author: Hero* relationship" in lyric poetry, and precisely, in the lyric poetry of the Romantic era). The *Ghost* plays the role of the one „*outside of me, whom I owe everything that I have inside*". The ghost does „stir" the life of the Survivor, bit it does remain a creature from the world beyond. Of that world one has no material evidence, since when one reaches it, one is not the same and one's consciousness is, most probably, no more, particularly if the *Other* (who is the true criterion for evaluating one's own identity) is not available there. As suggested earlier, this memorable sensuous epitome of the world beyond, which Charlotte Brontë cherishes, is also discovered, in the presence of the <u>*Nun – the deceased beloved – the female ghost – the dead muse*</u>, which many of her poems are centred round.

A few biographical details could throw light on some of the specificities of Charlotte Brontë's treatment of Mortality. Charlotte Brontë's last poems (including the undated ones – whose exact time of writing is a matter of speculation) go back to around 1844 – a time when significant poetic work – fine and mature – was still done (and lasted nearly until their deaths) by her sisters, Anne and Emily[3]. <u>Charlotte Brontë's poetic impulse seems to have been supplanted by a wish to write in prose, whilst</u>

---

[3] See, for instance, Anne's poem Self-Communion, 1847–1848, or „A dreadful darkness closes in" – 1849; or Emily's „Cold in the earth, and the deep snow piled above thee!" – 1845, or Julian M. and A.G.Rochelle – 1845, „No coward soul is mine" – 1846, or „Why ask to know the date – the clime?" – 1846.

considering the epic dimensions of Life: tracing the ontological growth of one man in relation to his/ her human milieu.

Curiously enough, the topics which Charlotte explored in the years 1836–1839, vary from those instilled with quietist overtones to those dominated by militant moods. The irregularities in the coherence of the dramatic structure of Angria hinder the critic's desire to employ a determinately chronological approach towards Charlotte Brontë's poetry. In addition, the Angrian dramatic cycle is not preserved in a thorough manner as to be truly indicative of the exact development of Charlotte Brontë's biographical involvement with the theme of Death in this context. Angria is a prose cycle of dramatic vignettes. It is the result of Charlotte and Branwell's literary partnership. Today, it can be found in a pack of novellas and stories, interspersed with poetry written by certain Angrian characters themselves.[4]. Some of the main characters were Branwell's invention, and were then developed by Charlotte. One such example is the riotous Alexander Percy, or Rogue – Viscount Ellrington and Duke of Northangerland, introduced by Branwell in 1831, while Charlotte was at Miss Wooler's school (Cf Winnifrith, 1984, p. xv; Cf Winnifrith, 1983, p. xix). It may, therefore, be necessary to refer to some of Branwell's poetic works – if and where appropriate. In 1837 Branwell reviewed his poetry and collected some of the Angrian poetic pieces in a poetic notebook. Reciprocally, Charlotte Brontë read through her poetry while she lived in Brussels (in the years 1842–1843). Many of Charlotte Brontë's poems are undated: they were written on loose leaves of paper, and were never conscientiously compiled in a poetic notebook. The ink smudges make some lines flow into one another, which prevents the critic from ascribing with certainty this or that verse to Charlotte Brontë (ibid.). Another immediate complication Tom Winnifrith discerned whilst preparing his 1983 edition of Branwell's poetry was that some poems had previously also

---

[4] The latter phenomenon is thoroughly examined by Victor Newfeldt, whose comparatively recent edition of Patrick Branwell's works is an attempt to recover the whole of the Angrian saga. This edition also tries to fit what was earlier considered as Branwell's singular poems within the logic of his dramatis personae's world. The edition in hand is: (ed.) Newfeldt, Victor, The Works of Patrick Branwell Brontë, in 2 volumes (New York and London: Garland Publishing Inc., 1999). I nonetheless cling to Tom Winnifrith's edition of Branwell's verse, which remained for a long time the first comprehensive guide to his poetry, namely (ed.) Winnifrith, Tom, The Poems of Patrick Branwell Brontë, for the Shakespeare Head Press, Basil Blackwell, 1983.

been ascribed to Emily Brontë (to whom Branwell was personally closer in real life than to any other of the three sisters; she was also the one to nurse him immediately before his death – Cf Winnifrith, 1983, p. xii). Also, when facing some unsigned manuscripts of Charlotte's poems, the possibility arises that they may be Branwell's, in which case thematic proximity with the rest of dated and signed poems, as well as coherence and legibility in writing and presentation have been the guiding motifs for categorizing some verse as part of Charlotte's writings (Cf Winnifrith, 1984, pp. x–xi).

Angria appears first in Charlotte's and Branwell's juvenile *The Young Men's Magazine*[5] – already a fact in 1829 (Cf Winnifrith, 1984, p. 80) and follows the lives of the ghostly personae of **Alexander Percy, Duke of Northangerland**, and his daughter **Marian Hume** – also wife of **Arthur Wellesley, Marquis of Douro, Duke of Zamorna**[6] (and later King of Angria). It is also the story about the charming but unscrupulous Lady **Augusta Romana di Segovia**, whose intention to eliminate her husband's father (i.e. Alexander Percy's father) is thwarted by her own death through poisoning, which is what makes possible Alexander Percy's further marriage to **Mary Henrietta Wharton** (Cf Du Maurier, Daphne, 1987, p. 60). Branwell decide to remove Mary, as he allotted her a lonesome and disgraceful end. Dared by her brother's literary boldness, Charlotte Brontë revived Mary again – openly and methodologically. She insisted that „Branwell's Author (Lord Richton) has only spread the rumour of her death in order to rouse the Angrians against Northangerland – their oppressor" (Barker, 1995, ch. 10). And although Mary was saved by Zamorna (who inspired Angrians to win victory), Mary

---

[5] The position and relationship among the participants of the Angrian story was determined as early as the Brontë children's juvenile plays. These are: Young Men (1826), Our Fellows (1827) and Islanders (1827) – Cf Gerin, Winifred, Charlotte Brontë. The Evolution of Genius (Oxford University Press, 1969), p. 25.

[6] A modern post-colonial interpretation of Angria would quite obviously be based on the examination of the origin of this particular character and on analyzing his position as a royal persona. One of Charlotte Brontë's juvenile stories, „The Twelve Adventurers. A Romantic Tale" (1829), relates the events around Arthur Wellesley's military victory over the Ashanti nation. Arthur Wellesley, Duke of Zamorna, builds a capital city on this newly acquired piece of land and establishes his power in an atmosphere of miscegenation, in which the adoption of Arthur's foster-brother, Quashia Quamina, is paralleled by the hideous murder of the mysterious figure of Finic, whose head Arthur Wellesley orders to lie „severed on a temporary scaffold". This is followed by the murder of Quamina himself, whose lifeless head makes a ghastly display of Zamorna's power as a colonizer (Cf Plasa, Carl, 2004, pp. 3–8).

remained dead (ibid.). The development of the theme of <u>Death could be seen as a battlefield for the two poets,</u> whose constant rivalry is evident to the critic in the dramatic atmosphere of uncertainties and murderous inclinations, in which Angria's main personae are immersed. The technique of eliminating main personae in Angria, and subsequently of resuscitating them, makes room for the emergence of *the ghost* as a persona in its own right. The female ghost's appearance seems to be more regular and more persistent than the male's in Charlotte Brontë's poetry. From an aesthetic point of view, a feminist would argue, the woman plays the role of the poetic muse, as she bears traits of the corporally existent beloved, yet the female is dead and mourned for, and so easier to take control of by the (male) Romantic poet (Cf Barreca 1990, p. 246). The dead female beloved is also easier to admire: she errs no more, she only represents the poet's aesthetic ideal.

In her personal experience, Charlotte Brontë was forced to consider the theme of Mortality rather early – both through her own family's involvement with Death[7], as well as during her life away from home. At the Clergy Daughters' School (at Cowan Bridge), the years 1824 – 1825 were marked by Death's gloomy visitations which took away many children that had come down with TB. Charlotte had been haunted by Death ever since the loss of her mother and her two beloved sisters (Maria and Elizabeth). Those events she would have been old enough to remember. Charlotte Brontë shared her feeling of being oppressed by the constant sight of Death in her personal correspondence with her closest friend Ellen Nussey, as well as in some letters between her and her publisher[8]. Charlotte Brontë's personal diary is another source of information, which proves that for Charlotte, the issue of children's Death must have been a crucial component in forming a complex understanding of a wholesome and full-fledged family happiness – something she never really had herself. Charlotte Brontë's literary aspirations, partly evident in her literary partnerships with her brother Branwell, as well as with her sisters Anne

---

[7] According to B. Babbage's 1850 report of Health in the village of Haworth, around 40 % of the population died before reaching the age of 6. By the age of 9, Charlotte herself had already seen off her mother and her two elder sisters (Cf Glen, Heather. Charlotte Brontë. The Imagination in History, Oxford University Press 2004, p. 18).
[8] Both were reflected in a detailed and comprehensive manner in Juliet Barker's The Brontës. A Life in Letters (Viking at Penguin Books Ltd, 1997).

and Emily (in the juvenile plays and in publishing their poetry first in the joined 1846 edition), were marked by another grievous memory. Charlotte remembered all her younger siblings' deaths, which she had to witness and keep in her memory forever (as her personal correspondence from the period 1848–1852 suggests)[ii]. In her art of drawing, Charlotte showed consideration for the theme of Mortality too[9].

As far as the genre representation of the theme of Mortality in Charlotte Brontë's poetry is concerned, ballads and elegies prevail over odes. Still, compared to Emily and Anne, her poems show a more pompous manner of reflecting Death through the death of great men and women, notable figures of Angria (e.g. *A National Ode for the Angrians* – 1834, Winnifrith, 1984, pp. 176–179). Compared to Emily's elegiac intimations and Anne's introspectiveness in her undisguised preference for the hymn, Charlotte's poetry demonstrates a more formal treatment of *Death*. The poet considers the role of Death in society – what it means for many individuals (who were in one way or another related to the dead Other). Many of the poems relevant to the theme of research are signed by Angrians. This is particularly easily observed in the poems which in Winnifrith's 1984 edition are categorized as: „Poems of Charlotte Brontë Published After her Death, from the Shakespeare Head Edition". Noticeably, some of those bear the signature of the Marquis of Douro. Confessional overtones and philosophical intimations are quite consistent throughout her poetic works.

At first, there is Charlotte Brontë's concern with, and lamentation at, Time's degenerative influence on man's efforts to ameliorate his/her attitude to Life. Gradually, there emerges the realisation that Nature is both destroyer and preserver: the configuration of certain natural phenomena, the repetition of certain scenes in Nature indicate its potential to store the memory of the happy days spent in the atmosphere of love and intimacy. The beloved's spirit outlives the Survivor, so to speak, as it is being engraved in the eternal spirit of Nature, a short glimpse of which the Survivor is allowed in his own lifetime. Charlotte Brontë describes a Survivor who is temporally dependent on the image of the deceased

---

[9] Some of her early drawings of 1828–1829 include: a juvenile picture of a boat stuck between two cliffs under a gloomy sky, then a sick-room filled with the air of the forthcoming death, a ruined tower and a solitary cormorant on a rocky coast (Cf Alexander & Sellars 1995, p. 154).

beloved who is indeed immortal because being one with the spirit of Nature, in which the Survivor could never really be integrated. Here, the individual is much more a victim of his/her own intellectual hubris, much more an orphan because of the composition and nature of his/her mind than an orphan in the physical sense of the word only. The urge towards self-appropriation, towards ownership of one's own life is stronger than in Anne Brontë's poetry, and therefore the perilous tendency to consider one's own consciousness as a self-sufficient form of existence proves rather greater a sin for one. The individual's encounters with the daemonic in Charlotte Brontë's poetry are summoned by man's own counter-empathetic desire to possess Life by defining it within the dimensions of his/her own lifetime solely. And the persistent presence of the Ghost – a creature traditionally considered to be a representation of the world beyond (unfamiliar and therefore threatening) – suggests the poet's determination to ontologically upgrade the self-sufficient individual, whose non-dialogic existence still holds a chance of self-improvement through the recognition of this *ghostly Other*. The Ghost is a reminder to the individual of a failed opportunity to prove faithful and dutiful to another human being, whose life ought to be seen as the „container“ of „My“ own life.

* * *

Mutability and Memory

If dead, we cease to be; if total gloom
Swallow up life's brief flash for aye, we fare
As summer-gusts, of sudden birth and doom,
Whose sound and motion not alone declare,
But are their whole of being! If the breath
Be Life itself, and not its task and tent,
(…)
O Man! Thou vessel purposeless, unmeant,
Yet drone-hive strange of phantom purposes!
Surplus of Nature's dread activity,
Which, as she gazed on some nigh-finished vase,
Retreating slow, with meditative pause,

She formed with restless hands unconsciously.
Black accident! Nothing's anomaly!
(…)
Be sad! Be glad! Be neither! Seek, or shun!
Thou hast no reason why! Thou canst have none;
Thy being's being in contradiction[10].

Charlotte Brontë's earliest indication of her interest in the theme of Death is evident in her preoccupation with the motif of *mutability*. In the years from around 1830 to 1837 she observes that, on the one hand, *mutability*, as a characteristic of Nature, reduces man's existence to the point of a mere incident in the natural world[11]. On the other hand, *mutability* makes stand out the certainty of the uniqueness of each individual's existence (in that each individual is given a certain amount of time, which is bestowed upon one as the possibility of achieving meaning within certain temporal definitions relevant through the presence of *Other* individuals). At first, there is the young individual's premature fear of the danger of an early death. Later, there is the silent and painful admiration of the unyielding principle of change in Nature. It is through such admiration man gains peace and his „*gall*" is „*distilled*". And out of this very admiration is born the feeling of <u>reverence for Nature – now the temple of the Survivor's memory of his beloved.</u> To the Survivor, the repetitiveness of Nature's seasons invokes repetitive recollections of the happiest moments spent with his beloved at certain times of year. In this way, *the dead beloved* is given the chance to outlive the Survivor, whose presence would

---

[10] Human Life. On the Denial of Immortality [? 1815], by S. T. Coleridge, quoted after Spiegelman, Willard, Majestic Indolence. English Romantic Poetry and the Work of Art (Oxford University Press, 1995), p. 79.

[11] Branwell Brontë is rather more militant in his resistance to the fact that man falls prey to the ravages of Time. Compare, for instance, his poem Song By Percy (Aug 27th–Nov 9th 1837, Winnifrith 1983, pp. 84–90), in which he expresses his indignation at Time the Destroyer:

(…)
Yet, Great Destroyer, whose will is dooming
All the world to be Thy prey,
Know thine own last our is coming
Faster still with our decay!

What Branwell is really saying, is that the limitations Time the Destroyer puts on man in making him mortal, do not do away with the fact that Time, as such, exists for and is contained in, man's consciousness above all.

only 'stretch' as far as the moment of his physical expiration. And it is this early voluntary acceptance of „Nature's great decree“ which opens room for the formation of the lyrical persona of the Mourner in Charlotte Bronte's poetry, whose early poetic works are very sensory, and much less religiously purposeful that Anne's when it comes to reflecting the principle *Death – Revival*. In her unsigned and undated poem „*All is change – the night, the day...*“ (Winnifrith, 1984, p. 275) she declares that „*all are fettered – all are free*“ – not through our own volition, but thanks to the principle of necessity inherent in Nature's constant regeneration. That principle of Nature ensures self-purification in that, eventually, it eliminates everything and all, including the evil, which otherwise may have threatened one to incapacitate one's spiritual potential.

Peculiarly enough, in Charlotte Brontë's poetry the individual seems to gradually grow more reluctant to come to terms with the idea of being mortal. Hard as one might try, one is unable to find justification for the knowledge that Death is spared no one. In the openly biographical poem, ***The Teacher's Monologue*** (12th May 1837, published 1846 – Winnifrith 1984, pp. 51–54), whilst she is evaluating the essence of her own existence, the teacher 'doubles up' and 'slips out' of her body in the shape of an observant *spirit*, who now acknowledges what is lost forever:

> *(...)*
> *Life will be gone ere I have lived;*
> *Where now is Life's first prime?*
> *I've worked and studied, longed and grieved,*
> *Through all that rosy time.*
> *(...)*
> *The morn was dreary, must the eve*
> *Be also desolate?*
> *Well, such a life at least makes Death*
> *A welcome, wished-for friend;*
> *(...)*[12]

---

[12] The note after the poem on p. 354 in Winnifrith's edition of 1984 suggests that this poem goes back to the time Charlotte Brontë spent as a student (and later, as a teacher, in 1836) at Roe Head – a period of poetic growth and existential maturation. Roe Head was, both for Charlotte and Emily, marked by a persistent feeling of loneliness and isolation.

The reader is faced with a Lyrical Self who interprets the philosophical problem of Death monologically: through the fear of her own death and loneliness (she is away from home, from the moors, where she is „*known and loved*"). Robert Keefe's monograph on Charlotte Brontë underlines that Charlotte's deep engagement with *solitude* could be seen in that a lot of the female personae in Angria become „chained within the dilemma of their loneliness" (Keefe, Robert, *Charlotte Brontë's World of Death* /Austin: University of Texas Press,1979/, p. 73). Such is the case with Mina Laury (in one of Charlotte's last Angrian tales of 1838). One of Zamorna's beloved, she is hidden and kept at a hunting lodge away from Zamorna's wife's wrath, where she slowly expires (ibid. p. 74).

The wistful and introverted female individual of Charlotte's early poetry seems to find shelter in the remotest nooks of Nature. Sadly, even in those places there is no escape from the realization that the principle of Dionysian rebirth is endorsed through Death – as inevitability, as imminence. In this context Mutability may become a driving force in Life. Nature alternates its „faces" by seasons and that ensures its coherence; yet nothing, which is a part of this seasonal change, ever remains the same:

(…)
She is thinking how that drifted snow
Dissolved in spring's first gleam,
And how her sister's memory now
Fades, even as fades a dream.

*(From **Presentiment** – 2ⁿᵈ July 1837, copied 1843, published 1846, in: Winnifrith, 1984, pp.49–51)*

The lyrical speaker's sister's memory might return to her with the arrival of the same season over a year and, again, the loss of her close friend will be felt – in a new way, yet bringing up the same feeling of loneliness and abandonment. In the above ballad, Jane (the Survivor) loses her sister, Emma, and she gradually realizes that what does bring her close to Emma (the one mourned) is not so much the memory of her (and of the natural scene of their happy times together), but that fact that Jane herself is drawing nearer to where Emma went, as she grows older and wiser („*To her shall Jane hereafter go,/ She ne'er shall come to Jane!"*). There is the obvious suggestion that „You" are to follow the *Other* – never the other way round. The motif of irrevocability is interwoven within the idea of the ontological duty – „You" seek to find and rescue the *Other* and cherish him/her inside „You", for he/she is your own rescue, your true Self. The thought of maintaining Otherness in this manner inside oneself brings one out of one's shell of self-sufficiency and self-content. Charlotte Brontë's further poetic works prove how the belief is sustained in that the reverence for the Past (which upgrades itself in an ongoing manner – as more and more pass away) ought to be a source for self-amelioration to the living, to the Survivor. The memory of *the dead one* requires that the living direct their efforts towards ontological maturation, of which the human being is fully capable[iii].

Death is implied in Nature with simply and wisely – something which is emphasized in many of Charlotte Brontë's very early poems, where the issue of man's temporal boundaries may be set in an Angrian context. The ballad *The Violet* (10th November 1830, Winnifrith, 1984, pp. 113–120) is signed by the Marquis of Douro, also called Arthur Wellesley, Duke of Zamorna and King of Angria (a proud and independent persona, whose three consecutive marriages shape the structure of relationships in the whole story of Angria). Here Douro reflects on the brevity of human life. He admits that a violet is a fleeting miracle of Nature, yet it has such a strong emotional effect upon the human mind. The violet is almost inconspicuous and lowly and cannot live forever. As a contrast, man's complexity may be seen to almost 'bursts up' into a determination to continue developing one' own potential in what is referred to as the *world beyond*. The violet only lasts as long as the season, which yields it. Yet Nature speaks „*condescendingly*" and advises man to wreathe a violet round his brow, rather than bind his temples with a laurel, because man's fate is set in a „*humbler sphere*" and the „*exalted mind*" will „*lie with the silent dead*, freed from „*withering blight*" and embalmed with the everlasting perfume „*the flower sheds*"[13] The violet's presence proves more lasting that man's

---

[13] The Lyrical Self's reflections and thoughts about Life expressed in this ballad are comfortably accommodated within the thematic context of the issue of poetic talent. The allusions to Greek history (Homer, Sophocles, Euripides and Æschylus) and to some later colossi of poetic might (like Virgil and Tasso) provide a solid creative background for the „sons of Albion", who „(…) deeply of

short-lived while, because it is a manifestation of the Eternal, which is hidden in the „silent" forms of Nature. The adjective „silent" is repeated (as in *„the silent dead"*, or *„silent tomb"*) and carries the idea of some secret revealed to the individual only through a special interaction with certain aspects of Nature which disclose to man the Eternal as hidden is what is generally perceived as *transient*.

Charlotte Bronte deepens her interest in what, if anything at all, does remain after Death. She acknowledges the fact that the human mind, by virtue of its generosity, is able to extract the good of a lifetime and keep it as a memory. Such memories harbour the dear dead, whose presence thus remains almost as feasible and as intact as in real Life. However, the reality of Death, i.e. the lack the dead person leaves behind, is what the Survivor has to face every day. And the luxury of exploring the World through the abilities to feel and think is allowed one through the unconscious awareness that one is still alive, that one has outlived an Other, that one's body still functions, in the physical sense of this word. In *Memory* (date unsure: either 2nd Oct 1835, or 2nd Aug 1835, or 13th Feb 1835 – Winnifrith, 1984, pp. 148–149) there oozes the thought that, ironically, man is confirmed to be alive so long as he is self-consciously able to negate Death, that is, so long as he is capable of qualifying himself as different to the ones whom we refer to as „the dead". The question is: why does one insist on keeping the memory of a dead person, when every such one departure from Life is practically irrevocable. Why should, as the lyrical speaker inquires, *„their memories remain"* with us, *„why should the spirit remember"* and *„why should the parted return"*? The answer does not linger:

---

the fount (…) drank:/ The sacred fount of Helicon!" The Lyrical Self (The Marquis of Douro, who claims to be the poem's author, and who – according to the chronicles of Angria, submitted this piece of poetry to Sergeant Tree, the publisher) reveals himself to be a Poet and summons Nature, the „Mighty Mother". Nature here reaches the Poet first with its voice, which „sweeps by on the wild wind", then „shadowy vapours gathered fast", the river's voice „proclaimed some prodigy was nigh", then a shape „more beauteous than the morn, (…) radiant with a thousand dyes" materializes as the vision of a woman. Again, the description suggests that this vision belongs not to the world of everyday reality, but comes from somewhere beyond the human mind. And, again, this poetic muse takes the shape of a beautiful and morally superior female creature.

(…)
Because that the fire is still shining,
Because that the lamp is still bright;
While the body in dust is reclining
The **soul** *lives in glory and light.*

I would argue that the „soul" referred to here is not only the soul of the dead, but also that of the living. There is a covert suggestion that „Your soul" is still glorious, i. e. alive, through the existential awareness „you" have acquired through the dearest person's death. The ability to confirm Death ought to become an ingredient in man's conscience, which ought to materialize itself into altruism. Since (following Levinas) *the realization of one's mortality makes one sensitive and sensible, and does not take away from the richness and the complexity of one's potential.*

In this early poetic period, Charlotte Brontë goes through the mental trials and tribulations of considering the insoluble question of whether the human mind is an independent viable unit of existence, or a temporally verified entity of contraries. Does the fact that man is capable of recognizing the phenomenon of Death limit one's potential in the knowledge that „you, too, will die," or does it, on the contrary, create positive opportunities for one in terms of developing one's capacities and faculties. In the poem „*The moon dawned slow in the dusky gloaming…*" (Unsigned, possibly 17th January 1834 – Winnifrith, 1984, pp. 268–271) there is an imaginary philosophic discussion between a river and the moon. The river can be taken as a representation of Life's permanence and continuity in life. It chants:

(…)
From the caverned earth I rose,
Mortal, like to thee;
Ever more thy torrent flows
Sounding to the sea;
Ever as thy career will close
In vast eternity.
(…)

And the moon „*bows its silver arch*" over the solitary grave of the unknown warrior, as it provides eternal „rest from the toil of life", which left him non-appreciated. The light, which his grave spreads over and around the streets, seems to reflect the moon's own benevolence, as the moon itself eulogizes the warrior's „*ancestral dust*". Broadly speaking, this poem is about the opposition *seasonal versus non-seasonal*, as well as man being part of both. The latter fact is, so to speak, „non-seasonal." However, the realization of it is „seasonal", i.e. unique in that it comes up once in every man's life: as the ultimate knowledge in every man's individual consciousness, which is what destabilizes man's life. Stability comes only with Death: as one ends up in one's „*last dark home.*"

In another poem, „*Well, the day's toils are over, with success*[14]" – 9th January, 1837 – Winnifrith, 1984, pp. 311–325), the Lyrical Self reflects over the brevity of human life, as he sees"*tyrants*" treading over the „*the fathers' graves.*" He then goes to recall the memory of his beloved, whose presence could still be sensed around the places she used to visit. „*The balmy gales*" and „*the pastoral walk*" utter to this man that his happiness is over. Mary is gone, „*like the spring shower's glitter of rain*". Although the man could feel Mary's presence at certain places, external Nature remains a mute and senseless void, which swallowed Mary's body, which is in the grave. And what in Nature reminds the Lyrical Self of Mary is exactly what emphasises the fact of the irrevocability of her departure. For, as Mary becomes one with Nature in the grave, she clearly interrupts her link to Life, and reborn – in his memory, or as an „apparition" – she inevitably leads the Lyrical Self to the notion of temporality. The danger, which lurks in the human mind's capacity to bring a close friend/ the beloved form the dead, is the human mind's own inevitable „crash" into the realization of the irrevocable loss of this missing Other. The Angrian context of the above poem reveals that it was most probably written by Arthur Wellesley, Marquis of Douro, and dedicated to Mary Henrietta Percy (his third wife and daughter o Alexander Percy), who withers and dies away from him, being the victim of the quarrel between her husband and her father (Cf Barker, 1995, p. 983). The vivid description of the unburied bodies, with which this ballad starts, soon

---

[14] The poem is analysed again, in more detail, at the end of this chapter, as an example of the crucial role the dead beloved's ghost plays in Charlotte Brontë's poetry.

flows into Arthur Wellesley's confession in his guilt in causing Mary's death. Condemning and accusing „*Percy, the demon*" of being the reason for this gory conflict soothes not the Arthur Wellesley. The greatest sin is that he conscientiously left Mary to die – imprisoned and alone, in order to revenge his enemy. The „*delusive dream*", in which Mary's image is „*stealing over [him]*" turns into his Life-in-Death (to paraphrase Coleridge). Seemingly, „*God gave the summons*" for Mary's end to come, yet Wellesley knows he caused her death. His feverish farewell with Mary's image in the last stanza of the poem promises no consolation to the existential guilt of Surviving *the Other* – One he loved and whom he caused to die unnecessarily. The complexity of the motif of loyalty to *the Other* unfolds here on the background of two interdependent problems: being loyal to death to one's fellow countrymen versus being loyal to the One „You" love on a personal level. The outcome is fatal, but there is the possibility that Wellesley's own willful character and insatiable thirst for power and recognition could be regarded as the source of this tragedy.

In Charlotte Brontë's works, as in Anne's works too, the Lyrical Self falls pray to re-experiencing Death whilst ruminating on the memory of the beloved. At the same time (as in the above poem), existential awareness is being „generated" through the individual's grievous observations of the vulnerability of the past „preserved" in the grave. It is man's privilege, as well as man's emotional punishment, to discover that the revelations about Life lie in possession of the grave, the tomb:

(…)
And dying dreams of light are sealed
In the marble urns, to be
No more to ear or eye revealed
Save, Memory, by thee.

(These lines were omitted from the last version of the poem *Winter Stores* – around 1837, copied 1843, published 1846 – Winnifrith, 1984, p. 362; see also the poem itself on pp. 65–66)

The way Charlotte Brontë imagines that Life is preserved is through *Memory*. The *memory of the beloved* becomes a memory of love, or rather, a metaphor of love, which is then carried and subsequently rediscovered throughout the ages by other human beings.

The hope of being ontologically rescued by an omniscient Otherness which these early poetic works of Charlotte Brontë's demonstrate is soon ousted by a Romantic hubris of abandoning a life which holds no future for the proud outcast (in Charlotte's later poems). Gradually, the faith in the possibility of amending Life through hope and through the memory of the beloved begins to wane. Ahead is a solitary journey in search for freedom – from all and everyone. Life appears an empty vessel, which tends to suck the spirit into a mundane existence of mediocrity and disguised Evil. The individual feels encouraged to believe that one has the right to choose when and how to quit *the life here and now*.

* * *

Death: Heroism, Hubris and Solitude

In the late 1830s–early 1840s Charlotte Brontë tends to discern in Death a possibility for a heroic victory over the World. Later, Death becomes man's chance to escape form a life of physical incarceration and spiritual vacuum. The equivocally silent grave is one the one hand a temptation for a possibility of a voluntary retreat from the Present, which is how the individual is hoping to triumph over the unpredictability of the moment of Death. On the other hand, the grave reminds one that it is through the physicality of the actual relationship with *an Other* that one could only feel as an integrated within Life. The Past emerges as the viable source of one's identity.

Charlotte Brontë must have undergone a personal conflict with society's conventionality and unfavourable attitude to the poetic genius. One personal letter of Charlotte's to her close friend, Ellen Nussey, written at Roe Head on 10th May **1836,** reads that Charlotte's „*fiery imagination eats*" her up and „*makes [her] feel society as it is, wretchedly insipid*" (Cf Barker, 1997, p. 37). The poem „*But once again, but once again*" (a part of a larger poem, *The Wounded Stag* – January 19th 1836, Winnifrith, 1984, pp. 289–298) describes a lost individual, who desires separation from the body, whilst seeking to find the way back home[15] and away from mediocrity and placidity:

(…)
I'll travel away, far away,
Where the dream in the darkness lies shrouded and grey.
Time shall not chain me,
Place not restrain me,
Mind is not matter, soul is not clay.

A careful insight into the poem would reveal its Angrian texture. The person who has got lost is one of Arthur Wellesley's subjects, who wishes to join him again and serve him until his last. He wishes to find his master, who *„ruled his thoughts right regally"*. The poem might be interpreted as a quest for the lost poetic inspiration, or generally, for the lost talent (as the reality that used to provide it is now gone). The desire to separate from the body is a result of the unbearable feeling of alienation in an environment deprived of an Author. As a contrast, the memory of the powerful Zamora is rather tangible. Still, it should be mentioned that the motif of *the orphan* was not as methodically and as fully researched in Charlotte's poetic works as it was investigated in Anne's and Emily's poetic heritage. Where this motif did find true recognition was in Charlotte's prose fiction. This particular poem is also a confession of the notion that self-consciousness, as such, is possible only so long as the Self partakes of a feasible consciousness of an *Other* (just as the „I" is linguistically confirmed as „I" in as much as it differs to „You")[iv]. In this sense, the „I" the Lyrical Self seeks to achieve in leaving his body, is immediately lost, because the body (a part of his whole being) is the physical container of his identity, which is whole only if a viable relationship to an Other is maintained even after the death of the Lyrical Self's own Other. In the same poem the relationship between the Lyrical Self and Zamorna is suggested also by the one between Zamorna and his beloved – as Helen fades, so

---

[15] As mentioned earlier in the present research, the motif of the separation of the soul/ mind from the body as a technique of overcoming Mortality, or Mediocrity, or Solitude, is Emily Brontë's, so to speak, „speciality". It is best observed in her poems: Day Dream (9 March 5th, 1844) and „I'm happiest when most away".

does Zamorna. Again, the glorious figures of Zamorna and Alexander Percy are analysed in this poetic work of Charlotte's.

Charlotte Brontë has a range of poems that treat the heroic deeds of famous historical figures. Both the poems *Death of Darius Codomannus* (2nd May 1834 – Winnifrith, 1984, pp. 158–166) and *Richard's Song* (in: *Richard Coeur de Lion and Blondel* – 27th December 1833, Winnifrith, 1984, 151–157) are based on the historical events of the two heroes' captivity. Richard Coeur de Lion is described as though he is helpless and unfit for Life: his „*heart is cold*," his soul – „*has lost its ancient might*," and „*dark despair's unholy night*" closes above him (Winnifrith, 1984, pp. 155–156). He is convinced that all natural phenomena – the stars, the sun, the breeze etc. – „live" in vain, for *he* himself feels „*a living tomb*." He considers himself someone of „the chosen of [God's] might," and therefore the realization of the likeliness of his death in captivity feels doubly bitter. The other historical persona, Darius Codomannus, has the expression of „*placid grace*" on his face, even despite the hideousness of his death through slaughter. „*A son bereaved, a childless sire*", Darius „murmurs" not like a slave. He blesses his conqueror, whilst he is praying for Asia to find a more worthy and able leader, so that it continues to be. What Charlotte Brontë seems to be concerned with here is apathy, which seizes one at the threshold of Death, and which is an evil greater than Death itself, for it hints at evading the responsibility towards the living. Life, at all times – even before the ghastlier and most horrible One Final Event – ought to naturally adhere to the principle of Being as Co-Being, ought never to shun this Duty towards the Other, ought to be a Life in active consideration of the consequences of each single act and thought of one's[v]. Branwell Brontë's famous elegy „*Cease, mourner, cease thy sorrowing for the dead*" (20th October 1837, Winnifrith, 1983, pp. 258–259) reiterates some of the ideas suggested in the above arguments.

Quite different is the sounding and message of Charlotte's poem *Lines Written beside a Fountain* (7th October 1833 – Winnifrith, 1984, pp. 149–150). The explanatory note to this poem (on page 380 in Winnifrith's 1984 edition) emphasizes the fact that, in the context of Angria, this poetic piece was written by Edward Sydney, and stolen by the Marquis of Douro. The poem is clearly signed by Charlotte Brontë and presents grievous contemplations over man's brief and transient hopes and expectations during Life, which dissolve into the imagined bliss and continuity in the *life beyond*. The quiet but persistent presence of *the dead* stirs the Lyrical Self's mind: as he presses his „*burning brow*" against the „*cool green grass,/ Freshened with spray-drops from the murmuring well*," „*strange wild musings from [his] spirit pass:*"

> *(…)*
> *High soars my soul from its chilled earthy bed –*
> *I hear the harmonious gates of heaven unfold –*
> *I see around me all the silent dead:*
> *Great ones who lived of old!*
> *(…)*

Hardly is it fortuitous that one of Charlotte Brontë's Angrian personae steals the above lines, which express so well and in such a condensed manner the Survivor's wish to „*expire*" „*amid untroubled silence (...) in stilly darkness*" and be received in due manner where – he thinks – he belongs. There is a dose of hubris in this, yet the importance of the memory of *the dead* is being amplified too – the source of quiet steady wisdom one seeks in the *after life*[16].

Two trends could be registered in Charlotte's poetry. One is the escapist philosophy, which maintains that Death is desirable because it might lead to salvation form earthly toil and routine. The other is Charlotte Brontë's growing desire to consider Death as an impetus *to live and to give*, in the context of which one could hear Lucy Snowe saying: „*I might suffer; I was inured to suffering: death itself had not, I thought, those terrors for me which it has for the softly reared* (*Villette*, ch. VI, pp. 42–

---

[16] In his sonnet „Why did I laugh tonight?" Keats is rather open about his belief that, of all earthly experiences, Death is the ontologically truest, the one which completes Life:
(…)
Why did I laugh? I know this Being's lease,
My fancy to its utmost blisses spreads;
Yet would I on this very midnight cease,
And the world's gaudy ensigns see in shreds;
Verse, fame and Beauty are intense indeed
But Death intenser – Death is Life's high meed.

43). Lucy embarks on a quest for her true self and for the meaning of Life as she offers freely the whole of her creative human potential to Madame Beck in the *Pensionnat* in Labassecour. Lamonica Drew interprets Death as an open-narrative technique, which, she claims, Charlotte used in constructing *Villette*, where Death becomes the metaphor for spiritual shipwreck. In *Villette* (as in some of her poems, one of which could be the one analysed above) there is not a full and unequivocal answer the question: „Is the castaway still alive?" Like most of the central characters in her novels, the Lyrical Self in Charlotte Brontë's poetry is made a Mourner – through the loss of the member of the family, or a close friend, or the beloved. The individual is more often than not the victim who survives the metaphorical shipwreck: as an orphan or a widower. As Lucy travels through an imaginary Styx and on Charon's vessel towards a cataleptic self-negation in Labassecour, so does the Lyrical Self, who finally understands that a return to, and communion with, the dead is the route towards self-acquisition and self-cognition (Cf Drew, Lamonica, 2003, pp. 179–195). On the whole, however, the nature of Charlotte Brontë's lyrical personae (as demonstrated in her early poetry) is introverted; they strive to overcome their self-centeredness and hubris, but they never quite reach the self-negation and humbleness that her brother Branwell Brontë managed to extract from the notion of Death[17].

* * *

Orphanhood and the Anticipation of the Life Beyond

What this sub-chapter focuses on is Charlotte Brontë's treatment of the motif of *orphanhood*, while there is an attempt to achieve a philosophic explanation of the anticipation of *the life beyond* – a rescue from the coarseness and chaos of the parentless Present. Particularly obvious is the motif of the lost child who seeks God's benevolence as a way of self-completion and of quenching the incompatibility of its own character with the general attitudes in the world of the living. The first poems that offer relevant „substance" to the theme in hand emerge around 1836–1837. The

---

[17] Refer especially to Branwell's poem The Triumph of Mind over Body (1841–1842, Winnifrith, 1983, pp. 122–129), especially lies: 199–263.

mature ones, however, come after a decade – around 1846. Most of the poetic pieces bear no links to the Angrian context. Death is anticipated as the individual desires to both gain redemption for the sins admitted, as well as to find in the *world beyond* that missing *Other*, whose presence motivates, so to speak, the world Before and After. The feasibility of the existence of *an Other* is the evidence and the reason for one's own existence – physical and spiritual[vi].

In the Charlotte's very early poem ***The Vision*** (13th April 1830 – Winnifrith, 1984, p. 95–97), the Lyrical Self falls into the state of daydreaming, in which she gets intoxicated with the thought of the harmony and melodiousness of Heaven, whence „*sweet voices, not like human sound*," come and „*a zephyr soft*" breathes on her. Here, God's imminent and unconditional benevolence merges with the description of the arrival of the day, the Sun and gives the Lyrical Self a feeling of spiritual completion and protection. She is loath to lose this heavenly vision. God's „*bright chariot*" and his „*glorious company*" have managed in truth to „*gild each wide-branching oak*". The majesty of heaven's heraldry is reflected in the epithets quoted above. The description is intense, dynamic and so gives the idea of the rapidity and ampleness, with which the heavenly is projected onto the Earth, which, as that is typical for Emily Brontë in particular, begins to equal Heaven itself.

Around the early 1840s – the time when Charlotte Brontë was engrossed in writing in prose[18] – one finds the individual in her poetry in a more existentialist frame of mind, as many of her confessional pieces demonstrates. The feeling of abandonment turns into a permanent state of mind, into a *camera obscura* for the possible interlocutor, whom the Lyrical Speaker does not allow fully in:

> *Unloved I love, unwept I weep,*
> *Grief I restrain, hope I repress;*

---

[18] In the 1993 introduction to the edition of Charlotte Brontë's unfinished novels Dr Tom Winnifrith points out that in 1839 Charlotte had already „bidden farewell to the burning clime of Angria", whilst her novel Ashworth was written between 1840 and 1841 (Cf Winnifrith, T. in: Brontë, Charlotte, Unfinished Novels /Alan Sutton Publishing Limited & The Brontë Society, 1995/, pp. vii–viii).

Vain is this anguish, fixed and deep,
Vainer desires of means of bliss. [19]

My life is cold, love's fire being dead;
That fire self-kindled, self-consumed;
What living warmth erewhile it shed,
Now to how drear extinction doomed!
(…)
Have I not fled that I may conquer?
Crost the dark sea in firmest faith
That at last might plant my anchor
Where love cannot prevail to death?

(*Reason*, possibly 19th January 1836 – Winnifrith 1984, pp. 243–244.)

The lines in the second stanza quoted suggest that the inescapable grief the Lyrical Self is experiencing (over her unrequited love and feeling of abandonment) is somewhat self-inflicted. This is a confession of an interrupted link with reality in the absence of someone who could love her. But also, to remember Bakhtin, there is the danger that, as there seem to be no Other, the Lyrical Self's ability to empathize might be atrophied. Really, what she longs for is *to ache indeed, to ache whilst loving* and thus to exist, to belong to reality, so that the „fire" inside her is no more „self-kindled", but were ignited by an *Other*. One is left with the impression that there is an Other, who, sadly, seems to be non-responsive to the Mourner's grief. And although she wreathes with grief over the fact of this imagined *Other*, to whom her love is „unasked", she still declares that she „*shall be strong to-morrow*", since faint she will not, „*nor yield to sorrow; /Conflict and force will quell the brain*".

On a superficial level, one might argue that Charlotte Brontë's poetry represents the individual's struggle to overcome the threatening competition a solid interlocutor's presence would provide. In this sense,

---

[19] In Winnifrith's 1984 edition, the note on p. 243 emphasizes the fact that the word „means" here can also be read as „dreams" in Charlotte Brontë's writing.

the unknown *Other* could be overpowered if one merges with this Other's self. Thus, the danger of interacting with the independent consciousness of any such opponent–Other would be eliminated. A deeper insight into the poems, however, would confirm that Charlotte Brontë intends not to absorb that *Other* in order to neutralize him/ her. Rather, there is the confession that loneliness paralyses one's senses and the wholesomeness of one's spirit: one becomes dependent on, and chained within, the notion of the imminence Death. In the already quoted poem *The Teacher's Monologue* (12th May 1837 – Winnifrith, 1984, pp. 51–53) the teacher declares that she is helpless to restore what has been taken away from her by a power she could never master anyway: „*Life will be gone ere I have lived.*" The reason why the ontological significance of *the Other's presence* could be insisted on in Charlotte Brontë's poetry is that the feelings of desolation and abandonment analysed in a number of poems of hers are a consequence of – and not a deliberate approach to – circumstances of Life. The individual mourns his/her orphaned Life, as though that is an event, which has already occurred, i.e. she does not „plan" it. The Past is of primary concern: in the Past the Other's presence is stronger. The Present, metaphorically speaking, stares at the Past in order to reach some clarity as to how to approach the Future.

The search for the *Other* appears particularly interesting when it is linked to the motif of matrimonial loyalty and love. In the poem *The Wood* (published 1846, Winnifrith, 1984, pp. 18–22), husband and wife are about to embark on a dangerous journey, which would test their dedication to each other, as they endeavour to remain together and thus achieve self-completion[20]. Their desire to return to their home, to the „*point obscure*" (to „*Bretagne*") is situated within the unfolding theme of accepting God's benevolence as the only criterion which sets boundaries to man's life. The wish that „*our souls*" should „*flow along the self-same line*" builds towards the poem's leitmotif. Namely, that the humble worshipper should realize that the „*dreamless ease*" and the „*divinest peace*" can only be achieved if the husband and the wife pass through life's „*conflict and turmoil [...] as God shall please.*" Death waits at every corner here: there is the risk that „*our mutual blood/ May redden in some lonely wood/ The*

---

[20] The explanatory note to this poem on p. 342 in Tom Winnifrith's 1984 edition emphasizes that the manuscript of the poem is untraceable.

knife of treachery". The discussion of the problem of orphanhood is hidden within the reflections on the theme of mutual loyalty, of the matrimonial vow. Death threatens the two outcasts not so much in the physical sense of the word: Death waits to sneak into the mind of either of them, should he/she forget about the duty to protect the Other, who has a parental (i.e. protective) role too. And the voluntary acceptance of God's ultimate authority implies a readiness to come to terms with the fact that happiness may only be temporary as a feature of a human being's life[21]. The thought that „*God shall please*" to determine one's fate shows that the Lyrical Self is on the watch for another human being, whose fate would challenge „Your" life's seeming intactness and unfinalizability[22].

Many of Charlotte's poems provide evidence that she links the theme of *orphanhood* to the individual's inability, or rather unconscious refusal, to break free from the dungeon that the feelings of independence and self-centeredness represent for one. Branwell Brontë would address the latter as „*a life [...] confounded to inward thought and outward eye*". He is afraid not of the „*eternal gloom*" that awaits his body „*in the tomb*," but of the lost trust in God, since that would open an „*awful [yawning] void,*" in which man would be „*launched all aidless*" (Cf Branwell Brontë's poem *Harriet II* – 14th May 1838 – Winnifrith, 1983, pp. 90–100). In her turn, Charlotte Brontë's poem **Stanzas on the Death of a Christian** (27th July 1837 – Winnifrith, 1984, p. 328) offers a way out of the cowardly mundane existence, which dominates the World. The listener is persuaded to believe that a fearless and proud acceptance of the fact that God reigns *above* does not limit the capacities of the self of a human being. Also, that the body, as well as the soul, go to the ontologically appropriate place at the moment of the actual happening of death:

(...)
Dust, to the narrow house beneath.
Soul, to its place on high.

---

[21] See also Charlotte's ballad „Long since, I remember well" (probably 19th January 1836 – Winnifrith, 1984, pp. 275–288).
[22] Of all four surviving children, Charlotte Brontë stood closest to her father. As such, she would have been familiar with the Rev. Patrick Brontë's concern to always follow „the good old plan". The Rev. Brontë taught his children to be zealous yet plain, judicious yet not keen on innovation (Cf. Barker 1995, ch. 11).

They that have seen thy look in death
Will never fear to die[23].

The death of the unknown Christian is described as an example one should try and emulate. The Christian is no eminent Angrian hero; in fact it remains unknown throughout the poem whether Charlotte Brontë had any specific persona of Angria in mind. I think there is a deliberate emphasis on the incidental character of the Christian's death – any Christian's death – a point which would be welcomed by the reader who looks at her poetry through the optics of ontophilosophy and existential ethics.[24]

In Charlotte Brontë's poetry, the yearning for the lost parent/ friend (mother, father, God, the beloved) has to do also with man's desire to find appreciation in life[25]. Like Lucy Snowe (*Villette*), Charlotte Brontë's Lyrical

---

[23] Defiant young Jane somehow refuses to accept that even the traditionally cherished Heaven might be her best friend's „long" home (Cf Wheeler, M., 1990, p. 38). She herself is loath to accept that Death, even when in brings salvation and heavenly peace, is a gift, an award. Jane seems to be loath to accept Death as the expected, or deserved, or even natural way of the Self's completion. That is why in chapter 9 of Jane Eyre Jane questions Helen about the meaning of Life until they fall asleep and rest to her tormented mind comes naturally. Jane asks Helen whether she knows where she is going, and Helen answers: „I believe; I have faith: I am going to God. (…) I rely implicitly on his power. (…) I am sure there is a future state; I believe God is good; I can resign my immortal part to him without any misgiving. God is my father; God is my friend: I love him; I believe he loves me" (Cf JE, Vol. I, ch. 9, pp. 94–95). Whilst Jane is non-disguisedly hesitant about the validity of the doctrine of salvation through Death as the innermost ingredient of Man's fate, Helen's reflections contain a dose of doubt too. From the above words it becomes clear, that her image of God's benevolence seems to be a product of her own unyielding faith and religious perseverance, rather than a blind image of God imposed on her from without. Charlotte Brontë's individual always questions, doubts, hesitates and wishes to verify the given, to somehow sieve it through his/her own mind, which makes him/her miserable and an outcast, and that is evident in her poetry, too, and in the poem quoted above.
[24] Branwell Brontë's philosophy is tinged with the gloomier conviction that even the knowledge of the moral load Death carries for man is yet no guarantee for the elimination of the persistent feeling of loneliness, from which the human being suffers:
(…)
And friendless, sightless, left alone,
I go where thou hast gone before,
And yet I shall not see thee more.
(…)
(Cf Branwell Brontë's poem Misery, Part II (2nd March 1836 – Winnifrith, 1983, pp. 23–33).
[25] Other poems of Charlotte Brontë's relevant to the thematic focus of this sub-chapter are: The Orphan Child and Rochester's Song to Jane Eyre (published 1847 – Winnifrith, 1984, pp. 71–73), The Orphans (February 1843, published 1850 – Winnifrith, 1984, pp. 74–76). The latter three are termed „poems from Jane Eyre". Another one is Parting (29th January 1837, copied 1843, published

Self is in a mental state of captivity, exacerbated by the fear of *„being no more loved, no more owned,"*[26] and she is trying to „stir" the stillness and unresponsiveness of life, which is comparable to Lucy's attempt to move the barque of Life in *„a harbour still as glass"*[27]. There lurks a realisation that the existential opposition *fate-freedom* could only be dismantled through one's own death[28].

*   *   *

Self-Appropriation and the Mortal Trap of Consciousness

In many of her mature poems Charlotte Brontë explores the capacity of the human mind as an active element in the formation of the Self in a temporally limited lifetime, which is preordained for each human being. The self-negating genius becomes the dominant persona, who could be described as someone enclosed within the framework of his/ her own mind and driven by the fatalistic urge to abandon the „dead" body, which enhances a transition into the state of ghostliness. Ghostliness is a quality sought, because it allows observation of one's self from a distance, from *outside*; ostensibly, it allows the quality of *transgredience* being executed upon oneself from within. However, the desire to separate from the body is a consequence of the persistent feeling of insurmountable solitude which the „inhabitant" of that body experiences. Although such separation is provoked by the individual's wish to look for continuation of meaning in the after life, it is doomed, because such practice excludes dialogism, it excludes *the Other* as an active participant in the formation of the Self. Unlike the individual of many of Emily Bronte's verse, the individual here is not as prone to suicidal thoughts. There are nonetheless indications of the poet's discontent with the spiritually poor Present. There is the hope that death voluntarily embraced, death experienced in advance, would cure the suffering spirit. A real insight into many of Charlotte Brontë's poems reveal

---

1846 – Winnifrith, 1984, pp. 61–62), which is in harmony with the above quoted poem of Charlotte's.

[26] Cf V., ch. XV, pp. 145–147.

[27] Ibid. ch. IV, p. 29.

[28] Terry Eagleton argues that the latter is valid because Death is both preordained, and yet incidental in its concrete happening (Cf Eagleton, 2003, p. 121).

an individual who has no reason to rejoice over death, yet there is the wish to flee from the carnal „frets" the body represents for a self whose creative potential would materialize better in a time and a space freely manageable and beyond ordinary life. Sadly, the Self is a Self only as it is being differentiated from *Others,* who participate in his/ her ontological journey, which is always temporally verifiable.

Whether the futile existence the individual chooses to abandon is something which has been inflicted upon the person 'externally', i.e. by circumstances of Life, or whether it is provoked by a feeling of some inner hidden existential guilt, remains an arguable issue. In the poem ***The Ring*** (May 1837 – Winnifrith, 1984, pp. 197–201) the Lyrical Self suffers from an insatiable thirst to match his creative potential to the „*world's turmoil and strife*", whilst in fact his spirit has been decaying „*unmarked, unloved and fated*"[29]. He therefore wishes to „*shake off time's encumbrance*" and „*roll back*" the years pased in an attempt to respond to a supreme *Other* (the mysterious He of this poem is most probably an amalgamation of the image of God and that of the missing/dead beloved, whose „*curl of chestnut hair beset with pearl*" he is holding). For, to the *Other* is one accountable in the long run and *the Other* has the ultimate capacity to define a task for one in one's life. „*Shaking off time's encumbrance*" would lead the Lyrical Self to nothingness, yet he wishes to renovate his self by starting everything afresh, through a more pious and persistent trust in the Deity in his heart, where indeed godliness and female grace and benevolence merge. Death is associated with the anticipation of spiritual rebirth. An alternative interpretation of this poem, which has rather vague references to Angria, might read it as a meeting between, most probably, Zamorna, and one of his vassals, the vassal singing his story of life and eventually meeting his sire, to whom he sings a ballad[30].

It is around 1837 that the individual in Charlotte Brontë's could be perceived to demonstrate a proneness to self-reflection through observation of his/her own Self after abandoning its body and turning into a

---

[29] Similarly, Lucy Snowe refers to her future as a „catalepsy and a dead trance [in which] I studiously held the quick of my nature" (V., chapter XII, p. 99). Lucy Snowe tends to visualize her fears about her solitude and uselessness in chthonian imagery, a most obvious example of which is the silent ghostly NUN – an image ubiquitous for Lucy even at the remotest nooks of the pensionnat.
[30] See also Branwell Brontë's poem „Man thinks too often that the ills of life" (Winnifrith, 1983, pp. 228–231).

spirit. As might be expected, such striving for Death is not deprived of a certain dose of narcissism. Thus, the elegy „*Is this my tomb, my humble stone*" (4th June 1837 – Winnifrith, 1984, pp. 212–215) is a lament over the great deeds and valour that a certain mortal person who is now dead was predestined for. The place and the whole atmosphere of the body's last abode appear somewhat inappropriate for the powerful spirit the body formerly harboured. The „death-chamber" has been dug too „*deep*" – it contains neither „*hope*", nor „*fear*", just morbid „*sleep*":

Is this my tomb, my humble stone
Above this narrow mound?
Is this my resting place, so lone,
So green, so quiet round?
Not even a stately tree to shade
The sunbeam from my bed,
Not even a flower in tribute laid
As sacred to the dead.
(…)

The episode where the body's erstwhile vigour is cut short is expressed through a sinisterly vivid metaphor, which makes the reader almost smell the scene of murder. Namely: „*(…) Who then disrobed that worshipped form? / (…) / Who turned the blood that ran so warm/ To Winter's frozen sleet? (…)*". The dead lady, who is the narrator of the story of her own life, is tormented by self-pity – that she lost her „princely hall" and lavish lifestyle, but looking at the contents more carefully, she laments over the fact that she is mortal – i.e. she laments over an existential dilemma, and not so much over the problem of her changed social status after her death. Finally, she admits she „*know[s] no hope*", and no „*fear*" either: „*I sleep – how calm I sleep*".

The longed for death in Charlotte Brontë's poetry – to use Terry Eagleton's interpretation of the latter – is to do with the individual's desire to appropriate his/her own death „*in order to live more fully*"[xii]. There is a wish to somehow stretch the boundaries of Life by analyzing what remains of the person in *the utmost borderline situation* (as Derrida would call that) – *Death*. When there is reached a clear awareness that each one life is to end at some point, there emerges an opportunity to check the worthiness of one's lifetime against the background of other lifetimes which draw the ontological boundaries to one's life. There is a natural curiosity as to how, after „My own" expiration, that *Other* person's Being would recognize and modify the fact of „My" life and „My" death. However, the *first* death in one's lifetime is always the death of another person, and only THAT death could one witness from outside (Cf Levinas in: Derrida, *Apories*, 1998, p. 60). Finally, what may seem a proneness toward describing death as happening to „Me" in Charlotte Brontë's poetry in fact indicates a laborious journey towards self-cognition – through experimental self-observation: as though the abandoned Self were *the Other*.

One of the most widely discussed poems of Charlotte Brontë's is her mature ballad **Frances** (around 1843, publ. 1846 – Winnifrith 1984, pp. 22–30). The lyrical persona of Frances in this poem is somewhat of an early version of Lucy Snowe (*Villette*)[viii], who laments over the loss of the ability to perceive meaning in living and admits to the fact that the death of her spirit is something her self-corrupted mind is responsible for, with its capacity to both „*erase pain*" and „*bliss*":

> (…)
> '*For me the universe is dumb,*
> *Stone-deaf, and blank, and wholly blind;*
> *Life I must bound, existence sum*
> *In the strait limits of one mind;*
>
> '*That mind my own. Oh! Narrow cell;*
> *Dark – imageless – a living tomb!*
> *There must I sleep, there must I dwell*
> *Content, – with palsy, pain, and gloom.*
> (…)
> '*Must it be so? Is this my fate?*
> *Can I not struggle, nor contend?*
> *And am I doomed for years to wait,*
> *Watching death's lingering axe descend?*

'And when it falls, and when I die,
What follows? Vacant nothingness?
The blank of lost identity?
Erasure both of pain and bliss?
(…)
I know at heart there is no dying
Of love, and ruined hope, alone.
(…)

This is a prayer in which Frances is asking for God's help in her „grievous need", in her „inward pain". She hopes, but she is not entirely convinced that man would find „hope on yonder coast", and „bliss", and „love", and would be released from „penal sufferings". If that were the case, Frances is prepared to „endure [her] weary frame". Her „unused strength (…) demands a task;/ Travel and toil, and full exertion/ Are the last, only boon I ask"[31]. In the world beyond she also hopes she would be able to find her beloved. Frances' consciousness represents for her a mortal trap, in which she is fettered[32]. Frances seems to employ the idea of the world beyond in her desire to peruse the meaning of the life that she has at present. Potentially, one could imagine what follows after death. However, one could not experience death conscientiously, i.e. as a part of one's identity and therefore in an emotionally meaningful way, one could not. Again, the „lost identity" Frances refers to is an identity lost because of the absence of an *Other*, whom she has truly known and who she wishes to join in the „sunny climes".

In Charlotte Brontë's mature poetry, then, there is hidden the idea that the human mind's capacity to project the Self after death is in itself death because of the accompanying involuntary exclusion of others who

---

[31] It might be worth comparing the Lyrical Self's prayer to God in one of John Donne's Holy Sonnets – Sonnet #4: „(…) if (…) my sins abound,/ 'Tis late to ask abundance of thy grace,/ When we are there; here on this lowly ground,/ Teach me how to repent; for that's as good/ As if thou hadst sealed my pardon, with thy blood." – Cf Donne, J., 1990, p. 175. Compare also Anne Brontë's poems: Self-Communion (1847–1848) and „A dreadful darkness closes in" (1849).

[32] Compare Tennyson's In Memoriam: „(…) And all the phantom, Nature, stands – / With all the music in her tone, / A hollow echo of my own, – / A hollow form with empty hands.' // And shall I take a thing so blind, / Embrace her as my natural good; / Or crush her, like a vice of blood, / Upon the threshold of the mind?" (Cf In Memoriam, III).

may define the Self here and now. The eternity, which the individual desperately seeks, is only possible as an idea relevant in its social dimensions. A link to someone completely *outside* one – in the physical sense of the word – and yet a part of one as an indispensable ingredient of one's inner world (Cf Levinas, 2000, p. 298). In *Frances* this is reviewed in detail. The state of „lonely microdialogue", or of „hyperactive inner dialogue," in which one finds the solitary genius in Charlotte's poetry, may lead (like that happens to Dosteyevsky's characters) either to suicide, or to religious conversion. Here the latter seems more likely (as Charlotte's prose fiction characters confirm that, too). As Caryl Emerson observes in her analysis of Bakhtin's philosophic category of *dialogue*, existence with *an Other*, i.e. in dialogue, does not necessarily bring truth, or happiness, or beauty. But it brings out concretization, which albeit temporary, implies the possibility of „change, of some forward movement." Living in dialogue means that there are „options" for the Self. And although there can still be deceptions and lies, yet „by having a real other respond to me, I am spared one thing (…): the most cumulative effects of my echo chamber of words" (Cf Emerson, Cary, *The First Hundred Years of Mikhail Bakhtin* /Princeton, New Jersey: Princeton University Press, 1997/, pp. 151–153).

* * *

The Daemonic and Death

One interpretation of Death which could find substance throughout Charlotte Brontë's poetry is that the persistence of images of Death signify *the omnipresent daemonic*. At first (in the years 1829–1837), the presence of the daemonic signals the individual's spontaneous fear of the abrupt and oftentimes completely unmotivated death of certain individuals. In Charlotte's mature poetry there appears the lyrical persona of *the ghost* – a representative of the borderline zone between life and death. The ghost's presence becomes desirable, almost indispensable in the individual's reconsideration of the meaning of Being. The *Mourner* and the *Ghost* exist in Charlotte's poetry as they complement each other in man's growing anticipation of *the End*. It gradually becomes clear that the Ghost is meant as an examiner, nay a moral inquisitor, of the Mourner's nature.

The ghost intimates to the Mourner some features of the world beyond, which makes the latter more familiar. The actively responsible and responsive realm, which the Ghost inhabits, is further juxtaposed to the unresponsiveness and placidity of man's everyday existence, which, in a reverse manner, begins to appear to man *demonised*. This sub-chapter is proposed to the reader as a preparatory introduction to the next sub-chapter, which deals in detail with the role of the Female Ghost in Charlotte Brontë's ontological quest.

The importance of the lyrical persona of the Ghost could be discerned in the early ballad *The Churchyard* (24th December 1829 – Winnifrith, 1984, pp. 83–85). After the general historical introduction (about the heroic past of the British, who went to meet the Saracen and free the „*sacred land of Palestine*"), the narrator secretly observes a strange female mourner, whose story is inserted into the general narrative. The female Mourner laments her sister's death, and describes herself as: „(…) *a sad mourner/ On this dark earth to stay*". Like the will of the wisp, her dead sister's ghost is that inaccessible reality, of which the Mourner had a taste, but which then vanished, leaving her to continue the toilsome journey towards ontological maturation on her own. On the higher level – in terms of the structure of the whole poem – the disappearance of the Mourner obviously leaves the narrator in a state of contemplation over the meaning of Life. The intimate and ontologically fruitful scene of the lyrical speaker's encounter with the mourner is counterbalanced by the introductory part in which the poet speaks of the British chivalry riding steadily and confidently to „*free the land of Palestine*" from the „*unhallowed presence of the Saracen*". The initial feeling of political grandeur and national pride pale before the power of the existential intimations about mutuality and fraternal closeness which are brought forth in the second part of the poem through the Mourner's memory of her dead sister.

In the light of Derrida's *Apories*, the Ghost seems to be the strongest factual support to the concept that Death is a borderline situation. Unlike the Ghost in Emily Brontë's poetry (which tends to blur the boundaries between self and non-self), here the Ghost is never fully present yet always sensed, as it urges one to analyse one's existence. In the process of this active analysis one's nature is subject to alterations on ontological level.

One is invited to believe that the Ghost somehow reads and deciphers man's various moods and patterns of existence in order to confirm the existential formula that „*being has no gate through which one could step out of once and for all*" (Cf Levinas, 2000, p. 39). Charlotte Brontë draws the image of the Ghost in a manner reminiscent of a late medieval preoccupation with the idea of the purgatory, following which there is a natural tendency to affirms the role of the revenant in promoting one's moral code[ix]. Charlotte Brontë's interest in the image of the Ghost unfolds on a grand scale in her prose fiction. In *Villette*, the *ghostly nun, who* haunts Lucy, possesses the capacity to juggle ingredients of her memory and consciousness. The nun is one projection of Lucy's unquenched thirst for recognition, for being loved and missed by someone, but she is also a proof of Lucy's propensity for projecting her personality in images of Death[33].

The Ghost is one form of furthering the existence of a heroic personality, who left life unavenged. In the poem **Stanzas on the Fate of Henry Percy** (15th June 1834 – Winnifrith, 1984, pp. 166–175) Henry's death is enveloped with the air of the unknown, of ghostliness. The fact of his death is only alluded to „by sign and token." So in a way, this story in poetic form is a record of the events around his death (Winnifrith points out that Henry was murdered by one of Alexander Percy's minions – Cf Winnifrith, p. 381) and around his interrupted relationship with his wife – Marian Hume In Emily Brontë's *Wuthering Heights* (1847), Cathy's and Heathcliff's ghosts appear to prevent the sheep from crossing the heath-covered moor: they are intangible yet a challenge to man's desire in the regularity and simplicity of *the world here and now*. In Charlotte's poem, Henry is said to sleep „*beneath the green sea-foam*" which smiles at sailors in a daemonic way:

(…)
But how he died no tongue can tell:
No eye was there to see;
Yet the winds that were his requiem knell
They moaned him mournfully.
(…)

---

[33] For instance, the roof of the Pensionnat seems to Lucy a „tomb slab" and the white beds in the dormitory – spectres (Cf Drew, 2003, p. 196).

In the last stanza of the poem Henry is said to lay intact in his tomb as he is caressed by the balmy „*enkindling sound*" of the church bells. In this lengthy elegy there could be sensed relief that Henry would stir the piece of the living on earth no more. Henry's bride, Marian, „*deems her bridegroom dead*" and goes into raptures when his death is announced. When knowing his son is dead, Henry's own father „*smiled a demon's smile*" and in his eye there sparkles „a glimpse of hell." Originally, Henry Percy must have been designed as a character both intimate and repulsively ferocious. In 1834 Branwell Brontë writes that Henry says to his wife, Augusta: „*Augusta, if there be a Satan, I am he*" (Cf Barker, 1995, ch. 8). Henry Percy is one manifestation of Charlotte's intention to use the Ghost persona as capable of modifying men's consciousness. Even though Henry's absence pacifies the world, yet his lack leaves a gap of unfulfilled a future in man's world of warring human passions[34].

As mentioned before, there are a few instances where some major lyrical personae from Angria disappear and then are revived. The case with Henry Percy is a good hint at how Charlotte focuses on the problem of *empathy* in the light of her treatment of *Death*. Henry's disappearance is projected onto the natural environment to such an extent that the reader is made to believe that after his death the whole of reality is transformed into a direct successor, a receptacle, of his spirit (through, for instance, the animated sea and the wind that stir people's minds). He thus becomes a reality against which people could begin to verify the feasibility of their own Being. Henry's beloved somehow fulfils her self through absorbing the identity of her *Other*[x]. At this stage, Death forbids the possibility of physical consummation of their relationship yet it ominously brings spiritual completion to Henry's beloved.

Another poetic work of Charlotte's worth looking into is the poem *Pilate's Wife's Dream* (published 1846, Winnifrith, 1984, pp. 3 – 8). This is Pilate's wife's confession of her equivocal attitude towards her husband – at first her inspiration for living, but mostly her spiritual gaoler, who „*robs her youth*", „*crushes her mind*" and „*slays [her] freedom*"; „*[her] soul abhors his mien*". The „*clear and red*" morning she is dreaming of is accompanied by the remembrance of a dreadful future

---

[34] Another poem which discusses the same event is Charlotte's „Lady-Bird! Lady-bird! fly away home" (around 1837, Winnifrith, 1984, pp. 302–308).

foretold for Pilate: the red gore-stained snow around her husband's dead body ripped apart by wolves. Factually, there is no direct evidence of the woman's wrongdoing. Yet the fact that she has imagines so vividly her husband's death torments her now, because she willed his annihilation in her mind, which thought acts fast in unravelling and crushing her own identity:

> *(...)*
> *I said I had no tears for such as he,*
> *And lo! My cheek is wet – mine eyes run o'er.*
> *I weep for mortal suffering, mortal guilt,*
> *I weep the impious deed, the blood self-spilt.*
> *(...)*

She is convinced in her husband's crime in ordering „*this Hebrew Christ*" Jesus' death. She almost canonizes Jesus as she broods over his „*spotless (...) goodness*" (yet Christ's „*lineage, doctrine and mission*" remain to her unknown); she admits the old faith is „*rotten*". She nonetheless mourns in advance, so to speak, her husband's future death too. Her husband's experience on earth may be crime-ridden, yet if he died, she herself would cease to mean... Pilate's wife's devotion for this controversial *Other* is additionally complicated by the fact that she connects the idea of *Otherness* with the image of Christ. On the other hand, if Pilate died, the woman would be undeniably deprived of her youth and of a past filled with the hope of a future of shared happiness. Even though Pilate's punitive death would be a way of rectifying his crime towards Christ, yet it would not really bring solace to his wife. The woman seeks to suffer an unachievable „*mortal guilt*" herself, i.e. to have done something, which could be considered her true experiential link to reality, which link is always emotionally burdensome. The last stanza of the poem tells us that Pilate's wife is waiting for the „*night*" when she would know „*what path and guide*" to follow.

Pilate's wife is a variation on *the Mourner* persona, for whom the notion of death serves to test her potential for an altruistic, i.e. generous, forgiving attitude towards Life.

In the poem *The Death of Lord Hartford* (January 1838, Winnifrith, 1984, pp. 227–229) the reader is allowed to partake of Lord Hartford's last moments of life, after Zamorna has shot him for loving his mistress, Mina Laury (Cf Winnifrith 1984, p. 229). Lord Hartford speaks of himself as though he were already dead and about to return on earth as a ghost. He is determined to gain his mistress' love in the dimmest and darkest of woods, at night, if only „*she confessed [her] heart [his] own*". The refusal to gain peace in Heaven and the decision to stir the life of the living brings this persona close to Heathcliff's fiendish hopes of merging with dead Cathy in Emily Brontë's *Wuthering Heights*. Determined to verify Catherine's unceasing beauty and spiritual might, Heathcliff performs the sacrilege of exhuming his beloved's body. In Charlotte's poem, the reader is offered Lord Hartford's confession of his devotion for his beloved's soul and nature, which he feels, was left incomplete. Harford's „*wild brain*" produces the sombre delusion about the possibility of returning back to earth is his way to „mend" the latter fact (he would „*buy*" the bliss of love „*with blood*"). He maintains a belief in his capacity to remodel reality in case he re-joined the living. The last stanza of the poem is sinisterly vivid in its description of his expiration: his eyes are „*up-turned,*" his lips are „*white*", his aspect – „*wan*", „*stricken with agony*". Again, the scene is reminiscent of Nelly Dean's description of dead Heathcliff, whose body she finds anguished and stark after the storm at Wuthering Heights. Hartford is alone in his last moments because in his life he failed to acknowledge God's free gift in man's ability to love unselfishly, unconditionally and without expecting the *Other* to conscientiously reciprocate (at one point he admits neglecting the fact that his beloved confessed to him „*she never loved but one*" – most probably Zamorna). As far as imagery is concerned, both in *Pilate's Wife's Dream* and in the latter poem Charlotte Brontë demonstrates an ominous zest for physical concreteness, for narrowly specific descriptions of the physicality of Death happening. In Charlotte Brontë's poetry, the presence of the Ghost „daemonizes" reality, as it insists on a „flexible" borderline between Life and Death, the crossing of which yields ontological revelations onto the Mourner.

* * *

The Female Ghost and its Role
in Charlotte Brontë's Ontological Quest

To „*extend reality*" into the realm of the unknown and the eternal is one of the functions of the Female Ghost in Charlotte Brontë's poetry[xi]. Doubtless, in this there are traces of the Romantic cult towards the muse as female (a replica of the once corporally existent beloved woman for a traditionally male poet). On a superficial level, ghostliness is a way to capture, to preserve the ambience created by the beloved's spirit. From the point of view of the feminist critic, the latter allows the poet to „take ultimate control over the departed woman'"[xii]. In Charlotte Brontë's philosophy, however, the female ghost is given the task to establish the fact of the individual's indifference towards the ontological Duty of *Being as Co-Being*. The Ghost is there to sanction a listless attitude towards Life, which would otherwise allow existence as granted unconditionally and would require one to fulfil no obligation with regard to one's fate (which is believed to be something beyond man's control). As might be expected, in a significant number of poems the Lyrical Self, who is speaking, is the *Mourner*, for whom the World has turned into a wilderness after the death of his erstwhile beloved. It is now within the Ghost's power to lead the Mourner towards spontaneous admission of his guilt, which is the only way his spirit could hope to reach his late beloved's soul. There is a conscientious attempt to re-initiate a male sinner into a feasible reality where the spontaneity of feeling would be subjugated to the mind's conscious desire to donate the best of one's potential to an *Other*. The process of overcoming the limitations of the singularity of one's mind is paralleled by the purgatorial practice of sharing one's Life with an *Other*, of taking the Eucharist[xiii]. The ghost's elusive presence, it would appear, is the Survivor's punishment and reward. Punishment, because the Survivor could never equal the woman's existence, which is complete and spiritually ampler that the Survivor's own (which is also incomplete at the moment the reader is allowed to look at it). Reward, because the Survivor's realization of his guilt towards the deceased woman could elucidate his road towards ontological maturation. Time on earth is limited anyway, it is never enough for one person's spirit to reach perfection and absolute fulfilment of his/ her potential, but it could be perceived as advantageous only through the realisation of each man's opportunity of self-concretization through Co-Being.

The poem *Matin* (12th November 1830 – Winnifrith, 1984, pp. 125–127), signed by the Marquis of Douro (the Duke of Zamorna), is dedicated to his late beloved and wife Marian Hume. Opium-like and intermingled with Nature's harmonious melodies, Marian both pacifies and disturbs Zamorna's sleep, which is unsettled by Zamorna's feeling of guilt in neglecting his young wife who died from grief[xiv]. The female is revered as the Redeemer. This attitude of the man towards the woman is reiterated in another poem, *Marian* (21st July 1837 – Winnifrith, 1984, pp. 217–219). Dying, the lady takes away man's chances for happiness, but instead provides his spirit with an opportunity to „upgrade itself" whilst building faith in the Christian belief in Heaven's benevolence towards, and protection of, Man. There is no need to open „*the grave-sheet's fold, / Nor lift the coffin-lid*". Instead,

(…)
If you wish to think again
Of her who loved and died,
Oh! Look upward to the plain
Of heaven expanding wide.
(…)

From the aesthetic point of view, the beloved's death is necessitated by the poet's need for creative growth (structurally evident, for instance, in Charlotte's tendency to embark on lengthy detailed descriptions of the appearance of certain personae of Angria). Ethically, however, the beloved's death dismembers the intactness, fixedness and superficiality of man's reality as composed only of facts. The man becomes an „exile," he feverishly clings to the image of his beloved, whose death he is bound to re-experience as he gazes at the perfect natural shapes which could be seen to reflect the woman's beauty. The acknowledgement of death is to him the value of life acknowledged.

In the ballad *The Rose* (around 1839 – Winnifrith, 1984, pp. 250–251) it is suggested that the beloved's death is caused directly, or indirectly, by the man[35]. On a grander scale, one who is at first unable to recognize *the Other's* ontological significance, or else one who is for one reason or another spiritually incomplete, may turn into a sombre melancholic likely to be visited by the „*silent Nun*" (the „*silent guest*"): „*comrade and confidante*," who fills with her presence the „*vacant gloom*" in every room (Cf „*The Autumn day its course has run*" – May 1843 – Winnifrith, 1984, pp. 239–240). Charlotte Brontë's frequent employment of the persona of the Ghost suggests a trust in a power, which could aid man's spirit *from without* – *the Other's* ameliorative influence over the Self. The ghost both counteracts absence, loss and Death, and at the same time emphasizes it[xv].

The re-appearance of this „silent confidante", the dead beloved, lead the reader to the impression that the acceptance and reconsideration of the Other's death signals at the fact that Life's dimensions have been acknowledged[36]. Following Griakalov's rather modern interpretation of the category of *the Other* in Bakhtin's works, the female ghost for Charlotte Brontë might be defined as one that occupies what is known as „*the space of the third person*". That space provides a background, is the chronotope, where the Lyrical Self's confessions unfold in a way which indicates the development of his own identity[xvi]. Charlotte Brontë's insistence on the existence of a space which holds this unique confessor has to do with her belief in that reality, Being, is impossible within the enclosure of a single mind, but could only *happen* when the mind partakes of, and donates to, another mind. This „*space of the third person*" listens actively, so to speak, and absorbs, the Mourner's confessions. It harbours an invisible third person, an ever-present interlocutor, who is actually a participant in the Lyrical Self's conscious life. This space cannot answer

---

[35] In this case, the rose dies of grief for its former master (and its natural milieu), who is now supplanted by a King, who „was the worm that withered thee" and made the rose die upon „exile earth", whilst its „crimson leaves" were covered with dew which looked like tears.

[36] In Villette, Lucy Snowe „measures out" her place in the universe according to the way the story of the Nun unfolds at the pensionnat. She records her life alongside her involvement with the story of the Nun's pervasive presence (and her tragic death) on the premises of the Pensionnat where she lives. In Charlotte Brontë's poetry, too, the appearance of the „Nun" „parallels" the pace in the main character's ontological quest.

back, yet it contains the dead beloved's spirit, which can still be physically sensed. In other words, *„the space of the third"* is also *the mortuary of the Second (i.e. of the Other)* who is now dead.

In the ballad *„Well, the day's toils are over, with success"* (9th January 1837 – Winnifrith, 1984, pp. 311–325), there are certain natural „modifiers" which hint at the dead lady's presence. The *„driving sleet, (…) emerald plain, (…) lingering sun, (…) freshened foliage, (…) Eden-breeze"* – all of those reiterate the spirit of Mary Percy, daughter of Alexander Percy, and Duchess of Zamorna, third wife of Arthur Wellesley. The unfortunate victim of the quarrel between her father and her husband, she is sent in exile where she dies of a broken heart[xvii]. Within the theme of love forsaken the reader could again find the motifs of infanticide and of national pride in times of war. Nature around reiterates the fact of Mary's non-remonstrative and tragic end, which aggravates the Mourner's own fate (of how he managed to appropriate Percy's daughter, then loved her and „resigned" „the bright deposit." Tempestuous Nature accepts Mary the victim, who reproaches Adrian of loving her yet killing her (l. 223). Adrian realises that he was oblivious of the detrimental effects his departure would have over Mary, whom he now sanctifies (l. 261). Two stanzas of the poem clarify that even despite the haunting memory of Mary, which torments Adrian's spirit, he thinks he „needs not repine," since she has found the place where there is no grief, and that he must forget her. This elegy is not merely an attempt to restore Mary's lifetime presence. While the man's grief and sadness are projected onto Nature, Mary's recurring image does not fight the fact of her loss[xviii], but emphasizes the irreversibility of her death. Adrian declares that *„god gave the summons"* for Mary to perish and therefore he must no more think of her (at one point – ll. 150–158 – he recalls how he even prepared to slay her himself, but could not). Yet in his attitude one could clearly sense guilt and existential despair: he is somehow drifting towards self-chastisement, as he hints that there might have been a chance to save Mary, and that Mary actually should have been saved[37].

---

[37] As far as Charlotte's art of drawing is concerned, a relevant sketch relevant to the ideas suggested above might be that of The Atheist viewing the dead body of his wife, 1835–1836 (Cf Alexander & Sellars, 1995, p. 243).

Charlotte Brontë develops her interest in the image of *the revenant* – a representative of the intermediary stage between Life and Death, as it contains the concept of change, of transformations happening, and whose intrusion in the life of the living „shatters" men's self-centred belief in owning the World[xix]. To the living, such ghostly presence might appear threatening, for it makes one face the obligation to reconsider oneself as never the sole proprietor of Life. Another thematic support of the latter could be found in the poem *Young Man Naughty's Adventure* (probably 14th October 1830 – Winnifrith, 1984, pp. 111–112). Naughty, the young Angrian hero, is sent on an errand to the witch but when he arrives he finds her dead (possibly after being shot). The whole poem is filled with the dead woman's spirit, whose encounter the young man dreads. He dreads that as one dreads to meet an alternative of what is familiar but which lives in the world and questions man's spiritual wholeness[38].

In Charlotte's lengthy ballad **Gilbert** (around 1843, published 1846 – Winnifrith, 1984, pp. 31–43) the dead Elinor acts as both the Mourner's salvation and punishment. Gilbert's existential guilt is revealed only later, as it is outlined against the background of the idyllic warmth of the family hearth in his house, now identified with his charming wife and children. His remembrance of Elinor, whom he abandoned when a young man, eventually summons her ghost. The encounter between Gilbert and Elinor's ghost happens at night, when all is still and he is by himself. He deliberately searches for Elinor, but when he does meet her ghost, he is overpowered by its sightless power. Elinor's eyes are „*hollow*", but she holds a candle out to Gilbert, which, symbolically, opens his eyes. The encounter with Death proves to be the moment of insight into the meaning of Life, whereupon the merits (if any) one's own life are specified. Elisabeth Bronfen would offer a feminist interpretation on the issue of the woman's death. In the context of the above poem, Gilbert would be the masculine Survivor, who would identify himself as „alive", rather than dead, in comparison to the sightless and ghostly Elinor, whose dress is „*dripping wet*" with water: „(…) *if the dead woman is also 'perfect', she simultaneously comes to signify the surviving man's imperfection*"

---

[38] See Mary E. Coleridge's poem The Witch (as suggested in: Gilbert & Gubar, 1984, p. 307). In it the witch is an embodiment of the young woman's solitary spirit, her heart's desire having been neglected whilst she was alive.

(Bronfen, 1992, p. 129). Initially, Gilbert is presented as distantly proud and powerful, somewhat reluctant to receive Elinor's devotedness. In part 3 of this ballad („*The Welcome Home*") he ends his life shamefully, as he perishes in prayer to the ghost and, obviously, to God:

(…)
Across his throat a keen-edged knife
With vigorous hand he drew;
The wound was wide – his outraged life
Rushed rash and redly through.
And thus he died, by a shameful death,
A wise and worldly man,
Who never drew but selfish breath
Since first his life began.

It is suggested that Elinor's death was precipitated by Gilbert's neglectful attitude to her. She maybe left her home and maybe drowned herself. Albeit not entirely confirmed, Elinor's death precipitates Gilbert's own death which has a purifying role to his spirit. Elinor's death was unnecessary and Gilbert's death is shameful. Gilbert's death is his true punishment not so much because his life is interrupted so suddenly, but because it leaves an „ontological gap" in the possible completion of his moral search. By committing suicide, he also commits a crime towards the ones whom he bears responsibility for – his present family. In this sense, the female ghost's „hollow eyes" also probe into Gilbert's worthiness as father and husband. The Female Ghost terminates Gilbert's life as it exposes the „mesh" in his conscience. In Charlotte Brontë's novel *Jane Eyre* Mr. Rochester goes through the purgatory of the great fire at his home, which leaves him blind but wiser[39]. Similarly, Gilbert seems to „open his eyes" and see that it is within the Other's capacity to complete his life in the aesthetic sense of the word, which in this case is accompanied by the fact of Gilbert's

---

[39] Karen Rowe compares the purgatory effect the fire at Thornfield Hall has on Rochester to the insight as to the true state of affairs that the Earl of Gloucester receives after he is blinded, and subsequently rescued by his own son, Edgar (Cf Rowe, Karen, „Fairy-born and human-bred": Jane Eyre's Education in Romance, in: Abel, Hirsch & Langland, The Voyage In: Fictions of Female Development /Hanover & London, The University Press of New England, 1983/).

own literal termination of his life. In Gilbert's case, the physical loss of *the friend/ the beloved/ the Other* stirs his memory, and the latter – his conscience[40].

The poems discussed in this sub-chapter indicate that in Charlotte Brontë's poetry the individual's wish to re-unite with his dead beloved equals a desire to gain wholeness whilst re-creating his conscience. The promise of spiritual wholeness is issued to man from the liminal realm of *Death/Non-Death*: the female revenant's abode[xx]. The process of mourning the dead female beloved is paralleled by the man's own senses being made more acute, his conscience being stirred, and reality being objectified to him. The contacts with the dead beloved's ghost both alleviate and deepen his sense of gloom and solitude, which in its turn confirms that there can be no meaning of one's life which is one's own alone (Cf Eagleton, 2003, p. 64). *The Other* here is always *the deceased Other*, and so the longing for that *Other* is comparable to the longing for peace and Heaven. The Survivor's redemption is conditional upon his conscientious request for pardon from the Ghost of the dead beloved lady, whose lifetime he *owns* after her death.

* * *

The present chapter aimed to offer an extensive survey of the specificities of the presentation of the theme of Death in Charlotte Brontë's philosophy, as revealed in her poetry. It felt logical to divide the thematic variations of the poetic material analysed into sub-chapters in order to outline separate philosophical motifs that logically illustrate the individual's growing ontological awareness through a preoccupation with Mortality. The discussion of the theme in hand was positioned, to a certain extent, within the context of the dramatic world of Angria – the field for Charlotte's and Branwell's literary collaboration and rivalry over creating and modifying the relationship between certain dramatic personae's lives. Charlotte Brontë's perusal of the theme of Death may be defined as centred on *the death of the friend* (but in particular on the death of the female beloved). The experience of such one death proves for the Survivor a

---

[40] Compare Branwell Brontë's poem On Caroline (1837 – Winnifrith, 1983, p. 65).

'cathartic investigation' of the meaning of Life and of the wholeness of his/her identity, which is simultaneously being frustrated and upgraded.

In Charlotte Brontë's treatment of Death there is no obvious and immediate urge for one to be released from the carnal limitations the body imposes on the Self (as that would be the case with Emily Brontë). Neither is her treatment of Death so thoroughly focused on a perusal of the motif of spiritual salvation through the image of Christ – as that is the case with Anne Brontë. For Charlotte, Death's moral imperative is illustrated through the dead beloved's ghost, whose visitations mould the Lyrical Self's conscience and consciousness. The clinging to the ameliorative effect the ghost has on the Survivor must have been born out of Charlotte's intention to prove that there is a real opportunity to enervate the carnal urge for individuation that the Self is prone to through the elimination of *the opponent, of the Other.* The moment of Death, which heralds the individual's natural ending, could also be seen as his purpose because thus one might hope to reach the silent and heavenly abode of the beloved[xxi].

Charlotte Brontë's early lyric pieces (e.g. *The Violet, Presentiment, Memory*) demonstrate her interest in the principle of Mutability as Nature's driving force (hidden in Nature's Dionysian rebirth). The natural alternation of seasons and moods invokes the Lyrical Self's remembrance of the dead beloved, whose significance is strengthened by his growing awareness of the vulnerability of Time, and particularly of one's own time on earth. The preservation and absorption of the beloved's presence becomes the man's ontological task, which engenders a responsible attitude towards Life. On another level, the opportunity to gain uniqueness of identity through a heroic death (which is misguidedly thought to be the ultimate remedy against an uneventful and placid Present – „*But once again, but once again*", *Richard's Song*) is gradually quenched with the realization of the need for perseverance in caring for *an Other* – as long as one's life lasts and allows that.

In Charlotte's poetry individuation both happens through, and is suppressed by, persistent introspection (man's fire is „*self-kindled*", „*self-consumed*"; e.g. *Reason*). There is felt the need to find an external receptacle for one's spiritual potential: to find another human being to whose Authorial Otherness one may yield and who one may cherish and weep for. This Other, whom Charlotte's Mourner/Survivor is looking for, makes life finalizable for the Survivor. That is so because the Survivor's experience on earth is now to be determined and valued as an ingredient of another's limited time on Earth (e.g. *Stanzas on the Death of a Christian*). Ironically, it is the finalizability of one's life that 'opens it up', i.e. makes it capable of bearing sense, meaning. An attempt to subsist on the recesses of one's own mind only, away from *an Other*, restricts the Self's spiritual development. Frances feels her mind to be a „narrow cell" (Cf *Frances*), which stifles her, as she pines away in loneliness. She desires death as a rescue from the nought life has come to be to her; yet death coveted is the Self's own death in the first place. „*Travel and toil*", i.e. employing one's potential actively in sustaining Life, is the real remedy against the proneness towards mortification of one's own Self through exclusive introspective self-analysis.

Achieving meaning in Life through the interpretation of the significance of the phenomenon of Death becomes particularly evident when the definition of the concepts of devotion and love intersect with the issue of daemonic in man's mind. The poem *Pilate's Wife's Dream* illustrates the ontological trial Pilate's wife goes through, as she wishes for her husband's death, which act of vengeance might be seen as justified with regard to his inhumane deeds in life, but unjustified with regard to the moral code of Life which forbids ruling out another living creature's existence (even in one's mind only). A positive appropriation of the phenomenon of Death would resists a negative action, because it would ultimately desire to maintain Good in Life, which would be accompanied by Man's whetted capacity to understand and empathise[41].

The notion of Death ought to engender empathy: the encounters with the '*silent Nun*' or the '*holy confidante*' in Charlotte Brontë's poetry contain a chance for man to find meaning in Life. Povided that one recognizes the ontological value inherent in the transgredience of the *Other* („*Well, the day's toils are over, with success*"; *Gilbert*). '*The space of the Other*' crosses and defines the space of the Present. It urges the Survivor to contrast the Present with an unfinished and forsaken Past without which

---

[41] On 9th October 1848 Charlotte Brontë makes an entry into her diary about her recent experience of witnessing her brother Branwell's death: „(…) Till the last hour comes, we never know how much we can forgive, pity, regret a near relative. All his vices were and are nothing now. We remember only his woes" (CF Gaskell, 1928, p. 254).

the present seems meaningless. On the aesthetic level the latter is seen in the Poet's revision of the event of death in certain major Angrians' lives (e.g. Marian Hume, or Mary Percy). On the level of ethics, there could be sensed a feeling of guilt which broods over Charlotte Brontë's poetry – the Survivor's guilt in outliving the Other, without whom the stability and singularity of one's mind are threatened. Hence the recognition that, if *Being* were to be achieved at all, then that would have to be a *dialogic* mode of Being (i.e. Co-Being).

NOTES:

[i] Cf Gaskell, 1928, pp. 323–324.
[ii] Cf Drew, Lamonica, 2003, p. 180.
[iii] Cf Ricoeur, Paul, 2004, p. 170.
[iv] Cf Clark & Holquist, in: Bakhtin, *Pro et Contra*..., 2002, p. 68.
[v] Cf Ibid., p. 51.
[vi] Cf Abrams, 1973, p. 296.
[vii] Cf Eagleton, 2003, p. 104.
[viii] Cf Winnifrith, 1984, p. 342.
[ix] Cf Boyadziev, 2000, p. 307.
[x] Cf Patterson, Charles: *Empathy and the Daemonic in Wuthering Heights*, in: Goodin George, /ed./ *The English Novel in the Nineteenth Century. Essays on Literary Meditation of Human Values* (University of Illinois Press, 1974), p. 84.
[xi] Cf Beach, 1936, p. 285.
[xii] Cf Barreca, Regina, *Sex and Death in Victorian Literature* (Macmillan, 1990), p. 246.
[xiii] Cf Bakhtin, KFP, 2003, pp. 16–17.
[xiv] Cf Barker, 1995, pp. 982–983.
[xv] Cf Bronfen in: Bronfen & Goodwin, 1993, p. 106.
[xvi] Cf Griakalov in: Bakhtin, *Pro et Contra*... *2002*, p. 344.
[xvii] Cf Barker, 1995, p. 983.
[xviii] Cf Bronfen & Goodwin 1993, p. 106.
[xix] Cf Bronfen, 1992, pp. 295 – 296.
[xx] Cf Bronfen, 1992, p. 67, p. 218.
[xxi] Cf Langan, Celeste, *Romantic Vagrancy. Wordsworth and the Simulation of Freedom* (Cambridge University Press, 1995).

Section III

Emily Brontë

The investigation of Emily Brontë's treatment of Mortality in her poetry is a major undertaking for the critic. To Emily I have chosen to dedicate the whole of section III in part II of this study. As with Anne and Charlotte, the motifs I have chosen to analyse will be separated in sub-chapters. It is only reasonable that those sub-chapters are lengthier in view of the more abundant thematic material relevant in Emily Brontë's poetry. In fact, they could almost be given the status of separate chapters, rather than sub-chapters; however, in this case, that would dissolve the contextual tightness of the presentation of the empirical, so to speak, poetic material. Naturally, where appropriate, quotations and reference will be made to Anne's, Charlotte's and Branwell's works, as I intend do demonstrate that *Mortality* is that philosophic discourse, which accommodates comfortably all the Brontës.

It nonetheless appears, that Emily was the one to mould the dominant persona of the **Gondal saga, A.G.A.** *(Augusta Geraldine Almeida),* as a multi-functional image of Death which includes both thematic interpretations of Death (e.g. the daemonic in nature, or the mother who murders her own babe, or the image of the Christian sinner), as well as the poet's own attitude towards the structural layout of Gondal. Taken in its poetic value, Gondal is a poetic cycle with one dominant lyrical persona, whose many personifications, elimination and resuscitation show the poet's own struggle with the problem of the „authorial surplus of vision" (following Bakhtin) which has the capacity to initiate, as well as to complete the life of a literary hero/lyrical persona. On the technical level, there is also the immediate problem of what portion of the Gondal saga is available to the critic at present. Emily Brontë is known to have provided prose notes for the Gondal story. If so, it should be reminded that at present they are missing[1]. Gondal, as a whole, is, for various reasons, in a

---

[1] Like Angria, the toponym Gondal stands for a kingdom in its own right in the Northern Pacific, situated on the isle of Gondal, populated by „a passionate, freedom-loving race". In the thematic introduction to Hatfield's 1941 edition of Emily's verse, Fannie Ratchford specifies that Gondal was a confederacy of provinces or kingdoms, each with a hereditary ruling family, which was involved in a „deadly rivalry". Gondal first developed as a play of Emily's and Anne's. „*Emily's and Anne's extensive prose literature of Gondal, constituting a full and detailed background for their somewhat cryptic poems, has been lost, and their verse now stands alone, scantily supplemented by a short journal fragment signed by both girls when they were about fifteen and sixteen; the notes they exchanged on Emily's birthday in 1841 and 1845; and Anne's lists of*

fragmentary state, it is incomplete. Being incomplete, however, it still preserves its status of the main texture of her poetic heritage. Gondal's fragmentarity imparts to Emily's verse the quality of being episodic, which is additionally endorsed by the fact that Death seems to mainly regulate the progress of Life in this dramatic world. A world where in man's mind are married malice and devotion; and the striving to gain attention is a tragic attempt to restore the lost time of one's youth and innocence – the time of embryonic indefiniteness and freedom from the moral responsibilities of one's temporal definitions. In Emily Brontë's Gondal the dominance of the theme of Death signifies a constant search for meaning – both by the lyrical personae and by the poet. Emily arrives at the idea of Death as inspiring the dialogic intention of Being as Co-Being after toil and deliberations, so that for a long time Co-Being remains a goal only. Yet the abundance of ballads and elegies in Emily's poetry proves that the poet is constantly „on the watch": she is constantly looking for *an Other*, who could fill the ontological gap in which the Survivor has fallen.

The fact that, compared to Anne's and Charlotte's poetic works, Emily's have been a true battlefield of contrasting critical viewpoints and literary approaches, is reflected in several issues which need to be mentioned at this introductory stage of presentation of Emily Brontë. The first issue is the long-lasted argument about whether the whole of Emily Brontë's verse should be classified as Gondal (that is, does each poem have a place in the Gondal saga) or Non-Gondal (that is, the poems could be seen as independent, as not necessarily belonging to the Gondal saga). Then, if her poetry were classified as Gondal, what would be the right order of events and incidents around which there can be grouped thematic clusters of poems, and how many main personae are there in Gondal. On the other hand, if the Gondal story were to be disregarded, there would emerge other ways of grouping the poems (e.g. chronologically, or with regard to the biographical specificities of Emily Brontë's poetic development, or else with regard to given philosophical motifs that can be traced in the poems). Many of the poetic pieces could be seen as independent, and extremely „self-absorbed". The literary historian and critic Philip Davis maintains that poems like „*Often rebuked, yet always*

Gondalan place names and personal names" – Cf Ratchford, F. in: /ed./ Hatfield, C.W., *The Complete Poems of Emily Jane Brontë* (New York: Columbia University Press, 1941), pp. 14–15.

back returning" (unsigned), *„Cold in the earth"* (1845) and *„No Coward Soul Is Mine"* (1846) are examples of lyrics without an immediately recognizable context. The only thing, which unites those poems, is the feeling of „a self whose deep inner mystic resources are bared by its very closeness to finding death". As is the case with Charlotte and Branwell, there is also some uncertainty as to the authorship of some poems of Emily's (some have been ascribed to, or bear the qualities of, Branwell's verse[2]). Also, how deep was Charlotte Bronte's editorial intervention in the 1846 and the subsequent 1850 editions of Emily's poetry? The edition of Emily Brontë's poetry followed throughout this thesis is ***The Complete Poems of Emily Jane Brontë, edited from the manuscripts by C. W. Hatfield[3] (New York: Columbia University Press & London: Oxford University Press, 1941).*** Although not the most recent edition, I think this is the most comprehensive one so far, as it makes allowances for major biographical, critical and graphical specificities of the emergence of the poems. It includes Fannie Ratchford's version of the Gondal saga (one of the Brontës' best equipped scholars – Cf Hatfield, 1941, p. 13). It also groups the poems around major events and personae in the Gondal saga (pp.17–21 of Hatfield's 1941 edition). In my opinion, Hatfield's edition is a pioneering work, which enhances the process of recognizing the importance of the theme of Death in Emily Brontë's poetic heritage. Hatfield was also the first Brontëist to put Emily's poems in their right chronological order, restoring their original headings (Cf Ratchford, F., 1955, p. 36).

For all my professional interest in the critical guild of „the Gondalians", I would argue that it would be more appropriate to rearrange Emily Brontë's verse in a manner, which would allow for observation of

---

[2] Clement Shorter investigated those and selected them in accordance with the poet's handwriting style (Emily's or Branwell's), or in accordance with previous opinions, which categorized some poems as belonging to either Branwell or Emily. He also marked the fact that, for instance, some hymns of Anne's had previously been printed as Emily's. – Cf Shorter, Clement, *The Complete Poems of Emily Jane Brontë* (London: Stoughton LTD, 1923).

[3] All quotations of Emily Brontë's poems in the present research follow Hatfield's 1941 edition. Normally, a poem will be quoted by title and/or first line, followed by the date of creation (if there is one that can be confirmed) and the page/pages it is to be found on in Hatfield's edition. When necessary, its number will also be mentioned like this: e.g. H121 (i.e. poem No 121 in Hatfield's edition quoted) – a commonly accepted technique of quoting Emily's verse when Hatfield's 1941edition is refereed to.

sub-themes and motifs in clusters of poems. Such approach would not diminish the significance of the Gondal context as the most solid thematic field, which nourished the formation of the philosophic discourse of *Mortality*. Yet, it is necessary to state that even outside Gondal, the thematic bias towards Death is as strong and as purposeful, so that groups of poems could be seen to cling to common motifs related to Mortality, and – in most cases – traceable chronologically within a certain period of time in Emily Brontë's ontological development. This is not to say that Emily's poetic heritage should be completely „de-Gondalised" – for the simple reason that it is exactly with the context of Gondal in mind that her poetry can be viewed as a preamble to her masterpiece *Wuthering Heights*. Undoubtedly, Gondal and *Wuthering Heights* represent a thematic dichotomy, in which many parallels are possible between certain characters' fates (as shall be observed later). *Mortality* is both in Gondal and in Emily's novel a regenerative technique and a „linking device"; Emily's characters' and lyrical personae's desire for self-completion depends on the acceptance of the presence of Death as an ingredient of Being as Co-Being.

Editions of Emily Brontë's Poetry and Their Relevance to the Themes of *Mortality*

It is crucial to spare some time over certain variations in the editors' efforts to restore Emily Brontë's poetic heritage. To begin with, there is the widely known 1846 edition of The *Poems of Currer, Ellis and Acton Bell* (London: Aylott and Jones, May 2nd 1846), one invaluable reprint of which is the Wordsworth Poetry Library 1995 one (with an introduction by Kathryn White). The subsequent selection of Emily's verse, which Charlotte Brontë made for the 1850 edition (the new edition of *Wuthering Heights* and *Agnes Grey*, which also included some poems of Emily's And Anne's), was accompanied by numerous alterations: changes of words (and therefore of the meaning of whole passages), as well as added words[4]. Mr Clement Shorter's contacts with Charlotte's husband, the Rev. Arthur Bell

---

[4] The existence of a second novel of Emily Brontë's is conjectural, yet if there had been one, Charlotte might well have destroyed it. That incomplete novel might have had the gloomy texture that Gondal had (Cf Barker, 1995, ch. 18).

Nicholls, lead to his subsequent purchase of a large number of manuscripts, which encouraged him to venture his 1910 edition of *The Complete Works of Emily Brontë (Vol. I – Poetry*, London: Hodder and Stoughton – Cf Hatfield, 1941, pp. 4–13). C.W. Hatfield's investigation of Emily's verse was enhanced by his meetings with H. H. Bonnell of Philadelphia, who owned an impressive portion of the Brontëana manuscripts. C. Shorter's 1923 edition of Emily Brontë's poems was assisted by Hatfield, who on this occasion provided the bibliography and the notes, and later, in 1941, himself published Emily's complete poetic works. Hatfield's edition pays due respect to the fact that for some of the poems of the three sisters no manuscripts were ever found. Mr Arthur Bell Nicholl's own transcripts were not really reliable, as they caused the texts to differ in certain ways from the originals, and titles were added to poems (ibid.). Hunting after the original manuscripts is not an aim of the present thesis. It should only be stated that Hatfield's edition is the only one so far that presents to the critic a full compilation of all poems of Emily's extant – whether from original manuscripts or from transcripts. It is therefore the one which ought to be used for the purposes of a serious critical attempt to analyse Emily Brontë's philosophy.

In Barbara Lloyd-Evans' 1992 edition of Emily's verse are to be found only the poems Emily herself chose to keep in her three poetic notebooks, in which she transcribed and grouped the poems herself (Cf Lloyd-Evans, Barbara, *The Poems of Emily Jane Brontë* /London: B. T. Batsford LTD, 1992/, pp. 7–13). Those were:

a/ the *Ashley Notebook* (poems Emily transcribed from the ones she wrote between 26 July 1837 and October 1839; the same Edward Chitham calls *book C* – Cf Chitham, 1998, p. 33)

b/ the *Emily Jane Brontë – EJB Notebook* (in it Emily transcribed poems she wrote up till February 1844 – *book A* in Chitham's terms – Chitham ibid.)

c/ the *Gondal Notebook* (poems written up till March 1844 – *book B* for Chitham – Chitham, ibid.)[5].

---

[5] In the manuscripts many of Emily's poems are „crabbed and constricted to save space", which hinders critical investigation (Cf Chitham, Edward, *The Birth of Wuthering Heights. Emily Brontë at Work* /St. Martin's Press, 1998/, pp. 8–9).

The last notebook is obviously the one that most pertains to the Gondal saga[6], but is not the only one that illustrates the relevance of *Mortality* in Emily Brontë's poetry[7]. Another well known fact is that Emily made some alterations to her verse for the first, the 1846 edition of her poetry (the joint edition of the three sisters' poems) in a conscientious attempt to conceal any obviously personal traces in her mythical world of Gondal. She nonetheless certainly left enough evidence in those notebooks to show she was not indifferent, shall we say, to Death. Eventually, Death became for Emily a trope: a trope that comprised other major themes such as: *Time, Space, Nature, Soul, Home, Heaven and God.*

The most fervent supporter of the Gondal-saga structure of Emily's poetry is <u>Fannie Ratchford</u>. In 1955 she published her version of Emily's poetic heritage, which she chose to call: *Gondal's Queen. A Novel in Verse by Emily Jane Brontë* (University of Texas Press). Arranged to logically present the context of the Gondal saga, Emily's poems formed a coherent whole with its history and novel-like progress of plot. The importance of Emily's and Anne's joined efforts in creating Gondal was emphasized. In addition, there was included a comparative presentation and analysis of both Emily's and Anne's poems pertaining to *the Republican – Royalist War in Gondal* – one of the most crucial events in the spine of the Gondal saga[8]. The only remnants extant of Emily and Anne's Gondal nowadays are

---

[6] Juliet Barker argues that Emily continued re-transcribing her verse into volumes until May 1848, so that Gondal must have been alive till at least 1847 for sure (Barker 1995, chapter 15).

[7] One proof is the much anthologised „*Cold in the earth, and the deep snow piled above thee*", which appeared on 3rd March 1845, i.e. after the Gondal notebook.

[8] The Republican-Royalist War was commented by Anne and Emily in prose notes (and in the so-called 'birthday notes'). This war, like the essence of the story in the saga of Angria, was based on historical events the Brontë children established; later, they provided commentary on those events as on historical truth (Cf Lloyd-Evans, 1992, p. 11). This event emerged from the Brontë children's juvenile plays, which they started with the set of 12 wooden soldiers their father the Rev. Patrick Brontë brought home from Leeds on 5th June 1826. Each child is known to have chosen a soldier and given it a name. Emily's was originally dubbed *Waiting Boy*, and was also called Sir William Edward Parry (after the real person, an Arctic Explorer who lived 1790–1855). Parry's palace would have been one literary predecessor of the house at Wuthering Heights in Emily's novel (Cf Ratchford, 1955, pp. 14, 19). The game with the wooden soldiers yielded *The Young Men's Plays*, which lasted for 6 years. Further on, the Brontë children developed two imaginary worlds: Angria and Gondal. Of the two the latter was more legendary. Angria was more civilized. While Charlotte and Emily shared 'secret plays' at bedtime, Gondal was most probably started in 1831 (and developed further by Emily and Anne), when Charlotte left for Roe Head (Cf Knapp, Betina, *The Brontës* /New York: Continuum, 1992/, p. 102).

their poems, as well as the so-called *Diary notes*, or *Birthday notes*[9]. Those are diary notes Emily and Anne decided to write every four years on/near Emily's birthday (30th July), and were each to be opened and read 4 years later. The papers were written in 1834 (jointly), 1837 (jointly), 1841 (separately) and 1845 (separately – Cf Lloyd-Evans, 1992, p. 11).

Fannie Ratchford's determination to re-create Emily's verse as one narrative was motivated with the fact that the Gondal saga was built on the life, relationships and tragic liaisons of one central persona called *A.G.A (Augusta Geraldine Almeida, Queen of Gondal)*. Fannie Ratchford also suggested to additionally group Emily's poems around other significant personae they refer to (eg. A.G.A. group, Julius Brenzaida group, poems about political and territorial events etc). Nowadays, A.G.A.'s personifications, as well as a detailed list of all Gondal characters and places can be found in Barbara Lloyd-Evans' edition of Emily Brontë's verse (Cf Lloyd-Evans, 1992, Appendix 1, pp. 180–183). What is also available at present is two versions of the Gondal story. First, there is W.D. Paden's one. Paden drew a genealogical diagram of the Stuarts of Exina – the main participants in the Gondal saga. The other one is Fannie Ratchford's account of A.G.A.'s life as linked mainly to her love relationships with Alexander, Lord of Elbë and to Lord Alfred of Aspin Castle. Paden's version is chronological – it endeavours to place the Gondal incidents and events in a period of about 50 years, the initial point of reference being the beginning of the nineteenth century. Paden pinpoints poems relevant for each event in Gondal. There is a detailed account not only of A.G.A.'s affair with Alexander and with Alfred, but also of her many personifications as Rosina, also called Geraldine (who was loved by the heroic and victorious invader and king of Gaaldine, Julius Brenzaida, from whom she had a girl). Augusta's other love affairs are elucidated too (i.e. those with, respectively, Amedeus and Fernando, who was sent by her in exile). Paden also pays attention to the following events: Augusta abandoning her own daughter; Augusta's death from grief after Alfred's death, Augusta's subsequent resuscitation and Augusta's final assassination by her rival Angelica (Cf Pinion, F. B., *A Brontë Companion* /Bristol: Macmillan 1975/, pp. 371–373). Gondal's stern nature reminds one of the West Yorkshire Moors –

---

[9] See also Ratchford, 1955, p. 22.

the land where Emily lived all her life and where she must have drawn inspiration both for her poetry and her novel.

Unlike the versions of the two critics discussed above, many an influential 20th-century Brontëist have argued that an adequate approach to Emily Brontë's verse is not necessarily one which should embrace the Gondal saga as a preamble. In <u>Maureen Peeck-O'Toole's monograph</u> on aspects of lyric in the poetry of Emily Brontë there is a division of the poems into Gondal, non-Gondal, hybrid, Gondal with hybrid elements and Non-Gondal with hybrid elements (Cf Peeck-O'Toole, Maureen, *Aspects of Lyric in the Poetry of Emily Brontë* /Amsterdam: Costerus New series, Volume 79, Rodopi, 1988/, p. 12). Additionally, within each group are outlined certain thematic similarities which lead to grouping Emily's poems into clusters. Robin Grove's opinion is that „a first requirement" for a good investigation of Emily's poetic heritage would be to ignore its Gondal canvas (Cf Grove, R. in: Smith, Anne, /ed./ *The Art of Emily Brontë* /Vision and Barnes & Noble, 1976/, p. 41). In this case, again, there is a proneness to group the poems in accordance with the dominant theme. Two opponents of Fannie Ratchford's and of Hatfield's seem to be <u>Derek Stanford and Muriel Spark.</u> In their biographical and critical book about Emily Brontë they insist on the „*de-Gondalisation*" of Emily's verse. They believe that the unique blend of „*(…) various currents of thought which Emily entertained in her verse…*" provide a safer key for analysing and selecting her poems (Cf Stanford & Spark, *Emily Brontë: Her Life and Work* /Arrow Books LTD, 1985/, pp. 144, 167). Those are: „*stoicism, pantheism, Christianity, and a form of personal Quietism…*" (ibid. p. 167).

The Issue About *Gondal's* Main Lyrical Persona and How this Relates to the themes of *Mortality*

A strong reason to adhere to a thematic grouping of the poems is that Gondal (like Angria) must have grown from incident and character, rather than from narrative design (Chitham, 1998, p. 203). The Gondal poems were not written chronologically, i.e. there was not the intention of following the Gondal story as we have it nowadays after the critics' reconstruction of it. Gondal is a blend of instantaneous occurrences, flashbacks and glances forward. It reads as an **epic** and as such does not have linear time, but „adheres to the reality of human consciousness in recalling and forecasting time" (ibid. p. 68). When a poem is dedicated to a dead persona and is „spoken" by another persona, this very poem may reflect as much fact as it would represent fiction. Thus the poem H143 is about *The Death of A.G.A* (January 1841–May 1844). Yet poems H150 *Geraldine* (August 17th, 1841) and H151 *Rosina* (September 1st, 1841) tell of the same persona (A.G.A, also known as Rosina of Alcona, or Geraldine, or „Sidonia's deity" – Cf Hatfield, 1941, p. 15) as if she were still alive[10]. The latter **Jill Dix Ghnassia** would categorise as an example of paramnesia (a phenomenon that occurs when a person's capacity to memorise real events and differentiate them from fantasy is in disorder – Ghnassia, 1994, p. 22). The obvious mixture of fact and fantasy in Emily Brontë's poetry, however, is rather more intricate. It seems to be a literary device: the subversive role Mortality is used to examine a person's Self which with Emily tends to dissolve into the multitude of other selves, the ones which constitute history and therefore memory.

Emily Brontë's refusal to systematize Gondal and her rejection of linear time makes Gondal feel like a whole that consists of „a variety of passionate moods" (Cf Hardy, B., 1985, p. 108). To remember Bakhtin again, in Romantic lyric poetry the lyrical persona is never complete[ii]. There is the poet's attempt to catch that persona in a moment, in a glimpse – when he/she is most himself/herself. In this respect the function of Death as the boundary to a lifetime story, i.e. in its liminal status, becomes irrelevant. The form that clads the content is fragmentary and flash-like. Hence Emily clinging to symbols (rather than to images). The symbols help the poet build up the main lyric persona as unique: they emphasize only what is more or less constant and impervious to Time, and thus help create a unique environment for the lyrical persona. Symbols here stand out at times of peak fusion of fates and lives of other personae with that main one[11].

---

[10] On the whole, Augusta's love relationships are represented in a mixed and scattered order in Emily's poetry extant (Cf Paden, 1958, p. 24).
[11] Of all the symbols she develops, Emily attaches the greatest significance to *the wind*. This ghostly confessor brings back the longed for reality (e.g. that of erstwhile happiness in childhood). It also provides the speaker with an insight into the future. As shall be discussed later, the wind plays a major role in at least 28 poems of Emily's, in which in one way or another it also represents the

A.G.A.'s life is „a life in flashbacks" and is reflected by other Gondalians, by the poet and by Augusta herself. It is a life of absences and cravings after individuals who perish for her and because of her. A.G.A. could be seen as a Romantic persona. She surrenders to Emily Brontë's desire to penetrate deep into her and invest her own frame of mind into her character. A.G.A. needs to amalgamate her self with the poet's self in order to find a still harbour for her tempestuous nature, which in a way isolates her. She is active and domineering to the point where she nearly merges with the poet. The occasions of her death and revival keep up with the pace of the poet's ontological progress in considering the problem of Mortality. A.G.A. is the most absorbent of all characters Emily Brontë ever created in her life and she concretizes the poet's search for Otherness. A.G.A. is in a diffused state, she is ubiquitous in Gondal, she cannot be arrested, just as Death cannot be arrested: she is unpredictable yet recurrent... A.G.A. dismantles what Bakhtin refers to as „the surplus of vision" an author/poet possesses in respect of a hero/lyrical persona. From the aesthetic point of view, A.G.A.'s presence seems to an obsession for the poet: she is *the Other* who could never be caught for good in order to be analysed and therefore to be fully subjected to the author's self and, eventually, rescued.

It is also possible to argue that Emily Brontë wished to, imaginatively, merge with A.G.A. in order to „(...) 'contain' death" – through this indomitable and ambiguous woman: „death's agent, elegist, (...) a victim" (Cf Chichester, T.L., 1991, in: /ed./ McNees 1996, Vol. I, p. 588–592). This opinion defines A.G.A. as the structural aim, the axis of Emily's Gondal cycle. The elimination of *the other personae*, Teddi Lynn Chichester argues, their „demise", is what secures the perpetuity of the development of A.G.A.'s character. A.G.A. 'reigns' the plot of the Gondal epic so steadily and surely that, Cecil Day Lewis argues[iii], one would begin to see in her authority Emily's covert efforts to equal the status of a man[12].

Self's *otherness;* the wind is the wise voice which brings the individual back to reality and makes one consider one's value in regard to other human beings. Symbols, as Arnold Kettle observes, leap beyond logical thought and are richer in their capacity to touch more of life at one time (Cf Kettle, *An Introduction to the English Novel* /Hutchinson University Library, 1957/, Volume 1, p. 140).

[12] In Freud's terms, Augusta could be perceived as a narcissistic type of person, whose main interest and goal is self-preservation, but who is not deprived of conscience. She is not afraid of Life, which she is able to model through her actions. True, she prefers to love and to be the leader on the level

The Gondal personae's deaths, however, are not the only deaths in Emily's poetry, approached in the broader sense of the word. Ominously, whilst Death happens, new selves emerge (including the spectral selves of A.G.A. herself), themes and motifs are formed.

The above arguments lead to the discussion of whether Emily Brontë's Gondal has one central lyrical persona, and if it does, then what is the most adequate way he/she should be referred to. As the prose fiction „portion" of Gondal is missing nowadays, it seems to me that Gondal is best described as *an epic in poetic form*. Its loose structure, however, merits A.G.A., whose presence is strong and steady: A.G.A. is *a hero*. However, as the present study investigates Gondal in its quality of lyric poetry too, I would prefer to refer to A.G.A. as to *the main poetic persona of the Gondal cycle*. It would be worth mentioning Lyn Pykett's observations: that Emily Brontë stands out as a chameleon poet, who experiments with a variety of dramatised situations, moods and emotions and the main Gondal personae are not very discrete, which is why they may be taken as the alternative selves of one and the same persona (Cf Pykett, Lyn, *Emily Brontë* /Macmillan, 1989/, p. 18). One way to look at Emily's poetic heritage would be to see it as the poet's obsession with Death as unfolding as a narrative about the fates of the participants of the Gondal saga.

Most probably, the Gondal saga had come to a close before *Wuthering Heights* was published (at the beginning of December 1847, by Thomas Cautley Newby[iv]), yet there is a possibility Emily Brontë's correction and work over the poems may have run parallel to her drafting her novel. For example the end of chapter 9 of the novel (where Catherine Earnshaw confesses to Nelly that Heathcliff is „*more myself than I am (…) I am Heathcliff*") was probably written after Emily wrote the poem *No coward soul is mine*, 2nd January 1846 (Cf Chitham, 1998, p. 127). Like Catherine, A.G.A. seeks to achieve eternal peace and quietude in the presence of the beloved person. There is the covert hope that there would be someone else, someone who would summon back to life the Mourner's perished self. One thing which strikes the eye whilst one reads Emily's poetry is that the desire to overcome the carnal limitations which the body imposes on

---

of emotions than to be loved. She both constructs (Gondal) and annihilates (Co-Being). – Cf Freud, Sigmund, (translation in Bulgarian) *Otvad printzipa na udovolstvieto*. sastavitel prof. Luben Nikolov. Sofia. Naouka I izkoustvo. 1992, p. 203.

the self, and to pass into the realm of free thought and imagination, alternates with the self's equally strong desire to find unity in addressing *an unknown listener, an viable Other,* whose presence equals Heaven to the Mourner. An *Other* who is ubiquitous in Nature and is a shelter for the Survivor's impoverished self. And being in Nature, this Other will consume the self but it will also complete it.

Gondal is tragic in its essence. Not because there are so many personae killed or forgotten. And neither is it tragic because Emily's last poem (H192: „*Why ask to know the date, the clime...*" – 14th September 1846) is about the death of a military leader and his orphaned and God-forgotten child. Gondal is tragic even regardless of the fact that A.G.A. is a Coleridgean Geraldine of a villain[13]. Gondal is tragic because A.G.A.'s life is tragic. Her death does not come as social punishment, but is dictated by personal motifs. Augusta is killed by her rival Angelica, who cajoles her lover Douglas into plotting together against Augusta (Cf Lloyd-Evans, 1992, p. 181). The other factor which makes Gondal tragic is seen in the other Gondal personae's conflicting attempts to fit into a world which is essentially A.G.A.'s own unique realm – Gondal. Augusta's love transgressions break the code of chivalry (Cf Turnell, M., 1949, in: /ed./ McNees, 1996, Vol. I, p. 532). Still, in Levinas' terms, A.G.A. would be seen to maintain and secure the existence of Gondal by re-confirming it with her disappearances and tragic endings as examples of a life interrupted, yet indivisibly chained to the world and authentic (Cf Levinas, 2000, pp. 268–269). After her death Gondal remains a remembrance of Augusta.

There is also another aspect of interpreting the broken linearity of chronology in Gondal. There is a feeling that Man is, more or less, prepared for the imminence of Death. There are numerous poems of Emily Brontë's where the individual does not merely crave to join those who have been granted eternal peace and wisdom. There is a strong belief – almost in a declarative tone of voice – that the contact with the dead and with certain physical representations of their world (i.e. *graves, tombs* – the

---

[13] „*For Aristotle and most other critics, the death of a villain would not be tragic, whereas for a certain strain of existentialist philosophy death is tragic as such, regardless of its cause, mode, subject or effect*" (Eagleton 2003, p. 9). A.G.A. the villain bears striking similarities to Coleridge's Geraldine from *Christabel* (Cf Chitham, in: /ed./ Chitham & Winnifrith, 1983, ch 6, p. 72): she is deadly attractive, compellingly beautiful, and she combines the features of a mother and a witch, to whom the victim seems to naturally yield.

latter word comes up in at least 21 poems of Emily's) should happen during one's lifetime: as part of the steady and conscientious preparation for Death (for instance see the poem H126 – „*Start not! Upon the minster wall*" – Cf Hatfield, 1941, p. 134–135; see also poems: H32, H35, H41, H90, H97, H101, H136, H177, and H188). Therefore, although in many poems death is tragic, because it is sudden and unjustified, there is evidence that Emily Brontë's thought hovered over what Philippe Ariès[14] would term „*the humanized death of the early medieval period*". Such Death is logical, expected, discussed and therefore not unfamiliar; it is Death which makes the person consider Life and his/her relationships and usefulness to other people. The *memento mori* theme is present in two thirds of Emily's poems, a large number of those being ballads. In some poems, one could say, Emily Brontë draws close to the traditional image of the Christian notion of the Saviour expecting the penitent after the moment of physical expiration, the penitent himself/herself striving diligently to deserve God's grace and benevolence. Yet the reason why Emily Brontë's poetry captures the reader is because she claims that there cannot be reached an unequivocal definition of God as unaffected by Time and therefore by Mortality. A.G.A.'s daemonic nature alone comes in support of that. The daemonic yields a greater variety of impersonations. What matters is Death's recurrence and variability, and not so much the fact that an event of Death is final or insurmountable. On a surface level, there may be noticed a poet who took pleasure in eliminating and then resuscitating her main poetic persona. The latter phenomenon, however, seems to be dictated not so much by the poet's own volition, but rather by the existential gaps which, reality in Gondal claims, are only to be „filled in" by the presence of *one* particular creature, whose own death feels like a major catastrophe.

---

[14] Cf Ariès, 2004. Robin Grove also notices that the motif of reconciling with Death stands out more obviously in Emily's early poetry (Cf Grove in: /ed./ Smith, A., 1976, p. 58). The way Emily develops the latter motif makes it possible to compare her to Emily Dickinson, Robin Grove argues.

Some Biographical Details of Emily Brontë's Life Relevant to the Theme of the Present Investigation

The biographical data about Emily Brontë shows that her social life was much more limited that that of her sisters' and that she left home less often. Cowan Bridge, Roe Head, Law Hill and Pensionnat Heger (Brussels) were the major experiences she had and (except for Law Hill) shared with her sister Charlotte. She spent a great deal of time at home, in Haworth parsonage, where she looked after the house, her father and – immediately before his death – after her brother Branwell.

Law Hill was a significant period in Emily's life. She had the demanding role of teaching 40 odd students aged 11 to 15. The Law-Hill poetic period (1838) yielded many well-known verses like, for instance, the poem „A little while, a little while" (H92, 4th December 1838), in which Emily must have poured out her feelings of desolation and abandonment, as she was away from home. Whilst she worked at the Law Hill girls' school (at Southowram, near Halifax), in the late hours she produced many poems relevant to the theme of the present study. Some of those bear biographical hues in their elegiac tone of voice, others pertain more specifically to the Gondal saga[v]. The Belgian period (1842), in its turn, yielded her *Belgian devoirs* which, as shall be demonstrated in due course, far exceeded the demands of the *devoir* M. Heger assigned to Emily. They proved to be not just a student's homework in French, but in fact a primary philosophical exercise in treating certain major themes like Mortality. Emily's estrangement from, and hostility to, *the world without* was ominously reiterated by the fact that in her last hours she forbade her sisters to call a doctor and suffered stoically until the end. Charlotte remembers that her sister „*made haste to leave us. Yet, while physically she perished, mentally she grew stronger than we had known her. (…) stronger than a man, simpler than a child, her nature stood alone. (…) while full of ruth for others, for herself she had no pity; the spirit was inexorable to the flesh*" (Barker, 1995, chapter 20).

As far as the matter of the <u>periodization of Emily's poems is concerned</u>, it was already mentioned that recent studies tend to group her poems thematically, which partly does away with the notion of a clear chronological structure of creative periods. I think, however, that there can be isolated certain clusters of poems which would demonstrate some specificities of Emily's treatment of Mortality in certain periods. Emily Brontë's earliest Gondal poem is likely to have been written in 1834[vi]. One of the most prolific periods of composing verse was for Emily the post-Brussels period – the years 1842–1845[vii] – which yielded, for instance: *H154 „How do I love on summer nights", H155 Self-Interrogation, 157 „How Clear She Shines..."*, *H163 „In the earth, the earth thou shalt be laid", H167 Castle Wood, H168 My Comforter, H170 A Day-Dream, H174 To Imagination, H177 I.M. to I.G., H179 M. Douglas to E.R. Gleneden, H181 The Philosopher, H182 R. Alcona to J, Brenzaida („Cold in the earth and the deep snow piled above thee"), H183 „Death, that struck when I was most confiding", H184 Stars, H190 Julian M. and A.G. Rochelle („Silent is the House – all are laid asleep"), H191 „No coward soul is mine", H192 „Why ask to know the date – the clime?"*

When exactly Emily ceased to write poetry is questionable[15]. Jill Dix Ghnassia divides Emily's poetry in 4 major periods (I – 1837, II – late 1837–1842, III – 9 months of 1842 in Brussels, IV – 1843–1848 – poems plus the novel; Cf Ghnassia, 1994, pp. 21–22). One thing is clear: that the poetry is a preamble to the novel and so some major specificities of the treatment of Mortality in Emily's novel *Wuthering Heights* draw on her poetry, mainly on the role A.G.A. plays in the life of Gondal. It would be curious to note that the verses dedicated *to* A.G.A. (and written by other Gondal personae) are fewer than the confessional lyrics or poems composed *by* A.G.A. herself (and addressed to other personae). Once again: the elegiac verses which mourn A.G.A. are fewer than the ones in which she herself ponders on the theme of Death and investigates – through her *many selves* – its effects on the people around her.

---

[15] Edward Chitham suggests that that happened in late 1846, so that between September 1846 and May 1848 Emily would have written no poetry (Cf Chitham in: /ed./ Chitham & Winnifrith, 1983, ch. 8, p. 86).

*   *   *

The Authority of Time and the Mirror of Nature

When I am dead, my dearest,
Sing no sad song for me;
Plant thou no roses at my head,
Nor shady cypress tree:
Be the green grass above me
With showers and dewdrops wet;
And if thou wilt, remember,
And if thou wilt, forget.
(…)

(From *Song* by Christina G. Rossetti[16].)

This initial sub-chapter deals with some dozen of Emily Brontë's poems, which reveal her interest in the link between Death and revival, as ingrained in Nature's cyclical progress, and how those two phenomena are paralleled by the progress of man's own fate. Of the three Brontë sisters, Emily is the one most interested in the concept of Death as a *principium Nature*. Some of the poems analysed here are what might be referred to as landscape poetry (those are Emily's earliest poems). Some pertain vividly to the Gondal cycle. Most of those poems were written between 1837 and 1839, which means that Emily's interest in Nature as a thematic field of research of Mortality is traceable in the earliest period of her poetic development. What Emily notices is that the *death-revival* principle in Nature is not just an external perpetuity of recurrent and interconnected events – the cyclical progress of Man's own life is an essential part of this mechanism[17]. The melancholy, which accompanies the reflections on the

---

[16] Quoted from: Leighton & Reynolds, (eds.) *Victorian Women Poets. An Anthology* (Basil Blackwell, 1995), p. 357.
[17] In his *Ideen ze einer Philosophie der Natur* Schelling writes: „*So long as I myself am identical with Nature, I understand what a living Nature is as well as I understand my own life. (…) But as soon as I separate myself, and with me all ideal being, from Nature, nothing is left to me but a dead object, and I cease to comprehend how life is possible outside of me*" (Cf Beach, J.W., 1936, p. 357).

above phenomenon, is inevitably linked to the fact that man plays a crucial role in Nature. There is also the grievous realisation that Nature outlives man (see poem H3).

Poems H2, H3 and H4 most probably refer to the birth of a child later named A.G.A. – the main poetic persona of Gondal (Ratchford, F. in: Hatfield, 1941, p. 17). The poem *Will the day be bright or cloudy* (H2 – 12th July 1836, Hatfield 1941, pp. 29–30) is a reflection over the human fate as dependent on Nature's cyclical progress[18]. In accordance with whether there will be bright „*summer vapours*" or whether „*Apollo (…) darkens*", the child's life is either to proceed happily or to be interrupted. Human life follows Nature's life, in which all things bright and beautiful spring up to last but a short while: „*(… Flowers may open, buds may blossom:/ Bud and flower alike are vain; (…)*" Vanity is seen not only in the fleetingness of human relationships and ambitions, but it is also present in a natural indefiniteness and short-lastedness which, in effect, could not be overcome. From the formal point of view, the poem reads as an enquiry in the conditional mood. There is a rhetorical question to the reader in the opening line and then three times – in the three consecutive stanzas – there is the „*If….*". sentence. If Apollo is happy then the child will be happy too and vice versa. A few poems of Emily's start with a question, as though the reader is somehow expected to know, or to guess what has already happened, or what the talk is about. That is to support the statement that the fragmentary nature of her verse is to be explained with the fact that Emily intended to present her poems as 'bits' of most significant events and occurrences in reality, which she chose to put down on paper. And as fragments, they commemorate the rises and falls in human fate, of which Death is but one. Thus, the cyclical changes, in which Death is an occurrence, demonstrate the quality of eventness of Emily's

---

[18] Jill Dix Ghnassia notes that the connection between man's fate and terrestrial phenomena is redressed vividly in a later poem: H122 – *There should be no despair for you*, „where the bond is made again between the seasonal cycles and man's common fate" (Ghnassia, 1994, p. 46). Another good example of the Brontës' belief in man's fate as dependent on the cycles of Nature is to be found in Branwell Brontë's tale *The Madman*, written by his famous character Captain Bud, and published in *Branwell's Blackwood's Magazine*. In a state of intoxication after a heavy drink, Captain Bud meets a madman who confesses that his destiny is as cloudy as the sky overhead and that this sudden overcast sky suggests his future death (Cf Branwell's Blackwood's Magazine, *The Glass Town Magazine*, edited by Christine Alexander /Juvenilia Press, Edmonton, 1995/, pp. 32–33, p. 41).

verse. *Nature's progress* is like a Bildungsroman, which also contains man's gradual maturation, to the point where man becomes physically independent, yet in his deeds – dependent upon one's conscience. In poem H3 **Tell me, tell me, smiling child** (Hatfield, 1941, p. 30) a wise child notices that Time is a sequence of natural vignettes, whose mosaic layout confirms that there can be no fixedness or security in Life, nor can there be an escape from the unfamiliarity that Death stores. In the child's response, the Past is an autumn's evening with a wind that „*sighs mournfully*", the Present is a „*green spray*" where a bird sits ready to fly away, and the Future is a mighty sea „*stretching into infinity*". [19]

Those early poems are possibly the earliest examples of the *sic transit Gloria mundi* motif in Emily Brontë's poetry (Cf Ghnassia, 1994, p. 53). What is also easily noticed is a covert indignation at man's dependence on predestination. Not so much on Nature's cyclical framework itself, indeed, as on man's own predisposition to cyclical existence. To Jill Dix Ghnassia the latter fact contains evidence that those poems of Emily's, as well as other ones, reflect a kind of ontological rebellion. To investigate the scope of Mortality might appear somewhat futile and truly impossible because no one, whilst alive, is granted the chance to have a direct personal experience of Death as an event. However, things seem different if one were working towards researching the ontological value of Death. Death contains a possibility for accomplishing the potentials of a human life conscientiously, of *Dasein* (Heidegger's term). A *Being* which realises its temporal limits is the only kind of being that ventures to delve in infinity and mortality as categories of the mind (Cf Derrida, *Apories*, 1998, pp. 79, 82). The reflections on Nature's cyclical frame suggest the feasibility of Emily Brontë's reflections on whether the temporal restrictedness of man's memory could assist man in his conscientious attempt to develop a responsibility for preserving the authenticity of the Past, of Time, independent of whether it ran for one as felicitous or it brought misfortune.

---

[19] Rosalind Miles notices that in Emily Brontë's poetry there are quite a few phrases which contain a reference to infinity and indefiniteness: e.g. „*the sea of death's eternity*", „*child of dust*", „*portals of futurity*", „*a dying memory*" etc. (Cf R. Miles in: /ed./ Smith, A., 1976, p. 78). Obviously, the idea of Mortality is implied in all of those.

That Nature succeeds and thus „exceeds" man is evident in poems H 9 and H10. In H9 (**There shines the moon – at noon of night** – 6th March 1837, Hatfield, 1941, pp. 33–35) the moon overlooks Alfred's „unremembered tomb". The poem is an elegy composed by A.G.A. and dedicated to her beloved Alexander, Lord of Elbë, who found his death near Lake Elnor. A.G.A. describes the divinity and purity of the moon[20]. What Lord Alexander however says is that „*the heath alone will mourn*" above his unremembered tomb, while Augusta will forget his „*mouldering corpse*". Emily Brontë is oftentimes stern and severe in the physical descriptions she provides. „*Drear*" is probably the word that she uses most often to depict the dramatic changes in Nature or the severity of Life. With envy and regret Augusta admits that Nature itself will remain unchanged but „*How wildly Time has altered me!*" In H10 (*All day I've toiled, but not with pain* – Hatfield, 1941, pp. 35–36) possibly again A.G.A. absorbs the ampleness and serenity of Nature, which she is praying never to lose, as that gives her internal peace. Mortality would mean a loss of one's perceptions and of the capacity to contemplate the outside world, which has a regenerative influence over the mind[21]. In this poem Nature's divinity makes the Lyrical Self remain „*true*" to herself, yet „*curb [her] own wild will*". To Emily Time is Nature's time, and *Death* is a lack of link to that

---

[20] As Jill Dix Ghnassia notes, the moon here appears in a scene of agony, during Augusta's wake over Alexander's body. It is also associated with life (as in H184) but it springs up in moments of tension (Ghnassia, 1994, pp. 55–56).

[21] This is almost the opposite of Tennyson's conviction that „*Nature is a hollow echo of my mind*" (*In Memoriam*), suggested in a milder form in his poem *The Lover's Tale*:

(…) I should have died, if it were possible
To die in gazing on that perfectness
Which I do bear within me.
(…)
To me alone,
Push'd from his chair of regal heritage,
The Present is the vassal of the past:
So that, in that I have lived, do I live,
And cannot die, and am, in having been –
A portion of the pleasant yesterday,
Thrust forward on today and out of place, (…)

Quoted from: Colville, Derek, *Victorian Poetry and the Romantic Religion* (Albany: State University of New York Press, 1970), p. 179.

Time, which could also be lost in an attempt to harness it in an authoritarian manner within one's own lifetime[22]. Other relevant poems would be: H27 (*Alone I sat, the summer day* – August 1837 – Hatfield, 1941, pp. 48–49) and H54 (*O evening, why is thy light so sad* – Hatfield, 1941, pp. 66–67).

In a mature hymn of Emily's, **H147 *Shall Earth no more inspire thee*** (16th May 1848 – Hatfield, 1941, pp. 163–164) the Earth is seen as a source of wisdom and vitality one draws on in developing his/her identity[viii]:

> *Shall Earth no more inspire thee,*
> *Thou lonely dreamer now?*
> *Since passion may not fire thee*
> *Shall Nature cease to bow?*
>
> *Thy mind is ever moving*
> *In regions dark to thee;*
> *Recall its useless roving –*

---

[22] Like Tennyson, Sylvia Plath's poem *Wuthering Heights* (Cf Plath in: /ed./ Petit, J. -P., 1973, pp. 325–326) expresses the Lyrical Self's conviction that she is dependent on, yet above, Nature:

The horizons ring me like faggots,
Tilted and disparate, and always unstable.
Touched by a match, they might warm me.
(…)
But they only dissolve and dissolve
Like a series of promises, as I step forward.
(…)
(…) the wind
Pours by like destiny, bending
Everything in one direction.
I can feel it trying
To funnel my heat away.
If I pay the roots of the heather
Too close attention, they will invite me
To whiten my bones among them.
(…)
The sky leans on me, me, the one upright
Among all horizontals.
The grass is beating its head distractedly.

Come back and dwell with me.
(…)
Few hearts to mortals given
On earth so wildly pine;
Yet none would ask a Heaven
More like this earth than thine.

Again, just because the individual's spiritual growth has ground to a halt does not automatically mean that Time as such would stop. Quite the contrary – Nature and life on earth are seen as capable of restoring any man's capacity to feel and act. Who is the interlocutor in this poem is conjectural. It could be that the Earth is arguing back to the Lyrical Self's outspoken thoughts, or it could be that there is a second voice within the Lyrical Self – that of conscience. In the present research, the link between Nature's progress and Man's own Life was also examined with regard to Charlotte Brontë (in the sub-chapter *Mutability and Memory* in the chapter about Charlotte Brontë). Another idea suggested in the above quoted poem is the argument that the lifespan one is granted here and now – however limited and flawed it may be – is more valuable than any other „prolongation of Time" man might be granted in the traditionally acknowledged blissful eternity of Heaven[23].

Parallelly happening human death and dying in Nature[24] are the core of poem H14 (*I saw thee, child, one summer's day* – July 1837, Hatfield, 1941, pp. 39–40). It is a ballad pertaining to the Gondal story. According to Hatfield, Alfred's daughter, Angelica, adopts a boy of sorrow (Cf Ratchford, F., in: Hatfield, 1941, p. 17). The ballad is an adult's lament over a child's defencelessness, as „*childhood's flower must waste its bloom/ Beneath the shadow of the tomb*". On the whole, the poem could also be understood as a lament over the inevitability of growing up, of

---

[23] Charlotte believed otherwise. In a letter to Ellen Nussey, which she wrote following Emily's death, Charlotte declared her hope that, now that Emily's „wasted mortal frame" was gone, her spirit would have most probably gone to a „*place [which] is better than that she has left*". There was no more the need to „*tremble for the hard frost and keen wind – Emily does not feel them*" (Cf Barker, 1997, p. 218). Charlotte stated that the earthly, the physical, was transient, whereas the heavenly was superior and benevolent to man.
[24] A more detailed analysis of poems containing parallels between human death and death in Nature could be found in: Ghnassia 1994, p. 105.

losing one's naïve trust in Good. Ironically, the „shadowy fiend" referred to in the poem seems to be the Lyrical Self, whom the child is powerless to chase away. The sinister events alluded to (which are about to happen to the child) are preceded by the Lyrical Self's (in the Gondal context that would be Angelica) own gradual decay. „*Doleful winter*" has come to substitute the summer day of her youth, and the child's fate might not be too dissimilar to hers. The „*fluttering blast*" that „*shakes the leaves (…) round the gloomy wall*" announces the spectre coming. Angelica cannot help the child whose „tiny hands" attempt to repel the ghost's invasion. This scene looks like an early draft of the scene in chapter III of *Wuthering Heights*, where Lockwood (i.e. this time the adult) rejects Cathy's juvenile authenticity by making her ghost's tiny hands become grazed on the bars of the windowpane, upon which they eventually bleed.

Unlike the cyclical revival in Nature, every *disappearance of a human being*, largely referred to as *dying*, is irrevocable to the world. It is true that in her later poetry Emily Brontë insists that there could be no gaps in Nature as every form of being is transformed into another form, the *next* form. And that Nature's regenerative mechanism is valid inasmuch as man is taken to represent an integral and common part of it, and not something superior to it. Yet Man's melancholy seems to stem from the realisation of one more perished *Other*, whose lack could never be compensated. Ironically, poem H119 (***There was a time when my cheek burned** – October 1839, Hatfield, 1941, p. 129*) reads:

(…)
O in the days of ardent youth
I would have given my life for truth.
(…)
And now I calmly hear and see
The vain man smile, the fool deride;
(…)
My soul still chafes at every tone
Of selfish and self-blinded error;
Only I know, however I frown,
The same world will go rolling on.

Poem H183 (*Death, that struck when I was most confiding* –10th April 1845, Hatfield 1941 pp. 224–225) is a ballad with elegiac overtones in which Augusta is mourning her late beloved, Julius Brenzaida (Cf Ratchford, F., in: Hatfield, 1941, p. 18). She recognizes that „*the morning sunshine mocks [her] anguish*" and that „*other boughs [will] flourish where that perished sapling used to be*". The allegorical reference to Julius as a tree that was blighted by Time also includes the idea that there will be other trees that will blossom instead (other lovers, perhaps?). Finally, „*the perished sapling's mouldering corpse will nourish/ That from which it sprung – Eternity*".

In a poem whose Gothic atmosphere reminds one of Blake's *Fair Elenor* Emily Brontë recognizes the inescapable principle of mutability as ingrained in Life. The strongly biographical ballad H29 (*A sudden chasm of ghastly light* – 14th October 1837 – Hatfield, 1941, pp. 50–52) commemorates the image of the „ruined Hall", whose windows overlook the minster-yard and the urns, all covered by whiteness *and chill. Death and destruction are seen wherever one turns one's gaze:* „*the shrieking wind*", „*The smothering snow-clouds*", the „*wan moonlight*", the „*plundered churches [are] piled with dead*", there are „*roofless chambers splashed with blood*". „*Every star [stares] like a dying memory*" above the Earth, and, reciprocally, the great Cathedral rises „*in serene repose/ On its own realm of buried woe*". The poem is unsigned and is strictly personal. The Lyrical Self is clenched between reminders of the brevity and fragility of human life both in Nature and in terms of the conflict-ridden history of mankind (e.g. the churches are „*piled with dead*" from wars). There is but one sad black yew-tree whose „*ghostly fingers (...) rattle*" against the vault of the church, still resisting the tree's natural doom (again, there could be made a reference to the episode of meeting Cathy's ghost in chapter III of *Wuthering Heights*).

The paraphernalia of Death is contained in certain objects/ phenomena of Nature that recur in Emily Brontë's poetry. The trees, the earth and the wind – these are chronotopal elements, which mark the progress and protuberances of man's life: they are not merely objects provided to the lyrical personae, but are conditions for the unfolding of events[ix]. The concretization of the theme of Mortality is visible exactly through the juxtaposition of various objects of the external world, which thus loose their quality of objects and become subjective signifiers of human nature[25]. In the poem H155 (*The evening passes fast away* – 23rd October 1842–6th February 1843, Hatfield, 1941, pp.179–181)[26] Time becomes the victim of its own unfolding. Albeit strongly linked to its home on Earth, the spirit is forced into the grave. There lurks the hope that Death is only liminal, rather than categorically final, that it divides two realms, and does not interrupt the perpetuity of the Present with the unknown of the Future:

(…)
„*Time stands before the door of Death,*
Upbraiding bitterly;
And Conscience, with exhaustless breath,
Pours black reproach on me:

„*And though I think that Conscience lies,*
And Time should Fate condemn;
Still, weak Repentance clouds my eyes,
And makes me yield to them!"
(…)
„*Alas! The countless links are strong*
That bind us to our clay;
The loving spirit lingers long,
And would not pass away –
(…)
(…)
„*Much have I done, and freely given,*
Yet little learned to bear!"

---

[25] Deconstructivists might say at this point that Time seems to stop, metaphorically speaking, to embody itself in images, which also marks the fixation of language, the inability of the language to continue further on. When chosen, these images solve, so to speak, any knots in a narrative, and in fact they are the narrative's essence. Presence is carnal, rather than incarnated. Presenting reality in images through language is the essence of the creative act, deconstruction would argue (CF Manchev, Boyan, *Donner corps à la mort*, in: /ed./ Znepolski, Ivailo, *Okolo Jacques Derrida. Tchudovistniat Discourse* /Dom na naoukite za tchoveka ꙮ obstestvoto. Sofia. 2000/, p. 183).
[26] The note beneath the poem in Hatfield's edition suggests that it was dedicated to Aunt Branwell – the Brontë children's foster mother who died in 1842, whilst Charlotte and Anne were in Brussels.

Look on the grave where thou must sleep,
Thy last and strongest foe;
'Twill be endurance not to weep
If that repose be woe.

The long fight closing in defeat –
Defeat serenely borne –
Thine eventide may still be sweet,
Thy night a glorious morn.

Death seems to be treated by Emily as „a condition of permanent exile, but its very permanence is also an escape from life's constant change" (Cf Pykett, 1989, p. 50). There is also a covert desire to evade the responsibility which man's temporal boundaries impose on man, and which is accepted here (in the second stanza quoted here). There are long-forgotten sins alluded to here, which appear more gruesome in view of the knowledge of man's short-lastedness.

In this early period of hers Emily Brontë deals with the philosophic links between Nature's fragmentarity and man's fragmented existence. The references to the context of Gondal, however, and to some other historical events (like war) indicate a desire to present Life as a phenomenon subject to modification under the interaction between humans, rather than just under the spell of Nature.

Migravit Anima...

Emily Brontë's early tendency to see Death as ingrained in Nature's great decree (and so applied on the human being from without), as the stamp of the empirics of the physical world, now gives way to a growing conviction that it is within man's capacity to command and accomplish Death as an act of one's independent will. The relevant poems date back to around the same time as the ones looked into in the previous sub-chapter. These are the years 1837, then the early 1840s and 1845. Abandoning the demands of daily life, of the self' physicality, Emily turns to the world *within*. Within the Romantic ideology, that tendency is not a novelty. The

„gaze into oneself" is surely a kind of a gaze at the World, which always remains unaccomplished: at least because of the actual temporal definability of one's consciousness. In Emily Brontë's poetry, the individual is determined to resist the invasion of the outside world and to insulate himself/herself from it in an attempt to remain unchanged, whole, or else to precipitate physical change, to leave the carnal tomb of the body and thus abandon physicality altogether in a desire to remain oneself. In both cases this particular act of will is in the long run terminal, because it happens counter the logic of survival, which circumstances of Life may impose on Man. For Emily, the Spirit's abandonment of its physical definitions is to be explained with the intention to fulfil one's duty to join the beloved person forsaken, or to go back home, or to overcome the unbearable doldrums and alienation Life imposes on one. There also hovers the promise of a pre-conditioned mystic union with the individual's liberated spiritual potential, which, Emily believes, is impervious to temporal decay. There is, of course, the optics of the traditional Christian doctrine of the thematization of Death, which is, above all, somatologic,[27] and which could be a guide to Emily's fixedness on the oppositional dichotomy *spiritual : carnal*.

Poem H36 (***The night is darkening round me*** – November 1837 – Hatfield, 1941, p. 56) is a ballad about an individual who gets bound by a „*tyrant spell*" on the eve of a snowstorm that is about to come upon a wood of giant trees. The noneity awaiting the Lyrical Self is suggested in the following lines: „*Clouds beyond clouds above me, / Wastes beyond wastes below*". Although everything speaks of the coming of a death prescribed, yet the Lyrical Self turns this gruesome description of Death as an ordinance into an act of volition. The latter is a particular speciality of Emily Brontë's. The three stanzas of the poem end in a similarly identical way, but every time the man's will grows stronger, and in the end, the impossibility to go turns into a refusal to go. Namely „*(...) I cannot, cannot go*", then „*And yet I cannot go*", and finally „*But nothing drear can move me; / I will not, cannot go*". A disaster precipitated and imposed on the individual externally is skilfully re-modelled into a weapon against reality itself. In Emily Brontë's

---

[27] The most obvious proof of that is that the main myth ingrained in the New Testament is the one about resurrection – in blood and in body (Cf Demichev, A., 1997, p. 13).

understanding (and in fact in her personal experience of social alienation) living implies resisting external circumstances. The final goal is self-completion, yet such completion aims at the furthermost boundary called death[28].

For all the theatricality and inversion of natural feelings which Barbara Hardy discerns in the tone of voice of the above poem[x], I think it would be naïve and groundless to disregard Emily's skill in moulding Nature's voicelessness as an alternative to achieving death through speaking it out. Emily Brontë employs what Derrida would refer to as the verbal ability to „speak death out" – which, quite like the assumption that one might die, is in fact getting closer to an experience of Death (Cf Heidegger in: Derrida, 1998, p. 57). In this sense, the atmosphere of stillness and motionlessness in poem H36 are as active in suggesting death as is, for instance, the scene of the murder of Alexander, Lord of Elbë (Augusta's beloved) in poem H89 (*There swept adown that dreary glen* – Hatfield, 1941, p. 89). Like many other Gondal events re-iterated, Alexander's death is mentioned again in poem H 180 (*O Day! He cannot die* 2nd Dec 1844 – Hatfield, 1941, pp. 217–219). The two poems form a diptych. The first one is a ballad about Alexander's assassination; the second one is A.G.A.'s elegiac lament of her beloved (Cf Ratchford, F. in: Hatfield, 1941, p. 17). This is a good illustration of how the poet utilizes Death as a thematic framework, which 'tightens' the essence of the main events in Gondal. In poem H89 the sound of the weapons killing Alexander

---

[28] I am tempted to offer comparison with Byron's *Manfred* (1817). Summoned by evil spirits, Manfred cries out:

(...)

Thou never shalt possess me, that I know;
What I have done is done; I bear within
A torture which could nothing gain from thine:
The wind which is immortal makes itself
Requital for its good or evil thoughts –
Is its own origin of ill and end

(As quoted by W. Gerin, 1966 in: /ed./ McNees 1996, p. 460)

George Eliot is known to have made a statement which speaks of a man quite different to Emily's and Byron's self-contained individuals: „*it would be better if my life could be done for me, and I could look on*" (Cf George Eliot in: Willey, Basil, *Nineteenth-Century Studies. Coleridge to Matthew Arnold* /London: Chatto & Windus, 1961/, p. 250).

sweeps down the glen wilder than a mountain wind. Alexander's body is only a suggestion of its master's former self:

(…)
Down in a hollow sunk in shade
Where dark heath waved in secret gloom,
A weary bleeding form was laid
Waiting the death that was to come.

This is an intermediary state: there is not the body of a real person, but a *form,* anticipating its death. Death could not be confirmed, yet the Self has split and its *form* is active. Although the word „*form*" (my italics) implies some kind of fixedness and definiteness, some passivity, yet the form here „*awaits*" death. The metonym of the „form" awaiting death (instead of saying, for instance, „man" awaiting death) perfectly illustrates that death for Emily Brontë does not imply a purposeful Methodist preparation, but a spontaneity that curtails any conscientious attempt to reflect upon death and capture it – even linguistically this becomes impossible. Death appears as both feared and anticipated by Gondal personae. In poem H180 the description is more vivid and Alexander is depicted a stage earlier in his expiration than in the above poem. Nature's ampleness, beauty and harmony would suffer from his loss, and Augusta summons his spirit back to Earth, declaring that the promise of „*Eden isles beyond*" is false and he should turn to his „*own native land*". In this ballad Augusta seems to both lament Alexander's death in a course of events, which she is powerless to change, yet she seems to also almost precipitate his transition into a ghost, which is to haunt the native land where he was most himself. The separation from the body is inevitable yet also wished for – in order for Gondal's atmosphere of tempestuous passions and attachment to one's native home to remain intact.

The separation of the soul from the body at the moment of death is often provoked by the individual's desire to complete what in Life may have remained unaccomplished – unity of body and soul. Fernando De Samara tries to quench the agonizing process of expiring with his wish to transfer his „*pangs past*" to the person who is responsible for his present misery – A.G.A. The poem H85 (*F. De Samara to A.G.A.* – 1st November 1838,

Hatfield, 1941, pp. 85–87) is a message to A.G.A. from one of her lovers, Fernando, who is about to commit suicide because of Augusta (Cf Lloyd-Evans, 1992, p. 183). Looking at the contents of the poem superficially, one could say that Fernando is being punished by the north wind's piercing current in a rainy evening. Yet it is that wind which he himself summons, as if the wind is to extract his mind (his „*death-cold brow*") and carry it away from its body and to A.G.A. The deadly spell he casts on Augusta is that she might suffer in the same way as he did (his „*pangs are past, but Hers are yet to come*"). There is a confession that Death is something Fernando is doomed to, yet he chooses the moment of Death, by which he somehow challenges the Christian doctrine of salvation, which is granted one through Death from without, and is not chosen by one through Death: „*(...) / One task alone remains – thy pictured face to view; / And then I go to prove if God, at least, be true!*". If his spell on Augusta comes true, that would undermine (to say the least) Christ's omnipotent benevolence on all and everything. Whether Augusta's life is presented as able to be finalized, or not, is disputable. Fernando understands Death as final (stanzas 9 & 10), but Death is a part of the cycle of existence, where there is an ingredient impervious to time:

(...)
Unconquered in my soul the tyrant rules me still;
***Life** bows to my control, but **Love** I cannot kill!*

Life is assumed to be final in that it is definable through Fernando's own life and death, or through the relationship he has had with Augusta, which may also be perceived as final because of his own finality. *Love* he assumes to master Death because of the possibility of Love being represented as a philosophical abstraction. It is *Love*, and not *Life* in an abstract general meaning, where *Otherness* is first born[29].

---

[29] See also Charlotte Brontë's poem *Memory* (2nd October 1833, Winnifrith, 1984, pp. 148–149). Somewhat counter to the above quoted poem of Emily's sounds John Clare's longing for a total abandonment of any link with society whatsoever:
(...)
I am the self-consumer of my woes
(...)
I long for scenes where man hath never trod

In the ballad H91 (*Loud without the wind was roaring* – 11th
November 1838 – Hatfield, 1941, pp. 90–93) the Lyrical Self performs the
traditional for Emily Brontë duplication and merges with the wind's roar to
ventriloquize the legend of the souls lost in the wilderness and determined
to return home – to the moor. *„For the moors...“* is the opening line of
two of the stanzas in the poem and when the final destination – *the moors*
– is reached, it becomes clear that the moors, too, are prisoners: the
„brown heath“ complains, that *„grim walls enfold me“*. The poem turns
into an entangled knot of confessions in the Lyrical Self's unquenchable
desire to return home whilst abandoning an adult's self. The poem ends
with the hope that there is a spot in Nature – the *mountains,* where *„the
loved and the loving“* shall meet again. The self of the individual, who is
narrating, opens up to the wind's roar, which then opens up to the heath's
lament and an *„ancient song“* is sung – typically, under *„the waned
autumnal sky“* and through a *„cold rain“*. Thus each previous Self splits
and partly merges with the next one. And each next one speaks clearer and
keener of the antecedent Self's grief in solitude. In the last stanza, Death is
implied as a state of deserved and long cherished rest and peace in *„the
mountains“*; it is implied as the end of a sequence of accumulated grief:
„the loved and the loving shall meet“.

The latter idea is carried over to poem H126 (***Start not! Upon
the minster wall***, – Hatfield, 1941, pp. 134–135). Now there is no
ambiguity as to whether life's temporality is remedial. The sensation of
temporariness and fleetingness is quenched with the consolation that *„the
saints“*, over whose resting-places the mortals' pathway lies, shall protect
the living from *„harm“*. The Past (i.e. the saints) feels benevolent and
spiritually balanced, it regularizes the Present, which then appears but a
segment of futurity (in stanza III the *„tomb“* is referred to as man's
„future home“). A listener is implied, whilst the process of joining the
dead is presented as though the individual speaking is also looking from

---

A place where woman never smiled or wept
There to abide with my Creator God, (…)
(…)
(As quoted in: Watson, J. R., *English Poetry of the Romantic Period* /Longman, 1992/, p. 121).

without at his/her own future fate[30]. Further on, the ambivalence of the semantics of *the tomb* in Emily Brontë's poetry is developed in two well-known poems: H182 and H183.

In Emily Brontë's poetry the desire to separate from the body and to visualise one's possible appearance after Death arises through the need to overcome what in real life has presented itself as a threat to the integrity of the self, namely fragmentation through alienating everyday particularity (Cf Turnell in: /ed./ McNees, 1996, p. 570). The individual is seen as *„wean[ed] from life and [torn] away, [buried] in everlasting gloom"* (see poem H43, 1838, Hatfield, 1941, p. 63), yet the tomb rescues man from some heart problems, which may prove lethal (stanza III). The dungeon seems not entirely undesired. Again, Emily Brontë mocks the reader's sympathy and turns the states of banishment and exile into a position of a rescue for the spirit, and not categorically into a punitive device. There is a cluster of about 5 poems (H15, H43, H61, H167 and H179) which deal with the one's desire to abandon the memory of one's own former self and to get re-integrated within a new individuality whose voice and soul would both be respected for their uniqueness and at the same time have a spiritual patron. There is the fear that an individual, whose self-analysing power was neglected by others during his/ her lifetime, should seek for an alternative of Life through Death (CF H167, *Castle Wood*, Hatfield, 1941, pp. 194 – 195). *Dasein*, in Heidegger's understanding, strives for Death as its very opportunity to be through not-being-here-any-longer (Cf Heidegger in: Derrida, 1998, pp. 96–97, p. 99). Emily Brontë explores Death as *Dasein's* most real possibility of defending its verity, which, ironically, is also *Dasein's* very impossibility of *Being*.

In Emily Brontë's universe the mind has the capacity to surmount Death, whilst the Spirit becomes the pure representation of a person's self, so that man's status of a mortal is somehow abolished. The many poems where the soul transgresses the boundaries of physicality prove that. Yet there is never an open declaration that Nature is a mere extension of man's synthetic capacity for knowledge[xi]. Because in the poems referred to above

---

[30] Van Gennep's rites of passage argue that the person who accompanies a dead body to the grave goes through 5 phases of experiencing Death from without. Namely: *the deathbed = the moment of death = the period of transition (~ of the body: – from home to the graveyard) = the Burial = description of the grave* (Cf Wheeler, 1994, p. 69).

Death is summoned not merely as a device for indulging the limitless capacity of the human mind, but as a *last* resort, i.e. after one has run out of power to suppress the thought of being unloved and uncoveted:

(…)
I mourn not heaven would blast my sight,
And I never longed for ways divine.
(...)
But I was bred the mate of care,
The foster-child of sore distress.

No sighs for me, no sympathy,
No wish to keep my soul below;
The heart is dead since infancy,
Unwept-for let the body go[31].

(From **Castle Wood** – *2nd February 1844* – Hatfield, 1941, pp. 194–195.)

Byron's reply to the above would have been:

(…)
The beings of the mind are not of clay;

---

[31] In *Call me away; there is nothing here* (24th January 1845 – in: Chitham, 1979, pp. 107–109) Anne Brontë recognizes the fact that the idea of remedial death is only justified with the intention to find the person upon whom one can bestow one's love. Death desired for this reason is a kind of attempt to overcome the individualistic urge of one's own mind. In *Sleep, mourner, sleep! – I cannot sleep* (13th January 1837, Winnifrith 1983, pp. 48–51) Branwell Brontë complains of „*dying away in wild decay*", and being „*a withered leaf on autumn's blast*". The romantic poet Laetitia Elizabeth Landon (L.E.L.: 1802–1838) sang:

Orphan in my first years, I early learnt
To make my heart suffice itself, and seek
Support and sympathy in its own depths.

(CF *Lines of Life*, by L.E.L. – 1829, as quoted in Feldman, /ed./ *Anthology of British Women Poets…, 2000, p. 376*)
See also Emily Brontë's poem H118 – *O between distress and pleasure* – 15th October 1839, Hatfield, 1941, p. 128.

Essentially immortal, they create
And multiply in us a brighter ray
And more beloved existence. That which Fate
Prohibits to dull life in its own state
Of mortal bondage, by these spirits supplied,
First exiles, then replaces what we hate:
(...)

(From *Childe Harold: 4.5*, as quoted in: Batten, G., 1998, p. 35)

Like her younger sister Anne, the Mourner in Emily's poetry endeavours to fill up the gap left after the *Other's departure*. The Mourner in the above quoted poem *Castle Wood* is an orphan, because no *Other* could be detected who could rescue this perished soul and raise it from its state of apathy and isolation (there is the confession that „*I never longed for ways divine*"). For Anne Brontë, the deadliest punishment of all would be if „*my life remains to me*"[32]. When solitude is prescribed, the only alternative seems to be a voluntary retreat from Life.

In H61 (*A.G.A. to A.S. – O wander not so far away!* – 20th May 1838 – Hatfield, 1941, pp. 70–71) Augusta laments her lover's death. That may be, Alexander Elbë' (Cf Ratchford, F., in: Hatfield, 1941, p. 17), or it may well be Lord Alfred of Aspin Castle (judging by the initials „*to A.S*". before the poem). Augusta says that „*(...) too dark for thee/ Are the hours to come, the joyless hours, / That Time is treasuring up for me*". The climax of revelations and reflections upon the issue of Mortality comes when Augusta concludes that if Alfred sinned, then he must have done so urged by circumstances or in the general spirit of a particular living environment (here: „*the dust of thy drear abode*") and that his soul will leave this earth „pure" again and ascend to God. The moral responsibility the Past inevitably bestows upon one prohibits one to ascribe any sin whatsoever to a dead man. Augusta's mind has travelled the distance between the Past and Future through the memory of this dead person. In this poem Augusta could be seen as a true believer in the traditional Christian sense of the word. In the first stanza of this poem is suggested the

---

[32] Cf Anne Bronte's poem *An Orphan's Lament* – 1st January 1841 (in: Chitham, 1979, pp. 78–79).

fear of living, and effectively of dying, in solitude. In the last stanza one notices that the focus has been transferred entirely onto *the Other*: his death is feasible and final, whilst the fear of one's own life and death in solitude is seen as *„this selfish tear"*. There is true *lack* when another person is missing, since his/her personality is the Mourner's true link to Life and to reality (Cf Bakhtin, AIG, 2003, p. 179).

There are several more poems of Emily's that round off, so to speak, the motif of the separation from the body and the escape from physicality. Factological probability and verifiability of events, it would appear, are not concepts that are essential in this case. What matters is, that once the limits of the defining status of Time are overcome, the individual is free to migrate in an ageless realm where only mind and spirit are welcome. In H44 – *I'm happiest when most away* (Hatfield, 1941, p. 63) Emily demonstrates proneness to subjective idealism in believing that Space is but a form of man's perception and that its feasibility is a consequence of, rather than a prerequisite for, the existence and development of, man's mind[xii]. How much Space could be enlarged and modified depends on how far the faculties of the mind could reach[33]:

I'm happiest when most away
I can bear my soul from its home of clay
On a windy night when the moon is bright
And the eye can wander through worlds of light –

When I am not and none beside –
Nor earth nor sea nor cloudless sky –
But only spirit wandering wide
Through infinite immensity.

When one reads this poem one feels as though it is not Life which flows and unfolds in Time, but that Life gives meaning to Time[xiii], concretizing and personalizing it within the limits of one mind and one system of feelings. A state is reached close to daydreaming/dreaming, in

---

[33] In poem H170 (*„On a sunny brae alone I lay"* – 5th March 1844 – Hatfield, 1941, pp. 198–201) the Lyrical Self „takes her heart to herself" and they „together sadly sank / Into a reverie", in which they reflect upon the themes of temporality and resurrection.

which Time stretches and flows more intensely than it ever could in reality. Mortality, in its traditional understanding, becomes irrelevant. The mind is active even beyond Death. In fact to die would mean to stretch Space further whilst making it more private than ever. Charlotte Brontë's poem *But once again, but once again* (19th January 1836) expresses the same idea, arguing that time and place could not „*chain*", or „*restrain*" one, and that „*mind is not matter, soul is not clay*" (Cf Winnifrith, 1984, p. 291). On the other hand, following Derrida, the inevitability of dying, the singularity of each one death, the uniqueness of each one man dying helps one gain knowledge about oneself, about one's true essence, even if this essence should simply unfold as estranging oneself from the World and from other people. This is „*the individualising interiorization*" which solitude and dying presuppose [xiv].

On a deeper level, however, the Lyrical Self in the above poem is not completely alien to any idea of *Otherness*. The way the soul is referred to makes it play the role of a second participant, as though it were another person who deserves to be looked after and rescued „*from its home of clay*": ultimately, this counterbalances the suicidal notes in the second stanza. What is confusing is that such an *Other* is the product of an almost schizophrenic division of the Self, the product of a spiritual malady and defenselessness. The critic is left utterly perplexed at the Lyrical Self's desire to transcend not only the external natural world but all physical phenomena, including one's own self [xv]. There is tension felt at this strong internal dialogue, which threatens the wholeness of the Self in the physical sense of the word. After all, the Self's physicality is a pre-requisite for the Self being split.

Emily Brontë's poetry praises the *world within* (i.e. one's inner world) and (as in poems H168, H174 and H176) there is the belief that Life, in the general sense of the word, is impoverished after each individual's expiration. In H168 (*My Comforter*[34] – 10th February 1844 – Hatfield, 1941, pp. 195–197) the Lyrical Self, being „*concealed within*

---

[34] Branwell Brontë is known to have claimed that happiness and misery have their origin within our own souls solely and that the human mind is entity self-sufficient and self-contained (CF Barker, 1995, ch. 3, p. 68). Both Emily and Branwell, writing under the strong influence of Protestantism that dominated their household, would have been encouraged to value the private Self as „the sanctuary of illumination" (Cf Davies, S., *Emily Brontë* /Harvester Wheatsheaf, 1988/, p. 19).

[her] soul", and drinking a concoction of a *„seraph's song"* and a *„demon's moan"*, declares: *„**What my soul bore, my soul alone/ Within its self may only tell"**.* In fact, she is torn between *„Heaven's glorious sun"* and *„the glare of Hell"*. Later, in H174 (***To Imagination*** – 3rd September 1844, Hatfield, 1941, pp. 205–207) she laments:

> *(…)*
> **So hopeless is the world without**
> **The world within I doubly prize**
> *Thy world where guile and hate and doubt*
> *And cold suspicion never rise;*
> **Where thou and I and liberty**
> *Have undisputed sovereignty*
> *(…)*

Again, an unknown benevolent Other is implied, whose *„kind voice"* brings *„hovering visions"*, *„call[s] a lovelier life from death,/ And whisper[s] with a voice divine/ Of real worlds as bright as thine"*. The addressee here seems to have been absorbed by the speaking Self whose internal balance, again in an ambiguous manner, depends on maintaining the existence and image of this superior Other (in one sense this poem raises human imagination to the status of an autonomous human being).

The rhetorical question comes in H176 (***O thy bright eyes must answer now*** – 14th October 1844 – Hatfield 1941, pp. 208–209):

> *(…)*
> *And am I wrong to worship where*
> *Faith cannot doubt nor Hope despair*
> **Since my own soul can grant my prayer?**
> *Speak, God of Visions, plead for me*
> *(…)*

„[Casting] the world away" and indulging the companionship of this *„intimate delight"*, the individual drifts further and further away from real life and from people. It is doubtful whether, left to itself, the soul could

be its own penitent and confessor – a dichotomy impossible and bound to destroy the wholeness of the Self, so that Death would come not as a request, but as inevitability. The Lyrical Self seems to have been enslaved by something/someone which/who is both „comrade" and „King" and which/who has become and integral part of her own will and identity.

Doubts are gradually creeping over the poet's faith in the Self as impervious to Mortality. There is search, albeit still not entirely declared, of an external referee, a regulator and objectifier of reality, a dialogic observer who possesses „the surplus of vision" Bakhtin speaks of. It is indeed only within the capacity of an „outside mind" to grant the Mourner eternal peace. Unable to find that external point of reference, one tends to hide *within*, where one also gets imprisoned, whilst trying to create an ethical model out of one's own inner world. And the above practice is doomed as it would result in a loss of the ability to perceive: Death would come as self-inflicted, rather than achieved. Emily Brontë seems to have been looking for a way out of the traditional existence, a door into Non-being. *Sadly, there is no such way. For, to realise the thought of Non-being means not to be any more at all, because there would be no one to confirm the latter for a fact* (Cf Levinas, 2000, p. 39). And *to Be* at all means to *Not Be through facts*, but to *Be* because of an *Other* human being: always *Other* and therefore always present, thanks to whom Death happens as particular events and is not a permanent state of mind (Cf ibid. p. 301). The poetic material analysed above contains evidence that Emily Brontë moved within this realm of philosophical thoughts and reflections.

Physical Matter: Limits and Limitations

A group of poems of Emily Brontë's speak vividly of her undisguised interest in chthonian representations of the theme of Mortality. Some of the poems are early works (1837), whilst others include some of the mature ones. The thematic points of reference in this sub-chapter will be: the presence of the ghost; the symbolic value of the night and the nought; the role of the grave (or the tomb) in the formation of man's philosophy of Being. One angle of looking at this portion of Emily's works would be to position her within the 17th- and 18th-centuries' Christian tradition of gathering, analysing and reflecting Death's paraphernalia through Art (Cf

Aries, Ph., 2004, book II, pp. 70–72). The Romantics took over: they were certainly tempted to decipher that „closed" and restricted part of the universe – *the realm of the dead.* Additionally, the poet's interest in discussing Death in terms of the physical particulars of its happening would have been encouraged by the theological unrest which was obvious, for instance, in the warring viewpoints and doctrines of Calvinism v/s Methodism on the issue of after Life as reward versus punishment[35]. Romantic poetry discovered a philosophically and aesthetically fruitful area in Nature as containing the concepts of nothingness and non-being. Following the recognition of the graveyard as a place for meditation, Emily Brontë dedicated to the latter both a substantial part of her poetry, as well as significant episodes of her novel *Wuthering Heights*[36]. Rooted in her native land and dedicated to a life beyond alike, Emily Brontë's inner sources of living seem to have „burst" the boundaries of the Self. Being interested in the chthonian side of existence for Emily meaned probing into what was beyond the visible[xvi], what would have been violent because unfamiliar to man and so hidden in the liminal estate of ghosts. Emily was interested in Death because she must have been interested in the non-human.

The validity of the concept of *non-being* is suggested as early as 1837, in the poem H12 (*The night of storms has passed* – 10th June 1837 – Hatfield, 1941, pp. 37–38). What is peculiar about this poem is not so

---

[35] Eighteenth-century Western Europe was stirred by the proliferating medical experiments over bodies in private conditions. Dissection had become a common practice at certain people's homes, because of which bodies were reported stolen from graveyards. The French poet Chateaubriand shared in writing how he was disturbed by the frequent knell of the church bell at night-time, as it announced that yet another corpse was stolen from the graveyard which was situated opposite the house, where he lived in London in 1793 (Cf Aries, 2004, book II, pp. 95–99).

[36] Ph. Aries notes that Edgar Linton mourns his wife Catherine at her grave when there are no other witnesses (Cf ibid. pp. 306–307). Entirely and hostilely alienated from society, Heathcliff's almost necrophiliac obsession with Catherine's body drives him to the point where he orders the sexton at Gimmerton to exhume it so he could check whether Cathy is still whole. He bribes the sexton to remove one side of Cathy's coffin so that when he himself is buried next to her they could both merge, which would be facilitated by the fact that their corpses would have changed by the incoming air (Cf *WH*, chapter 29). Michael Wheeler argues: „*Like Cathy's substitution of her heath for an orthodox Christian heaven which in her dream did not seem to be her 'home' (chapter 9), Heathcliff's idea of bodies dissolving into each other displaces a „vertical" spiritual transcendence in favour of a consolation which is rooted in natural process*" (Wheeler, M., 1990, p. 58).

much that Emily Brontë uses the dream-vision method of narration, as the fact that she discovers a space neither „*of earth or time*", nor categorically of the dead. The Lyrical Self's words „*die in a voiceless moan*" amidst „*the sea of death's eternity, / The gulph over which mortality/ Has never, never been*". Ghosts, she declares, gather at this time of year to grieve, and she meets one of them – „*a shadowy thing (…) dim*", whose eyes make her blood „*curdle*", upon which she begins to pray – without success. Although ghosts are revenants, and so creatures whose former appearance was once definable within the traditional parameters of Time and Space, yet now they inhabit that non-defined expanse which is impervious to Mortality. This phantom realm is threatening because its energy could not be harnessed or directed to serve any practical purpose man could think of. Both earth and heaven „*shrink*" and „*shiver*" beneath this power. What Emily Brontë describes in this poem is what Levinas would call „**the IL y a of the night**". The phrase has already been explained in connection to Charlotte and Anne's works. It refers to the impersonality of the night (syntactically reflected best in the impersonal construction "*there is*", which is what the above phrase means in French*)*. The night's darkness and stillness and motionlessness, the voiceless objects – these elements expose man to his/ her own self, upon which man tends to lose the capacity to hide in the *world within*. The night – so ardently defended by poets as the realm of protective calm – hinders one from making assertions about Life, because it gives one away, exposes one to the threatening dimensions of Non-Being (Cf Levinas, 2000, pp. 34–37). In this poem of Emily's there is plenty of activity even in the evening in the Lyrical Self's dream. Yet there is the fears that one may not be one's own self any more in the face of this nameless immortal continuum, which is impenetrable and incapable of being defined or mastered[37].

What is needed is a space where Time could be defined in that one's soul could be „*wrapt away*" (see the above poem). Yet the tomb proves to have no such status (compare also poem H58 – *Darkness was overtraced on every face* – [unfinished] May 1838, Hatfield, 1941, p. 68). The search for an adequate representation of termination of Time is frustrated by the presence of a *third party*, which is always implied in the Lyrical Self's

---

[37] Rosalind Miles interprets this poem as an individual's mystical experience, accompanied by a state of paralysis (Cf Miles, R. in: /ed./ Smith, A., 1976, p. 87).

story/ confessions. This *third party* witnesses the Lyrical Self's anxiety at being observed[38], being criticised, which is what gives this invisible witness the status of a ghost and guarantees its existence[xvii]. The obsession with ghostliness also discloses another kind of fear too: that, somehow, the importance of the dead, of *the missing Others* in the Survivor's life might be weakened, i.e. the individual might lose the connection with the Past. And the dead have an active role in Emily Brontë's poetry, as they contain that moral imperative which the Past stores for man[39]. The grave, the night and the wind (as a mediator between Past and Present) contain the notion of the superiority of *someone Other than the speaking Self.*

In Emily Brontë's philosophy *the grave* holds that *Other* who could be described as „an inverted representation of good", and whom men shun for fear of being unworthy of, or unprepared to face. The chthonian dimensions of *Otherness* become relevant when man's incapacity to accept his temporal definitions surges. Both poems H95 (***The night was dark yet winter breathed*** – 12th January 1839 – Hatfield, 1941, pp. 99–101) and poem H153 (*H.A. and A.S.* – 17th May 1842, Hatfield, 1941, pp. 173–175) are based on the above argument. In poem H95 one encounters a female ghost, whom the lyrical speaker meets after setting his horse free amidst Gondal's wilderness. Inserted in the main narrative is the story about the ghost's benevolence, which rescues souls, lost amidst the moors. For example, the ghost relates the story of a shepherd, who „*had died on the mountain side, / But my ready aid was near him then: / I lead him back o'er the hidden track, / And gave him to his native glen*". Whether the ghost did bring the shepherd from the dead is conjectural, but it did restore him to his native land. To Emily, one of the most crucial elements of the ritualistic side of Death is dying at one's native place, out of which

---

[38] The persistent image of the ghostly Nun at the school where Lucy Snowe teaches (in Charlotte Brontë's novel *Villette*) for a while dominates the development of the plot of the novel. Lucy's covert fear of, as well as her subsequent defeat over, the Nun are a part of Lucy's own maturation and self-liberation. She nearly masters Death, the thought of which seems to otherwise threaten and limit her life. Yet even the end of the novel is in itself emotionally burdened with the gloomy premonition of the loss of Paul Emmanuel – Lucy's mentor, and, possibly, her future husband.

[39] Compare Branwell Brontë's poem „*O God! While I in pleasure's wiles*" – 19th December 1841 (Cf Winnifrith, 1983, pp. 137–138), as well as Charlotte Brontë's poem *Winter Stores* (around 1837 – Winnifrith 1984, pp. 362–363). In both poems the dead are treasured as the Past which holds the golden key to interpreting the Present. In both poems there is the fear that man's self-centeredness might be the reason to loose that Past.

the World seems an unwelcoming wilderness. The ghost assures the lyrical speaker that she brings „care", but not „despair": „To a silent home thy foot may come / And years may follow of toilsome pain; / But yet I swear by that burning tear / The loved shall meet on its hearth again". The ghost also relates how she saves stray sheep with a „powerful charm". In Wuthering Heights (end of chapter 34), Nelly Dean's insistence that local people are afraid to cross the moors because of Cathy's and Heathcliff's ghosts wandering there is one return to, and inversion of, the contents of the present ballad. On a deeper level, this ballad reads like a lament over man's inability to capture the momentary and the instantaneous manifestations of altruism hidden in the awesome part of Nature. The lyrical speaker's fear of the ghost (he is „confounded and distressed" – a common state of near paralysis during man's encounter with a ghost in Emily's works – but he is also „wakeful" and anxious to meet the ghost) is contrasted to the mellowness and femininity the ghost's image emanates. There are suggestions to the sexual attraction and near physical intimacy kindled between the lyrical speaker and the ghost (the ghost's „bare shoulders" shine „like clouds round the moon" and her feet are „noiseless (…), like melting sleet"). This ghost ominously reminds one of Cathy's ghost in the way she appears in chapter III of Wuthering Heights: she returns to summon Heathcliff to join her and thus complete what was left unaccomplished in their lifetime. The „silent home" alluded to in the last stanza is a projection of that momentary vision of lack of any evil intent, which is something the relentless linearity and rapidity of real-life Time fails to keep. In H153 there is another early variation – again in reverse order – of the tragic events in Emily's novel. There is a female mourner who laments her beloved's death, over a „covered grave", upon which the grass grows „grave"[40]. It seems ominous that the tomb is neither „girt by Gondal's wave / Nor arched by Gondal's sky" – i.e. it is in a non-definable realm, it is nowhere, it inhabits a ghostly space, yet the metaphors above suggest particularity and physical concreteness. The play with epithets of colour („dark/light" v/s „fair/raven" in the description of the two lovers' appearances – their hair and their faces) is another proof how Emily both imitates and mocks a

---

[40] In addition, in H153 there is the theme of the irrevocably lost innocence of childhood – a time when the dividing power of Death feels to one less insurmountable.

traditional expectation of physical concreteness and exactness in describing Death – what she describes so vividly is ghostliness, rather than real Life.

What the individual in Emily Brontë's poetry strives for is to meet and partake of a power, which outlives all and everything, a power non-dependent on earthly things that are subject to the degenerative influence of Time. Such power appears to be **the Wind** – a much discussed multi-functional trope which has both contextual, as well as structural significance in Emily Brontë's interpretation of the theme of Mortality. Lyn Pykett manages to stipulate the following major roles, which Emily Brontë gives to the Wind: *a muse, an interlocutor, an ancient bard, a source of vision* (Cf Pykett, 1989, pp. 62–64). In her intriguing survey of the works of Emily and Charlotte Brontë Irene Tayler argues, that Emily attached to the Wind both religious and moral value: in her poetry it is often *called „angel", or „guide", or „messenger", or „comforter".* Apparently, the Wind also symbolises a possibility to return to the mother' it may also aid the longed for transition to eternity (Cf Tayler, 1990, pp. 45–46). In summary, I would defend the following roles of the Wind in Emily Brontë's works:

• The Wind contains a summon to <u>liberty</u>, which involves a planned transgression of physicality (i.e. a breach of man's temporal definitions): poems H36, 44, 83, 144, 162, 169, 190;

• The Wind reveals a secret path to <u>eternity</u>, which, in some instances, may demonstrate an open rebellion against the form of a present life: poems H26, 42, 45, 83, 140, 148, 173;

• The Wind possesses the capacity to restore the Lyrical Self back either to his/ her dearest beloved, or else to the days of authenticity of his/ her youth: poems H91, 95, 120, 126, 139, 154, 175, 177;

• The Wind brings a sensation of balance and peace which the Present lacks; it transfers the Lyrical Self to another world, which could be described as *Non-Present*: poems H89, 114, 117;

In H148 (*Aye, there it is! It wakes tonight* – 6th July 1841, Hatfield, 1941, pp. 165–166) the Wind is a visible a source of eternal spiritual regularity which is timeless. Traditionally, the wind is a physical element – it is a Natural source of energy, and as such it could be physically registered. Yet it could not be captured, it could not be contained in a single vessel; it seems to defy the philosophical concept of temporality. It could last a certain time but its beginning and end are not to be grasped with undeniable precision. It has no capacity to inflict time on itself. In other words, it embodies the notion of immortality:

(…)
And thou art now a spirit pouring
Thy presence into all –
The essence of the Tempest's roaring
And of the Tempest's fall –

A universal influence
From Thine own influence free;
A principle of life, intense,
Lost to mortality.

The wind „*dashes*" the memory of the world from the Lyrical Self's friend's mind. And when she is no more, the Wind shall make „*dungeon*" and „*mould mingle*" and carry her soul up into Heaven. <u>The Wind seems to consume Death and make the notion of man's temporariness irrelevant</u>[41]. Similar is the status of the Polar Star in Branwell Brontë's poem *Ode to the Polar Star* (26th June 1832 – Winnifrith, 1983, pp. 3–5). To Emily, The Wind is *the container of the third party*. Both in Charlotte and in Emily Brontë's poetry the already discussed *space of the third* – i.e. the listener, the invisible witness & confessor[42] – can be interpreted as the

---

[41] The soothing and domesticating influence of the Wind that brings the Lyrical Self back to her native land is also mentioned in the poem *Stanzas* (*Often rebuked, yet always back returning* – Hatfield, 1941, pp. 255–256). The authorship of this poem is uncertain. Charlotte Brontë may well have written it: its manuscript has not been found among the other manuscripts of Emily Brontë's poems.
[42] In contrast to Charlotte Brontë's poetry, where the ghost is exclusively a confessor, in Emily's works the ghost can be both the confessor and the confessing party. H95 – the ballad about the ghost's story – proves that. In *Wuthering Heights* Cathy's ghost is the confessing participant, but the confession is bilateral: her ghost precipitates Heathcliff's recollection of his beloved as well as Lockwood's memory of his blunt and non-gentlemanly refusal to accept a young lady's company when he was on holiday.

mortuary of *the second*, i.e. *the Other* (the beloved) who may be dead, but in other ways still active[43].

Edward Chitham's analysis of the above poem of Emily's (H148) maintains that, in a Shelleyan platonic way, the spirit is being liberated from the body[xviii]. A deeper comparative analysis of this poem and of *Shelley's Ode to the West* does suggest how Shelley, in his own fashion, must have taken an earnest interest in Mortality. In its *Ode to the West Wind* the Lyrical self, like the corpse of a *„dead leaf"*, is being dug out of his grave and swirled away from mundane existence by the wind, which is referred to as *„destroyer and preserver*[44]*"*. As the year is dying, the Lyrical self's soul is shrinking and he is praying that the wind *„drives his dead thoughts over the universe (…) to quicken a new birth"* and that his words may be spread like *„ashes and sparks (…) among mankind"*.

There are three poems of Emily Brontë's (H34, H158 and H184) that deal with **the grave** as the thematic core in the treatment of the themes of Mortality[45]. On the surface, Emily's poetry might seem a hermetically sealed environment, driven solely by the self-maintaining principle of dying and decaying. The persistent presence of the grave and the tomb in her works aims at a kind of liberation from the doldrums of earthly life, but it also implies total irrevocability and disappearance. Emily Brontë also associates the tomb with the hearth: in many poems (e.g. H9, H14, H28, H43, H56, H63, H133, H136, H143, H156, H163) *tomb* rimes with *home*[46]. Here A.G.A. seems to hover over the liminal world of ghosts,

---

[43] See Charlotte Brontë's poem *Stanzas on the Fate of Henry Percy* (15th June 1834, Winnifrith, 1984, pp. 166–175). Here the wind is the receptacle of Henry's spirit.

[44] Similar is the subject matter of Charlotte Smith's *Sonnet XLIV* (in: /ed./ Feldman, 2000, pp. 686–687). She envies the liberation the *„village dead"* have achieved: the blast that has risen from the Western cave and has then carried away their bodies into an undifferentiated mass of sea-weed, shells and corpses – all free of the oppressive *„life's long storm"*.

[45] Almost every other poem of Emily's contains a reference to Death through specific words semantically related to the idea of Mortality. The words *„death/ dying/ dead"* come up in poems: H5, 9, 16, 19, 29, 32, 34, 41, 50, 61, 63, 72, 73, 74, 75, 79, 85, 88, 89, 91, 98, 101, 194, 108, 109, 117, 119, 123, 124, 125, 126, 133, 136, 150, 151, 152, 153, 154, 155, 157, 167, 169, 170, 172, 173, 175, 177, 178, 179, 180, 181, 183, 185, 188, 190 and 192. The word *„grave"* comes up in poems: H9, 10, 41, 48, 110, 126, 151, 153, 156, 188 and 190. The word *„tomb"* comes up in poems: H9, 12, 14, 28, 43, 56, 58, 63, 102, 111, 125, 133, 134, 136, 143, 149, 153, 158, 163, 170 and 182.

[46] In those poems the *tomb* signifies both enclosure as well as a kind of abatement of existential tension, which a child would feel once it has returned to the hearth, to its home.

which is confirmed by the fact that she accepts the grave as something familiar and coveted both in an early poem (H34), and in one of the last poems Emily wrote (H184). A.G.A. has the qualities of the Romantic lyrical persona. She contains negativity – through denying the Present she also denies the general ontological validity of the Past – the time in which the Present may see/seek its origins.

The mystic visionary approach is employed again in H34 (*A.G.A.* – November 1837, Hatfield, 1941, pp. 54–55) where Augusta complains: „*sleep brings no joy to me, (…) no rest, (…) no hope, (…) no strength, (...), no friend to me/ To soothe (…)*"[47] The six stanzas of the poem each start with the anaphoric „*sleep brings no... to me*". The gradation reaches the point where even the mortuary where Augusta fancies herself to be, the grave (where she would otherwise „*knit / [her] harassed heart*") promises no remedy against the misery of living. The „*doleful imagery*" the dead bring to her is but a reproduction of the gloomy imagery real life carries for her. Her „*only wish is to forget/ In sleep of death*". Sleep represents a liminal state for the Lyrical Self. A state dense with such existentialist insoluble questions as: the burden of the Past (which broods over her with the presence of the dead, whose ontological aid her waking eyes fail to grasp), hopelessness and cowardice, lack of friends and alienation. Augusta is hoping that Death would be her final sleep and so would provide for her that timeless security which is an escape from the phantom of *the Other* – in the case where one has refused to recognize *the Other's* significance in the principle of *Co-Being*, i.e. *being in a dialogic manner*[xix]. Yet the *Other* is the one really mourned in this poem.

That *the grave* is not the escape from the ultimate existentialist question is clear from both H158 (*To A.S.* – 1ˢᵗ May 1843 – Hatfield, 1941, pp. 186–187) and from H163 (*In the earth, the earth, thou shalt be laid* – 6ᵗʰ September 1843 – Hatfield, 1941, pp. 190–191). In H158, the hope that „*a grave never shuts its dead/ From heaven's benignant smile*" is contrasted to the „*eternal midnight*" and the actual „*gloom*" of the space beneath the earth's grass in spring. The sight of „*the blessed sleep*" of the

---

[47] Edward Chitham categorizes this poem as a „mystic experience of feverish dreaming". He argues that that method is typical for Emily Brontë and is sometimes accompanied by a „nightmare of the incubus type" (Cf Chitham in: Chitham & Winnifrith, 1983, p. 113).

dead causes not peace, but in fact „*bitter woe*". In H163 „*heaven laughs above, / Earth never misses thee*". The grave promises no rescue from the anonymity and impersonality the Lyrical Self has experienced during one's lifetime:

> *In the earth, the earth, thou shalt be laid,*
> *A grey stone standing over thee;*
> *Black mould beneath thee spread*
> *And black mould to cover thee.*

She is nonetheless dreaming of her „*sunny hair*" twining with the „*grass roots*". This brilliant metaphor reflects her desire to belong to something firm and eternal. She finally admits that *that place* is where her sworn friends will „*own*" her and „*prize [her] memory*" (unlike the „*chill world*", in which „*sworn friends fall from me*"). The suicidal note is linked to the Lyrical Self's realization of her incapacity to keep her friends and of her inability to live without them. She believes that being in the grave, Banquo-like, she would be able to return to Life and stir it, restoring friendship[xx].

As A.G.A. deserts Lord Alfred for Julius Brenzaida, it is possibly Lord Alfred that summons back the night in H184 (*Ah! Why, because the dazzling sun* – 14th April 1845, Hatfield, 1941, pp. 225–227). Muriel Spark and Derek Stanford argue that the solitary, private and Gnostic communion with his beloved could only happen at night – the time which has been denied him[xxi]. The „*hostile light (…) does not warm but burn–*" (this light „*drains the blood of suffering men;/ Drinks tears, instead of dew;*" – these metaphors convey the image of a vampire). The day makes „*the pillow glow*" and sets the whole world for him on fire. The solemnity and intimacy the night are now ousted by the draining and exposing power of daylight. Privacy and divinity – features, typical of the night time in Emily Brontë's understanding – are in direct link to the grave, or the death bed, as an alternative form of *Being*, where the Lyrical Self is hoping to find *the Other* (both Augusta, and his „*departed*" friends – see stanza I).

The preference for, and exploitation of, chthonian elements (the grave, the tomb, the night, the wind) in Emily Brontë's poetry reflect her wish to explore the limits of physical matter in the process of gaining awareness of *Being as Co-Being*. Throughout the present sub-chapter it was argued that Emily Brontë's interest in the general theme of Non-Being unfolds as the individual's desire to escape the emptiness of earthly existence and to join *the missing Other*, the dead. There is the unyielding presence of the *ghost* – a reminder of that missing *Other* who is pronounced to inhabit a liminal realm – neither that of the living, nor that of the dead. The poetic glorification of *the wind*, as the power that incapacitates Time, expresses a desire to join an *Other* whose existence is not restricted within physicality either, is non-defined and therefore timeless. At that, Emily Brontë makes no allusions to Heaven as the personification of a timeless good. The grave is believed to not merely be the gate through the Present and into the Past (as the true abode of *the Other*). She dreams, naively, of a realm where, there would be no differentiation between *me* and *Other*. For, only in reaching that non-differentiated dichotomy could one reach finality, and only in that dichotomy Time becomes an irrelevant concept. Otherwise, there is always the fear of a temporal boundary: *the one* and *the revered Other* are always on two opposite sides, and when *one* joins *the Other*, then *Otherness* is eliminated.

The Place of Death in Emily Brontë's Idea of Home

Although the poems that are to be discussed vary in their date of composition, they were mainly written in 1839, with a subsequent growth of interest in the link between *home and death* around 1845. In at least four of those A.G.A. is a direct participant and in most of the others the events described are indirectly linked to her life. The strongest sub-motif here seems to be *infanticide* (see especially poems H42, H96 and H108) – a motif also sustained throughout Emily's novel *Wuthering Heights*. Another significant sub-motif is that of orphanhood[48]. If Charlotte Brontë and Anne Brontë deal with orphanhood as a theme spoken out by orphaned lyrical personae themselves, Emily Brontë is seriously engaged in revealing the nature of the person that causes orphanhood. She is interested in the attitude of the adult towards the child-orphan. She focuses

---

[48] The theme of orphanhood is the subject matter of about a dozen poems of Emily's, which are: H11, H14, H36, H100, H108, H152, H164, H179, H186 and H187.

her attention particularly on the disintegration of the sense of family because of the child's death as caused by the mother. The adult's responsibility for the future, the process of ageing and being alienated from the young generation, the opposition between family and non-family, the problem of how to preserve the memory of home under Time's degenerative influence – these will be the points of analysis in the present sub-chapter.

Poems H42 (*O mother, I am not regretting* – 14th December 1837 – Hatfield, 1941, pp. 60–62), H96 (*A.G.A.* – 27th March 1839 – Hatfield, 1941, pp. 101–102) and **H108** (*A Farewell to Alexandria* – 12th July 1839, Hatfield, 1941, pp. 114–115) are centred round the motif of infanticide as performed by Augusta. The author of the first of these poems, H42, might be a child of Augusta's. It could be that the Survivor here is a female individual who was very attached to her brother, whose death she laments. Alternatively, it might be a young lady's rebuke for the heartless mother who has left the young lady's beloved (possibly A.G.A.'s own child) to die. Fannie Ratchford accommodates this particular poem in the group of poems which deal with the relationship between A.G.A. and Fernando – a youth whom Augusta „enslaves and betrays" (Cf Ratchford, F. in: Hatfield, 1941, p. 19). In this brilliant ballad the Lyrical Self declares she has no regrets about „*leaving this wretched world below*", but that she is still lingering because the winter night is speaking „*of thoughts that should not stay*". In a dream vision she imagines herself to be buried beneath the church stone, and predicts that the mother shall soon „*dry*" her tears. Further on is suggested the mother's most probably impersonal and passionless adieu with Fernando (stanza X, p. 61). Finally, the Lyrical Self admits to have learned to cope with „*thoughts I could not once endure*" – she has obviously come to terms with Fernando's death, although in the last stanza she declares that she should like to join him forever. Possibly, the theme is reiterated again in H96 which tells of „*crime, / Long lost, concealed, forgot for years*"; Time will be „*[cancelled]*" and there will be „*unavailing tears*". The most powerful of the three poems is H108, in which Augusta leaves her own child, Alexandria, to die in the snow. Trusting that God is guarding her child, Augusta leaves the babe in the deadly frozen snow, which muffles the mother's lullaby and the child's limbs and breast „*freeze*" under the „*pall*" of snowflakes: „*And coldly* *spreads thy couch of snow, / And harshly sounds thy lullaby"*. The funeral imagery emphasises the mother's evil intent. She abandons her child in the middle of the storm in the mountains, *„unblessed"*, as she declares, in a way, which stuns one with its lack of mercy and maternal care. At the same time, she declares that she *„cannot bear to watch thee die!"* It would appear that A.G.A.'s evil deed is suggested as early as poem H79 (*Fall, leaves, fall; die, flowers, away;* – Hatfield, 1941, p. 82): the lyrical speaker admits that she prefers the snow to kill the blossoms of the rose. It is as though she is chanting a spell, which should seal all processes of growth (*„Fall, leaves, fall; die, flowers, away; / Lengthen night and shorten day;"*). Both H108 and H79 could, for instance, be juxtaposed to Coleridge's feeling of bliss at his babe asleep in *Frost at Midnight* (1798). The babe's *„gentle breathings (…) fill up the interspersed vacancies/ And momentary pauses of the thought"*. J. Hillis-Miller argues, that in H108 Augusta performs infanticide as a remedy against the natural law by which the new generation replaces the old one. Nature's proliferation, Augusta realises, involves constant destruction evident in each instant of emergence of new life[xxii].

In *A Farewell to Alexandria* the mourner is the mother who is not simply mourning the death of her child – she is doing that in advance, whilst the child may still be alive, as if to speed up its death. The moral responsibility the adult carries seems to dissolve in her conviction that she is helpless to defend her child anyway: there is *„no gleam to say that God is nigh"* (in poem H108). In Emily Brontë's poetry there is sensed a lack of universal maternal instinct. In her novel, too, Heathcliff's biography is a cuckoo's story, and mothering feels like a social constriction (Mellor, 1993, p. 208). The lack of maternal instinct leaves a mesh in the pantheism Emily Brontë is traditionally claimed to have developed. Through that mesh squeezes in the existential doubt in the worth and worthiness of man's existence; the certainty of the existence of a universal protective instinct is undermined. Death becomes not simply inevitable: it looses its capacity to evaluate man's Life within certain temporal definitions. Death is the unruly regulator of man's fragmented existence. It would be interesting to note that Emily Brontë's art of drawing demonstrates the same kind of ruthlessness and lack of mercy in treating a child's death as many poetic pieces of hers do. One such example dates from 1838: a man is holding a whip in his hand and with the other hand – a child by its hair; there is also another man who is watching the scene listlessly. Another piece of drawing shows a man who is being flogged severely (Cf Alexander & Sellars, 1995, p. 381). Emily's drawing of a fir tree from 1842 is memorable too: man-like, the tree is reaching with its uppermost branches for the sky: the top has been cut and the roots have been laid bare (ibid. p. 387). Here one would recall again the motif of orphanhood: i. e. when a child is left alone and deprived of any possibility of further growth and is doomed to perish in the lack of parental spiritual guidance. After Hindley's death, Heathcliff takes over The Heights and over the upbringing of young Hareton (*WH*, chapter 17). He turns The Heights into a fiendish abode to suit his gloomy and gruesome nature. As an act of revenge for his own life, which was conscientiously maimed (in that its spiritual props were destroyed by the confiscation of Cathy, so to speak), Heathcliff is quick to cut Hareton's few opportunities to grow and develop better than what his environment may dictate[49].

The motif of *infanticide as performed by the mother* has its own cultural history. The Russian philosopher Andrej Demichev notes that in the folklore of the Russian people there have been recorded numerous lullabies, in which Death is summoned to take away the child. This could be seen as a socially motivated method of the demographic policy of ancient tribes, where the child's stamina and fitness to survive in harsh conditions were thus tested through Art. Those „deathly lullabies" were a kind of a sentence to an infant who was ill, weak, or was treated as redundant etc. It is important that those lullabies were performed by the mother, who is (as Bakhtin would argue) the first and foremost protective Author/Authority, the first tutor of empathy, the first *Other*, and when she fails to perform her functions, the child's life is doomed[xxiii]. One immediate instance of a death lullaby is when Nelly Dean is singing to young Hareton in chapter 9 of *Wuthering Heights*: „*It was far in the night, and the bairnies grat, / The mither beneath the mools heard that*",). Another easily recognized one is Bessie's song to young Jane in Charlotte Brontë's

---

[49] Heathcliff scowls at infant Hareton: „*Now, my bonny lad, you are mine! And we'll see if one tree won't grow as crooked as another, with the same wind to twist it!*" – *WH*, ch. 17, p. 136.

novel *Jane Eyre*[50]. The negative impulse, which comes form the mother-murderer and is being transferred onto her child, paralyses the child's physical and spiritual potential and deprives the little individual of chances for survival[xxiv]. At this stage of its early development, the child's status as an *Other* in respect of the parent/ the Mother is still rather embryonic, rather feeble. Yet for the mother the child is always more than just an „I" (in psychoanalytical terms). The child's status is unstable and therefore challenging to the adult, because its emergence trespasses the borderline between Life and Death on a large scale. The child is the bearer of hope; it is capable of discovering new philosophic horizons in man's thought[xxv]. Another interesting cultural specification of the daemon- mother, the Bulgarian philosopher Tzotcho Boyadziev argues, is the significance of the *Lamia* (a female vampire). During the Middle ages, *lamias* (also *bonae res/ bones dames*) were women who were thought to raid a hearth at night, break objects, throw the babes out of their cradles, and in the worst cases – find and swallow people at night[xxvi]. Another problem in a merciless and callous attitude to a child is when a child dies unblessed[51]. In *A Farewell to Alexandria* the mother (the adult) feels discouraged to defend the child – it is out of God's reach, out of the power of good; but then the first manifestation of good which should come through the mother herself is also missing. One should not exclude the possibility that in the ambivalent and ventriloquist texture of Gondal infanticide works as a weapon against the plurality of interpretations that the instability of verbal and visual signs otherwise carries (Cf Bronfen, 1992, p. 151). In other words, if the child is eliminated, one has eliminated the possibility of a future where the androgynous nature of Gondal's main lyrical persona (A.G.A.) would multiply and cause Death to happen again. Indeed, Death in Gondal is little reminiscent of what in the middle ages was known as –

---

[50] In chapter 3 of Volume I, Bessie rends to young Jane the sad cadences of a funeral hymn about a babe, whose „*feet are sore*" and „*limbs are weary*" – it got lost in the mountains, after it was sent away to the grey rocks on the moors by itself. The „*poor orphan child's*" sole hope is God the father, who could shelter it near his „*bosom*".

[51] Tzotcho Boyadziev quotes one English medieval collection of chronicles and stories, in which a Richard Rounty of Cleveland is described to have spent one night in a forest. Hearing the drone of animals' feet, he shortly sees a procession of people riding horses, oxen sheep etc. and at the very tail – an infant babe – Richard's own son, who was doomed to eternal peregrinations and solitude because he was buried unblessed, i.e. he was not baptized (Cf Boyadziev, 2000, p. 333).

Mors repentina[xxvii] – the accidental death, the worst of evils, because it frustrated man's strife for orderliness and peace in dying and leaving the world before man has made his will, before he has passed on his message to the world.

That the experience of witnessing and contemplating Death (caused/not caused by a crime) saddens and burdens one's memory is reflected in three poems that all have the Gondal context. Those are H97 (*From our evening fireside now* – 17th April 1839 – Hatfield, 1941, pp. 102–103), H99 (H99 – *Lines* – 28th April, 1839 – Hatfield, 1941, pp. 104–106) and H156 (*On the Fall of Zalona* – 24th February 1843, Hatfield, 1941, pp. 181–184). In H97 R. Gleneden is left to mourn his brother's death. The elegy ends with the words: *„one being absent saddens all"*. Poem **H99** assures the reader that:

> *(…)*
> *(…) crime can make the world grow old*
> *Sooner than years of wearing woe;*
> *Can turn the warmest bosom cold*
> *As winter wind or polar snow.*

In the state of daydreaming the Lyrical Self remembers a boy who was very attached to his affectionate mother, but who is mysteriously burdened with a sin, which is mentioned in stanza XI. To him are indeed addressed the lines quoted above (the close of the poem). The motif of the unspecified crime is suggested again in *Julian M. And A.G. Rochelle (1845)*, which is discussed further in this sub-chapter.

H156 is a lament by the countrymen of Zalona, a kingdom invaded by the victorious Julius Brenzaida – one of Augusta's lovers. The people of Zalona lament the fact that they will not even be allowed to die on their home land. They are tempted to stay near those *„glorious, longed for graves"*. What they care most about are their children, whom they cannot leave to be slaves. They hope God is going to forsake Julius' armies as he once forsook their own armies. Albeit hidden in this curse, the motif of infanticide is being juxtaposed to the motif of parenting here. Peculiarly enough, in Emily's works one would normally observe not a mother parent, but either a father/male parent, or else a „collective parent", whose voice is that of the patriot defending his native land. The overall significance of the topos of the native land is greater than that of the sole parent for Emily Brontë. The many personal lyrics show devotion to home, yet not necessarily to a home as parented by a mother. Home for Emily Brontë is characterized with certain typical features of Nature (e.g. the wind), and it is the place where one is allowed to praise *the world within* (see esp. poem H102). Home is a place where one could contemplate one's own inner world, undisturbed by the unyielding duty to respond to someone. And inevitably, Emily Brontë reaches the same deadlock that her sisters Anne and Charlotte do. Namely, that man is responsible for, and owes something to, *someone Other than oneself* in the sense that one is free to accept, or to ignore, the universal call for an answer to *other human beings*, who constitute and maintain the familiarity of the World and of one's identity. Really, at all times one is being summoned for an answer for one's deeds: even when Death snatches away the source of wisdom and protection.[xxviii] Man's presence in the World is registered not just through man's physicality, but rather through one's active and conscientious participation in it, which presupposes always *Being with*, and *for the sake of*, someone else.

The above reflections are confirmed by poems H101 (*May flowers are opening* – 25th May 1839, Hatfield, 1941, pp. 107–108), H113 (*Mild the mist upon the hill* – 27th July 1839 – Hatfield, 1941, pp. 122–123), H114 (*How long will you remain? The midnight hour* – 12th August 1839 – Hatfield, 1941, pp. 123–124) and H189 (M.A. *Written on the Dungeon Wall – N. C.* – August 1845 – Hatfield, 1941, pp. 234–236). They all deal with Fate, whose strongest and most unyielding prescription is Death. Yet the awareness of Mortality fosters man's conscience and consciousness. The poet's „*cold heart longing to be at rest*" in the deeply biographical In H101 the Mourner wishes heaven to „*rain*" on her „*that future storm of care*" in order that „*their fond hearts were free*", yet neither „they", nor she could „flee" the future fate. In H113 the golden days of youth (also longed for in H114), with the damp in the grass „*thick as morning tears*", pass fragrance on to „*other years*" (i.e. the experience of growing and ageing is hereditary and as such is passed on future generations). Poem H189 contains the climax: the lyrical speaker „*chides*" with her soul, which says that she should forget friends since they have forgotten her. She masters her selfishness by saying that it is better that her friends *„dream on"*, and she *„pines alone in the prison gloom"*, than if she were free, but would pine at the sight of them being imprisoned. There is no suicidal trace in this, but a desire to save *the Other*.

The above idea is suggested as early as poem H11 (***I am the only being whose doom*** – 17th May 1837 – Hatfield, 1941, p. 36). It is a brilliant companion piece, in which the Lyrical Self dwells on loneliness – the basis of man's loss of faith and meaning in Life. Here the wistful young person's first lonesome eighteen years have *„slipped away"* with the prospect that not much will be different in the future. Sadly, after *„the hope of youth melted off"*, one is able to see that *„truth in mortal bosoms never [grows]"*. Experience teaches that *„hollow mankind"* provides no friends, yet incomparably worse is to discover that one's own mind bears *„the same corruption"*. The poem is a confession into the inability to exist in the lack of another human being upon whom one is programmed, so to speak, to bestow one's potential. What is being looked for is found and defended in **H102 (*Lines by Claudia* – 28th May 1839, Hatfield, 1941, pp. 109–110):

(…)
In English fields my limbs were laid
With English turf beneath my head;
(…)
(…)
My mortal flesh you might debar,
But not the eternal fire within.

Here, the process of dying is but a reiteration of the process of birth – it reaffirms the love for the home and the land – at once a desired place of dwelling and a source of creative energy and freedom, where the Other also dwells (here „My Monarch"). The home's physical definitions not only do not bind: they liberate *the fire within*[52]. The heath-covered moors at The Heights are Catherine Earnshaw's haunt and home[53].

There is the gradual tendency to draw the world of the living closer to that of the dead: not just because the world of the dead is the unreachable homeland. The dead inhabit a world active and informative: it could guide and protect orphaned souls, who seek their home. Poem H152 (*A.S. to G.S.* – 19th December 1841, Hatfield, 1941, pp. 172–173) reads like a contemplative letter of mourning, written by one of, possibly, two brothers whose mother is dead. One of the brothers, A.S., believes that the mother, though her brow is „*changed and cold*", still sees them and guides and guards them from „*that world of heavenly light*". The significance of the memory of home, of friends, and of childhood escalates in three marvellous poems of Emily Brontë's – H120, H172 and H190. In H120 (***The wind, I hear it sighing*** – 29th October 1839 – Hatfield, 1941, pp. 129–130) the „old feelings" gather upon the Lyrical Self „*like vultures round their prey*". This sinister metaphor suggests the completeness and wholeness that, most probably, the time of youth held for her in the presence of the „*dearest treasures*", whose death she now mourns. She wishes to „*buy past woe's oblivion*" with past pleasures. Although she is hoping to find „*another love*", the poem overall conveys the feeling of inescapable alienation to which the Lyrical self was sentenced after her friends' death. According to Fannie Ratchford's classification, which Hatfield adopted for his 1941 edition of Emily's verse, this poem might refer to Augusta who has regained the throne of Gondal, but is tormented by feelings of loneliness and remorse (Cf Ratchford, F., in: Hatfield, 1941, pp. 18–19).

H172 (***Come, walk with me*** – Hatfield, 1941, pp. 203–204) emphasises that once the mystic union of a circle of comrades has fallen apart, existence becomes aimless:

---

[52] In poem H33 (*Now trust a heart that trusts in you* – November 1837 – Hatfield, 1941, pp. 53–54) the mountain peasant cherishes the heath better than the „*richest plains beneath; / He would not give one moorland wild/ For all the fields that ever smiled*".

[53] In Chapter 12 of *Wuthering Heights*, delirious **Cathy**, in a state of nervous breakdown, declares her devotedness to her home. She is so obsessed with The Heights that she is capable of denying herself life in order to join her counterpart, Heathcliff, who also embodies her home. Furious, yet helpless, she says to her husband Edgar Linton: „***What you touch at present you may have; but my soul will be on that hill-top before you lay hands on me again***".

(…)
But Death has stolen our company
(…)
So closer would my feelings twine,
Because they have no stay but thine.

In the lack of *others*, man's existence becomes questionable: *„time parts the hearts of men"* surer than the most *„dreaded dwelling"* – *„the narrow dungeon of the dead".* The union of two people is deprived of the wholeness and mutuality the union of friends contained. That union of friends could again be interpreted as a surrogate family, which again was protected by the native land.

The most significant poem of those three is **H190 (*Julian M. And A.G. Rochelle – Silent is the House – all are laid asleep* – 9ᵗʰ October 1845** – Hatfield, 1941, pp. 236–242). One of Emily's best ballads, this major poetic work could be taken to summarize her perception of the link between such philosophical concepts as Mortality, Freedom, Love and Pardon. According to Barbara Lloyd-Evans' interpretation, Julian is Rochelle's friend from childhood (Cf Lloyd-Evans, 1993, p. 182). He has come to visit Rochelle, who is imprisoned and abandoned. Negotiating with the gaoler, Julian manages to spend enough time near Rochelle's cell in order to hear the grievous story of her imprisonment cheered only by the *„messenger of hope"* – a ghostly visitation the western winds bring to her with the *„evening's wandering airs".* Namely, that she could be liberated. Moved by her story and by the recollection of the golden time of their childhood, Julian breaks the prison bars and frees Rochelle. He then takes her to his place where he hides her for over three months. In a state of total dedication to his beloved, he forsakes military glory as he passes it on to a braver „man". What he gains, however, is Rochelle's love. The latter considers to be the most meaningful event in his entire life. What awakens Julian's dormant conscience is what Rochelle has hardly the power to utter, yet she utters it with *„scorn".* Rochelle manages to frustrate Julian's firm beliefs in his righteous and victorious lifestyle by saying that she holds *„a hidden ghost"* within:

(...)
„My friend", she said, „you have not heard me mourn;
When you my parents' lives – my lost life, can restore,
Then may I weep and sue – but never, friend, before!"

Life has been violated and denied Rochelle. Death she links to the destruction of her family unit: her parents are said to have been consumed by death. Death, then, has imprisoned Rochelle's *source of wisdom – the first Other (the parent)*.

Rochelle's face resembles the sculptured marble face of a saint and of a *„slumbering, unweaned child"* at the same time. The representations of Death and of stillness, which Julian sees in Rochelle, bear comparison to the idea of maternity and of the protectiveness of home. Home appears to be a place where Time slows down its relentless ride, which draws man closer to his end. The state of orphanhood interrupts man's ability to think and act in an adequate way; it digs into the props of man's aim of living. In this sense, the ghost, which brings over to Rochelle *„visions"* that *„kill [her] with desire"*, most probably restores the completeness of spirit she must have possessed when a child. It is only when she is delirious and her *„outward sense is gone"* (she might be comatose) that her *„inward essence feels"*, her eyes open. This visionary experience is almost lethal. While it re-charges Rochelle's self and liberates her, it destroys her suffering mind and makes hell and heaven merge. She only wishes the *„divinity"* of Death to materialise.

Julian experiences an unexpected flow of closeness and solidarity with Rochelle: although he knows that liberating Rochelle would mean making her independent and powerful (*„the bird would go"*), yet he does that upon the conviction that otherwise he would *„seal her woe"*. Conscious that he may rue his deed, he sets her free, because he realises that if Death set her free – which would be the only other alternative – that would be irrevocable. He thereupon gains an *„unasked embrace"* from her. Stupefied by such a priceless reunion, he admits to his former callousness and cowardice. From the point of view of psychoanalysis, one could speak of Julian's sense of guilt, in which the Super-Ego dictates to Julian empathy, which also however subjects him to Rochelle (Cf Passi, I., in: Freud, S., 1991, p. 18). From the point of view of ontophilosophy, however, Julian rediscovers – in a painful and toilsome way – his own Self through the acceptance and the rescue of daemonic Rochelle, in whose imprisonment is implied an unknown crime she probably committed.

The poem is not about imprisoned virtue. Rochelle's admissions of her ghostly and uncontrollable yearning for freedom and of her unholy union with her visitant – the wind, bring her close to such Romantic women-daemons like Geraldine in Coleridge's *Christabel*. Also, Rochelle could be interpreted as a double of the two imprisoned Catherines of *Wuthering Heights*. Catherine Earnshaw's yearning for home escalates to the point of deliriousness and results, eventually, in a nervous breakdown that kills her. Yet, whilst dying, she „doubles up" and produces the second Cathy who herself becomes imprisoned at The Heights. Charles Patterson interprets Cathy's and Heathcliff's relationship as empathic: one identity is swept away, and at the same time completed, by another. Similarly, one could argue that Rochelle's identity is negated and at the same time restored by the Wind. Such simultaneous regeneration and loss of one's selfhood through an *Other* is not far from the notion of a sexually consummated relationship[xxix].

It is obvious that the theme of orphanhood is not merely suggested but reviewed in detail in this mature poetic work of Emily's. In this respect, it is worth mentioning Martin Turnell's observations over the poem. He rightly argues, that the film of snow at the beginning of the poem appears to be the „*alien substance that smothers life*" – a „symbol of constriction", i.e. there is an external representation of the prisoner's inability to restore her world of childhood[xxx]. The way Rochelle achieves completeness through her almost suicidal meetings with the ghost gives enough substance to Edward Chitham to recall Shelley's *Epipsychidion*. In it Shelley's love for Emilia Viviani, Chitham insists, is expressed as Emilia lures the poet to death: her voice kills with passion[54]. Rochelle admits that only her parents

---

[54] Compare:
(…)
She met me, Stranger, upon life's rough way
And lured me towards sweet Death; as Night by Day,
Winter by Spring, or Sorrow by swift Hope,
Led into light, Life, peace. (…)
(…)
from *Epipsychidion;* Cf Chitham in: Chitham & Winnifrith, 1983, p. 61.

could regenerate her fragmented self, as they are the only ones who could make her life worthwhile and objectify it. In Rochelle's speech there emerges the realisation that man's life on earth is limited and that those temporal limits should raise one's awareness of *Other* human beings. That is evident in Rochelle's mourning for the parents, but mostly in Julian's decision to free Rochelle. It is true that Rochelle is asking for help, is admitting to her former sins (possibly even to a murder long forgotten); in that sense the request for pardon meets Julian's equally well grounded decision to give Rochelle pardon. That is, forgiveness in this case is factually real, because there is a sinner, who does admit to her evil deeds (Cf Ricoeur, *La mémoire...*, 2004, pp. 634–635, p. 637). Julian's act of will in liberating Rochelle is that demonstration of altruism, which frees him of his self-centredness (the extreme of which is the suicidal drive – ibid. p. 503). It is a case of Julian acting in spite of Death (Levinas), rather individualistically drifting towards it (Heidegger). On a deeper level, however, Julian's act of mercy almost reaches what Derrida calls the „madness of the impossible" – i.e. ideally, the pardon should come even when unsought for. Even the greatest evil should be granted pardon: even when it is a case of the most unforgivable deed, such as murder is (Cf Derrida, 2001, p. 107, p. 113). Since Justice ought to imply care, so long as Justice insists on the uniqueness of each individual. It is a case of an endless and eternal process of getting ontologically indebted to an Other, which indeed would make one recall Levinas' argument about one's Duty to an Other (Cf Ricoeur, Paul, *Soi-même...*, 2004, p. 319). A further hermeneutical interpretation of the poem would add that what Julian realises is that no one dies as poor as to have bequeathed absolutely nothing to his/her inheritors, in the philosophical sense of the word. Even daemonic Rochelle will do so. At least because she will leave a memory about herself which ought to be somehow acknowledged (Cf Benjamin, W., in: *Stranitza*, 1999, p. 48). Rochelle's story is that legend, which one should be open to in the highest stage of the hermeneutical experience. Julian's consciousness is truly historical in that it does not claim self-sufficiency of the mind, it strives to know Rochelle as *Other*. Julian allows Rochelle to speak and listens to her, which presupposes openness of mind. The hermeneutical consciousness gains completeness not in the methodological self-confidence, but in the readiness to partake of experience, of real Life, which inevitable leads to the realization of Life's limits. The experienced individual, and not the dogmatically self-sufficient one, marks the ontological significance of Death (Cf Gadamer, H.-G., *Wahrheit Und Methode*, 1988, pp. 425–426).

Emily Brontë's perception of *family* includes the direct relatives, the friends, the comrades and the native countrymen. A tragic accident may have stolen a friend. As a contrast, infanticide, as an act of will, leaves an existential gap in which the doer of the crime sinks and vanishes. The Mother is no longer the ultimate source of protection, so that the individual is much sooner made vulnerable and gets isolated quicker. There sneaks in the realisation that the experience of witnessing crimes and murders which concernt one's friends and closest relatives makes man age, rather than mature. In addition, torn from one's natural milieu, from the homeland, one is left with no object to correlate to, no receptacle to bestow one's potential upon. Where there is no friend the land is foreign land: in it the dichotomy of *Being for the sake of, and through, the Other* is violated.

In the poem *Julian M. and A.G. Rochelle* the compensatory mechanism for the parents' death is the orphaned child's delirious state of self-completion through day-dreaming – a state encouraged by the ghostly visitations (of the wind). The irrevocability of the parents' death could only be made up for by a spontaneous act of benevolence of one man towards another man (which seems to be Julian's attitude in respect of imprisoned Rochelle). Julian's spontaneous altruism is close to Levinas' interpretation of an ethical attitude, which is non-allegorical, real, self-denying, as it demonstrates true care (Cf Levinas, 2000, p. 88). Such attitude represents an attempt to bar Death's accidental power over man. In this regard, Julian appears a direct opponent of A.G.A., who performs infanticide. His desire to achieve Co-Being is redemptive, purgatorial, it is like taking the Eucharist – both for himself and for Rochelle (Cf Bakhtin, KFP, 2003, pp. 7–8, pp. 14–15).

The Inversion of the Self: Death and Emily Brontë's Other

When I am dead, and doctors know not why,
And my friends' curiosity
Will have me cut up to survey each part,

When they shall find your picture in my heart,
You think a sudden damp of love
Will through all their senses move,
And work on them as me, and so prefer
Your murder, to the name of massacre.
From *The Damp,* by John Donne

The present sub-chapter is meant as a summary of the theoretical observations already made in regard to Emily Brontë's treatment *Otherness* as she deals with *Mortality*. The poems relevant vary in their dates of composition: from 1837 up until 1846; and the most significant ones date back to after 1840. One thematic focus here will be the specificities, which the notion of *temporality* imposes onto an individual's attitude to the child, the parent, the friend and the beloved. The subject context of most of the poems reviewed in this sub-chapter is Gondalian, and, as might be expected, Augusta Geraldine Almeida plays a central role. One preliminary statement could be that, more often than not, the Lyrical Self is a woman hovering at the deathbed of her beloved[xxxi]. Predictably, another peculiarity of the motif of mourning here is the preference for the experience of mourning in the environment of external Nature, where mutuality and affection are oftentimes stronger than they can be in the official strictly social practice of mourning in the human world. Sometimes, it is the deceased one whose presence is felt in a spirit's ominous striving to rejoin the world of the living and help a living partner. The dead companion objectifies reality to the Survivor, whose obsession with the world beyond turns into a way of interpreting the world of present. The most interesting motif is the philosophic dichotomy *sin:forgiveness*. The issues of *redemption* and *penitence* are interwoven in the fabric of the Emily Brontë's specific treatment of the ontological superiority of the *Other*. The awareness of the temporal limits imposed on one's life by the phenomenon of Death are finally seen as an impetus to correct one's nature, one's consciousness, which would otherwise swerve into self-indulging introspection.

Two relatively early poems of Emily's provide evidence of the sharpness, with which the poet conveys man's practice of mourning at the frequent encounters with Death in external Nature. I would suggest that

Emily partly went counter Coleridge, for whom is typical spontaneous transference of the ungovernable fragmentation of man's spirit outside man and onto Nature's chthonian and preternatural side. There is something of Wordsworth in her: the belief in the wise and spiritually fulfilling influence of external Nature on man's mind. Both in poems H73 (*Coldly, bleakly, drearily* – Hatfield, 1941, p. 77) and in H124 (*The wind was rough which tore* – 23rd November 1839 – Hatfield, 1941, p. 133) the natural vignettes and episodes follow in a chaotic order. There is felt a lack, a spiritual gap in Nature itself. For instance, in H73 as the evening *„dies on Elbë's shore"*, so the winds *„sigh and mourn*[55]*"*. In H124, a leaf is *„torn out of its parent tree"* and its *„withering corpse"* is carried mercilessly to the Lyrical Self, whose heart sinks with grief. Both poems contain the theme of the irrevocable death of the child/the beloved. Yet the grief, which one experiences whilst observing Nature in these cases seems to be informative *to* one. Man's empathy is being stimulated as he/she delves into examples of loss and regeneration in Nature. The two poems quoted may make the reader to remember Blake's belief that each particle of the universe displays the same conscientious whole and in this sense the loss of each such particle equals death on as grand a scale as the universe's own possible annihilation[56]. If I were to interpret Coleridge's *Dejection* correctly, if there is a lack or an irrevocable loss that Nature exhibits, then that should be because of a mesh in the supposed orderliness of man's own mind (*„O Lady" we receive but what we give, / And in our life alone does Nature live"* – Cf Furst, L. 1969, p. 162). Apparently, in Emily's understanding man is to be made aware that loss, as an ingredient of Life, should be contemplated even on the level of everyday sight of the death of a leaf[57]*"* (see also poem H170 – *On a sunny brae alone I lay* – 5th March 1844 – Hatfield, 1941, pp. 198–201).

---

[55] The poem is in the tone of voice of A.G.A. mourning Alexander, Lord of Elbë's death (Cf Ratchford, F., in: Hatfield, 1941, p. 17).

[56] In *Auguries of Innocence Blake* says:
To see a World in a Grain of Sand,
And Heaven in a Wild Flower,
Hold Infinity in the palm of your hand,
And Eternity in an hour.
(Cf Furst, L., 1969, p. 165)

[57] See also poem H145 (*Methinks this heart should rest awhile* – Hatfield, 1941, p. 162), in which the death of the shrinking leaves prefigures man's own death.

That Emily Brontë sees the attitude to the dead as a key element in man's ontological journey is readily observed in two poems. Those are H41 (*Lines* – December 1837, Hatfield, 1941, pp. 59–60) and H177 (*I.M. To I.G.* – 6th November 1844, Hatfield 1941, pp. 209–212). In both poems the grave combines temporality (it does not yield back its inhabitants) with timelessness (it functions as the threshold to eternal and boundless wisdom which man should, if he were prepared for that, accept[58]). In H41 the dying lady is lamenting the fact that she should leave her beloved in this „sea of gloom":

> *(…)*
> *Weep not, but think that (…)*
> *(…)*
> *[I] have anchored safe (…)*
> *Where tears and mourning cannot come.*

> *'Tis I should weep to leave thee here,*
> *On that dark Ocean, sailing drear*
> *(…)*
> *We part below to meet on high*
> *Where blissful ages never die.*

The promise is not simply of a realm devoid of care and corruption, but a realm where the idea of time is irrelevant as that place continues the ages of erstwhile bliss, which have withstood the vicissitudes of fate. The imagined Heaven is in fact the realm of eternal and limitless Good.

H177 is a dialogue between a father and his daughter about the significance of the phenomenon of Death and the dimensions of the

---

[58] Ph. Ariès reviews in detail how Emily Brontë sees Death and dying as both eternal rest and ghostly unrest. He also observes that 19th-century Western European culture already tended to see the contact with the dead beyond the established prism of the Christian doctrine of *damnation/salvation*. People would communicate to the dead person's spirit, who would be an informant, as well as a comforter – in a way, which showed deviation from classic eschatology. By the end of the 18th century Hell, as an alternative to Heaven, had ceased to represent a possible abode for the dead relative/companion (Cf Ariès, 2004, book II, pp. 197, 215). Man's senses of solitude and of alienation swelled and the only possible place of dwelling for the dead companion was thought to be a realm of peace and timeless bliss (i.e. Heaven). Hell was becoming a state of earthly existence.

concept of liberty. It is the child who seems to be instructing her own father about how to come to terms with the death of a dear person. To the father, the „*winter's blast*" brings the memory of his native land where the dear dead lie far away (on „*the moor and misty hill*"). The child reassures him by claiming that the dead, unlike the living, have „*nothing to dread*". She argues, that, although they lie in the „*drear*" grave, their „*dust is mingled with the sod*" and they have thus joined God. Iernë remembers her father's words that the seed that lies dead in the earth will yield fertile boughs that will spring up into „*the breezy sky*". She assures her father that they shall both meet on that „*eternal home —/ The steadfast, changeless shore*" and shall both be restored into the Deity. Ominously enough, the child appears not to be afraid to join the dead: she would confirm to her father that there is a land of eternal life and peace. The poem resembles more a dream vision narrative, in which the father is himself a child visited by his own child, whose role is that of a protector and instructor. The poem is one preamble to that episode in *Wuthering Heights*, in which Cathy's adolescent ghost's hand breaks through Lockwood's window and „reaches for" his dormant conscience, whilst begging for sympathy and reminding him of a child's unconditional trust in man' altruism. The child, who is the informant, exemplifies what Meyer Abrams, analysing Shelley's idea of love, defines as „a sensuous object outside the self" – the only remedy against man's ingrained selfishness[xxxii]. To quote Jill Dix Ghnassia, Emily Brontë places man in „an ontological vice" – i.e. between the notions of transcendence (through omnipresent observers – ghosts etc.) and immanence („the /.../ image that brings logical significance by empirical verification")[xxxiii].

Four poems of Emily's most vividly demonstrate her pervasive belief that the beloved person's death plays a particularly important role in activating man's conscience and in directing man's potential towards developing ontological awareness. These poems are: H86 (*O Dream, where art thou now?* – 5th November 1838 – Hatfield, 1941, pp. 87–88), H136 (*I'll not weep that thou art going to leave me* – 4th May 1840 – Hatfield, 1941, p. 142), H180 (*From a D – W – In the N.C.* – 2nd December 1844 – A.G.A. Sept. 1826 – Hatfield, 1941, pp. 217–219) and H182 (**R. Alcona to J. Brenzaida – Cold in the earth, and the deep snow piled above thee** – 3rd March 1845, Hatfield, 1941, pp.

222–223). H136 is in the feminine tone of voice of a young woman who is lamenting the imminent death of her beloved. She declares that she will not weep over the fact that „*thou art going to leave me*". She knows that she will be lonely and unloved, yet she seems more concerned not about her own fate, but about whether her beloved would really find peace, rather than suffering in the world beyond. She seems helpless and this grieves her: her beloved might need her assistance in the world beyond. The tears she would shed over his deathbed are over her inability to join him, rather than over her own state of abandonment. The Lyrical Self's sense of care for *the Other* is thus extended beyond the grave, which shows a subtle doubt in the Christian doctrine of salvation after death (according to which God's benevolence is not to be questioned). There is a unique kind of self-denial and self-negation here. To reiterate Bakhtin, the Survivor's active care for one goes even beyond the beloved person's Death. For, it is after the death of another human being that the Survivor gains ownership of one's life in that the latter is transformed into the Survivor's Past and becomes an active ingredient of his/her memory. The dead person's memorial maintains the Survivor's memory, in which *the dead person* should be present ethically (i.e. as a point of informative and morally obliging *outsideness*. What ought to be emphasized and cherished is the positive, rather than the negative, in the deceased's lifetime experience, which is now free from temporality and from ontological tasks[xxxiv]. The Survivor's activity after *the Other's death* ought to continue and the aesthetic ought to now dominate: it ought to be able to discern the good in the life of the one who is no more other than in the living individuals' minds.

For every man there is always *an Other person* who, and only who, could justify his/her time on Earth, because that *Other person* partakes of man's joy and misery. On the other hand, it is only *an Other person's* death which could potentially be observed from outside. Only that death a Survivor could verify empirically[xxxv]. In the lack of that *Other*, man's existence feels not simply challenged: it is violated (see also poem H86)[59].

---

[59] The Survivor's inability to come to terms with the fact of the beloved's death raises the dead to the position of a *ghost*. So A.G.A. does in H180, where she cannot let Alexander, Lord of Elbë, die. She is praying that his death were delayed by at least an hour. Although he dies in her lap, his features remain ominously unchanged (his eyes never „*move*", or „*close*"). The reader is left with the sensation that he will rise again (see especially lines 41–48). Similarly, in the closing chapter of *Wuthering Heights* (ch. 34) Heathcliff's eyes refuse to close long after Nelly has found him dead.

In H182 (***Cold in the Earth...***) Rosina Alcona (one of A.G.A.'s impersonations – in her relationship with Julius – Cf Ratchford, F., in: Hatfield, 1941, p. 18) laments Julius' death. She admits to „*Time's all-wearing wave*": she is afraid she might be floating away from the memory of her beloved, after „*fifteen wild Decembers have passed*". In an elegiac form, she is asking forgiveness from her dead beloved, since

> *(...)*
> *Sterner desires and darker hopes beset me,*
> *Hopes which obscure but cannot do thee wrong.*
> *(...)*

She confesses: „*all my life's bliss is in the grave with thee*". The tomb, which presses Julius' body feels „*already more than [hers]*". She is forced to „*wean her young soul from yearning after [his]*": her turn has not yet come. Following Bakhtin, Rosina's consciousness is being activated with Julius' death, when „*the golden days have perished*". She has been forced to „*strengthen and feed existence without the aid of joy*". She admits that she had to, artificially, i.e. using her own decreasing spiritual resources, inject meaning in her life in her beloved's absence"

> *(...)*
> *And even yet, I dare not (...)*
> *Indulge in memory's rapturous pain;*
> *Once drinking deep of that divinest anguish,*
> *How could I seek the empty world again?*[60]

---

[60] Compare the following lines from John Donne's *Song* (from *Songs and Sonnets*):
(...)
When thou sigh'st, thou sigh'st not wind,
But sigh'st my soul away,
When thou weep'st, unkindly kind,
My life's blood doth decay.

It cannot be
That thou lov'st me, as thou say'st,
If in thine my life thou waste,
Thou art the best of me.
An excerpt from another one of Donne's poems (*The Dissolution*) reads:

It is easy to notice that the separation from the beloved somehow reminds one of a separation from the parent. The Lyrical Self is an orphan. In Emily Brontë's philosophy parenting unfolds as endless and selfless friendship for which, once broken by Death, there could be found no remedy (such is the case with the relationship between Catherine Earnshaw and her partner Heathcliff in *Wuthering Heights*). And, to recall Levinas' aesthetics, whatever the resources of man's own being, it is the life and the death of the beloved, of *the Other*, that represents the central ontological experience for every potential Survivor[xxxvi]. In the above poem the Lyrical Self has the premonition that her own end might be drawing near[61].

The relationship between *death, sin* and *forgiveness* is best illustrated in poems: H133 (*F. De Samara, Written in the Gaaldine Prison Caves to A.G.A* . – 6th January 1840 – Hatfield, 1941, pp. 137– 140), H134 (*Far, far away is mirth withdrawn* – March 1840, Hatfield, 1941, pp. 140–141), **H143 (*The Death of A.G.A.* –** January 1841, May 1844 – Hatfield, 1941, pp. 150–161) and H179 (*M. Douglas to E.R. Gleneden* – 21st November 1844 – Hatfield, 1941, pp. 215–217). Two of the poems are directly linked to Augusta's life, and all the poems reveal Emily Brontë's treatment of the theme of Divine intervention in man's life, as one prone to sin, but with the possibility of subsequent repentance. H133 is a song by Fernando de Samara – one of Augusta's lovers (who, according to Barbara Lloyd-Evans, commits suicide because of her[xxxvii]).

She is dead; and all which die
To their first elements resolve;
And we were mutual elements to us,
And made of one another.
My body then doth hers involve,
And those things whereof I consist, hereby
In me abundant grow, and burdenous,
And nourish not, but smother.
(…)

[61] Norman Sherry interprets this poem as an example of how the poet wants to „suppress the memory of love" and continue forward, as the essentials of the finality of death have already been declared (Cf Sherry, 1970, p. 103). Irene Tayler argues that the subject matter of this poem might be that of Emily's remembrance of her dead mother (Cf Tayler, 1990, p. 30). David Holbrook believes the same, and he also observes how that is comparable to Heathcliff's desire to merge with Catherine Earnshaw in the grave, which, in its turn, could be interpreted as an emphasis on the issue of parentlessness in Emily Brontë's own life (Cf Holbrook, 1997, p. 97, pp. 103–104).

Parallel to the admission of a life of sin, Fernando declares his conviction that death, although it may not bring salvation, should definitely terminate his sufferings, which were enough on Earth. Fernando claims that his „*sin was purified by woe*" (i.e. by his woe at being mistreated by Augusta) and that „*if there be a God above (…) / This hell shall wring thy spirit too*" (to Augusta). He knows that his misdemeanour precipitates his end. However, he „*kneels not*", there seems to be no „*mercy*" from above available to him. The poem subtly subverts the idea of Heaven as a dome of virtue, which one may/may not be destined to join. Heaven, to Fernando, is the exclusive abode of one master who does justice, in person, to every separate individual. Fernando is not sure whether God always necessarily sees that justice is done to each and everyone. All Fernando is asking for is to stay alive a little longer – even mad (ll. 41–44). What he remembers most vividly is the crime done to him by the lady, which is stronger than Heaven's capacity to ameliorate one's spirit („*(…) All Heaven's undreamt felicity/ Could never blot the past from me*"). In its overall sounding, the poem is rather similar to Emily Brontë's **Belgian Essay** *The Butterfly* (11th August 1842; refer to Lonoff, 1996, pp. 176–178). In it there is the grievous observation that at the bottom of the Divine principle of universal love and mercy there lies an ominous mechanism: death. Death drives Nature forward: the loveliest flower would spring up each time only to be devoured by a newly fledged butterfly, which it once protected[62]. She says: „*It is true that there is a heaven for the saint, but the saint leaves enough misery here below to sadden him even before the throne of God*". It is Emily Brontë's conviction that a human being's lifetime experience – with its at times intentional wrongdoings – is chastisement enough for one. Therefore, whatever follows after living should spare one's spirit further torture.

In H179, the Lyrical Self claims that compared to his guilt, the whole of his outlawed race will have to be pardoned for their insignificant errors.

---

[62] For Arthur Schopenhauer God was not a personality, he was merely will – deprived of „*intelligence and goodness, blind and indifferent to any purpose whatsoever except existence and, (…) indifferent to the sufferings of living things*". „*Thus does the will tirelessly create, and death tirelessly dissolve, in an endless cycle that achieves nothing beyond the pain and travail of what is thus raised up and abolished. The same meaninglessness is found throughout the whole of nature, and human life is no exception*". (Cf Arthur Schopenhauer, in: /ed./ Smart, N., *Nineteenth Century Religious Thought in the West* /CUP, 1985/, pp. 160–161, p. 168).

He is prepared to give his „*heart to death*" to keep his honour fair, yet he cannot give his „*inward Faith*" his Honour's name to spare:

(…)
I know the path I ought to go;
I follow fearlessly,
Enquiring not what deeper woe
Stern Duty stores for me.

So foes pursue, and cold allies
Mistrust me, every one:
Let me be false in other's eyes
If faithful in my own.

Both poems point at Emily's fluctuations between ideas of individuation through introspective self-observation and self-praise, and, on the other hand, individuation through Christian self-denial and readiness to suffer for the sake of *the Other's* well being. Poem **H143** (***The Death of A.G.A.***) contains the idea that although man is free to model his own fate, and therefore in some sense free to act according to his own will in general, internal freedom lies in the readiness and determination to constantly grow and learn whilst assisting and absorbing the negative from the identity of an *Other* human being[xxxviii]. A.G.A.'s death is caused by Angelica (who was brought up with A.G.A.) and Douglas, who is drawn into Angelica's evil plot to eliminate her rival[xxxix]. The ballad includes the following episodes: the plot against A.G.A., her actual murder, and the moment of Douglas' remorse over his crime.

Using the fact that Douglas has always felt alienated and orphan-like, Angelica cajoles him to assist her murder Augusta, as she thus promises him recognition from Augusta's foes, as well as a restoration of their erstwhile happy childhood union. She admits she was about to kill Augusta herself when a wild bird woke Augusta up and frustrated her evil intent. Whether the bird, which wakes up Augusta, is really what frustrates Angelica's evil intent, or whether Angelica herself summons not enough courage to complete what she has planned (to eliminate this superwoman named Augusta), remains uncertain. At that point the poem comes to an abrupt pause and then the episode of the actual murder follows in detail. The ballad reads like a condensed novella about an ominous deed, in which more prominent appears to be the mental torture of the murderer than the scene of the murder itself. Despite the lark's song, the sun is sinking, heralding Augusta's imminent death. In a brilliant metaphor Emily Brontë confirms Douglas's equivocal attitude to his future crime: the moors and sky seem to him „confused and strange and drear". He hears the „cry of agony" which declares he has „overpassed the sea/ That none can pass again". The latter is an allegory of crossing over, or acting against, one's own conscience in depriving another human being of the right to live. Such deed seems unpardonable. In the retardation, where the poet „inserts", so to speak, the episode of the actual murder, there is a sinister description of Augusta bleeding to death: the blood is running down her „coal-black hair". The parallel between Augusta's own evil nature and the Devil is obvious. She recognizes her murderer. Typically for Emily, there is no certainty that Death has put an end to the mind of this powerful person. Is Augusta dead in truth or not? Does the observer's mind accept fully and unquestionably the fact of her death, or does he re-experience it (and, so, does he bring her back to life over and over again)? Augusta's pulse is still „playing on her forehead" under the light of the full moon and the day-like sky. Albeit „unconscious", Augusta's body provides to the onlooker enough evidence that „she did not pass at rest". As Douglas is looking into Death's eye, he is expiring himself (Augusta „marks and knows him" and his „own heart's ensanguined dew/ Must slake her vengeance now"), experiencing „hopeless agony". The poem ends with a sweeping finale of philosophical reflections over the significance of Death, spoken out, possibly, by Lord Eldred (of Augusta's men), or better, by the poet herself, disguised as an impersonal and helpless onlooker. Alternatively, Douglas' own remorse, strongly tinged with the authorial comment of the poet, could be seen to constitute this last philosophical bit. In it is summarized that Death does not only terminate the opportunities a self may have had for unfolding its potentials. The sight and knowledge of death kills a part of the survivor's self, who could only hope to continue life despite the remembrance of such a ghastly event, and so forget the actual victim. In a more general sense, the Mourner, whose reflections are brought to the reader in the final section of this ballad, laments not what Augusta was, for what she was did not hold much good. He mourns *what she may have become*, if future had been allowed her[63]. The Mourner admits that Augusta's death *„has wronged us more than"* Augusta herself ever did. The fact that a man supposes that Augusta might have turned good if no intervention in her life had terminated it, proves that Emily Brontë is considering Death as an event which activates, rather than disables, man's capacity to sympathise and thus to *Co-Be*. Remembering Bakhtin through Caryl Emerson's interpretation, „another's consciousness is not only a language. Once contract is made with it, it opens up in ways that cannot be „learned" by any norm-driven grammar at our disposal" (CF Emerson, C., 1997, p. 161). Not to forget to think about the dead person, even though his/her death might not feel undeserved, is what man ought to do if he were to remain a full-fledged human being (see also poem H134, esp. stanzas 2, 6 and 8). What is most important is the moral ban – the voice of conscience – which here obviously remembers the Christian call for protecting Life (God's ten commandments), and which contains an element of subjectivity too (as to what is allowed outside „what is forbidden" through the commandments). In a way, subjectively determined are the two participants: the criminal and the victim. There is a degree of initial dissymmetry and accidence, in which the categorization of one as bad or good curtails the potential of each of those two sides (Cf Ricoeur, *Soi-même…* , 2004, p. 345–346). Yet, as Derrida argues, the access to Death is an access to the dignity of the human mind and to the dignity of man, who, unlike animals, lives in accordance with Law (Cf Derrida, in: /ed./ Znepolski, Iv., 2002, p. 33). Comparable to Emily's poem are her sister Anne's Vanitas *Vanitatis* – 1845 (which stresses man's task to *„assist his friends and forgive his foes"*) and *Self-Communion – 1847–1848* (which warns man against his *„worst enemies"* – the ones *„within my breast"*).

Three poems of Emily Brontë's seem to deal with the dichotomy *sin: forgiveness*; here, the treatment of the link between sin and punishment is not typically Christian, not fully Orthodox. The motifs of murder, euthanasia

---

[63] In Branwell's poetry there is the idea, too, that often, it is quite difficult to categorise a person as either good or bad. Death is sometimes hard to verify. See the poems *„Alone she paced her ancient hall"* (1837) and *Harriet II* (1838). Similarly, it is difficult to determine one's attitude to this persona – that of a victim, or that of a criminal.

and death for the beloved native land appear in: H37 (*I'll come when thou art saddest* – Hatfield, 1941, pp. 56–57), H75 (*Douglas' Ride* – 11th July 1838, Hatfield, 1941, pp. 77–80) and most importantly **H192** (*Why ask to know the date – the clime?* – 14th September 1846, Hatfield, 1941, pp. 244–252). Those maintain a discussion which includes such issues as: the right to impose one's will and power over a person's life (to the point of murdering him/her) and the dimensions of the term „crime", particularly when it has to do with a person's wish for termination of suffering.

That the sufferer might be considering the possibility of euthanasia is evident in poem H37. The Lyrical Self – effectively a ghost – promises to pay regular visits to the sufferer who would thus creep out of the depressive state of melancholy and gloom. The ghost's „*influence*" shall be „*stealing over*" the sufferer: it would be „*grief deepening and joy congealing*" and will „*bear thy soul away*". The ghost's presence would aggravate the sufferer's life, yet it would also act as an antidote to the utter spiritual desolation the sufferer has been locked in. As Marianne Thormählen observes, Death is being presented as a „much-desired sleep" which, chosen freely and achieved with another man's help, could cut man's road off from Heaven, but would at least lead to earthly love achieved[xl]. Emily Brontë's ghost is a liberator but a liberator with certain daemonic features. The ghost seems to be capable of hastening and executing the sufferer's wish to die in a way that challenges the Christian belief of cherishing the life of *the Other* – always and at all costs. What Emily Brontë implies, however, is that the ghost only does what man considers possible, but has not got the necessary determination to do. Death is an escape from imprisonment and solitude. In order to gain liberty, the sufferer needs an external projection of his/her own self's capacity to gain freedom. That external projection is the ghost – here possibly the ghost of the dead beloved. The Survivor is expected to yield to the ghost, by which an ominous power capable of terminating life would be activated and re-union with the dead beloved would be achieved.

The subject matter of H75 is that of A.G.A.'s murder again. Here, Douglas is chased by Augusta's men after her murder and there is a detailed account of his subsequent crafty but narrow escape (Cf Ratchford, F., in: Hatfield, 1941, p. 19). Peculiarly enough, the poem tells of an episode that most probably follows after Augusta's murder, so that, according to the chronology of Gondal – and until poem H143, Augusta should still be alive. The poem reviews the theme of sin and of repentance. Douglas is being chased and nearly caught by his foes, who seek justice for their monarch's death. Douglas topples a tree over his pursuers, who sink in shade and gloom. He „*neither shrinks nor flies – / He need not fly the dead*". Douglas is presented as being deprived of any sense of guilt: his „*coal-black*" horse (comparable to Augusta's „coal-black hair" in H143) pursues its relentless ride, carrying him away from his foes. Nature is singing a threatening song through the roar of the foaming river: an unknown voice is reminding him: „*death comes on every wind*". Although the poem ends with the assurance that the dead are harmless (i.e. Douglas „*need not fly the dead*"), the last stanza does not unequivocally confirm Douglas' pursuers' death.

Poem H192 demonstrates how Emily Brontë draws close to her sisters Charlotte and Anne, who both reach the realisation that the discovery of *Otherness* makes one's own existence both finalizable and at the same time „opens it up", which is Death's merit and curse. Man's life is only valued as an active ingredient in *an Other* human being's life, and that *other human being* broadens man's life by providing a field for one's potential and spirit to unfold[64]. Poem H192 is a ballad about the captivity of a young military leader whose last hours are attended by a person from the enemy camp – the lyrical speaker – confessor and murderer in this story. For a short while, the captured leader regains power when a man enters and announces that the lyrical speaker's son is about to be killed. The young military leader signs a document with which he saves the lyrical speaker's son's life and that is his „latest prayer". In return to this noble act of conscience, the lyrical speaker obliges himself to look after the military leader's orphaned child. However, incapable of carrying his promise through to the end, he lets the child go – unattended and into the wilderness. The lyrical speaker admits that his desire to fight was urged by his „*thirst for things abandoned now*": he „hated rest" and most probably desired active application of his inner power, yet:

---

[64] See again Charlotte Brontë's poem *Stanzas on the Death of a Christian (1837)*.

(…)
(…) I grew hard – I learnt to wear
An iron front to terror's prayer·
I learnt to turn my ears away
From torture's groans, as well as they.
By force I learnt – What power had I
To say the conquered should not die?
What heart, one trembling foe to save
When hundreds daily filled the grave?
Yet, there were faces that could move
A moment's flash of human love;
And there were fates that made me feel
I was not, to the centre, steel –
(…)
The blood spilt gives no pang at all;
It is my conscience haunting me,
Telling how oft my lips shed gall
On many a thing too weak to be,
Even in thought, my enemy;
And whispering ever, when I pray,
„God will repay – God will repay!"

From the start the reader is invited to partake of the lyrical speaker's feeling of remorse, of guilt. Although he is convinced that *„the conquered should die"*, yet he prolongs the wounded military leader's life. The sufferer's face is like *„a moment's flash of human love"*. The turning point is the realisation that the captured leader is a father too. The captive leader scornfully generalizes, that sufferings are rarely spared to a poor wretch, who may only be granted prayer by chance, whereas the rich are made to *„buy/ The pleasant privilege to die"* – possibly, provide material wealth for a death wish to be fulfilled. The poem contains the grievous reflections of a man who, faced with a dying foe, realises how short and ungrateful man's memory is: men forget good and bad alike, but in fact:

(…)
(…) Justice holds in store

Reprisals for those days of gore;
Not for the blood but for the sin
Of stifling mercy's voice within.

Conscience-stricken and Lady Macbeth-like, the lyrical speaker sees blood and death everywhere: in the water in the basin, and in his food dyed „*crimson*". He hears all the time: „*God will repay – God will repay!*" The dying leader's words that he „*would not cause [him] equal woe*" reverberate in his mind, as he is watching the leader's lifeless corpse. At this point I could hear Jacques Derrida say that it might be lawful to kill a foreign enemy in a time of war, even in a country, where the death sentence has been abolished. Yet how and why is a foreign enemy defined as enemy remains rather unclear (Cf Derrida, in: /ed./ Znepolski, 2002, p. 36). Now the lyrical speaker has to face his enemy's death in the presence of the enemy's own child.

The lyrical speaker is the murderer, but in effect he remains a repetition of the leader's orphaned child. He is left without what Bakhtin calls *the point of reference through an Other. The other dead*, the lyrical speaker loses his option to gain selfhood through a viable link to Life. In regard to the lyrical speaker, the captive military leader performs what the mummy from the *medieval dance macabre* does to the dying man, who looks utterly lost at the sight of Death. The mummy is holding the dying man's arm whilst leading a dance, whose purpose is to enliven the petrified man's conscience and consciousness. The mummy urges man to accept Death as a point of reference, in accordance with which man should measure the proportions and consequences of his actions in life[xli]. The point of this „dance" is for man to be able to face death with the conviction that a wholesome existence is one geared towards „serving" another human being. The lyrical speaker ignores Life's summon towards Co-Being by letting the dead leader's orphaned child go „*one moonless night*". What remains a goal only in this poem is the act of pardon, which, as Julia Kristeva argues, could truly interrupt the continuity of cause and effect, punishments and crimes: pardon does overcome Time and actions, whilst it opens a new space (not the space of the wild unconscious, which strives for killing, but the space of love harmony – Cf Kristeva, 1999, p.213).

Emily Brontë declares her belief in that there should be *another human being* who should serve to objectify meaning in life for one. As Tatjana Shtitsova argues (interpreting Bakhtin), „two voices" constitute the minimum of Life, the minimum of Being. It is only in dialogue that one reaches the truth about Life: one possesses no sovereign territory of Being which could be termed his/her „OWN" only. One always exists on a borderline: as one looks into one's inner world, one looks at the Other or through the Other (Cf Shtitsova, T., 2002, pp. 174–177). In this there shows a swerve away from the romantic proneness to seek individuation through a voluntary retreat from existence, in which the dependence on others would appear stifling. The poems analysed in this sub-chapter provide evidence that Emily Brontë knows that in the lack of *an Other* one's existence becomes aimless. Sadly, it is often after that *Other* expires that he/she becomes a recognized *point of reference* for the Survivor. The *Other's death* has the effect of a boomerang upon the living: it returns and haunts man, like a ghost, as it endeavours to exterminate the roots of man's evil and selfishness. The latter is accompanied by an almost self-inflicted admission to proneness to crime. A murder leaves an existential gap in the murderer's mind. The murderer considers the possibility that whoever is referred to as „enemy" might be more of a projection of one's own degenerating consciousness.

The Deity: Emily Brontë's Idea of Heaven as Seen through the Prism of Death

Most of the poems relevant may bear little or oftentimes no trace of Gondal (if Fannie Ratchford in Hatfield's 1941 edition is to be relied upon). They have a confessional tone of voice and reveal Emily Brontë's mature reflections on both the merits and the inadequacies of the traditionally built idea of Heaven as the dome of salvation, ruled by an omnipotent and virtuous master. The majority of poems were written after 1840, when metaphysical ideas seem to have been burgeoning in Emily's mind. This sub-chapter is the last in the overall structure of the investigation of *Mortality* in Emily Brontë's poetry. The idea is to show an evolving consideration of Life whose point of reference lies beyond the visible and the physically palpable, of Life whose basis is the acceptance of a supreme being. There also gets involved the understanding that Life is not unlimited, but has a boundary (physical and philosophical), traditionally referred to as „Death", in view of which one ought to gear, to direct and utilize one's potential. Death, in its liminal status, divides existence: it appears to be the threshold before the realm which contains a mechanism believed to „amend" Life's gaps and errors, a mechanism which has the ability to prolong Life as heavenly bliss or, in any case, to see that justice is done to each individual, according to one's deeds. Both Emily Brontë's poetry and her prose works demonstrate good theological awareness on the matter of the Heavenly institute and on the common perception of Heaven's recuperative significance over man's Life. Where she deviates from tradition is in her understanding that Heaven and Hell do not inevitably and unquestionably function as opposites and do not even necessarily ensue, after the person expires. To Emily, Heaven seems to bear traces of Hell in its selectivism. She considers toils and tribulations on Earth enough a trial and a punishment – both for virtuous and for sinful people alike, so that the idea of purgatory/Hell in the afterlife becomes, largely speaking, unacceptable. „Temporality" versus „Eternity", „Captivity" versus „Freedom" – in Emily Brontë's works those terms seem to absorb and to substitute traditional notions like „Hell" and „Heaven". Emily Brontë's anti-Calvinism is also visible in that, on the whole, the theme of forgiveness in her works is understood not really as forgiveness granted first and foremost by God (who would have been the conventionally regarded ultimate regulator of man's moral and spiritual growth). It is clear that the persistent presence of the phenomenon of Death in man's life ought to unleash the positive potential of man's conscience. However, the sources of such regeneration of spirit, she argues, are also to be sought in the Life at present and on Earth, which is man's true abode[65].

As mentioned earlier, Emily Brontë confirms that there is a borderline that cuts existence in two, which could be referred to as Death. As Death has liminal status, it invites one to sum up one's existence and admit to any existential gaps and meshes one has allowed in Life. The

---

[65] Jill Dix Ghnassia observes how, whilst some Brontë characters cherish faith in the existence of some sort of after-life, they nonetheless reject salvation and hell „and find heaven a poor substitute for life on this earth" (Cf Ghnassia, 1994, p. 137). Such is the case with Rosina in the already discussed H182, as well as with Cathy, who dreams of her Heaven on „that hilltop – the Heights".

poems relevant here are: H85 (*F. De Samara to A.G.A.* – 1st November 1838 – Hatfield, 1941, pp. 85–87), H146 (***Riches I hold in light esteem*** – 1st March 1841 – Hatfield, 1941, p. 163), H154 (*Written in Aspin Castle – How do I love on summer nights* – 20th August 1842 & 6th February 1843 – Hatfield, 1941, pp. 175–179), and H181 (*„Enough of Thought, Philosopher;* – 3rd February 1845, Hatfield, 1941, pp. 220–222).

Fannie Ratchford argues, that poem H85 is connected with the fate of Lord Alfred, who kills himself in exile (Cf Ratchford, F., in Hatfield, 1941, p. 18). Barbara Lloyd-Evans' specification of the context of this poem appears more logical: it was probably written (as the initials before the poem indicate) by Fernando De Samara – in love with A.G.A. and about to commit suicide whilst being imprisoned because of her (Cf Lloyd-Evans, 1993, p. 183). He is standing at the threshold of Death, determined to view his beloved's face yet again and then he goes *„to prove if God, at least, be true".* Torn between his dedication and venom for A.G.A. (both his beloved and the reason for his imprisonment), Fernando sets himself the task of proving whether there is a Supreme Being whose omnipotence regulates the relationship between people. He is not merely a passive observer of Life happening to him. He believes that the Present is capable of flowing further, of attacking the future: he believes that his own deeds would dare that Supreme Mind and redirect the course of events. In stanza VII Fernando is dreaming of Augusta undergoing equal grief, which would alleviate his own grief. What he feels will outlive him is his equivocal *Love* for A.G.A., whereas *Life* could „bow" to his control. Looking at Fernando's character from one perspective, one could say that he is a representation of the typical for the Romantics hubris driven self-confident individual/outcast (Manfred, Cain etc.), who acts as though God were the emanation of the human spirit, rather than an independent supreme mind (i.e. the Superman has the power to regulate Life).

The value of the temporal framework, within which man finds his life to be set, is the subject matter of one of Emily Brontë's most anthologised poems – **H146 (*Riches I hold in light esteem*).** Earthly pleasures, such as „Love", or „Fame", are neglected. As one is reading these lines, one could hear a non-Christian prayer:

Riches I hold in light esteem
And Love I laugh to scorn
And lust of fame was but a dream
That vanished with the morn –

And if I pray, the only prayer,
That moves my lips for me,
Is – „Leave the heart that now I bear
And give me liberty".

Yes, as my swift days near their goal
'Tis all that I implore –
Through life and death, a chainless soul
With courage to endure!

The poet does admit that man's existence is measurable in accordance with the certainty and imminence of Death, yet it ceases not with Death. If a wholesome being is to be achieved, the soul should be liberated in *life* and *death* alike. Herbert Dingle argues, that what the Lyrical Self is asking for here is not a universal freedom of spirit, but a personal unity with her heart (*„Leave me the heart...etc"*[xlii] – my bold type throughout the poem). The soul will outlive the body and thus man's concrete physical representation on Earth. The awareness of Death's imminence does put limits and limitations on one's life (line 9), but just because life ends does not mean that life has utilised its options (it would be worth remembering other poems of Emily's such as: *Julian M. And A.G. Rochelle,* or *The Death of A.G.A*). The need to ask for prolongation of existence in the after-life arises because a lifetime's abrupt end may never come on time: it always comes before a human Self has fully exhausted its potential...[xliii]. Emily Brontë hypothesizes over a possibility for the Self to continue the process of maturation and creative development – after Death.

Counter to the above, in H154 is discussed the motif of finality, of irrevocability. Late Lord Alfred's portrait shines like a spectre through the windows on *„the moonbeam, chill and blue".* The description of Lord Alfred's dead body suggest finality in the physical sense: *„those eyes are dust, those lips are clay; / That form is mouldered all away".* If one were to follow Fannie Ratchford's explanation in Hatfield's edition of Emily's verse, the (1941 – p. 18) the context might be that of Lord Alfred's loss of his former wife, and his subsequent marriage to A.G.A., which proved lethal for him. Whether the description of Lord Alfred's beloved (very probably A.G.A. by this time) also implies her own death, or merely emphasizes physically her evil nature (in the lyrical speaker's attitude toward her), is unclear: „*there is no worm, however mean, / That, living, is not nobler now/ Than she, Lord Alfred's idol queen, / So loved, so worshipped, long ago*". Finally, the lyrical speaker, who relates the story of Aspin castle's ghosts, invites the reader to turn to Nature's „*face divine*", which is visible in the golden „harvest moon" – the same which lights up Sidonia's journey back to Earth as a spectre, as an ambivalent creature not completely deprived of certain dose of daemonic.

Although the individual in Emily Brontë's poetry wishes for eternal life for the soul, it seems that man is also looking for a realm where the perpetuity of legibility of things would be destroyed, where there will be no more the incessant call for verification of meaning[xliv], where harmony would be self-explanatory, homogenous and non-verbal. H181 (*The Philosopher*) perfectly illustrates that. The philosopher wants to sleep, but to sleep „*without identity*" (stanza II). He admits that neither Heaven, nor in fact the finality of Hell could quench his ardent desire for knowledge and for finding a Spirit which surpasses everything and exists independent of man's stereotypes oppositess (evil and good). Such a Spirit, he imagines, could hold within the three rivers the philosopher describes to the interlocutor/Seer (i.e. *the Golden, the blood-like, and the Sapphire-like*). He admits that he himself could no longer hold inside the three warring Gods and that he should „*forget [his] present entity*" and „*never suffer more*". The Spirit he is looking for is not quite traditional, compared to the Christian God. He is not merely looking for a Spirit whose power is untouched by Time. He reaches his hand for an outside/transgredient rescue, for a respite from the endless strife for knowledge that promises no finality. He is yearning for eternal simplicity (so that „*vanquished good*" and „*victorious ill*" might be „*lost in one repose*"), devoid of the intricate link between good and evil that is only temporally verifiable.

Emily Brontë's picture of Heaven is exclusive in that it considers not external participants in it: it is a Heaven private which tends to hold two persons in an entity – sensuous and feasible, which failed to happen during their own lifetime. There are four poems that illustrate that best. These are: H109 (*Come hither, child – who gifted thee* – 19th July 1839 – Hatfield, 1941, pp. 116–117), H137 (*At such a time, in such a spot* – 6th May 1840; 28th July 1843 – Hatfield, 1941, pp. 143–144), H157 (*How clear she shines* – 13th April 1843 – Hatfield, 1941, 184–185), H188 (*How beautiful the earth is still* – 2nd June 1845 – Hatfield, 1941, 231– 234). In H109, the lack of *an Other* (in this case, the parent) is compensated for in the orphaned Lyrical Self's dream of Gabriel taking her to her father's home. In **H137** Augusta imagines Heaven as lit by God's pure light, which is to shine for her and her love, Alfred of Aspin Castle. When she admits to him that *„heaven's sun shines in thee"*, she is preparing the reader for the much discussed image of the Deity of poem H191, *No Coward Soul Is Mine*, i.e. possibly the beloved or a perfect projection of the Lyrical Self's (Cf *„every existence would exist in thee"*). In H137 Augusta says:

(...)
Let others seek its beams divine
In cell and cloister drear;
But I have found a fairer shrine
And happier worship here.

By dismal rites they win their bliss –
By penance, fasts, and fears;
I have one rite: a gentle kiss;
One penance: tender tears.

(…)
I'd ask for all eternity
To make a paradise for me,
My love – and nothing more!

In a more traditional way, the lyrical self would demand (in poem **H157**) that the *„stormless sea"* of the glorious night-sky substitutes *„all the woe Creation knows"*. Heaven would be that realm which would not allow for any negatives typical of the „*Dark world*" of the Present. In that imaginary better world „*Wisdom never laughs to Love*", and „*Virtue never crouches to Infamy;*" „*peace is not the lethargy of grief*" and „*Life is not a labour void and brief*", and „**Death is not the despot of the whole**". In Charlotte Brontë's novel, *Jane Eyre*, in chapter IX, Helen Burns' tombstone contains the sentence „**Resurgam**" („*I will rise again*"). This sentence sounds both like a challenge that aims at verifying the recuperative capacity Heaven holds for the innocent's spirit, as well as like an ominous threat that the spirit shall rise again to complete what has not been completed in a Life which teaches that the virtuous God is the one to possess the capacity to exterminate Evil.

Poem **H188** demonstrates the mature perception that what really matters is not so much whether ideas of Heaven are likely to materialise. Far more important seems to „*long till life be done*" and never to let one's „*Spirit tire / With looking for What is to be*". She admits that „*it is Hope's spell that glorifies (...) / All Nature's million mysteries – / The fearful and the fair*". Hope makes one „*strong to undergo / What I am born to bear*". Optimism is intermingled with fatality in the above lines. However, the more „*unjust*" present life is, „*the more my spirit springs elate*", as it „*anticipates rewarding destiny*". Emily is hoping, rather, that what follows this life is another life on the very same Earth (and not in Heaven), but modified to satisfy the quenchless will of the Spirit to unfold its potential and to create Life as a private and mystic union of friends. In Charlotte Brontë's novel *Shirley* Caroline Helstone seems to trust the potentials of a Self which holds God in a pervasively intimate way[66]: „*Does virtue lie in abnegation of self? I do not believe it. Undue humility makes tyranny; weak concession creates selfishness*"[xlv].

Four poems of Emily's illustrate best the boundaries of Emily Brontë's perception of God and of the dichotomy *Heaven:Hell*. These are: H140 (*The Night-Wind: In summer's mellow midnight* – 11th September 1840 – Hatfield, 1941, pp. 146–147), H159 (*E.G. to M.R.* – *Thy Guardians are asleep* – 4th may 1843 – Hatfield, 1941, pp. 187–188), **H183 (*Death, that struck when I was most confiding* – 10th April**

---

[66] About the theory that Emily Brontë's God is immanent, rather than transcendental see: Hillis-Miller, 1963, p. 172.

1845, Hatfield 1941, pp. 224–225) and **H191** (*No Coward Soul Is Mine* – 2ⁿᵈ January 1846 – Hatfield, 1941, pp. 243–244). In all of those Heaven is the phenomenal realm, which restores the wholeness of the spirit that was fragmented during Life. To Emily, Heaven does not necessarily imply regeneration through a conscientious self-chastisement and abnegation of the self's lifetime pride. To her, Death could lead man into a Heaven which is a prolongation of earthly bliss – with the best times and events of earthly life repeated there.

In H140 Emily Brontë demonstrates yet again her proneness to mysticism, as she employs the dream vision method[xlvi]. The poem is a dialogue between the night wind and the woman who is exposed to the wind's description of Heaven. The wind promises „*glory*" in Heaven, as contrasted to the „*fair*" „*sleeping Earth*". The woman begs the wind to play „*with the scented flower*", but to leave her feelings „*in their own course to flow*". The wind is trying to persuade the listener to yield to its own power so that she reaches quicker the realm of reveries. But in fact the wind is an embodiment of the listener's own will, which could be perceived to be seeking completion. The wind promises her that when she dies,

(...)
I shall have time enough to mourn
And thou to be alone.

What will follow after death is expected to complete the self, and for some that implies the serenity of being left alone from the aggressive intrusiveness of *external reality*, of *the world without*. In the same context, poem H159 argues, that neither the traditionally established omen of Hell, nor the promise for bliss in Heaven, could incapacitate and „rob" two people in love of their past, of their memory, of the viable link to their own private Heaven. There is the belief that the mind is impervious to the time-curtailing essence of Death[67]. Most strongly the latter idea is developed

---

[67] In Felicia Hemans' poem *Arabella Stuart* (1828) Death is only a „*fabled fruit*" which Arabella is free to ignore, because in fact she knows that „*the world within me*" holds the cure against death. However, she admits that her soul is a „*gulph*", which holds „*fierce forms*", which she is hoping to

in poem **H191** (*No coward soul is mine*). Difficult to classify as a Gondal poem, it is a hymn – in poetic form and in content, too. There is glorification of the endless capacity and potentials of the human mind, which holds a Deity of its own *within*, which is what immortalises a human being. Most literary critics come to one of two opposing conclusions about this poem. Some, like Jill Dix Ghnassia, consider it to be an affirmation of Emily Bronte's unyielding belief in the immeasurable depth of the human soul. The soul is seen as capable of making the Self *„the creator of the world"*. Ghnassia argues, that Emily Brontë turns the Orthodox creed of God's omnipotence into heresy by claiming that it is upon man to create Him[xlvii]. Others, like Norman Sherry and the Rev. Dr Bruce, consider that the poem depicts the threshold of Death, at which the spirit submits to God. Also, that Emily's much sustained agnosticism yields to the redemptive power of the Supreme mind of The Creator[xlviii]. Or, that the poem is a product of Emily Brontë's belief in „a brave independent soul" – „a part of God and his universe"[xlix]. Really, it remains unclear whether Emily means *„God within my breast"* as the God of Christianity (as reflected in her self in particular), or that the soul itself has the power of a Deity. I tend to cling to the latter of the two interpretations, because the last stanza cancels Death out of God's scheme of existence. And to cancel Death would mean to cancel the Christian idea of the liminal state which is believed to divide Time and confirm the relevance of the opposition between good and evil, actual and deserved, fact and fiction. Ironically, that would also mean (following Heidegger and Bakhtin) to negate the capacity of Death to confirm the sense of selfhood:

> *No coward soul is mine*
> *No trembler in the world's storm-troubled sphere*
> *I see Heaven's glories shine*
> *And Faith shines equal, arming me from Fear*
>
> *O God within my breast*
> *Almighty ever-present Deity*

---

brave through strength of prayer in order to *„o'ersweep the grave"* and meet her beloved again (Cf Hemans in: /ed./ Feldman 2000, pp. 314–316).

Life, that in me hast rest
As I Undying Life, have power in Thee

(...)
(...) thy infinity
(...)
The steadfast rock of Immortality

(...)
Thy spirit animates eternal years
Pervades and broods above,
Changes, sustains, dissolves, creates and rears
Though Earth and moon were gone
And suns and universes ceased to be
And thou wert left alone
Every existence would exist in thee

There is no room for Death
Nor atom that his might could render void
Since thou art Being and Breath
And what thou art may never be destroyed[68].

God materialises as the emanation of the spiritual potential that is latent within the self, rather than situated outside of the self. I here feel the

---

[68] Compare he following lines from John Donne's poem *A Fever* (*Songs and Sonnets*):
(...)
But yet thou canst not die, I know;
To leave this world behind, is death,
But when thou from this world will go,
The whole world vapours with thy breath.

Or, when thou, the world's soul, go'st,
It stays, 'tis but thy carcase then,
(...)
(...) I had rather owner be
Of thee one hour, than all else ever.

need to quote Rilke: „*The world is large, but in us it is deep as the sea*"[69]. The poem is also reminiscent of Cathy's canonization of Heathcliff. She declares that if he were annihilated, the universe would turn for her into „*a mighty stranger*" (*WH*, chapter 9). There is a Hegelian trace in Emily's idea that man is a predicate of God, of the Deity; yet man is the one to attach meaning to this omnipotent *Other*. The Deity thus exists as one whole in its many particles that constitute the essence of the Spirit as such (Cf Hegel in: Panova & Donchev at al. *Antoligia...* 1988, pp. 315–320). The endless alternation of change, constancy, disintegration, creation and growth (as seen in the stanza in bold type) appears like human consciousness, which, being immersed in endlessness, projects onto the world its own endlessness (Cf Feuerbach in: ibid. p. 589). Unlike Emily, Charlotte Brontë would insist on the traditional God who punishes and rewards, and whose mystic appearance at one's deathbed alleviates the physically torturous realisation that Death implies a lethal outcome (refer again to *Stanzas on the Death of a Christian* – July 1837). Nonetheless, there is felt in Emily's poem the doubt that there is some *Other*, both inside one's mind and physically verifiable outside one, who sustains Life[70].

Seemingly, poem H191 does away with the idea of Temporality and of the dependence of man's mind on external resources. It still does not unequivocally claim that Time, as such, is a parameter that is entirely irrelevant to humankind. The phrase „*eternal years*" proves that: it implies both timelessness and eternity, as well as the realisation that man's

---

[69] Quoted from: Bachelard, Gaston, *The Poetics of Space* (translated from French by Maria Jolas, /Boston: Beacon Press, 1969/, chapter 8). Disputing the issue of whether the world was an entire product of one's conscience, or whether external reality came prior to an individual's perception of it, Hallam Tennyson wrote to his father: „(...) *the Spiritual is the real; (...) You may tell me that my hand and my foot are only imaginary symbols of my existence, I could believe you; but you never, never can convince me that the eye is not an eternal Reality, and that the Spiritual is not the true and real part of me*" (quoted from Colville, Derek, *Victorian Poetry and the Romantic Religion*, /Albany: State University of New York Press, 1970/, p. 192).

[70] When Paul Ricoeur reflects on Descartes' theory about the evil genius (the reverse image of true God as demoted to the status of a mere opinion), he stresses Descartes' conclusion that even the extreme state of doubt is down to the fact that there is some One, who must guide and regulate this doubt. Ultimately, the hypothesis about the existence of the great conjurer is contained exactly in that whilst I doubt the certainty of my existence, I am in fact practising thinking, I am reflecting. There is ontological intention contained in doubt. If man doubts that he may be imperfect, then that is because he has some awareness or premonition about perfection, which is the eternal, which can only be God... (Cf Ricoeur, P., *Soi-même...*, 2004, pp. 16–22).

existence must be happening within certain dimensions, within certain definitions ("years"), out of which it could not be perceived or described. That man's existence is defined within certain temporal dimensions is also clear from **H183**, which mourns the fact that Death is an agent of *"Time's withering branch"* that divides existence by taking friends away and into non-being for ever. Time is seen in the development of the leaves of a tree, which *"blossom"* (as when A.G.A. enjoyed her happy days with Julius Brenzaida[i], when he was still alive), or *"droop"*, when Death strikes. The poem ends with the scene of Augusta imploring Death to *"strike"* once more and so make sure that *"the sapling's mouldering corpse"* (by which she implies both her own body and that of her beloved, Douglas) might return to whence it came – *"Eternity"*. Also, Blake could be heard here: in the idea of one living organism becoming food/prerequisite for another in the chain of existence (e.g. *The Book of Thel*). By mourning her beloved, the woman here recognises the fact that the idea of the Eternal (in the light of which Death becomes a mere test of endurance of human devotedness) is only relevant inasmuch as it implies Eternity on a social level. *Eternity* would mean to turn to, and to be voluntarily absorbed by, a being completely outside one's own being. Such steadfast *outsideness/Other*, to remember Emmanuel Levinas yet again, guarantees eternity to the Self. The Self partakes of this *Other*, yet seems incapable of holding the immensity of such an *Other* oneself. Man's partaking of Eternity appears not a privilege, but a fundamental characteristic of man's identity. Man's identity ought to be cultivated to accept and cherish the fact that it is an identity thanks to, and for the sake of, *an Other*. Such responsibility leads to individuation[ii].

In Emily Brontë's philosophy, individuation is only possible on Earth. Not because life on Earth could be verified at all times. She admits to Nature's numerous mysteries, but she knows that on Earth only does one find that unity of Being which is hidden in the unique union of native souls. Life on Earth, not always one of entire virtue, appears to be chastisement enough so that the Inferno ought to be spared. Emily has an unequivocally critical attitude to the system of Heavenly judgement, which determines the moment and the form of Death. That is also suggested in her *Belgian essay* *"The Cat"* (15th May 1842). In it she condemns the fact that a noble lady should embrace her child in transports when the child – ostensibly an embodiment of heavenly innocence – is crushing a beautiful butterfly between its fingers. The narrator tells Madame that if she could provide for her and her child a cat with a rat half-devoured by it, then that picture would be a good replica of her child's act. Heavenly innocence cannot exist alongside cruelty. Heaven is not exemplary if it allows for violence. One would not dream of joining such Heaven. As Lyn Pykett observes, Emily Brontë subverts both the Romantic theory of the fragmentation of the self that awaits its union with its *otherness* through Death, and also the Evangelical view of death as an escape from the „vale of tears"[lii].

What Emily rejects is the finality of Earthly life, which is immanent in a God-dominated system of ethics, where it also has a punitive function. Relevant are the poems: H111 (*Shed no tears o'er that tomb* – 26th July 1839, Hatfield, 1941, pp. 120–121), **H149** (*I see around me tombstones grey* – 17th July 1841 – Hatfield 1941, pp. 166–168), and H185 (*A thousand sounds of happiness* – 22nd April 1845 – Hatfield 1941, pp. 227–228). In poem H111 Heaven is described as not only incapable of providing a shelter for the souls of the dear dead, but it sends down on Earth „*even darker clouds*". Compassion is said to „*reign a little while*", whilst „*revenge – eternally*". There is the powerful memorable rhetorical question:

(…)
Is it when good men die
That sorrow wakes above?
Grieve saints when other spirits fly
To swell their choir of love?

What is frowned upon here is the Christian idea of salvation and mercy as based upon the consequentialist understanding that an individual's overall righteousness/sinfulness is confirmed upon the moment of expiration. Unrest and disobedience is also sensed in Jane Eyre's reply in an episode from Charlotte Brontë's novel *Jane Eyre*. When asked by Mr Brocklehurst what she is supposed to do to in order to avoid Hell, little Jane answers: „*I must keep in good health and not die*". Like Jane, the Lyrical Self obviously knows that Death is a prerequisite for arriving at either of the two destinations – Heaven or Hell[liii]. In Byron's *Cain* (2.1.52)

Cain declares that to create human beings who are to die one day is in fact to preach Death (Cf „*For what must I be grateful? / For being dust…*")[liv].

In H149 the Lyrical Self sees herself surrounded by „*tombstones grey stretching their shadows far away*". She treads beneath the turf, where low lie the silent dead. Utterly sunk in grief, which she has experienced on Earth, she admits her wounds „*could never heal again*". Yet she declares:

(…)
Let me remember half the woe
I've seen and heard and felt below,
And Heaven itself, so pure and blest,
Could never give my spirit rest.

The „*native land*" is sweeter than „*any world beyond the Tomb*". She is dreaming of a „*lasting rest*", or else of a wake in which she would „*share a mutual immortality*" with the Earth – the mortuary of her dearest people. Albeit limiting in its physicality, the Earth symbolizes eternity against the background of Heaven's limitative selectiveness in prolonging earthly bliss. Earthly life does imply finality, yet finality preferable to Heaven's stubborn unresponsiveness to man's lifetime travail. The term „*mother*" in line 29 most probably refers to the Earth – the only one to value man and recognize each man's uniqueness (*„No – Earth would wish no other sphere / To taste her cup of sufferings dread; / She turns from Heaven a careless eye / And only mourns that we must die!*"). For, it is only on the Earth that a direct execution of the principle of *Otherness* is possible[71]. The rebirth (*„Or waken but to share with thee/ A mutual immortality*"), which the Earth could provide for man (instead of the traditionally believed resurrection in Heaven) is not quite of the platonic type that Edward Chitham describes[lv]. Emily Brontë lays stress upon Earth's physicality and feasibility: Earth's „*kindly breast*" is sweeter than Heaven's spiritual might (it accepts man as he is: with „*gloomy*

---

[71] In *Wuthering Heights* Catherine Earnshaw says to Nelly: „*I've no more reason to marry Edgar Linton than I have to be in Heaven*" (quoted from: Thormählen, M., 1999, p. 104). It is only on the Earth, at the Heights, that Cathy feels herself, since that was the place where her union with Heathcliff should have developed in a lifetime.

guests", *„torments and madness, tears and sin"* within). She believes that there is a good reason for the individual to become one with Earth, yet she does not affirm a spiritual rebirth as a consequence (*„let us be laid in lasting rest..."*). Man's best wish is for an earthly hereafter[lvi]. Death would lead to a heritage better than Heaven's dome[lvii].

How different, indeed, does the above poem sound in comparison to what, say, the famous children's writer Edith Nesbit (1858 – 1924) says in her essay entitled *The One Thing Needful*. In it she argues, that *„man's life and the will of God are like a poem"*: God creates and man gives that creation the finishing touch (as the poet composes a line more). When the poem rhymes, there is harmony, and when man's efforts do not rhyme with God's intent, then man must only rest assured that the Author knows man made his best[lviii]. To Emily Brontë Death comes to confirm man's desperate love for Life on Earth and in the present moment[lix]. It is only because such love cannot be accomplished in the absence of *Others* that Death is sought as the final answer. That is what poem H185 tells us. Earth's *„vocal joy"* is immediately hushed by the death of one single human being, whose *„groan"* causes the world *„misery"*. Although expected to come to terms with her beloved's death and to acquiesce, the Lyrical Self finds not rest, as she cannot *„call the cold corpse from its funeral pall*[72]*"*. Again, in discussing the fact that Death *„smites" „the loved and the blest"* is sensed rebuke to the Almighty's system, whose purgatory mechanism is driven by death's reductive power over man[73]. And again, the Lyrical Self implores for *„one arrow more"* to be launched by Death, and for *„a quiet bed"*, granted to the one who *„yearns to be beside his early stricken dead"*.

The concept of Heavenly forgiveness upon Death is rejected. Instead, Death is anticipated as a revenge against Death itself, or in other words, against God's punitive mechanism. This attitude of Emily's implies that

---

[72] In *The Borderers* (III, v. 83–88) William Wordsworth rages against the fact that a leaf's death (just like any other death) is soon forgotten, as though the thing *„had never been / Whose shadows gnaw us to our vitals"* (Quoted from: Paley, Morton, 2003, p. 227).
[73] In *To Cowper* (10th November 1842) Anne Brontë asks the same question: is Heaven so *„severe"* as to let a glorious soul such as Cowper's get *„lost"*. Mathilde Blind (1841–1896) goes further in her poem *The Prophecy of St Oran*. In it she declares that *„there is no God"* and heaven is *„deaf and dumb to prayer and praise"*: man is simply given the *„burden of eternity"*, which the philosophical abysm of death opens before him (Cf Blind, in: Shattock, Joanne, *Women and Literature in Britain (1800–1900)* /CUP/, 2001, pp. 176–177).

Death can be desired actively, but cannot be performed to mach its active anticipation. At that, man's active anticipation of Death does not necessarily imply suicide because to „achieve" Death would mean to reach a deadlock. The realisation of the inescapability of one's own death does not necessarily, unlike that is in Christianity, teach Emily Brontë's lyrical personae humility (Cf Goritcheva, in: *Bakhtin, Pro et Contra...* 2002, p. 352). What it does cultivate, however, is a rebellious attitude against temporality, which on the whole, manifests itself in even greater a zest for developing one's potential to protect and ease the life and pains of the *Other* (the friends, the beloved, the family) – as that is evident in Emily's mature poetry (e.g. H143, H149, H172, H182, H183, H190, H192).

* * *

The aim of this chapter was to <u>investigate the treatment of the themes of *Mortality* in Emily Brontë's poetry</u>. I employed the method of <u>thematic re-grouping</u> of the poems with the purpose of specifying certain philosophical concepts and outlining certain philosophical parameters within which the given thematic field could be accommodated and examined. The dramatic world of <u>Gondal</u> was used as a main context of discussing the contents of some major poems of Emily's. One motif for doing that was that Gondal appears to have been built upon semi-deliberate and semi-spontaneous elimination–resuscitation of one major lyrical persona – Augusta Geraldine Almeida (A.G.A. = Rosina of Alcona = Sidonia's Deity = Geraldine/ Rochelle). The development of A.G.A.'s individuality appears to have been the driving force in the progress of Gondal. The intricacies in Gondal around rivalry for power and independence, it would appear, leave Death as the only possible tool for moulding A.G.A.'s character. In regard to this central lyrical persona, the poet's „surplus of vision" could be seen as suppressed. The poet's position of authority over this persona (who can be defined as Romantic) is minimal, and the reader's attention is driven to Augusta's inner world, which nearly merges with that of the poet[ix]. A.G.A.'s consciousness appears unfathomable, so that Death is but a test for its firmness. Yet the lyrical persona's independence and self-confidence are frustrated by the physically felt *lack of an Other*. Gondal, as a preamble to *Wuthering Heights*, could be taken to represent the poet's laborious journey towards restoring *that Other* whose presence is essential to the wholeness of the universe. Bearing in mind that Gondal itself exists in fragments only, the theme of Death becomes doubly relevant. But even independent of Gondal as a strong thematic background of investigating *Mortality* in Emily Brontë's poetry, it should be noted that almost every other poem of Emily's demonstrates the poet's interest in Death, dying and in the idea of the End. At this point, I am tempted to remember and rephrase Rilke's formula of dying. That would mean to say that the lyrical self in many of Emily Brontë's poetic works is faced with the dilemma of how to die truthful to one's own nature and personality without betraying the truth and the ontological essence of Death itself[74].

In external Nature Emily Brontë finds examples of fragmentation that allegorically allude to fragmentation in man's mind (see especially poems H2, 3, 4, 9, 10, 14, 27). The lack that each human being's death leaves behind in the universe proves irreparable. Each lack of a thing living is destructive to the stability of the whole. In this sense, Emily Brontë deviates from the pantheist conviction that immortality is a feature guaranteed each and everyone by a natural re-absorption and re-integration of each spirit. The soul is released from its „carnal case" (see especially poems H15, 36, 43, 61, 85, 91, 126, 167, 168, 179 and 180). It may now be admitted into a realm where the traditional chronology of Earthly life is ousted by the phenomenology of the liberated spirit which achieves a mystic completion of man's Self. Thus, man's personality gets liberated from the limitative effect temporality has had on it. This division of the Self is enhanced by certain natural conditions (e.g. a windy night), but it is not pre-planned. Emily Brontë's poetry affirms that the knowledge of the essence of one man's Self is „closed" within the Self; there is also the insistence on the voluntarily chosen moment of self-division – an alternative to traditional Death (which tends to be seen as imposed on man by circumstances). Yet even when Death is conscientiously chosen, it is irreversible and cannot really be fruitful to the Self: the external point of reference lost, any intention to act in a certain manner becomes divested of sense.

The abode of the dead (poems H12, 58, 148, 158, 163) is immediately sensed at night when man's self is exposed to its own „face" –

---

[74] Cf Blanchot, Maurice, *L'Espace Littéraire*. [translated in Bulgarian] *Literaturnoto prostranstvo*. LIK. 2000. pp. 126–127.

in the lack of complete visibility of other objects beside which it otherwise exists. The night – which is the time of the dead – is when, indeed, the spatial characteristics of Life are more easily and readily accessible[lxi]. The grave is inhabited by what may indeed be referred to as „the third party" – the *dead friend/companion/beloved/relative/countryman*, who refuses to keep to his/her own abode and plays the role of *the missing Other*. This „third party" is listener/witness/confessor to the living and suffering man, to the Mourner. The *tomb* is *home*. It yields not its dwellers back. Sadly, the notion of Death stimulates man's potential for ontological growth much more than actual Life itself does.

Otherness is first and foremost discovered and fostered within the *Family*, at *Home* (relevant poems include H11, 42, 79, 97, 99, 101, 102, 108, 113, 114, 120, 172, 156, 190), where only a stable basis for true Being (i.e. Co-Being) is formed. This particular thematic focus of the treatment of *Mortality* in Emily Brontë's poetry was intended to demonstrate how she gradually arrives at the conclusion that Death, in ontological terms, is the most crucial event in everyone's existence, which ought be existence shared. With the death of the parent, or especially of the child, there emerges an existential „vacuum". At this point there is a possibility for projecting Death everywhere – as a spontaneous reaction against the feeling of loss. Augusta may will her own infant's death in order to master the unyielding and interminable destructiveness of Death in man's life in general. Yet infanticide terminates the possibilities of the Self from a moral and ethical point of view. Death in the family is the Survivor's sure spiritual death. Man is invited to sustain one's humaneness by looking for someone upon whom one should bestow one's love and care (see poems H37, 41, 73, 75, 86, 124, 143, 177, 180, 182, 192). Only an *Other* could grant one the sensation of Time happening.

Emily Brontë's idea of *protective outsideness*, which fights Death, does not necessarily imply the image of the traditional Christian God. Instead of God – as a point of ontological reference – there is the Earth – man's instructor and true protector. Despite man's sinful life on Earth, existence on Earth is preferred to the chastisement and selective redemption and salvation which the arrival at Heaven through Death heralds. Both Emily Brontë's poetry and her Belgian essays demonstrate her belief that suffering on Earth is penance enough and that therefore the idea of dying in order to make penitence in the life beyond appears unacceptable. She dreams of an Earthly hereafter, where Life's Evil would be ameliorated and transformed into a source of aesthetic productiveness. Heaven is on Earth, where it is the Heaven between two people, in the Native land, which the Lyrical Self of many of Emily's mature verse longs for. A „a chainless soul" is needed to reach the realm where the mind is most itself and most lasting; presumably, that realm is also the one where *Survivor* and *Dead Other* meet. If the awareness of Death teaches forgiveness and altruism, then that is not so much because Death is a statement in the inescapability of one's terminus, but because it lays emphasis on the irreversibility of each one existences on earth which has already been completed. No Survivor is as immaculate and as chaste as to be superior to someone who is dead. No dead man could be pronounced to have used up one's potential during one's lifetime: one could never really prove that there is guilt such as it should undeniably deserve Death[lxii].

NOTES:

[i] Cf Davis, Philip, *The Victorians*, The Oxford English Literary History, volume 8 (Oxford University Press, 2004), pp. 510–511.
[ii] Bakhtin, AIG, 2003, p. 230.
[iii] Cf C. D Lewis in: Pykett, Lynn, /ed./ *Emily Brontë* (Macmillan, 1989), p. 46.
[iv] Cf Barker, 1995, pp. 538–539.
[v] Cf Barker, 1995, pp. 294–295.
[vi] Cf Sinclair, May, *The Three Brontës* (London: Hutchinson & Co., 1912), p. 209.
[vii] Cf Gerin, Winifred, *The Brontës II – The Creative Work* (Longman, 1974), p. 18.
[viii] Cf Benvenuto, Richard, *Emily Brontë* (Boston: Twayne Publishers, 1982), p. 68.
[ix] Cf Bakhtin, AIG, 2003, p. 173.
[x] Cf Hardy, B., 1985, p 102.
[xi] Cf Kant in: Panova & Donchev et al., /eds./ *Antologia Evropeiska Filosofia.* 1988, p. 61.
[xii] Cf Panova, Donchev et al, 1988, pp. 76–77.
[xiii] Cf Nikitaev, Vladimir, 2005, p. 212–214.
[xiv] Cf Gurko, Yelena, [in Russian] *Jacques Derrida. Dekonstruktzia*, Minsk. Ekonompress. 2001. p. 157.
[xv] Cf Spark & Stanford, 1985, p. 185.
[xvi] Cf Knapp, B., 1992, pp. 105–106.
[xvii] Cf Griakalov in: Bakhtin, *Pro et Contra…2002*, pp. 330–331.
[xviii] Cf Chitham in: Chitham & Winnifrith, 1983, p. 58.
[xix] Cf Griakalov in: Bakhtin, *Pro Et Contra… 2002*, pp. 331–339.
[xx] Cf Miles, R., in: /ed./ Smith, A., 1976, p. 79.
[xxi] Cf Stanford & Spark, 1985, p. 199.
[xxii] Cf Hillis-Miller, 1963, p. 207.
[xxiii] Cf Bakhtin, *AIG*, 2003, pp. 128–129.
[xxiv] Cf Demichev, 1997, pp. 27–29.
[xxv] Ibid. pp. 31–32.
[xxvi] Cf Boyadziev, 2000, pp. 206–213.
[xxvii] Cf Ariès, 2004, book I, pp. 18–19.
[xxviii] Cf Clark, in: Bakhtin, *Pro Et Contra*, 2002, pp. 51, 53.
[xxix] Cf Patterson, Ch., in: /ed./ Goodin, 1974, p. 84.
[xxx] Cf Turnell, M., in: /ed./ McNees, 1996, p. 534.
[xxxi] Cf Peeck-O'Toole, M., 1988, p. 42.
[xxxii] Cf Abrams, 1973, p. 296.
[xxxiii] Cf Ghnassia, 1994, pp. 68–69.
[xxxiv] Cf Bakhtin, *AIG*, 2003, p. 181.
[xxxv] Cf Bakhtin, *AIG*, pp. 179–180.
[xxxvi] Cf Levinas, *Drougost i transtsendentnost*, pp. 168, 173.
[xxxvii] Cf Lloyd-Evans, 1992, p. 183.
[xxxviii] Cf Levinas, 2000, pp. 81–82.
[xxxix] Cf Lloyd-Evans, 1993, p. 181.
[xl] Cf Thormählen, M., 1999, p. 106.
[xli] Cf Ariès, 2004, book I, p. 161.
[xlii] Cf Dingle, Herbert, *The Mind of Emily Brontë* (London: Martin Brian & O'Keefe, 1974), pp. 35, 41.
[xliii] Cf Bolnoff, 1999, chapter XI.

[xliv] Cf Eagleton, 2003, pp. 256, 260.

[xlv] Cf Bodenheimer, R., 1988, in: /ed./ McNees, 1996, p. 553.

[xlvi] Cf Miles, in: /ed./ Smith, A., 1976, p. 88.

[xlvii] Cf Ghnassia, 1994, p. 198.

[xlviii] Cf Bruce, in: /ed./ McNees, 1996, pp. 486–487.

[xlix] Cf Sherry, 1970, p. 109.

[l] Cf Ratchford, F., in: Hatfield, 1941, p. 18.

[li] Cf Levinas, *Totalité Et Infini...*, 2000, p. 298.

[lii] Cf Pykett, 1989, pp. 68–69.

[liii] Cf Keefe, Robert, *Charlotte Brontë's World of Death*, Austin: University of Texas Press, 1979, p. 100.

[liv] Quoted from: Batten, G., 1998, pp. 39–40.

[lv] Cf Chitham in: Chitham & Winnifrith, 1983, p. 118.

[lvi] Cf Spark & Stanford, 1985, pp. 181–182.

[lvii] Cf Chichester in: /ed./ McNees, E., 1996, p. 594.

[lviii] Quoted from: Gates, Barbara, *In Nature's Name. An Anthology of Women's Writing and Illustration (1780–1930)* /Chicago & London: The University of Chicago Press, 2002/, p. 196.

[lix] Cf Ariès, Ph., 2004, book I, p. 191.

[lx] Cf Bakhtin, AIG, 2003, pp. 239–240.

[lxi] Cf Genette, Gérard, *Figures I, II, III* (sélection), [in Bulgarian] Figuri, Sofia. „Figura". 2001, p. 198.

[lxii] Cf Eagleton, 2003, p. 149.

Conclusions

The conclusions offered in this final part of the present research come with the hope that the following statements were defended. First, my intention was to demonstrate that the poetry of Anne, Charlotte and Emily Brontë could legitimately be presented as *one* literary whole – an entity of three constituents, which share and develop specifically one major theme – *Mortality*. Second, I argued, that in the poetry of Anne, Charlotte and Emily Brontë Death was elevated to the level of a philosophic discourse with the highest degree of ontological value. In terms of contents, this philosophic discourse unfolds in the formation of the image of the *Mourner/Survivor*, who could also be defined as the main lyrical persona in the poetic heritage of the three sisters. To this lyrical persona the interpretation of the *Other's Death* seems to be the basis of interpreting the more general concept of *Being* and for verifying and affirming *Being as Co-Being*[1]. Third, I believe that Angria and, especially Gondal – as autonomous literary constructs (indeed, dramatic worlds) and in particular in their quality as poetic wholes – serve as a unique and rather intriguing context in which the themes of *Mortality* generously evolve. Further on, each of the three sisters' personal poetic development obviously ran parallel to the development of presenting the theme of *Death*. All other motifs and topics related to issues existential, which the Brontës touch upon or discuss in detail, seem to be subordinate to that large main one. One would notice a gradual, not entirely unequivocal, and toilsome arrival at the idea of *Life as only and always Life in Dialogue* – attentive and open to *the Other*, whose transgredience in respect of the speaking subject proves rescuing and Life-maintaining. The perusal of the notion of *the Other's death* as a moral imperative to the Living speaks of an ethical attitude towards existence, it speaks of the formation of the feeling of Duty and gratitude to *the Other*, who defines, limits and concretizes in a fruitful manner „My" own Being.

I also believe that the theme of *Mortality* should be seen as the most adequate link between the Brontë sisters and their literary and philosophic environment which each of them moulds and enriches in a specific manner in her own prose fiction works. Indeed, *Death* here offers the widest

---

[1] The experience of Death situation is a truly historical experience of the highest degree, the necessity of which (as postponed in its happening) historicizes any other, ordinary experience in one's life (Cf Nikitaev, Vl., 2005, p. 218).

spectrum of critical ideas and links between the three sisters and their literary milieu. The beginning of this literary milieu is indeed the Pre-Romantic period, in which Death and the grave simultaneously inform, instruct and swallow Life irrevocably. The Romantics stress the euthanatic availability of Death (a chance for liberating the genius from the burden of Life's temporality and physicality, with the hope of self-completion and independence of spirit). Yet they also mourn the lost closeness to Nature – the spontaneity of feeling, accommodated in the warm environment of friends, family, the beloved, who are gone. One concrete expressions of the Romantic grief, which the Brontës doubtlessly share, is the problematization of the missing/destroyed family unit. There is also the Victorian tendency to „hear" Death in its social sounding (as a malady of a society which refuses to accept the idea of the End as making people closer and interrelated). With regard to their position in English literary history, I believe the Brontës could be placed in that phase of the thematic development of Death when its dialogic value was beginning to get destabilized and challenged.

I also think that the choice of *Mortality* as a theme of research hides a rather productive opportunity to track down, in a comparative manner, the formation of this one main philosophic discourse as dominant in the Brontë sisters' whole literary heritage, i.e. in their prose fiction too. Evidence could be found in the ontological quest, on which embark the main characters in novels like: *Wuthering Heights* (Emily Brontë), *Jane Eyre* and *Villette* (Charlotte Brontë), *The Tenant of Wildfell Hall* (Anne Brontë). These characters all share a zest for self-cognition, which is satisfied through the painful experience and need to interpret Death, *the Other's Death*.

Finally, I tried to show how the chosen theme of research allows the critic to embark on an interdisciplinary research, in which one specific part of English literature of the nineteenth century could be revised through the optics of modern European ontophilosophy and existential ethics (in the face of Martin Heidegger, Emmanuel Levinas, Jacques Derrida and Mikhail Bakhtin). And, reciprocally, that those main achievements of modern ontophilosophy and existential ethics could examine their critical applicability in the heuristic large-scale analysis of concrete literary material.

The <u>analytical approach</u> I chose to employ throughout the present research could be defined as non-formal, but one based on the contents of the poetic works of the three sisters, as well as on the context of the emergence of those works. I rejected the possibility of merely deconstructing a certain number of poetic pieces on the basis of formal verbal references to the theme of *Death*. I took into serious consideration the fact that Angria and Gondal each boast their central lyrical personae (e.g. Arthur Wellesley, Duke of Zamorna and Alexander Percy, Duke of Northangerland in Angria, and A.G.A. in Gondal). The formation and maturation of the inner world of those (mainly A.G.A.), I argued, verifies the ontological significance of Death, which evolved into a philosophic discourse in the Brontë sisters works. The analytical approach chosen embraced some major terms and concepts of <u>modern existential ethics and ontophilosophy.</u> This investigative apparatus was employed, because, as it puts on a pedestal the idea of *the Other* (to whom one is open and answerable at all time), it is the one to most strongly maintain the idea of *the Dialogic Being* as the only possible form of Being worth man's while. The innovativeness was in applying the latter theory on the specific literary material in hand for the first time.

The research pointed out that the early poetry of the Brontë sisters (mainly from the late 1830s) is centred around one issue which **Martin Heidegger** would define as „*Presence*" – a category of Space, which unfolds through a positive appropriation of the Past, which in effect, is the „container" of *the Dead Other*. More often than not, for the Brontës *Presence,* as such, becomes available, tangible, when *the Other* is no more alive, but has become, sadly, a fact. In this sense, *Being as Being through an Other,* may be seen to strive for Death as for the moment of ultimate self-completion. On the other hand, the experience of observing Death externally becomes the possibility of factual verification of the life of each one Survivor, who thus also confirms the uniqueness of his/her erstwhile *Other.* In itself, the striving to achieve Death is doomed, since *Death is the possibility of the total impossibility.* Quite ominously, in both Angria and Gondal the *Other* is the so-called *missing lyrical persona* – the dead beloved/parent/friend. The cognition of Death (and of the daemonic as one of its ingredients) summons man towards constant hermeneutical vigilance and responsibility towards present Life (as Eagleton put that).

Another trace of the Brontë sisters' treatment of Death in their poetry could be discerned in their belief which **Levinas** would define as *endless care and love for an Other – the only power capable of incapacitating even the factual imminence of Death.* A number of poems of the three sisters demonstrate how the Survivor's individuality looses its balance and objectivity after *the Other's Death.* A necessity emerges to follow an altruistic approach to Life, according to which the knowledge that „*You, too, will die*" maintains and regulates one's conscience and consciousness. Unlike their earlier poetic works, the Brontë sisters' mature ballads and hymns depict Death as futurity unexpected, overwhelming and, though productive, not conscientiously wished for or aimed at.

In Anne's and Emily's early poetic works is discovered an attitude, which **Derrida's** deconstructive theory would define as the insistence that each man's Life has the capacity to define its the purpose and limits. Ironically, the Survivor and the No-longer-alive are always on two opposite sides, which is why there could never be a witness who could draw a clear topographic line confirming with physical precision the threshold over which follows Death. Hence the element of option, which Death contains. Bio-ethics, which is in effect Thanato-ethics, is really Euthanato-ethics. This understanding synchronises rather well with the Romantic ideology. In some major poems of Emily Brontë's the factual verifiability and probability of Death seem to be devalued: there is the dream of a Heaven of one's own which may be non-fact for others, yet feasible for the Self's soul and including the cherished beloved. Ostensibly, the lack of a methodological apparatus for confirming the factuality of Death appears to eliminate the importance of the search for meaning after Death, which is this being read as the ultimate metaphor for incompletion. However, to re-iterate Derrida again, the *culture of the World, the Culture of Being, is in fact a culture of posterity, built on the cult towards the Dead.* Unconditional, unselfish and spontaneous pardon – even before the actual sentence has been pronounced in regard of the most unforgivable deed – is what could save humankind.

The Brontë sisters' mature poetry was purposefully analysed through **Bakhtin's** theory of *Otherness,* according to which no individual has an alibi in simply being for the sake of being. Without an outside referee, which is what the *Other* functions as (so long as he/she is alive), there is no true justification or objectification of one's Self. *Being* is a theoretical availability, and the non-recognition of *the Other's* presence from the very start curtails one's lifetime potential. As, the analysis of, say, Emily's ballad *Silent is the house*, or Charlotte's ballad *Gilbert* confirmed, selfhood could be achieved through the realisation that each one man owes life to someone that precedes him/her, someone who is *one's Author* – and one faces the task of becoming an Author to someone else further on. The fact that in Gondal and Angria Death regulates the murderous instincts of the main participants of the two stories is not really dissonant with what Bakhtin terms *crisis of authorship* (i.e. when the Romantic lyrical persona usurps and incapacitates the author's self who thus looses its aesthetic outsideness and authorial reliability). Whilst absorbing and „processing" in a biographical manner the Author's shaken and wistful vision of the fatality of Life, the Romantic persona projects mortality around. The individual's feeling of self-sufficiency urges him/her to wish to encompass the whole of Life *within* solely, to analyse it and possess it (i.e. to be able to terminate it), at which the dialogic principle of the *no-alibi-in-Being-to-the-exclusion-of-an-Other* is destroyed. On a broader literary scale, one tends to remember Coleridge's Ancient Mariner, Byron's Manfred and Cain and Emily's Augusta. The incompleteness of both the Angrian and the Gondal poetic cycles (suggested in the dominance of the lyrical persona of the ghost) was also refracted through Bakhtin's argument, that orphanhood (the state which best describes Angrians and Gondalians) is the earliest and most damaging reason to fail in achieving self-definition in the ontological sense of the word. Infanticide in Emily's Gondal was interpreted as deficiency in maternal care, which the Self both suffers from and somehow maintains. Another specificity of the Brontë sisters' poetics was seen in the role the grave/tomb plays – a „coagulant of time", which holds the *Dead Other*, the remembrance of whom could help one repair consciousness dialogically, i.e. into *co-consciousness*. The knowledge of Death thus becomes redemptive, purgatorial, and Eucharistic. Emily's last ballads argue that the knowledge of Death should teach forgiveness – limitless and ever active (see for instance *Silent is the house…*). At this point, again, Derrida's and Paul Ricoeur's observations on the dichotomy *guilt–pardon* would apply.

As already explained in this conclusive part of the present research, it seemed logical to position the investigation of themes of *Mortality* in the poetry of the Brontë sisters within the English literary context of early Romanticism – early Victorianism. Chapter I of Section I of Part II was devoted to the latter. There were established certain thematic links between the poets who could be defined as the Brontë sisters' immediate predecessors and contemporaries. A distant echo of *the graveyard school's* fascination with the graveyard and the grave as recognised spots for meditation and self-contemplation was suggested in the Brontë sisters' preoccupation with the grave/the tomb as the „container of the *Dead Other*" – the didactic source of forgiveness and care. Quoted were Young's *Night Thoughts (1742)*, and Gray's *Elegy Written in a Country Churchyard (1750)*, also Charlotte Brontë's *The Violet (1830)* and *Lines Written beside a Fountain (1833)*, and Emily Brontë's *I. M. to I. G. (1844)*.

The euthanatic availability of Death (as one feature of the Romantic ideology) was found in the Brontë sisters' early poetry, which may remind the modern reader of poets like Byron, Keats and Tennyson. The striving towards Death was defined as aesthetic, as non-communal, because it was seen as imagined to the exclusion of another participant. The roots of a voluntary retreat from Life were also sought in the misfortunes, which the individual's unbridled cognitive urge incurred. One tends to remember Byron's *Manfred (1817)* and *Cain (1821)*, as well as Tennyson's „internally dead" individual, for whom reality reflects the dissembled fragments of man's own expired spirit (Cf *Mariana – 1830, In Memoriam – 1834–1850* and *Maud – 1855)*. Relevant Brontë sisters' poems may include: Anne's „*Call me away...*" (1845), *Self-Communion (1847–1848)*; Charlotte's „*But once again...*" (1836), *Reason (1836)* and *Frances (1846)*; Emily's *Lines (1839)*, *The Philosopher (1845)*, „*I'm happiest when most away*" (?1838) and *To Imagination (1844)*.

In terms of symbols, which reflect the poetic interest towards *Mortality* in the given historical period, the Brontë sisters certainly share two with the Romantic poets. First of all, the wind – Shelley's ambivalent „destroyer and preserver" (*Ode to the West Wind*), Emily's prophet, „comforter", informant and guide, the bearer of the germ of moral insight (see also Emily's „*Loud without...*" – *1838*, or „*Aye, there it is*", *1841*).

The other symbol is that of sleep/daydreaming – the liminal state, in which the soul is carried away from the alienating doldrums of everyday existence. Sleep is also a state of providential intimations, in which the notion of *Being as co-Being* may be discussed (here, poems I referred to included: Keats' *Isabella – 1820*, Tennyson's *The Lotos-Eaters – 1832*, Charlotte's *Gilbert (around 1843)* and Emily's *Julian M. and A. G. Rochelle – 1845)*.

In terms of motifs, the one, which the Brontë sisters obviously have in common with the Romantics and the Victorians, is that of *orphanhood* (which, I believe, could also be referred to as *„the syndrome of the missing Authority/Author"*). For poets like the Brontës, Blake, Wordsworth and Byron orphanhood is linked to the individual's desire to overcome the state of disorientation reached at the loss of a feasible link with one's parents/one's child (see Wordsworth's *Michael – 1800, Intimations of Immortality – 1807, The Excursion – 1814, Vadracour and Julia – 1820* and *The Prelude – 1799–1850*, esp. book XII). Another major motif is the dichotomy *infanticide:fratricide,* both of whose components lead towards spiritual impoverishment, to orphanhood of the Self in a more general sense. Relevant works include: Blake's cyclical diptych *Songs of Innocence (1798) & Songs of Experience – 1794* (especially *the poems Holy Thursday, London, The Little Girl Found & The Little Girl Lost*); Byron's *Cain* (1821); Anne Brontë's *Retirement (1840),* and *An Orphan's Lament (1841);* Charlotte Brontë's *The Vision (1830)* and *The Missionary (1846);* Emily Brontë's *„I am the only being whose doom" (1837), A Farewell to Alexandria (1839)* and *„Why ask to know the date – the clime" (1846).* Yet another motif common for both the Brontë sisters and their literary milieu is the tripartite problem of *guilt:redemption:forgiveness*. Two points are worth emphasising here. First, the understanding that Evil contains the „germ of good", since it induces the desire to overcome Death as Life's ultimate negation, which in practice is possible through a caring attitude to an *Other* – the true beneficiary of a Self's positive energy. Appropriate poetic works include: Blake's prophetic *Book of Thel (1789)* as well *The Marriage of Heaven and Hell (1790)*, both of which could be seen to prefigure early Shelley's necessitarian faith that each instance of Death is counterbalanced by the fact that each next emergence of Life „*contains perfection's germ"* (e.g

Queen Mab – 1813). Second, the fact that nineteenth-century English literature suffers from a feeling of guilt in a way, which presupposes redemption through someone *Other*, who would brave to share one's ontological burden of fratricide with an unconditional and limitless Eucharistic readiness. As Adah does so in choosing to accompany Cain – the murderer of his own brother Abel – in Byron's mystery *Cain – 1821*, or as Emily Brontë's Julian, who rescues Rochelle in *Julian M. and A. G. Rochelle – 1845* (see also Charlotte Brontë's poem *Pilate's Wife's Dream – 1846*). Another aspect of interpreting the same motif would be to say that the 19th-century individual seems to hesitate in accepting the fact that Life does continue even after „My" Death (In *Maud, 1855*, Tennyson said: „*If I be dear, / If I be dear to someone else"*). Last but not least, in the obvious for the poetics of the nineteenth century re-actualisation of the notions of *Heaven and Hell* in literature, there could be outlined three main features, which the Brontë sisters share with their predecessors and followers. First, Nature's heavenly grip provides a lasting shelter from all earthly travail and from the existential burden of temporality (this is discovered in a comparative analysis of certain poetic works of Keats', Shelley's and early Anne's and Emily Brontë's). Second, there is a counterbalancing perception of the notion of immortality as hellish if deprived of the Otherness that would verify the existence of the Self on the Earth: *here* and *now* (see again mature Emily Brontë, Byron's *Cain and Manfred*, Coleridge's *The Wanderings of Cain – 1797–1798*). And third, the ambivalent nature of the female beloved. The female beloved may be a source of poetic inspiration, as she guarantees the poet eternal life (e.g. Shelley's *Epipsychidion – 1821*). She could also be the daemonic mother, capable of murdering her own babe (e.g. Coleridge's *Christabel – 1816*, Emily's *A.G.A.* persona). And all of those specificities evolving under the individual's constant struggle to find a point of agreement among the Evangelical insistence on sin as a part of the child's/man's identity, the Calvinistic doctrine of predestination, election and reprobation, and finally the Methodist faith in salvation available to all.

The investigation of *Mortality* in **Anne Brontë's poetic** works was chosen to be the first chapter with heuristic contributions to the Brontë studies. It was established that the earliest poetic period concerned with the above thematic area (1836–1840) demonstrates that Anne's vision of the End is refracted through the euthanatic urge. The familiarity of the *grave* was identified as the receptacle of a lost world of youth/childhood, which is juxtaposed to the hostilely alienating and friendless reality of the present. Whilst creating an early phenomenology of self-treatment through self-mourning, the lyrical self involuntarily strives to own her own fate, memory of which one could never really have. Particularly indicative of the latter were found to be the poems *Verses by Lady Geralda* (1836), *A Voice From the Dungeon* (1837), and *Lady of Alzerno's Hall* (1838). It was suggested that the idea of *Otherness* through the knowledge of Death was only latent in this early period, in which it could not have unfolded fully due to Anne's poetic concern with the End as merely the individual's *own* end, rather than as a general idea of the End of humanity. Anne Brontë's ideology of self-observation becomes enriched with a new range of ideas in the period 1840–1842. There was discovered a desire to join a missing *Other*, which was specified within the boundaries of the individual's strife to reach the revered better component of his/her disjoined self – the Dead Mother, and later, Christ. There was detected a variation of the customary for the Brontë sisters separation of soul from body in a moment, which documents the transition towards idealised heavenly bliss. A specificity emphasized is Anne's amalgamation of the images of the revered Mother with that of Christ.

At a later stage, there is a more quietist contemplation of Life, which, from a formal point of view, is evident in Anne Brontë's preoccupation with the poetic genre of the *prayer*, good examples of which are poems like: *Retirement* (1840), *An Orphan's Lament* (1841), *Despondency* (1841) and *In Memory of a Happy Day in February* (1842). The research also discovered that Anne Brontë took some time before she accepted the idea of Heaven as God's realm of perfection, which could be reached through Death as an instantaneous but conscientiously prepared-for phase of the existence of the Spirit. From around 1843 and as late as 1848 Anne Brontë's poetry could be seen to have maintained doubts as to the Methodist understanding of Death as a temporal component of God's just and wise reign over the Earth and of God's universal altruism. On the other hand, rejected also seems to have been the popular Calvinist concept of selective redemption through Death (i.e. that the access to holiness upon the body's expiration is a quality bestowed upon a chosen few). The earliest examples, which reflect the above controversies, were found to be Anne's hymn *To Cowper* (1842) and *A Word to the Calvinists* (1843). Bakhtin's and Levinas' concepts of *Otherness* were applied to show that Anne Brontë's mature lyrics might be seen as a poetic attempt to overcome the awareness of the corruption and instability that the individual's mind tends to project on reality. The best poems of the year 1845 and after demonstrate coming to terms with the notion of Death as the kernel component of accepting *Being* as *Co-Being* (i.e. amongst, and for the sake of, *Others*). Death no more invokes the fear of „My Own End", which would naturally paralyse the capacities of the Self. The knowledge that there is a *Dead Other* charges the Self with humbleness and empathy, with forgiveness – the core of Anne's system of ethics. The latter she builds on the understanding that Christ's death demonstrated the exemplary devotion to a next *Other*. The poems quoted at this stage of analysing Anne Brontë's works were: „Call me away" (1845), Confidence (1845), Vanitas Vanitatis (1845), Parting Address from Z. Z. to A. E. (1845), and Self-Communion (1847). A thought, which accompanied the investigation of Anne Brontë's perception of Death was that, given her upbringing in an Evangelically minded time and place, she was persistently inclined towards self-analysis to the point of self-chastisement. The latter fact seems to have been enhanced and at the same time aggravated by the immediate availability of Death in her own lifetime experience (through her father's profession and, as with the rest of the Brontë children, in the history of her family).

The analysis of the themes of *Mortality* in **Charlotte Brontë's** poetry was orientated towards, yet not limited within, the imaginary world of Angria. In this regard, the research emphasised the fact of Charlotte's and her brother Branwell's poetic rivalry in creating Angria (which, in one way, manifested itself in the elimination and resuscitation of a lyrical persona), whose main faces were those of Alexander Percy, Duke of Northangerland, his daughter Marian Hume, the Duke of Zamorna and Percy's wife – Mary Henrietta Wharton. Branwell Brontë's works were cited where appropriate. Angria's involvement with Death was somewhat more erratic than Gondal's. The research clarified that the central lyrical persona of Charlotte Brontë's poetic world could be defined as Mourner, who is in contact with the Ghostly nun/the Dead female beloved/the nightly female visitant – a variation of _the Dead Other_. This female informant brings about the Survivor's/Mourner's painful yet inevitable realisation of his inability to exist in an independent and self-sufficient manner. One specific feature of Charlotte's treatment of _Mortality_ was found to be the fact that her poetic zest ceased earlier than her sisters'. Another is that the Nun/Dead Female persona was later transferred to, and modelled further on in her novels (at first in _Jane Eyre_, but mainly in _Villette_) into _the missing Maternal authority syndrome_. Charlotte seems to have commissioned this persona on a quest, in which she had a solid authorial function: to complete the orphaned Survivor/Creator. This persona of Charlotte's was claimed to possess a certain dose of daemonicity. For, whilst enlightening man's Being through a remembrance of his duty to Others (a neglected dead beloved, or a forgotten friend, who might still be alive etc) and thus making it meaningful, it is also capable of terminating the Survivor's time through dragging it to the ultimate lifetime experience – the providential contact with Death.

As might have been expected, the earliest motif to do with Mortality in Charlotte's poetry was found to be that of _mutability_. From 1835 till 1840 Charlotte Brontë's poems demonstrate her concern for the brevity of human life. There is sensed uneasiness towards the fact that consciousness is a component of man's self, which is temporally limited (i.e. dependent upon physical verifiability), and threatens to unravel memory. Memory, in itself, seems to be additionally strengthened by the periodical reappearance of certain natural phenomena, which, ironically, only last a certain while each time. And memory is what maintains continuity for humankind, as it maintains the image of each Other. Alongside, however, Charlotte Brontë grows convinced that the irrevocability of a beloved person's Death (through which the Survivor is given the chance to qualify as non-dead) deepens the orthodox feeling of sensitivity to Life, of compassion and benevolence as dominant attitudes to potential „Survivors" after „You". The poems I chose to illustrate the above were: „_All is change – the night, the day_", _The Violet (1830)_, _Lament (1834)_, „_The moon dawned slow in the dusky gloaming_" (possibly _1834_), _Memory (1835)_, _The Teacher's Monologue (1837)_, _Presentiment (1837)_, and „_Well, the day's toils are over, with success_" _(1837)_. In contrast to Anne's and particularly to Emily's, the individual in Charlotte's poetry is not as keen on abandoning the body in order to reach heavenly perfection in a world untouched by destruction. If anything, the hubris-driven individual could be seen as desirous of a heroic escape from the World in order to conquer it, to master its compulsory temporality and physicality (see for instance the poem *The Wounded Stag, 1836*).

In the years 1836–1837, and then again in 1846, Charlotte Brontë explores the theme of <u>orphanhood.</u> Peculiarly enough, most of the poetic pieces relevant bear no direct link to the context of Angria. *„The silent dead"* (*Lines Written Beside a Fountain, 1833*) from the dreamed-for and anticipated World Beyond appear as an amalgamation of the grief for the missing parental authority and an imagined and cherished God. There is the voiceless confession into a kind of mortal guilt: that the *„fire"* of man's spiritual potential is *„self-kindled, self-consumed"*, i.e. that the individual does not ache enough (does not do enough for an *Other*) in order to feel existence for a fact. The near spontaneity in the willingness to bear the consequences of God's wrath was said to be directly linked to Charlotte's acceptance of the Other's moral superiority: the fact an Other „measures" and finalizes one's Life ought to be seen as a gift, rather than a punishment. Here, I referred to the poems: *The Vision (1830), Reason* (possibly *1836), Stanzas on the Death of a Christian (1837)* and *The Missionary (1846)*. Like Anne, Charlotte admits with regret to the narrowness of a consciousness that mortifies existence, instead of integrating it through the absorption of the possibility of Co-Being. Charlotte's mature poems (like *Frances* – around *1843*, or *Pilate's Wife's Dream* – published *1846*) were found to declare the individual's desire to achieve a relationship of *Otherness* (i.e. care, altruism) towards a human Being, who would appreciate, possibly outlive, one and would thus own the memory of one. It is an unequivocal journey that the individual travels to reach the latter realisation – here man *„weeps for mortal suffering"* and *„mortal guilt"*, as though wishing to stand out against the multitude of common mortals (who yield to fate without resistance), yet there is the awareness that one's own time on Earth is limited.

To sum up, Charlotte Brontë's treatment of *Mortality* in her poetry could be perceived as an amalgam of two evolving images – that of the *Survivor (the Self)* and that of a „mobile" observer, called the *Ghost (or, the Dead Other* – the objectifier of reality). The initial stage of this research also specified that this *ghost persona* inhabits the space of „the third person" – the grave/the tomb/the night/the recesses of the Survivor's memory. This space of the third, it would appear, is as active and feasible as the space of a hypothetically living *Other*. In most of Charlotte's poems relevant *the Other* is indeed the *Dead Other* – capable of both healing the Survivor, of counteracting loss, but also of emphasizing loss through reminding the Survivor of his selfish and inhumane attitude to a former beloved now lost, as in Charlotte's masterpiece *Gilbert* (around 1843). At one point, the ghost's punitive influence over the living individual drives him to self-annihilation. And suicide only displays the ontological mesh in a consciousness that has lived in an often-deliberate oblivion of the existence of an *Other* – the „moral inquisitor", to whom man is subordinate and answerable.

The whole of section III of part II of the present thesis was dedicated to **Emily Brontë,** as she was found to be the one with the deepest, most consistent and most thorough interest in *Mortality*. I argued that Emily's entire literary heritage (her poetry, her novel *Wuthering Heights*, and her *Belgian Devoirs*) shows an obsession with the philosophic discourse of Death – a discourse, against which the critic could indeed trace the evolution of her genius. The research claimed that the Gondal saga, now extant in the form of a poetic cycle (and also functioning as a specific thematic background for Emily's whole poetic heritage), should be treated as the main environment for motifs and sub-motifs of Death to develop. Gondal proves to have been both the poetic, as well as the experiential milieu, where A.G.A. was born. Augusta – Gondal's central lyrical persona – is notoriously known for her murderous instincts and interrupted numerous love liaisons, which obviously account for the fragmentary state of Emily's poetic heritage nowadays (at least for the Gondal portion of it). The research relied on W. D. Paden's, Fannie Ratchford's and C. W. Hatfield's arrangement of the Gondal saga, as well as on Barbara Lloyd-Evans' explanation of the characters and places in Gondal. It also made clear that the structural and contextual role the theme of Death plays in Gondal should not be a hindrance to a certain thematic rearrangement and possible regrouping of Emily's poems on a larger critical scale. A peculiarity of A.G.A.'s persona additionally emphasised was her capacity to usurp the poet's authority. A.G.A. claims to be the author of many poetic pieces and messages (by signing them), which reflect her lonely and desperate attempts to restore the happy moments of her past. On the other hand, the poet's creative tribulations over Augusta's nature show in the technique of alternating elimination/resuscitation of this main persona, who therefore appears under numerous names and titles in the poet's struggle with her as with an ambiguous bearer of the idea of *Otherness*.

Quite predictably, Emily Brontë's early interest in *Mortality* (during the years 1837–1839) was reflected in her concern with the motif of <u>*transitoriness*</u>. Unlike Anne or Charlotte, Emily faces stoically the fact that the presence of Death in Nature – evident in the regenerative appearance/disappearance of various natural phenomena – is superior to man's existence, which is also cyclically predisposed. A number of poems demonstrate certain parallels between changes in Nature and the various stages of A.G.A.'s life. Some of those include: *„Will the day be bright or cloudy"* (1836), *„There shines the moon – at noon of night"* (1837), *„A sudden chasm of ghastly light"* (1837), *„All day I've toiled, but not with pain"*, *„Alone I sat; the summer day"* (1837), *„O evening, why is thy light so sad"*, *„There was a time when my cheek burned"* (1839), *„Shall Earth no more inspire thee"* (1841), and *„The evening passes fast away"* (1842–1843). Yet, Death, as a characteristic of Nature's cyclical essence, is above all seen here in its value as a category of the relations between humans, which could be regulated, particularly when conscience is activated through contemplation of loci and symbols of Time/temporality (such as *the grave*).

Around the same time (1837, and then in the early 1840s) Emily Brontë develops the motif of <u>separation from the body</u>. The abandonment of physicality is motivated mainly by a duty to join a forsaken beloved, to return to the native place, or else to overcome the unbearable doldrums Life imposes on the lyrical Self. Ultimately, this abandonment of the body is expected to lead to a dreamed for reunion with one's true spiritual half in a realm which copies the blissful and protected state of childhood, now counterbalanced by the adult's state of orphanhood. The spirit is free to migrate in a timeless area, which, however, is very much characterised by certain physical criteria of real Life on Earth (the mountains, the wind etc.). Yet even in this private Heaven there lurks the doubt whether the soul could be both penitent and confessor – such a dichotomy, formed by an almost schizophrenic division of the Self is, as man realises, destructive, rather than ameliorative. At this point Death becomes non-optional, non-euthanatic, but unavoidable, because of the denial of a physically external *point of reference through an Other* individual (here Levinas was referred to in particular). I chose to illustrate the above ideas with the poems: *„The night is darkening round me"* *(1837)*, *„O God of Heaven, the dream of horror"* *(1837)*, *A.G.A. to A.S.* *(1838)*, *Castle Wood* *(1844)*, the masterpiece *„I'm happiest when most away"* *(undated)*, *My Comforter* *(1844)*, *To Imagination* *(1844)*, and *„O thy bright eyes must answer now"* *(1844)*.

In comparison to Charlotte, or even Anne, Emily Brontë devotes a massive part of her poetry to the already discussed concept of *„the space of the third person".* As with Charlotte and Anne, this is the mortuary of the now *Dead Other,* which functions as both a shelter from an alienating Present, as well as a source of wisdom in the process of self-analysis. This *chthonian side of Otherness* becomes particularly relevant when man's incapacity/refusal to accept his/her temporal definitions begins to constrict the spirit. In Emily's hermetically sealed environment the grave/the tomb is equalised with the hearth (often „tomb" rhymes with „home"). There the individual is often absorbed, whilst also being in the liminal state of sleep/daydream, in which the Self, almost physically, merges with the Earth (Augusta wishes to *„knit her harassed heart beneath";* or the lyrical Self dreams of twining her *„sunny hair"* with the grass roots). That is the space which carries one back to the familiarity of the Past, which holds one's closest people, but it is also a step one level higher – into futurity, ruled by a Deity not strictly orthodox, yet someone who has the capacity to join the dead and the living in harmony. Some of the poems analysed in detail included: *„Darkness was overtraced on every face"* *(1838)*, *„The night was dark, yet winter breathed"* *(1839)*, *H.A. and A.S.* *(1842)*, poems *H9, 14, 28, 43, 56, 63, 133, 136, 143, and 156* of Hatfield's 1941 edition, *A.G.A.* *(1837)*, *To A.S.* *(1843)*, and the famous elegy *„In the earth, the earth thou shalt be laid"* *(1843)*. An obvious symbol, which Emily uses to illustrate the transition to a superior *Other* is the wind. An element which precedes and exceeds Time, the wind is the nightly visitant that brings inspiration and liberation, the consumer of the notion of Death, the restorer of the lyrical Self's erstwhile bliss with a beloved or of the age of innocence. The reader's attention was drawn in particular to the poems: *„The wind, I hear it sighing"* *(1839)*, *„Aye, there it is! It wakes tonight"* *(1841)*, *I.M. to I.G.* *(1844)*, and the A.G.A. focused poem *Julian M. and A.G. Rochelle (1845)*. Other poems relevant are: *H26, 39, 42, 44, 45, 83, 91, 95, 114, 117, 120, 126, 139, 140, 144, 154, 162,* and *169*.

Two motifs appear to recur and form a dichotomy in Emily Brontë's poetic involvement with *Mortality*. In the years 1837 through to around 1845 one could observe the motif of *infanticide*, developed as a feature of the A.G.A. persona. This is reflected in a series of poems, namely: *„O mother, I am not regretting"* *(1837)*, *A.G.A.* *(1839)*, *„From our evening fireside now"* *(1839)*, *and A Farewell to Alexandria (1839)*. All of those were defined as focused on Augusta's murderous strife to exterminate the infant as, firstly, a replica of the parent (Augusta is aware of the daemonic grain of her own nature), and secondly, because of the child exemplifying the natural rule of substituting old with new (i.e. that a new Life emerges on the basis of destruction). At this point, Emily's Belgian essay *The Butterfly (1842)* was also examined. *A Farewell to Alexandria (1839)* is the poem most indicative of the fact that Gondal suffers from a mesh in its ontological design – the lack of maternal instinct, as the first and foremost form of protective authorship in maintaining Being as Co-Being (Bakhtin was referred to extensively). The second motif that Emily Brontë develops alongside that of infanticide was found to be that of *home*. A part of the *memento mori* theme (suggested earlier by the symbolic presence of the grave/the tomb), home & parenthood is just the reverse of the motif of infanticide. It is to be found in about two dozens of poems of Emily's, the most significant of which I consider to be: *„I am the only being whose doom"* *(1837)*, *Lines by Claudia (1839)*, *„May flowers are opening"* *(1839)*, *„Mild the mist upon the hill"* *(1839)*, *„How long will you remain? The midnight hour"* *(1839)*, *„Come, walk with me"* (probably around *1844*), *„M.A. Written on the Dungeon Wall – N.C."* *(1845)*, and again the poem *Julian M. and A.G. Rochelle (1845)*. The lament for home is the lament for a now lost happy union of friends, of comrades, which may not always be parented by a mother/ father, but which illustrates the principle of *Otherness,* according to which Presence is Co-presence (as in the poem *Julian M. and A.G. Rochelle,* where Julian's magnanimity allots him the role of a surrogate parent to ambiguous Rochelle).

Ultimately, the desire to overcome the state of orphanhood to Emily is equalized with the desire to provide a confessor, a pardoner, an Author to an ostensibly independent individual, whose props of *Being* are about to collapse. The painfully informative ontological experience of the loss of an Author (beloved/friend/parent) is also meant by Emily Brontë as a stimulus for the Survivor to interpret his/her own existence by „measuring" it against the value of the completed *Dead Other's Life* (which the Survivor always owns). The latter was seen to be best summarised in four ballads of Emily's. These are: *I.M. to I.G (1844)*, ***The Death of A.G.A. (1841–1844)*** and ***R. Alcona to J. Brenzaida ("Cold in the earth, and the deep snow piled above thee", 1845)*** and *„Why ask to know the date – the clime"* (1846). Again, the fact is reiterated that the child is a living reminder of a parent's obligation to provide Life with altruism, with spiritual balance. Also, that one is worth nothing in the absence of an outside point of reference (i.e. when there is not found a /preceding/ Other). And finally, that forgiveness – particularly towards a Death sentence ostensibly „deserved" – is a kernel component of a decision to maintain and protect Life (Derrida was quoted here). Forgiveness was summarised to be that attitudinal ingredient of a consciousness whose dialogic vision of the World allows not for a deliberate termination of Life. In a Dostoyevskian manner, Emily declares that a murder in mind equals a murder in truth – it kills mercy and empathy, which are the innermost ingredients of the integrity of the Self. The research also emphasised that, from a formal point of view, Emily's skill in composing ballads is her tribute to the dialogic discourse, because the ballad is that poetic genre, which allows for the greatest degree of *Otherness*. Mostly devoted to the themes of *Mortality*, these are always poems about at least two people and about threatened/lost mutuality at the fact of Death – caused deliberately, or registered as accidental.

The final part of the analysis of *Mortality* in Emily Brontë's works dealt with the poet's struggle with the concept of the Heavenly institute (starting in 1840 and lasting until 1846). The research found out that, firstly, Emily claims that an unequivocal definition of a God as unaffected by Time, i.e. by Mortality, could not be reached. Further on, that Emily deviates from traditional theology in her understanding that Heaven and Hell do not necessarily function as opposites. She rejects Heaven's selectivism, because she argues that Earthly toils are tribulation and penance enough for any soul. The element of purgation in the traditional Christian idea of the after life is hereby counterbalanced by the reverie about a return to the Earth where, at familiar places and in the companionship of the dearest people, true regeneration of Spirit may only be possible. Hence the dream of a Heaven which replicates, rather than refutes, Earthly existence – with its many contraries, but without the constant need for verification of meaning, without a temporally verifiable link of good and evil, but containing a Spiritual outsideness very much physical – the beloved person who would be the only other participant in this private Eden. Poems considered appropriate to defend the above statements are: *F. de Samara to A.G.A. (1838)*, „*Shed no tears o'er that tomb*" *(1839)*, „*At such a time, in such a spot*" *(1840/1843)*, **„*Riches I hold in light esteem*" *(1841)*, „*I see around me tombstones grey*" *(1841)*,** „*How do I love on summer nights*" *(1843)*, „*Enough of thought, philosopher;*" *(1845)*, **„*Death, that struck when I was most confiding*" *(1845)*,** and „*No Coward Soul is Mine*" *(1846)*.

Finally, the juxtaposition of <u>*temporality* and *timelessness*</u> in Emily Brontë's poetic heritage could be categorized as almost obsessive. On a formal level, that is noticeable in the structural specificities and thematic concreteness of the Gondal poetic cycle. On the ideological level, Emily (as is the case with her sisters) realises that Death self-inflicted cannot be fruitful to the development of the Self, because of the lack of the *rescuing authorial surplus of vision through an Other*. The state of orphanhood is detrimental to the spirit, but infanticide (as a planned decision to regulate Nature's progress) is a sure and irreversible annihilation of the Self's potential and future. In Emily's poetry the individual wishes to pass into a state in which the soul would no longer be subject to a Life of contraries. The latter craving is complicated by the fact that there lurks the doubt as to the legitimacy of a traditional Christian vision of Death as the ultimate form of deserved punishment. I believe that, given the philosophic and religious specificities of the time and place in which Emily Brontë's poetic genius was formed, it is rather unique to find a woman, who would argue that no dead man could be seen as having used up his/her potential entirely by the time Death arrives. And that therefore there could not exist a deed such as would undeniably deserve death (see Eagleton). It is in fact quite startling to discern such level of ontological maturity in fostering the notion of forgiveness.

* * *

During the course of the investigation of the themes of *Mortality* in the Brontë sisters' poetry, certain ideas emerged for possible further research, within the same critical context, but in directions, which, it seems to me, have not yet been explored. These ideas could be summarised as follows:

• It is possible to search for remnants and reverberations of the Romantic poets' amalgamation of the images of Death and of the female beloved in later Romantic and Victorian poetry. The intricate link between such qualities of the female beloved as the source of poetic inspiration, on the one hand, and daemonic consumer of the guilty lyrical Self's soul, on the other, give enough substance for the latter. Charlotte Brontë's Nun/ghost persona and Emily's A.G.A. could be positioned within a Pre-Raphaelite context of perceiving the closeness between the themes of *marriage* and *death* (the *matrimonial* element of dying), evident in the Pre-Raphaelite poets' sensuousness in depicting Heaven, or life beyond. It seems logical to suggest that such research could be extended into a comparative study of representations of the above ideas both in poetry and in the fine arts too. Some obviously relevant poetic examples may include: some of D. G. Rossetti's poetic works (e.g. *The Blessed Damozel – 1847*, or the poem *Nuptial Sleep* etc.). Some relevant paintings may be: D. G. Rossetti's *Beata Beatrix Envisioning Her Own Death*, Edward Burne-Jones' *The Depths of the Sea* and John Everett Millais' *Ophelia*. Also, some of Algernon Charles Swinburne's works could be cited, such as: *The Garden of Proserpine (1866)*, *Itylus (1866)*, and, possibly, *Laus Veneris (1866)*, in which *the female* ingredient (the daemonic side of it) in the idea of the End is noticeable. Earlier variations on the theme of marriage & death could be discerned in works like: Byron's *Oriental Tales (e.g. The Giaour, The Bride of Abydos – both 1813)*, or *Corsair* – published *1814)*, Shelley's *Epipsychidion (1821)*, Keats' *Endymion* (published *1818)*, *Lamia (1819)*, or *Isabella (1819)*. At that, the role of sleep, as a providential liminal state-transition from one modus vivendi into another, may be considered.

- The theme of <u>orphanhood</u> (discussed in detail in relation to the persistence of *the missing-authority syndrome* – both on the level of form and contents) in the Brontë sisters' poetic works could become the subject field of a larger comparative study of the poetry of some major Romantic poets. One obvious example would be some major works of Byron's, but the references could be extended to Wordsworth, Coleridge (*Christabel – 1816*) and further, to certain works of Alfred Tennyson's (e.g. *In Memoriam*). Orphanhood is detected in the feelings of loss and disorientation, which the poet Matthew Arnold conveys in a work like **Dover Beach (1867).** In it there is a description of a land void of spiritual values and of a remedy for pain, a land full of images of death, and a land, in which Nature seems hostile and finite, because „*incognizable*". Other works of Arnold's worth mentioning may include: the poem *Human Life (1852)*, and *Tristram and Iseult (1852)*. The broader understanding of orphanhood as the lack of a „spiritual precursor", which seems to have been a particular malady of the 19th-century poetic genius, would inevitably lead to a study of this motif in the prose fiction heritage of the Brontës. That is, in their novels: Emily's *Wuthering Heights*, Charlotte's *The Professor, Jane Eyre, Shirley* and *Villette*, and Anne's *Agnes Grey*, and *The Tenant of Wildfell Hall.* Other prose fiction masterpieces of the 19th-century worth looking into may include some of Charles Dickens' novels (e.g. *Oliver Twist – 1837, The Old Curiosity Shop – 1841, Dombey and Son – 1848* and *David Copperfield – 1850*) and, for instance, George Eliot's (*Adam Bede – 1859 –* the motif of infanticide, *The Mill on the Floss – 1860,* and *Silas Marner – 1861*). It might also be rather challenging to trace certain earlier writers' interest in *orphanhood* (latent, say, in some works of the Gothic trend of English fiction – e.g. Ann Radcliffe's *The Mysteries of Udolpho –* 1794, Horace Walpole's *The Castle of Otranto –* 1765, Charles Robert Maturin's *Melmoth the Wanderer –* 1820). A late decadent example could be Oscar Wilde's *The Picture of Dorian Grey (1890).* For the reasons explained earlier, the investigation of *orphanhood* leads to an analysis of the theme of fratricide/infanticide, a concern with which most of the above – both prose and poetic works – show.

- Without limiting oneself by feminising the theme of Death (by looking exclusively into the Gothic texture of dying, or by looking into Death as a thematic expression of the extreme desire for liberation, which female poets may be perceived to foster in a male-dominated poetic world), it would be particularly valuable to position the Brontë sisters within the broader context of 18th- and 19th-century British women poets, who developed the theme in hand. Of those, the ones who definitely show consideration for themes of *Mortality* include: A. L. Barbauld (1743–1825), Charlotte Smith (1749–1806), Felicia Hemans (1793–1835), L. E. L. (1802–1838), Elizabeth Barret Browning (1806–1861), Christina Rossetti (1830–1894), Mary Coleridge (1861–1907) and Charlotte Mew (1869–1928). It would be certainly worth bridging the gap between those and the American poet Emily Dickinson, whose poetic heritage certainly makes an important contribution to developing the subject area of *Mortality*.

• It is certainly worth extending the research of the evolution of the themes of *Mortality* into a broader general overview on later Victorian and early 20th-century poetry. It would be particularly useful to investigate in detail how, for instance, later Victorian poetry becomes oblivious of the authorial status of Nature (both „*destroyer and preserver*“) and begins to show deeper sympathy for the purely human dimensions of the ontological problem of the *Dead/Missing-Other*. One ramification of this thematic focus would be the examination of the re-actualized motif of *murder* as linked to physical malady and social ills in the poetic works of Robert Browning. Possible examples may include: „*Childe Roland to the Dark Tower Came*“ (published *1855*) – in which the ontological quest to the Dark Tower symbolises the individual's striving to achieve self-completion and to cure his failed integrity of *Being*. Or, *The Pied Piper of Hamelin (1842)*, which may be seen as a critique on a world where the child is left to perish unprotected. Additionally, *My Last Duchess (1842)* and *Porphyria's Lover* (1842) demonstrate a typical for 19th-century literature inclination to capture beauty through seizing it in images of still life (following the individual's attempted homicidal ownership of Life, here the life of the beloved as the bearer of beauty). One more feature of Browning' works is, as Michael Wheeler notices, his typically Victorian hesitation over diagnosing Death. That is, whether what appears „dead“ is really dead, or it is something, which may be reformatted and reconsidered by human consciousness (e.g. *The Bishop Orders His Tomb at Saint Praxed's Church* – Cf Wheeler, 1990, p. 34). Another phenomenon worth noticing is the growing urban and matter-of-fact concreteness in the representations of the theme of Death in the works of poets like: James Thomson (the motifs of urbanized imbecility, eternal moral corruption and faithlessness – in *The City of Dreadful Night, 1870–1873*) and W. E. Henley (the clinical dimensions of Death – in his poetic cycle *In Hospital, 1873–1875*). It would also be interesting to see how far such analysis would reach if some works of Thomas Hardy's were considered. The feeling of redundancy; the painful search for the protective and authoritative influence of a Prime Supreme Other; the fear of finality and limitedness in the coming/happening of Death, which may engender a pitiful and ironic attitude toward a person's desire to mourn; the naturalism in describing man's cynical attitude to the grave as to a *„jumbled patch/Of wrenched memorial stones"*, in which a dog may bury a bone – here are some major aspects of Thomas Hardy's vision of the place of Death in man's Life, which may be observed in works, such as: *De Profundis (1901), In Tenebris I, The Levelled Churchyard (1882), In Death Divided, In the Cemetery ("Satires of Circumstance In Fifteen Glimpses" – V, 1919), „Ah, Are You Digging On My Grave", The Sunshade,* (Cf Wheeler, M., 1990, pp. 28–29, p. 65, p. 67). I believe that there will have to be made certain references to Hardy's prose fiction as well. Further on, it would be curious to note how the problem of faithlessness and of the lost Past unfolds in T. S. Eliot's poetry (especially in *The Waste Land, 1922*). Such a major critical venture might finish with a brief overview of how in the works of the English poets of World War I (Wilfred Owen, Siegfried Sassoon and Rupert Brooke) the attention of modern man's interest in Death was re-orientated towards the military dimensions of the notion of the End (the traditionally revered peaceful green churchyard was substituted with the impersonality and terror of the trenches – Cf Wheeler, 1990, p. 68). They developed the theme of the meaninglessness of Death in a time of War (one new variation of the idea of the inhumane in the act of limiting/owning an Other human being's life). On the ontological level, one human being's life cannot, and ought not to, be juxtaposed to another human being's life[2].

---

[2] Worth considering are Wilfred Owen's: *Nocturne, A New Heaven, Inspection, Anthem For Doomed Youth, 1914, The Letter, Conscious, Dulce Et Decorum Est, Insensibility, Strange Meeting, The End, The Chances, Disabled, Soldier's Dream, Elegy in April and September,*

It is beyond doubt that, on the level of poetry, the roots of later and late Victorian engagement with *Mortality* could be sought in the heritage of the Romantics. In future studies of the given problem the Brontë sisters' input would stand out as obvious and captivating in its originality, exactly because *Mortality and Death* are the kernel constituents of their philosophy, which was formed in their poetic works, and was later developed in their novels. The philosophic discourse of *Death*, vastly and most uniquely explored in England by most poets of the later 18th–19th centuries, has not yet been made justice to by the critical guild: it is certainly worth examining in a large monographic study and, I think, the heuristic perspectives, which open up in this case, are sure and numerous.

Exposure. The specificities of Rupert Brook's treatment of *Mortality* could be observed in, for instance: *Sonnet (1909), Dust, The Life Beyond, Paralysis, The Funeral of Youth, II. Safety, IV, The Dead, V. The Soldier* (the last three from the *1914 sequence*).

Bibliography

Primary Sources

Text Editions in the English Language

- Abrams, M., (ed.), *The Norton Anthology of English Literature*, vol. 2 (W. W. Norton & Company: New York & London, 1986).
- Alexander, Christine, (ed.) *Branwell's Blackwood's Magazine: The Glasstown Magazine Written by Branwell Brontë With Contributions from His Sister Charlate Brontë* (Edmonton: Juvenilia Press, 1995).
- Alexander, *Christine*, (ed.) *Charlotte Brontë's High life in Verdopolis: A Story from the Glass Town Saga* (The British Library, 1995).
- Aldington, R., (ed.) *The Viking Book of Poetry of the English-Speaking World*, Vol. I (The Viking Press, New York, 1958).
- Armstrong, Isobel, (ed.) *Nineteenth Century Women Poets. Anthology* (Oxford, 1996).
- Arnold, Matthew, The Works of ~ (Wordsworth Poetry Library, 1995).
- Austen, Jane, *Sense and Sensibility* (London: Chatto & Windus, 1984).
- *The Complete Novels* (Penguin Books, 1996).
- Barker, Juliet, (ed.) *Charlotte Brontë: Juvenilia 1829–1835* (Penguin, 1996).
- *The Brontës. A Life in Letters*, (Viking at Penguin Books Ltd, 1997).
- Blake, William, *Poems and Prophecies* (London: J. M. dent & Sons Ltd; New York: E. P. Dutton & Co. Inc., 1945).
- *Selected Poems* (Penguin Books, 1996).
- Beer, John, (ed.) *The Poems of Samuel Taylor Coleridge* (J. M. Dent & Sons LTD: London and Melbourne, 1986).
- Brett, R. L., Jones, A. R., *William Wordsworth & Samuel Taylor Coleridge, Lyrical Ballads: The text of the 1798 edition with the*

additional 1800 edition poems and the Preface (Methuen: London & New York, 1984).

- Brooke, Rupert, *The Complete Poems* (London: Sidgwick & Jackson Limited, 1942).

- Brontë, Anne, *Agnes Grey*, in Four Novels of the Brontë Sisters (Swing Books: Butter & Tanner Ltd, 1976).

- Brontë, Charlotte, Emily and Anne, *Poems*, Printed for Private Circulation Only, (London: Thomas J. Wise, Hampstead, 1917).

- Brontë, Charlotte, *Shirley* (Wordsworth Classics, 1995).

- Brontë, Charlotte, *The Twelve Adventurers: A Romantic Tale*, ed. by members of English 455 at the University of Alberta under the general editorship of Juliet McMaster (University of Alberta, 1994).

- Brontë, Charlotte, *Unfinished Novels* (Pocket Classics, Alan Sutton Publishing LTD 1995).

- Brontë, Charlotte, *Villette,* with an introduction and notes by Dr Sally Minogue (Wordsworth Classics, 1999).

- Brontë, Emily, *Wuthering Heights* (Hertfordshire: Wordsworth Classics, 1992).

- Browne, Sir Thomas, *The Religio Medici and Other Writings*, (London: J. M. Dent & Sons LTD, 1956).

- Browning, Robert, *The Works of ~* (Wordsworth Poetry Library, 1994).

- Burns, Robert, *Selected Poems* (Penguin Books, 1996).

- ed. Chitham, Edward, *The Poems of Anne Brontë, with A New Text and Commentary* (Macmillan, 1979).

- Clare, John, *The Works of ~* (Wordsworth Poetry Library, 1995).

- Cowley, Bill & Wade, Gwen, Waddington-Feather, John, (eds.) *Dialect Verse from the Ridings* (The Yorkshire Dialect Society, Yorkshire, Ilkley: The Scholar Press LTD, 1970.

- Cunningham, Valentine, (ed.) *The Victorians: An Anthology of Poetry and Poetics* (Blackwell Publishers, 2000).

- Dickinson, Emily, *The Works of ~* (Wordsworth Poetry Library, 1995).

• Dobreé, Bonamy, (ed.) *Ann Radcliffe, The Mysteries of Udolpho* (Oxford University Press, 1980).

• Donne, John, *A Critical Edition of the Major Works*, edited by John Carey (Oxford & New York: Oxford University Press, 1990).

• Edgeworth, Maria, *Castle Rackrent, The Absentee* (Wordsworth's Classics, 1994).

• Feldman, Barbara, (ed.) *British Women Poets of the Romantic Era: An Anthology* (The Johns Hopkins University Press, Baltimore & London, 2000).

• Gates, Barbara, (ed.) *In Nature's Name: An Anthology of Women's Writing and Illustration – 1780–1930* (Chicago and London: The University of Chicago Press, 2002).

• Glen, Heather, (ed.) *The Professor, A Novel by Charlotte Brontë* (Penguin Books, 1989).

• Glover, A. S. B., (ed.) *Byron, George Gordon: Poems* (Penguin Books, first published in 1954).

• Hatfield, C. W., (ed.) *The Complete Poems of Emily Jane Brontë* (New York: Columbia University Press, 1941).

• Holmes, Richard, (ed.) *Shelley On Love. Selected Writings* (Flamingo: Harper Collins Publishers, 1996).

• *The Holy Bible, The New King's James Version* (New York: American Bible Society, 1990).

• Jain, Nalini & Richardson, John, (eds.) *Eighteenth-century English Poetry: The Annotated Anthology* (Harvester Wheatsheaf, 1994).

• Keats, John, *The Works of ~* (Wordsworth Poetry Library, 1994).

• Larkin, Philip, (ed.) *The Oxford Book of Twentieth-Century English Verse* (Oxford: Clarendon Press, 1974).

• Leigh, Vincent, (ed.) *The Norton Anthology of Theory and Criticism* (W. W. Norton & Company, New York & London, 2001).

• Leighton, Angela & Reynolds, Margaret, (eds.) *Victorian Women Poets: An Anthology* (Basil Blackwell, Oxford University Press & Cambridge USA, 1995).

- Lloyd-Evans, Barbara, (ed.) *The Poems of Emily Jane Brontë* (London: B.T. Batsford, LTD, 1992).
- Lodge, David, (ed.) *XXth-Century Literary Criticism: A Reader* (Longman, 1972).
- Lonoff, Sue, (ed.) *Charlotte Brontë, Emily Brontë. Devoirs – The Belgian Essays*, translated from French by Sue Lonoff (Yale University Press, 1996).
- Marsden, Hilda & Jack, Ian, (eds.) *Wuthering Heights, A Novel by Emily Jane Brontë* (Oxford: Clarendon Press, 1976).
- Mason, Michael, (ed.) *Jane Eyre, A Novel by Charlotte Brontë* (Penguin Books, 1996).
- *The Metaphysical Poets* (Wordsworth Poetry Library, 1995).
- Minogue, Sally, (ed.) *Villette, A Novel by Charlotte Brontë* (Wordsworth Classics, 1999).
- Newfeldt, Victor, (ed.) *The Works of Patrick Branwell Brontë*, 2 volumes (New York and London: Garland Publishing Inc., 1999).
- Owen, Wilfred, *The Poems of ~*, edited by Jon Stallworthy (London: Chatto & Windus, 1990).
- Peterson, Linda, (ed.) *Wuthering Heights, A Novel by Emily Jane Brontë*, with biographical and historical contexts, critical history and essays from five contemporary critical perspectives (Boston New York: Bedford Books of St. Martin's Press, 1992).
- Plowman, Max, (ed.) *Blake's Poems and Prophecies* (London & New York: Dent, 1970).
- Price, Martin, (ed.) *The Oxford Anthology of English Literature: The Restoration and the 18th Century* (Oxford University Press, 1973).
- Ratchford, Fannie, (ed.) *Gondal's Queen. A Novel in Verse by Emily Jane Brontë* (University of Texas Press, 1955).
- Shelley, P. B., *The Works of ~* (Wordsworth Poetry Library, 1994).
- Shorter, Clement, (ed.) *The Complete Poems of Emily Jane Brontë*, with bibliography and notes by C. W. Hatfield (London: Stoughton LTD, 1923).

- Stojceva, Tatjana, (ed.) *Readings in English Intellectual History and Civilization* (Sofia: The University Press of Sv. Kliment Ohridski, 1988).
- Swinburne, Algernon Charles, *Miscellanies* (London: Chatto & Windus, 1886).
- Tennyson, Alfred Lord, *The Works of* ~ (Wordsworth Poetry Library, 1994).
- Wain, John, (ed.) *The Oxford Library of English Poetry*, in 2 volumes (Oxford University Press, 1988).
- White, Kathryn, (ed.), *The Tenant of Wildfell Hal, A Novel by Anne Brontë* (Wordsworth Classics, 1996).
- Winnifrith, Tom (ed.) *The Poems of Patrick Branwell* Brontë (Basil Blackwell for the Shakespeare Head Brontë, 1983).
- Winnifrith, Tom, (ed.) *The Poems of Charlotte Brontë: A New Annotated and Enlarged Edition of the Shakespeare Head Brontë* (Basil Blackwell, 1984).
- Wordsworth, William, *The Works of* ~ (Wordsworth Poetry Library, 1994).
- *The Works of the Brontë Sisters,* with an introduction by Kathryn White (Wordsworth Poetry Library, 1995).

Text Editions in Bulgarian and in Russian

- Бронте, Эмили. *Грозовой Перевал. Стихотворения.* Москва. „Художественная литература". 1990
- Бронте, Энн. *Агнес Грей, Незнакомка из Уайлдфел-Холла,* Стихотворения. Харьков. „Фолио" и Москва. АСТ. 1998
- *Готически романи.* София. „Народна култура". 1986
  - Мери Шели, *Франкенщайн*
  - Хорас Уолпоул, *Замъкът „Отранто"*
  - Уилям Бекфорд, *Ватек*

- Дикенс, Чарлз. *Коледна песен*. София. „Отечество“. 1983

- Диккенс, Чарлз. *Оливер Твист*. Москва. „Икона“. 1993

- Дмитриев, А. С., *Литературные манифесты западноевропейских романтиков*. Москва. Издательство Московского государственного университета. 1980

- Рассказов, Ю. С. *Западная поэзия конца XVIII–начала XIX веков*. Москва. „Лабиринт“. 1999

- Сариева, Любка. *Въображение и свобода: Английски романтици за литературата и изкуството*. София. „Наука и изкуство“. 1982

- Стърн, Лорънс. *Сантиментално пътешествие*. София. „Народна култура“. 1981

- Улф, Вирджиния. *Своя собствена стая*. София. „Хемус“. 1999

Secondary Sources

General Reference

In the English Language

- Abel, Elisabeth & Hirsch, Marianne & Langland, Elisabeth, (eds.) *The Voyage In: Fictions of Female Development* (Hanover& London: University Press of New England, 1983).
- Abrams, Meyer, *Natural Supernaturalism: Tradition and Revolution in Romantic Literature* (New York & London: W. W. Norton & Company, 1973).
- – *The Mirror and the Lamp: Romantic Theory and the Critical Tradition* (Oxford University Press, 1971).

- Alexander, Meena, *Women In Romanticism: Mary Wollstonecraft, Dorothy Wordsworth and Merry Shelley* (Women Writers series, Macmillan, 1989).

- Allen, Walter, *The English Novel: A short Critical History* (Penguin Books, 1991).

- Auerbach, Nina, *The Woman and the Demon. The Life of a Victorian Myth* (Harvard University Press, 1982).

- Bachelard, Gaston, *The Poetics of Space, translated from French by Maria Jolas* (Boston: Beacon Press, 1969).

- Barreca, Regina, *Sex and Death in Victorian Literature* (Macmillan, 1990).

- Barnard, Robert, *A Short History of English Literature* (Oxford, UK & Cambridge USA: Basil Blackwell, 1994).

- Bate, Jonathan, *Shakespeare and the English Romantic Imagination* (Oxford: Clarendon Press, 1986).

- Batten, Guinn, *The Orphaned Imagination: Melancholy and Commodity Culture in English Romanticism* (Durham & London: The Duke University press, 1998).

- Beach, Joseph Warren, *The Concept of Nature in Nineteenth-Century English Poetry* (New York: The Macmillan Company, 1936).

- Beatty, Bernard: *'Reviewing Romanticism: The Sea and the Book'*, in Philip W. Martin & Robin Jarvis, (eds.) *Reviewing Romanticism* (Macmillan 1992).

- Bennett, Andrew, *Romantic Poets and the Culture of Posterity* (Cambridge University Press, 1999).

- Berry, Philippa, *Authorship Overshadowed: Death, Darkness and the Feminisation of Authority in Late Renaissance Writing*, in Biriotti, Maurice & Nancy Miller, (eds.) *What is an Author* (Manchester University Press, 1993).

- Blamires, Harry, *A Short History of English Literature* (London and New York: Routledge, 1994).

- Bloom, Harold, *The Anxiety of Influence: A Theory of Poetry* (New York, Oxford University Press, 1975).

– *The Ringers in the Tower: Studies in Romantic Tradition* (Chicago & London: The University of Chicago Press, 1971).

– *The Visionary Company: A Reading of English Romantic Poetry,* (Ithaca & London: Cornell University Press, 1971).

• Bohls, A., *Women Travel Writers and the Language of Aesthetics 1716–1818 (the introduction & chapter 3: Landscape Aesthetics and the Paradox of the Female Picturesque),* Cambridge University Press, 1995

• Botting, Fred, *Gothic* (The New Critical Idiom Series, London & New York: Routledge, 2001).

• Brewer, John, *The Pleasures of the Imagination: English Culture in the Eighteenth-Century* (Harper Collins Publishers, 1997).

• Bronfen, Elisabeth & Goodwin, Sarah Webster, (eds.) *Death & Representation* (The Johns Hopkins University Press, Baltimore & London, 1993).

• Bronfen, Elisabeth, *Dialogues With the Dead: The Deceased Beloved as Muse,* in Regina Barreca, *Sex and Death in Victorian Literature* (Macmillan, 1990).

• Bronfen, Elisabeth, *Over Her Dead Body: Death, Femininity and the Aesthetic* (Manchester University Press, 1992).

• Brooke, Stopford, A., *The Development of Theology as Illustrated in English Poetry from 1780 to 1830* (London: Philip Green, 1893).

• Burgess, Anthony, *English Literature* (Longman, 1985).

• Burke, Sean, *The Death and Return of the Author. Criticism and Subjectivity in Barthes, Foucault and Derrida* (Edinburgh University Press, 1998).

• Buxton J. & Davis, N., *The Oxford History of English Literature* (Oxford: Clarendon Press, 1990).

• Calder, Angus, Byron. *Open Guides to Literature Series* (Milton Keynes: Open University Press, 1987).

• Camm, Anthony, *Biographical Dictionary of English Literature* (Cornwall: Harper Collins Publishers, 1993).

- Caruth, Cathy, *Empirical Truths and Critical Fictions: Locke, Wordsworth, Kant, Freud* (Baltimore and London: The Johns Hopkins University Press, 1991).
- Cavaliero, Glen, *The Supernatural and English Fiction* (Oxford University Press, 1995).
- Cecil, David, *Early Victorian Novelists. Essays in Revaluation* (London: Constable & Co. LTD, 1948).
- Chadwick, Owen, *The Victorian Church: An Ecclesiastical History of England, Part I* (London: Adam & Charles Black, 1966).
- Clark, Colette, *Home At Grassmere: Extracts from the Journal of Dorothy Wordsworth Written Between 1800 and 1803, and The Poems of William Wordsworth* (Penguin, 1980).
- Clery, E. J., *The Rise of Supernatural Fiction: 1762–1800* (Cambridge University Press, 1999).
- Colville, Derek, *Victorian Poetry and the Romantic Religion* (Albany: State University of New York Press, 1970).
- Conrad, Peter, *Shandyism, The Character of Romantic Irony* (Oxford: Basil Blackwell, 1978).
- Cooper, Andrew M., *Doubt and Identity in Romantic Poetry* (Yale University press, New Haven & London, 1988).
- Cotsell, Michael, (ed.) *Creditable Warriors: 1830–1876* (London: The Ashfield Press, Atlantic Highlands, New Jersey, 2000).
- Clayton, Jay, *Romantic Vision and the Novel* (Cambridge University Press, 1987).
- Cuddon, J. I., *Dictionary of Literary Terms and Literary Theory* (London: Penguin Books, 1993).
- Curran, Stuart, *Poetic Form and British Romanticism* (Oxford University Press, New York – Oxford, 1986).
- Daleski, H. M., *The Divided Heroine: A Recurrent Pattern in Six English Novels* (New York London: Holmes & Meier Publishers, 1984).
- Davis, Philip, *The Victorians – volume 8 of the Oxford English Literary History* (Oxford University Press, 2004).
- Day, Aidan, *Romanticism* (London: Routledge, 1996).

- Dekker, George, *Coleridge and the Literature of Sensibility* (Vision, Clarke, Doble & Brendon Ltd, Plymouth, 1978).
- Derry, T.K. & Blakeway, M.G., (eds.) *The Making of Pre-Industrial Britain* (London: John Murray, 1973).
- Eagleton, Terry, *Sweet Violence: The Idea of the Tragic* (Blackwell Publishing, 2003).
- Easthope, Anthony, *Wordsworth Now and Then: Romanticism and Contemporary Culture* (Buckingham Philadelphia, Open University Press, 1993).
- Ellis, Kate Ferguson, *The Contested Castle: Gothic Novels and Subversion of Domestic Ideology* (Urbana Chicago: University of Illinois Press, 1989).
- Emerson, Caryl, *The First Hundred Years of Mikhail Bakhtin* (Princeton & New Jersey: Princeton University Press, 1997).
- Ermarth, Elizabeth Deeds, *The English Novel in History: 1840-1895* (London New York: Routledge, 1997).
- Evans, Ivor H., *Dictionary of Phrase and Fable* (Wordswoth Reference, 1993).
- – English Poetry in the Later Neineteenth century (London: Methuen & Co. LTD, 1966).
- Fields, Beverly, *Reality's Dark Drea:. Dejection in Coleridge* (The Kent State University Press, University of Illinois at Chicago Circle, 1967).
- Ford, Boris, *The Cambridge Cultural History, volume 6 – The Romantic Age in Britain, volume 7 – Victorian Britain* (Cambridge University Press, 1992).
- Ford, Boris, (ed.) *The New Pelican Guide to English Literature, vol. 5 – From Blake to Byron* (Penguin, 1990).
- Forster, E. M., *Aspects of the Novel* (Penguin Books, 1976).
- Fowler, Alastair, *A History of English Literature* (Basil Blackwell, 1989).
- Frye, Northrop, *A Study Of English Romanticism* (The Harvester Press, 1968).

- Frye, Northrop, *The Great Code: The Bible and Literature* (London Melbourne Henley: Routledge & Kegan Paul, 1982).
- Furst, Lilian R., *Romanticism in Perspective: A Comparative Study of Aspects of the Romantic Movements in England, France and Germany* (Macmillan, St. Martin's Press, 1969).
- Gamer, Michael, *Romanticism and the Gothic: Genre, Reception and Canon Formation* (Cambridge University Press, 2000).
- Garber, F. *Self, Text and Romantic Irony: The Example of Byron* (Princeton New Jersey: Princeton University Press, 1988).
- Gilbert, Sandra M. & Gubar, Susan, *The Madwoman in the Atti:. The Woman Writer and the Nineteenth-Century Literary Imagination* (New Haven & London: Yale University Press, 1984).
- Gibson, Andrew, *Reading Narrative Discourse: Studies in the Novel from Cervantes to Beckett* (Macmillan, 1990).
- Gilmour, Robin, *The Novel in the Victorian Age: A Modern Introduction* (London: Edward Arnold Publishers, 1986).
- Gilmour, Robin, *The Victorian Period: The Intellectual and Cultural Context of English Literature 1830–1890* (London and New York: Longman, 1993).
- Goodwin, Sarah Webster & Bronfen, Elisabeth, (eds.) *Death and Representation* (Baltimore & London: The Johns Hopkins University Press, 1993).
- Gravil, Richard, *Romantic Dialogues. Anglo-American Continuities: 1776–1862* (Macmillan, 2000).
- Gregor, Ian, *Reading the Victorian Novel: Detail into Form* (Vision, 1980).
- Gregor, Jan B., (ed.) *Gossip and Subversion in Nineteenth-Century British Fiction: Echo's Economies* (New York: St. Martin's Press, 1996).
- Haggerty, George E., *Gothic Fiction/Gothic Form* (The Pennsylvania State University Press, University Park and London, 1989).
- Hardy, Barbara, *Forms of Feeling in Victorian Fiction* (London: Peter Owen, 1985).

- Hewitt, Regina, *The Possibilities of Society: Wordsworth, Coleridge, and the Sociological Viewpoint of English Romanticism* (State University of New York Press, Albany, 1997).

- Hillis Miller, J., *The Disappearance of God: Five Nineteenth-Century Writers* (Cambridge Massachusetts: The Belknap Press of Harvard University Press & London: Oxford University Press, 1963).

- Holquist, Michael, *Bakhtin and His World. Dialogism* (London & New York: Routledge, 1991).

- Hull, Anthony, *English Romanticism* (Minerva Press, London, Miami, Rio De Janeiro, Delhi, 2000).

- Hunter, J. Paul, *Before Novels: The Cultural Contexts of Eighteenth-Century Englsih Fiction* (New York: W. W. Norton & Company, 1990).

- Jack, Ian, *English Literature 1815–1832* (Oxford: Clarendon Press, 1990).

- James, W. G. G., *„The Portrayal of Death and „Substance of Life": Aspects of the Modern Reader's Response to „Victorianism"*, in Ian Gregor (ed.) *Reading the Victorian Novel: Detail into Form* (Vision, 1980).

- Kearns, Katherine, *Nineteenth-Century Literary Realism: Through the Looking-Glass* (Cambridge University Press, 1996).

- Kenyon, J. P., *The Wordsworth Dictionary of British History* (Wordsworth Reference 1994).

- Kermode, Frank, *The Sense of an Ending: Studies in the Theory of Fiction* (Oxford University Press, 1968).

- Kettle, Arnold, *An Introduction to the English Novel* (Hutchinson University Library, Volume 1, 1957).

- Kiely, Robert, *The Romantic Novel in England* (Cambridge Massachusetts: Harvard University Press, 1972).

- Kostova, Liudmila, *Tales of The Periphery: The Balkans in the 19th Century British Writing* (Veliko Tarnovo: The University Press of Sv. Sv. Kiril I Metodij, 1997).

- Kroeber, Karl, *Styles in Fictional Structure: The Art of Jane Austen, Charlotte Brontë, George Eliot* (Princeton NJ: Princeton University press, 1971).
- Labbe, Jacqueline M., *The Romantic Paradox: Violence and the Uses of Romance 1760–1830* (Macmillan, 2000).
- Lane, Maggie, *Literary Daughters* (London: Robert Hale, 1989).
- Langan, Celeste, *Romantic Vagrancy: Wordsworth and the Simulation of Freedom* (Cambridge University Press, 1995).
- Laplanche, Jean, *Life and Death in Psychoanalysis*, transl. by Jeffrey Mehlman, (Baltimore and London: The Johns Hopkins University Press, 1976).
- *The Longman Dictionary of English Language and Culture* (Longman, 1992).
- Lynn, Bette, *Writing Double. Women's Literary Partnerships* (Ithaca and London: Cornell University Press, 1999).
- Man, Paul de, *The Rhetoric of Romanticism* (New York: Columbia University Press, 1984).
- Marwick, Arthur, (ed.) *The Arts, Literature and Society* (London & New York: Routledge, 1990).
- McCalman, Iain, (ed.) *An Oxford Companion to the Romantic Age. British Culture: 1776–1832* (Oxford University Press, 2001).
- McFarland, Thomas, *Romanticism and the Forms of Ruin: Wordsworth, Coleridge and Modalities of Fragmentation* (Princeton NJ: Princeton University Press, 1981).
- McGann, Jerome, *The Romantic Ideology. A Critical Investigation* (Chicago and London: The university of Chicago Press, 1983).
- – *The Poetics of Sensibility: A Revolution in Literary Style* (Clarendon Press, Oxford, 1999)
- Mellor, Anne, *Romanticism and Gender* (Routledge 1993).
- Merchant, Carolyn, *The Death of Nature: Women, Ecology and the Scientific Revolution* (San Francisco: Harper and Row, 1980).

- Mews, Hazel, *Frail Vessels: Women's Role in Women's Novels from Fanny Burney to George Eliot* (University of London, The Athlone Pres, 1969).

- Mincoff, Marco, *A History of English Literature*, part II (Sofia: Naouka I Izkoustvo, 1970).

- *The New Encyclopaedia Britannica*, Volume 11 (Chicago, 1994).

- *The New Pelican Guide to English Literature*, Volume 5 & 6 (London, 1990).

- Newlyn Lucy, *Paradise Lost and the Romantic Reader* (Oxford University Press, 2001).

- O'Neill, Michael, *Romanticism and the Self-Conscious Poem* (Clarendon Press, Oxford, 1997).

- Ousby, Ian, *Companion to Literature in English* (Wordsworth Reference, 1994).

- Paglia, Camille, *Sexual Personae: Art and Decadence from Nefertiti to Emily Dickinson* (Yale University Press, London and New Haven, 2001).

- Paley, Morton D., *Apocalypse and Millennium in English Romantic Poetry* (Oxford: Clarendon Press, 2003).

- Patterson, Charles (Jr.), *Empathy and the Daemonic in Withering Heights*, in George Goodin, (ed.) *The English Novel in the 19ᵗʰ Century. Essays on Literary Mediation of Human Values* (University of Illinois Press, 1974).

- Pite, Ralph, *The Circle of Our Vision: Dante's Presence in English Romantic Poetry* (Oxford: Clarendon Press, 1994).

- Pollard, Arthur, (ed.) *The Penguin History of English Literature, Volume 6: The Victorians* (Clays LTD, 1993).

- Poovey, Mary, *Making A Social Body: British Cultural Formation 1830–1864* (Chicago & London: The University of Chicago Press, 1995).

- Priestman, Martin, *Romantic Atheism: Poetry and Freethought – 1780–1830* (Cambridge University Press, 1999).

- Raimond, Jean & Watson, J. R., *A Handbook to English Romanticism* (St. Martin's Press, 1992).
- Roe, Nicholas, *Romanticism: An Oxford Guide* (Oxford University Press, 2005).
- Rorty, Richard, *Philosophy and the Mirror of Nature* (Oxford: Basil Blackwell, 1980).
- Ross, Marlon B., *The Contours of Masculine Desire: Romanticism and the Rise of Women's Poetry* (New York Oxford, Oxford University Press, 1989).
- Rosen, Charles, *Romantic Poets, Critics and Other Madmen* (Harvard University Press, 1998).
- Sambrook, James, *The Eighteenth Century: The Intellectual and Cultural Context of English Literature – 1700–1789* (London & New York: Longman, 1990).
- Sanders, Andrew, *The Short Oxford History of English Literature* (Oxford: Clarendon Press, 1993).
- Schapiro, Barbara A., *The Romantic Mother: Narcissistic Patterns in Romantic Poetry* (Baltimore and London: The Johns Hopkins University Press, 1983).
- Sedgwick, Eve Kosofsky, *The Coherence of Gothic Conventions* (New York & London: Methuen, 1986).
- Selden, Raman, *Practicing Theory and Reading Literature: An Introduction* (Harvester Wheatsheaf, 1989).
- Shattock, Joanne, (ed.) *Women and Literature in Britain: 1800–1900* (Cambridge University Press, 2001).
- Simpson, David, *Romanticism, Nationalism and the Revolt Against Theory* (Chicago and London: The University of Chicago Press, 1993).
- Smart, N., (ed.) *Nineteenth-Century Religious Thought in the West* (Cambridge University Press, 1985).
- Spiegelman, Willard, *Majestic Indolence: English Romantic Poetry and the Work of Art* (Oxford University Press, 1995).
- Stokes, Myra, *The Language of Jane Austen: A Study of Some Aspects of Her Vocabulary* (Macmillan, 1991).

• Taylor, Anya, *Magic and English Romanticism* (Athens: The University of Georgia Press, 1979).

• Taylor, Beverley & Bain, Robert, (eds.) *The Cast of Consciousness: Concepts of the Mind in British and American Romanticism* (Contributions to the Study of World Literature, No 24, Greenwood Press, 1987).

• Tillotson, Geoffrey, *A View of Victorian Literature* (Oxford: Clarendon Press, 1978).

• Van Ghent, Dorothy, *The English Novel: Form and Function* (New York: Rineheart & Company, INC., 1953).

• Ward, A. W. & Waller, A. R., (eds.) *The Cambridge History of English Literature, Volume 13 – The 19th Century* (Cambridge University Press, 1912).

• Watson, J. R., *English Poetry of the Romantic Period: 1789–1830* (Longman, 1992).

• Watt, Ian, *The Rise of The Novel: Studies in Defoe, Richardson and Fielding* (Penguin, 1972).

• Weisser, Susan Ostrov, *Woman and Sexual Love in the British Novel: 1740–1880* (Macmillan, 1997).

• Welburn, Andrew J., *The Truth of Imagination: An Introduction to Visionary Poetry* (Macmillan, 1989).

• Wheeler, Kathleen M., *Kubla Khan and Eighteenth-century Aesthetic Theories*, in: Peter Kitson, (ed.) *Coleridge, Keats and Shelley* (Hong Kong, 1996).

• Wheeler, Michael, *Death and the Future Life in Victorian Literature and Theology* (Cambridge University Press, 1990).

• Wheeler, Michael, *Heaven, Hell and the Victorians* (Cambridge University Press, 1994).

• Willey, Basil, *Nineteenth-Century Studies: Coleridge To Matthew Arnold* (London: Chatto & Windus, 1961).

– *The Eighteenth-Century Background: Studies on the Idea of Nature in the Thought of the Period* (Penguin Books & Chatto & Windus, 1972).

- Williams, Merryn, *Women in the English Novel: 1800–1900* (London: Macmillan Press, 1984).
- Williams, Raymond, *The English Novel from Dickens to Lawrence* (London: The Hogarth Press, 1984).
- Wimsatt, W. K. Jr., *The Verbal Icon: Studies in the Meaning of Poetry* (The Noonday Press, 1962).
- Wolfson, Susan J., *Formal Charges. The Shaping of Poetry in British Romanticism* (Stanford University Press, Stanford California, 1997).
- Zemka, Sue, *Victorian Testaments: The Bible, Christology and Literary Authority in Early Nineteenth-Century British Culture* (Stanford California: Stanford University Press, 1997).
- Zimmerman, Sarah M., *Romanticism, Lyricism and History* (State University of New York Press, 1999).

In Bulgarian and in Russian

- Ариес, Филип. *Смъртта от Средновековековието до наши дни.* В: Литературна мисъл. София. БАН. книга 5. 1993
- Ариес, Филип. *Човекът пред Смъртта* (2 тома). София. ЛИК. 2004
- Артамонов, С. Д. *История зарубежной литературы XVII–XVIII веков.* Москва, „Просвещение". 1967
- Батай, Жорж. *Литературата и Злото.* София. ИК „Аргес". 1995
- Бахтин, М. М., *Въпроси на литературата и естетиката.* София. 1983
- Бахтин, М. М., *К философии поступка.* Научный архив. Философия и социология науки и техники. Эжегодник (1984/1985). Москва. „Наука". 1986
- Бахтин, М. М., *Литературно-критические статьи.* Москва. 1986

• Бахтин, М. М., *Философия на словесността. Том 1. Автор и герой в естетческата дейност*. София. ЛИК. 1996

• Бахтин, М. М., *Эстетика словесного творчества*. Издание второе. Москва. „Искусство". 1986

• Бахтин, М. М., *Эстетика словесного творчества*. Москва. „Искусство". 1979

• Бахтин, М. М., *Собрание сочинений*.

– Том 1. *Философская эстетика 1920х годов*. Москва. „Русские словари". РАН. 2003

– Том 5. *Работы 1940х–начала 1960х годов*. Москва. „Русские словари". РАН. 1996

• Белецкий, А. И., *В мастерской художника слова*. Москва. „Высшая школа". 1989

• Бенямин, Валтер. *Разказвачът*. В: списание „Страница" – 2/1999

• Бенямин, Валтер. *Художествена мисъл и културно самосъзнание*. Съставител: Атанас Натев. София. „Наука и изкуство". 1989

• Бланшо, Морис. *Литературното пространство*. София. ЛИК. 2000

• Больнов, О. Ф., *Философия экзистенциализма. Философия существования*. Санкт-Петербург. „Лань". 1999

• Бочаров, С. Г. *Сюжеты русской литературы*. Москва: Языки русской культуры. 1999

• Бояджиев, Цочо. *Нощта през Средновековието*. „Софи-Р". 2000

• Брандес, Георг. *Литературата на XIX век*. София. „Наука и изкуство". 1980

• Бренън, Хърби. *Великата мистерия на живота*. София. „Бард". 2003

• Бучков, Атанас. *„Апории"-те в „Смъртта на една птица"*. ПУ „Паисий Хилендарски". България. Научни трудове. Том 41, книга 1. 2003

- Вернан, Жан-Пиер. *Индивидът, Смъртта, Любовта: Аз и Другият в Древна Гърция*. София. Нов Български Университет. 2004

- Волков, И. Ф., *Творческие методы и художественные системы*. Москва. „Искусство". 1978

- Гадамер, Ханс-Георг. *Истина и Метод. Основы философской герменевтики*. Москва. „Прогресс". 1988

- Георгиев, Никола. *Анализ на лирическата творба*. София. ДИ „Народна просвета". 1985

- Георгиев, Никола. *Образът на Другия в литературната комуникация: диалогизми, интерференции*, В: Литературен вестник. 8–14.12.2004.

- Грицнер, И. А. (ред.), *Историческая поэтика*. Москва. „Наследие". 1994

- Гурко, Елена. *Жак Дерида. Деконструкция: тексты и интерпретация*. Минск. Экономпресс. 2001

- Демичев, А. В., *Дискурсы Смерти. Введение в философскую танатологию*. Санкт-Петербург. ИНАпресс. 1997

- Дерида, Жак.
  – *„Аз съм във война със себе си"* – разговор на Жан Бирнбом с Жак Дерида. Превод на Любен Каравелов. Във: в-к *„Култура"*. 2004 – брой 35. с. 10–11.
  – *Апории. Умиране – очакване пределите на истината*. София. ИК „Критика и хуманизъм". 1998
  – *Вяра и Знание*. София. ЛИК. 2001

- Женет, Жерар. *Фигури*. София. „Фигура". 2001

- Засурский, И. Н., *Зарубежная литература 19ого века*. Хрестоматия. Москва. „Просвещение". 1979

- Знеполски, Ивайло /ред./. *Около Жак Дерида. Чудовищният дискурс*. София. Дом на науките за човека и обществото. 2002

• Игълтън, Тери. *Теория на литературата. Въведение.* София. Университетско издателство „Св. Климент Охридски". 2000

• Калчев, Иван. *Метафизика на Смъртта.* София. Библиотека „Нов Ден" – 3. 1993

• Коларов, Радосвет. *За автора – post mortem – изпитанията на теорията,* В: Литературоведски диалози. ИК „Александър Панов". 2004

• Кръстева, Юлия. *Черно Слънце. Депресия и Меланхолия.* Издателство „Гал-Ико". 1999

• Лаврин, Алескандър. *Енциклопедия на смъртта. Хрониките на Харон.* София. „Абагар" 2000

• Левинас, Э., *Время и Дугой. Гуманизм Другого Человека.* Санкт-Петербург. Высшая Религиозно-Философская Школа. 1998

• Левинас, Э., *De l'existence a l'existant. Totalité et Infini* /Тотальность и бесконечность. ТГНИИ ИНИОН. Российская Академия Наук. Москва, Санкт-Петербург. „Университетская книга"2000

• Левинас, Е.,
– *Другост и Трансцендентност.* СОНМ. 1999
– *Другояче от битието, или отвъд същността.* СОНМ. 2002
– *Собствени имена.* СОНМ. 1997
– *Хуманизъм към Другия човек.* СОНМ. 1997

• Манчев, Боян. *Руини. Посвещение.* Във: в-к „Култура". 2004 – брой 40/41. с. 5

• *М. М. Бахтин. Pro Et Contra, Творчество и наследие М. М. Бахтина в контексте мировой культуры. Антология* (том 2). Санкт-Петербург. Издательство Российского гуманитартого института. 2002

• Мелетинский, Е., *Историческая поэтика новеллы.* Москва. „Наука". 1990

- Михальская, Н. П., Аникин, Г. В., *История Английской литературы*. Москва. „Академия“. 1998

- Никитаев, Владимир, *Герменевтика смерти*. В: „Логос“ (философско-литературный журнал). Москва. 2005, 2 (47). с. 202–220

- Панова, Е., Дончев, Г., Стефанов, Е., *Антология Европейска философия (XVII–XIX век)*, част II, София. „Наука и изкуство“. 1988

- Паси, Исак. *За Красотата и изкуството. Фрагменти из историята на Западноевропейската естетика от Ренесанса до Романтизма (XV–XIX век)*. София. „Наука и изкуство“. 1975

- Протохристова, Клео. *Западноевропейска литература*. ИК „Хермес“. 2000

- Рикер, Поль. *Память, История, Забвение*. Москва. Издательство гуманитарной литературы. 2004

- Рикьор, Пол. *Себе си като някой Друг*. Плевен. „ЕА“ АД. 2004

- Розентал, М. М., Юден, П. Ф., *Философски речник*. София. 1968

- Стахорский, С. В., *Энциклопедия литературных героев*. Москва. Аграф. 1997

- Стоянов, Цветан. *Идеи и мотиви на отчуждението в Западната литература*. София. „Наука и изкуство“. 1973

- Тамарченко, Н. Д., Садецкий, А., Махлин, В. Л. *Бахтинский Тезаурус*. Москва, Российский гуманитарный институт. 1997

- Тертерян, И. А. (ред.). *История всемирной литературы. Том 6*. Москва. „Наука“. 1989

- Тодоров, Цветан, *Введение в фантастическую литературу*. Москва. Дом интеллектуальной книги. 1997

- Трендафилов, Владимир. *Неизличимият образ в огледалото. Актуалната българска рецепция на Англия,* англичанина и английската мисъл през XIX и началото на XX век. София. „Кралица Маб". 1996

• Тураев, С. В., *От Просвещения к Романтизму*. Москва. „Наука". 1983

• Тъли, Джеймс. *Престъпленията на Шарлот Бронте*. София. „Епсилон". 2000

• Уэллек, Р., Уоррен, О., *Теория литературы*. Москва. „Прогресс". 1978

• Фройд, Зигмунд. *Естетика, изкуство, литература*. Съставител: Исак Паси. София. Университетско издателство „Св. Климент Охридски". 1991

• Фройд, Зигмунд. *Отвъд принципа на удоволствието*. Съставител: Любен Николов. София. „Наука и изкуство". 1992

• Хайдегер, Мартин. *Бытие и Время*. Москва. Ad Marginem. 1997

• Шкловский, Виктор. *Избранное, в двух томах. Том 1 – Повести о прозе, размышления, разборы*. Москва. „Художественная литература". 1983

• Шурбанов, Александър. *Поетика на Английския Ренесанс*. София. Университетско издателство „Св. Климент Охридски". 2002

• Щитцова, Т. В. *Событие в философии Бахтина*. Минск. „И. П. Логвинов". 2002

• Янкелевич, Владимир. *Смерть* (перевод с французского). Москва. Литературный Институт им. М. А. Горького. 1999

• Яус, Ханс Роберт. *Изкуството като антиприрода*. – В: Яус, Ханс Роберт. *Исторически опит и литературна херменевтика*, СУ, 1998

Criticism on the Brontë Sisters

In the English Language

- Alexander Christine & Sellars, Jane (eds.), *The Art of the Brontës* (Cambridge University Press, 1995).
- Allott, Miriam, (ed.) *Emily Jane Brontë. Wuthering Heights. A Selection of Critical Essays* (Macmillan, 1994)
    - Allott, Miriam, *The Rejection of Heathcliff?*, 1958, source: Essays in Criticism, 1958
    - Blondel, Jacques, *Literary Influences on Wuthering Heights*, 1955, source: Emily Brontë. Expérience Spirituelle et Création Poétique, Paris, 1955
    - Drew, Philip, *Charlotte Brontë's Insight into Wuthering Heights*, 1964, source: Nineteenth-Century Fiction, 1964
    - Homans, Margaret, *Transcending the Problems of Sexual Identity*, 1980, source: *Women Writers and Poetic Identity. Dorothy Wordsworth, Emily Brontë, Emily Dickinson* (New York: Princeton, 1980).
    - Traversi, Derek, *Wuthering Heights After a Hundred Years*, 1949, source: Dublin Review 1949
    - Van Ghent, Dorothy, *Dark „Otherness" in Wuthering Heights*, 1953, source: *The English Novel. Form and Function*, 1953
    - Visick, Mary, *The Genesis of Wuthering Heights*, 1958, source: *The Genesis of Wuthering Heights*, 1958
- Barker, Juliet, *The Brontës* (London: Weidenfeld & Nicholson, 1995).
- Bentley, Phyllis, *The Brontë Sisters* (Longman Green & Co., 1959).
- Benvenuto, Richard, *Emily Brontë* (Boston: Twayne Publishers, 1982).
- Björk, Harriet, *The Language of Truth: Charlotte Brontë, The Woman Question, and the Novel* (C. W. K. Gleerup, LUND, The LUND Studies in English, number 47).

351

- Blondel, Jacques, *Imagery in Wuthering Heights*, in *The Durham University Journal*, December 1975, Volume LXVIII, 1; New Series, Volume XXXVII 1

- Boumelha, Penny, *Charlotte Brontë* (Harvester Wheatsheaf, 1990).

- Brown, Marshall, *The Cambridge History of Literary Criticism, Volume 5 – Romanticism* (Cambridge University Press, 2000).

- Burkhart, Charles, *Charlotte Brontë: A Psychological Study of Her Novels* (London: Victor Gollanz LTD, 1973).

- Dinsdale, Anne & White, Kahtryn (eds.) *Brontë Parsonage Museum, A Souvenir Guide* (The Brontë Society, 1998).

- Buxton J. & Davis, N., *The Oxford History of English Literature* (Oxford: Clarendon Press, 1990).

- Celly, Ashok, *Emily Brontë, D. H. Lawrence and the Black Horse* (Delhi: Pragati Publications, 1997).

- Chitham, Edward, *A Life of Anne Brontë* (Oxford: Basil Blackwell, 1997).

- Chitham, Edward & Winnifrith, Tom, (eds.) *Brontë Facts and Brontë Problems* (Macmillan, 1983).

- Chitham, Edward, *The Birth of Wuthering Heights: Emily Brontë at Work* (St. Martin's Press, 1998).

- Crump, R. W., *Charlotte and Emily Brontë: 1846–1915 – A Reference Guide* (Boston: G. K. Hall & Co., 1982).

- Davies, Stevie, *Emily Brontë* (Harvester Wheatsheaf, 1988).

- Dingle, Herbert, *The Mind of Emily Brontë* (London: Martin Brian & O'Keefe, 1974).

- Drew, Lamonica, „*We Are Three Sisters*": *Self and Family in the Writings of the Brontës* (Columbia & London: University of Missouri Press, 2003)

- Du Maurier, Daphne, *The Infernal World of Branwell Brontë* (Penguin Books, 1987).

- Eagleton, Terry, *Myths of Power: A Marxist Study of the Brontës* (Plymouth: The Macmillan Press LTD, 1975).

- Ewbank, Inga-Stina, *Their Proper Sphere. A Study of the Brontë Sisters as Early Victorian Novelists* (London: Edward Arnold Publishers LTD, 1966).
- Flintoff, Eddie, *In The Steps of the Brontës* (Newbury Berkshire: Countryside Books, 1993).
- Fotheringham, James S., *The Work of Emily Brontë, And the Brontë Problem*, in: Wood, Butler, (ed.) *Transactions and Other Publications of the Brontë Society*, vol. II, Parts IX to XV (M. Field and Sons LTD., January 1906).
- Frank, Katherine, *Emily Brontë: A Chainless Soul* (London: Hamish Hamilton, 1990).
- Fraser, Rebecca, *Charlotte Brontë* (Vintage, 2003).
- Gaskell, Elizabeth, *The Life of Charlotte Brontë* (New York: J. M. Dent & Sons LTD, 1928).
- Gerin, Winifred, *Anne Brontë* (London Edinburgh Paris Melbourne Johannesburg Toronto New York: Thomas Nelson & Sons LTD, 1959).
- Gerin, Winifred, *Charlotte Brontë: The Evolution of Genius* (Oxford University Press, 1969).
- Gerin, Winifred, *The Brontës: I – The Formative Years* (Longman, 1973).
- Gerin, Winifred, *The Brontës: II – The Creative Work* (Longman, 1974).
- Ghnassia, Jill Dix, *Metaphysical Rebellion in the Works of Emily Brontë: A Reinterpretation* (New York, St. Martin's Press, 1994).
- Glen, Heather, *Charlotte Brontë: The Imagination in History* (Oxford University Press, 2004).
- Gordon, Lyndall, *Charlotte Brontë: A Passionate Life* (London: Chatto & Windus, 1994).
- Hagan, John, *Control of Sympathy in Wuthering Heights*, in: Gregor, Ian, (ed.) *The Brontës: A Collection of Critical Essays* (New Jersey: Prentice Hall Inc., 1970).

- Hale, Will T., *Anne Brontë: Her Life and Writings,* in *Indiana University Studies, Volume 16,* 1929 (Bloomington Indiana: Indiana University Press, 1929).

- Harrison, Ada & Stanford, Derek, *Anne Brontë: Her life and Work* (London: Methuen & Co. LTD., 1959).

- Harrison, G. Elsie, *Haworth Parsonage: A Study of Wesley and the Brontës* (London: The Epworth Press, 1937).

- Harrison, G. Elsie, *The Clue to the Brontës* (London: Methuen & Co. LTD, 1948).

- Holbrook, David, *Wuthering Heights: A Drama of Being* (Sheffield Academic Press, 1997).

- Hoeveler, Diane Long, *Gothic Feminism. The Professionalization of Gender form Charlotte Smith to the Brontës* (The Pennsylvania State University Press, 1998).

- Holderness, Graham, *Wuthering Heights* (Philadelphia: Open University Press, 1985).

- Ingham, Patricia, (ed.) *The Brontës* (Longman Pearson Education, 2003).

- Kavanagh, James H., *Emily Brontë* (Basil Blackwell, 1985).

- Keefe, Robert, *Charlotte Brontë's World of Death* (Austin: University of Texas Press, 1979).

- King, Jeanette, *Jane Eyre: Criticism* (Open University Press, Milton Keynes: Open University Press, 1986).

- Knapp, Betina L., *The Brontës: Branwell, Anne, Emily, Charlotte* (New York: A Frederick Ungar Book, Continuum, 1992).

- Knies, Earl A., *The Art of Charlotte Brontë* (Athens: Ohio University Press, 1969).

- Kucich, John, *Repression in Victorian Fiction: Charlotte Brontë, George Eliot and Charles Dickens* (Berkeley & Los Angeles & London, University Of California Press, 1987).

- Langbridge, Rosamond, *Charlotte Brontë: A Psychological Study* (London: William Heinemann LTD, 1929).

- Lock, John & Dixon, W. T., *A Man of Sorrow. The Life, Letters and Times of the Rev. Patrick Brontë: 1771–1861* (Ian Hodgkins & Co LTD, London Meckler Books Connecticut, 1979).

- Miller, Margaret J., *Emily: The Story of Emily Brontë* (London: Lutterworth Press, 1969).

- Moglen, Helene, *Charlotte Brontë: The Self Conceived* (New York: WW Norton and Company, 1976).

- Maynard, John, *Charlotte Brontë and Sexuality* (Cambridge University Press, 1984).

- McNees, Eleanor (ed.), *The Brontë Sisters: Critical Assessments*, in 4 volumes (Helm Information LTD., 1996).

- Oates, Joyce Carol, *The Magnanimity of Wuthering Heights*, originally published in *The Critical Inquiry*, Winter 1983, Reprinted in *The Profane Art: Essays and Reviews* (Ontario Review Inc., 1983).

- Ocampo, Victoria, *Emily Brontë: Terra Incognita* (Buenos Aires: SUR, 1938).

- Paden, W. D., *An Investigation of Gondal* (New York: Bookman Associates, 1958).

- Peeck-O'Toole, Maureen, *Aspects of Lyric in the Poetry of Emily Brontë* (Costerus New series, Volume 70, Rodopi, Amsterdam, 1988).

- Peters, Margot, *Charlotte Brontë: Style in the Novel* (Wisconsin: The University of Wisconsin Press, 1973).

- Petit, Jean-Pierre, (ed.) Emily *Brontë: A Critical Anthology* (Penguin Education, Penguin, 1973).

- Pinion, F. B, *A Brontë Companion* (Bristol: Macmillan, 1975).

- Plasa, Carl, *Charlotte Brontë* (Palgrave, Macmillan, 2004).

- Pollard, Arthur, *Charlotte Brontë* (London: Routledge & Kegan Paul, 1968).

- Pykett, Lyn, *Emily Brontë* (Macmillan, 1989).

- Robinson, A. Mary F., *Emily Brontë* (London: W. H. Allen & Co., 1883).

- Romiew, Emilie & Georges, translated from French by Robert Tapley, *Three Vigrins of Haworth* (New York: E. P. Dutton Co.).

- Schorer, Mark, *Technique as Discovery: Wuthering Heights and Moll Flanders in: Modern Literary Criticism*
- Sherry, Norman, PhD thesis *Charlotte and Emily Brontë* (ARCO, New York, 1970).
- Shuttleworth, Sally, *Charlotte Brontë and Victorian Psychology* (Cambridge University Press, 1996).
- Sinclair, May, *The Three Brontës* (London: Hutchinson & Co., 1912).
- Smith, Anne (ed.), *The Art of Emily Brontë* (Vision and Barnes & Noble, 1976), includes:
  - Grove, Robin, „*It Would Not Do*": *Emily Brontë as a Poet*
  - Hardy, Barbara, *The Lyricism of Emily Brontë*
  - Miles, Rosalind, *A Baby God: The Creative Dynamism of Emily Brontë's Poetry*
- Spark, Muriel & Stanford, Derek, *Emily Brontë: Her Life and Work* (Arrow Books LTD, 1985).
- Stevenson, W. H., *Emily and Anne Brontë* (London: Routledge & Kegan Paul, New York: Humanities Press, 1968).
- Stoneman, Patsy, *Brontë Transformations: The Cultural Dissemination of Jane Eyre and Wuthering Heights* (Prentice Hall, Harvester Wheat Sheaf, 1996).
- Tayler, Irene, *Holy Ghosts: The Male Muses of Emily and Charlotte Brontë* (New York: Columbia University Press, 1990).
- Thormählen, Marianne, *The Brontës and Religion* (Cambridge University Press, 1999).
- Wang, Lisa, PhD thesis *The Use of Theological Discourse in the Works of the Brontë Sisters* (Birkbeck College, University of London, Submitted for the Degree of PhD in 1998)
- Weimyss Reid, T., *Charlotte Brontë: A Monograph* (London: Macmillan, 1877).
- Wilks, Brian, *The Illustrated Brontës of Haworth: Scenes and Characters from the Lives and Writings of the Brontë Sisters* (Willow Books, 1986).

Index